REVOLT OF THE RICH

Revolt of the Rich

How the Politics of the 1970s
Widened America's Class Divide

David N. Gibbs

Columbia University Press   New York

Columbia University Press
Publishers Since 1893
New York   Chichester, West Sussex
cup.columbia.edu

Library of Congress Cataloging-in-Publication Data
Names: Gibbs, David N., author.
Title: Revolt of the rich : how the politics of the 1970s widened America's
    class divide / David N. Gibbs.
Description: New York : Columbia University Press, [2024] | Includes
    bibliographical references and index.
Identifiers: LCCN 2023054349 (print) | LCCN 2023054350 (ebook) |
    ISBN 9780231205900 (hardback) | ISBN 9780231205917 (trade paperback) |
    ISBN 9780231556224 (ebook)
Subjects: LCSH: Wealth—United States—History—20th century. |
    Rich people—United States—History—20th century. | Conservatism—
    United States—History—20th century. | Deindustrialization—
    United States—History—20th century.
Classification: LCC HC110.W4 G53 2024 (print) | LCC HC110.W4 (ebook) |
    DDC 339.2/2097309047—dc23/eng/20240316
LC record available at https://lccn.loc.gov/2023054349
LC ebook record available at https://lccn.loc.gov/2023054350

Printed in the United States of America

Cover design: Milenda Nan Ok Lee
Cover photos: (*top*) AP Photo/Dennis Cook; (*bottom*) Hum Images/Alamy Stock Photo

Contents

REVOLT OF THE RICH

Introduction

Everybody knows the fight was fixed.
The poor stay poor, the rich get rich.
—LEONARD COHEN, "EVERYBODY KNOWS," 1988

The concentration of wealth among the richest Americans has become a potent political issue, animating such phenomena as the Occupy Wall Street movement of 2011 and the youthful enthusiasm associated with the presidential campaigns of Senator Bernie Sanders, an avowed socialist. Growing economic inequality has even elicited notice on the political right in recent years, breaking with past trends and blurring long-standing ideological distinctions. While proposed solutions to these problems remain issues of contention, the fact of rising inequality is now recognized across the political spectrum. This book will explore why resources have become so concentrated in America, focusing on political changes during the 1970s, which marked a basic turning point in U.S. history.

The evolution of inequality is shown in stark terms in figure 0.1, which presents compensation for workers, paired with the rate of productivity growth, from 1948 to 2021.[1] The story is clear. In the first phase, during the 1950s and 1960s, worker compensation grew steadily in tandem with productivity growth. Then in the 1970s, a crisis period emerged, with both compensation and productivity becoming essentially flat. Finally, in a third phase, beginning after 1979, a striking divergence opens between worker compensation and productivity, producing a "pay-productivity gap." In a break with past trends, working

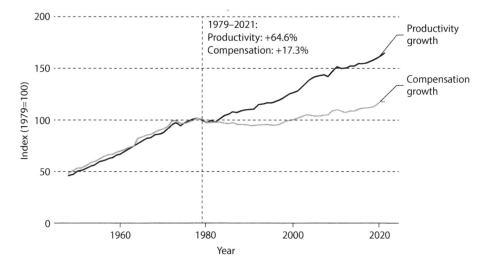

FIGURE 0.1 Growth in U.S. worker compensation and productivity, 1948–2021
Source: Graph from "The Productivity Pay Gap," Economic Policy Institute, updated October 2022, https://www.epi.org/productivity-pay-gap/.

people ceased to benefit from improvements in efficient production. Meanwhile, accumulated wealth held by the very richest Americans grew to levels not seen since the pre–New Deal era.[2] The trend of concentrated wealth was encouraged by government policies, which moved in a sharply free market direction. Beginning in the late 1970s, America's political economy assumed a strongly elitist character.

The facts raise a simple question: How was it possible to obtain such elitist results in a democratic polity with multiple parties, regular elections, and (mostly) universal suffrage? These results seem all the more surprising in light of public opinion polls from this period, which show broad support for progressive taxation and government programs to alleviate poverty, a support that remained strong through the end of the decade and well beyond. Polling data present no evidence that the public supported a conservative shift in economic policy.[3] Indeed, the conservative policy shift and resulting concentration of wealth occurred despite public opposition to these developments.

I argue that America's shift toward wealth concentration was the product of pressures from economic elites, not the general public. It resulted from a carefully crafted campaign to move economic policy in a laissez-faire direction, orchestrated by large businesses and wealthy individuals who were acting to advance their own interests at the expense of working people. The strategy was discussed openly. In 1974, for example, an article in *Business Week* declared that large portions of the American population might have to "accept the idea of doing with less so that big business can have more." To achieve this objective, the article emphasized "the selling job that must now be done to make people accept the new reality" of declining living standards while it acknowledged that the proposed redistribution of resources would prove "a hard pill for many Americans to swallow."[4] We will see that corporate interests did indeed mount the "selling job" advocated in *Business Week*, which achieved great success in guiding government officials toward free market policies despite the lack of public enthusiasm. It constituted a revolt of the rich against what they viewed as intolerable conditions.[5] Let us now look more closely at what led to this revolt.

A DECADE OF CRISIS

For America's richest citizens, the 1970s began as a challenging period. The rich were negatively affected by stagnant productivity rates[6] as well as "the unchecked and out-of-control rage of inflation," in the words of the historian Bruce Schulman.[7] It was widely presumed at the time that inflation harmed all social groups equally.[8] However, it was actually the wealthy classes that were most affected, a point confirmed in the memoirs of Herbert Stein, who served as chairman of the Council of Economic Advisors in the early 1970s: "The main losers [from inflation] are upper income people, whose assets decline most in real value during inflation."[9] Stein's claim is supported by an abundance of statistical data.[10] While rising prices harmed nearly all income groups to some degree, it caused greatest harm to the rich. As a result, the distribution of resources became considerably less skewed during the 1970s, producing one of the most equalized levels of income distribution in American history.[11] In addition, economic elites were confronted by declining rates of profit, which began during the late 1960s and continued through the 1970s.[12] Given the combined challenges of inflation and declining profits, America's wealthiest citizens mobilized to protect their interests. They were able to set aside their petty differences, coming together as a unified social class to lobby for basic changes in policy that would benefit them.

A key figure assisting this elite mobilization was President Richard Nixon. Using new documentation from the Nixon Presidential Library, I will show that Nixon quietly urged corporate executives to fund conservative think tanks with the aim of advancing free market ideas. Given their declining fortunes, business interests were happy to oblige. Nixon also seeded federal agencies with economists from the very conservative Mont Pèlerin Society (MPS)—associated with such figures as Milton Friedman and Friedrich von Hayek—for the first time engaging the MPS network in high-level policy making. These actions formed part of a concerted presidential effort aimed at building up a rightist counterestablishment, as explained in detail in confidential White House memoranda. And after Nixon's 1974 resignation from office following the Watergate scandal, business figures themselves directed the buildup of a rightist political infrastructure, all lavishly financed. Once galvanized, the business steamroller proved unstoppable, and it influenced a range of policy areas, while the MPS network of academics that Nixon had empowered would play decisive roles in shaping policy through the remainder of the 1970s and well beyond.

In addition, Nixon sought to establish a mass base for modern conservatism by mobilizing evangelical Christians and social traditionalists (who were heavily funded by business interests) while carefully fusing social and business conservatives into a unified right-wing movement of considerable force. Business conservatism held little mass appeal, but social conservatism proved far more popular. Nixon is often viewed as a cynical opportunist lacking ideological commitment, but I will show that he was in fact a deeply conservative president committed to free market ideals. He would play a central role in pushing America toward a more skewed distribution of wealth.

The 1970s also presented a series of foreign policy crises, beginning with the spike in international oil prices orchestrated by the Organization of the Petroleum Exporting Countries (OPEC). Later in the decade, the Iranian Revolution raised oil prices still further and added to the turmoil, while the 1979 Soviet invasion of Afghanistan presented yet an additional source of turmoil. The Afghan invasion was considered a particularly severe threat, given its supposed proximity to the

Persian Gulf, combined with a widespread suspicion that the Soviets would use Afghanistan as a staging area to launch attacks against the Gulf countries. By the end of the decade, these combined crises led to a dramatic change in foreign policy, with a large-scale military buildup in the Persian Gulf/Indian Ocean region and a substantial rise in overall military spending.

With regard to motive, it has been widely assumed that the U.S. move toward military force was an inevitable response to threats emanating from the Soviet Union, which was considered the main source of instability in the Middle East. The invasion of Afghanistan was seen in especially dire terms. The conventional wisdom is nicely distilled by Philip Jenkins: it was generally agreed that "the Soviets genuinely did pose an imminent threat to the United States, that the United States needed to rearm to resist that aggression."[13]

The foregoing interpretation is predicated on a myth. Based on newly declassified documents—from both U.S. and Soviet archives— we will see that the USSR's invasion of Afghanistan was undertaken for defensive purposes, posing no serious threats to U.S. or Western security. And in general, Soviet threats in the Middle East were greatly overstated. The main cause of the turn in U.S. policy was, once again, a massive corporate lobbying effort that argued for a military buildup while using alleged Soviet threats as a pretext to justify this buildup. At the level of impact, escalating military budgets served to lower federal spending on social programs while enriching weapons manufacturers, further skewing the distribution of income and wealth. Thus, the move toward militarism at the foreign policy level bolstered conservative programs being undertaken simultaneously at the domestic level. To state the matter simply: in all historical periods, government officials must choose between guns and butter; at the end of the 1970s, they chose guns.

In the story of the America's political shift, a central role was played by President Jimmy Carter, who succumbed to interconnected lobbying pressures and finally implemented a decisive change at the policy level. Carter's program brought liberalization of the financial sector, deregulation of industry, and the imposition of severe austerity measures that lowered working-class living standards. There was also a concerted effort to reduce the influence of labor unions. And finally, it was President Carter who implemented the rightward shift in foreign and military policy in favor of increased military spending. Recent studies of the Carter presidency, especially *The Outlier* by Kai Bird, present Carter as a centrist president who resisted ideological extremes. This book argues, in contrast, that the Carter presidency left a deeply conservative imprint on federal policy; he was not centrist at all. While President Nixon had laid the groundwork for the conservative policy shift—by mobilizing business and creating a conservative intellectual infrastructure—it was Carter who implemented that shift across a broad range of issues. President Ronald Reagan would later extend and deepen America's turn to the right; but in taking those actions, Reagan was building on a conservative policy foundation that had been laid by his Democratic predecessor.

This study also emphasizes the salience of foreign economic policy in reducing working-class living standards. An event of special importance was the deregulation of international finance. In 1973, the United States moved to a "floating exchange rate" system, whereby the value of the dollar would be set mainly by private currency traders on a free market basis, ending the system of regulated currencies that had been established by the 1944 Bretton Woods agreement. While previous studies have treated this deregulation as an accidental event, taken without any real forethought,[14] I will show that it was not accidental at all. The floating of the dollar resulted from long-standing efforts by conservative economists associated with the MPS—strongly supported by financial interests in the private sector—to empower the free market in setting the value of the dollar—to "free" currency trading from governmental interference.

The deregulation of international exchange rates set a precedent for the deregulation of domestic finance as well, culminating in the 1980 decontrol of interest rates. The cumulative effect of these multiple rounds of deregulation was to supercharge the U.S. financial sector, which saw impressive growth in profitability, while contributing to the decline of heavy industry, to the detriment of labor. Entire categories of high-paying industrial jobs were lost as a result, helping to skew the distribution of resources over the long term. I will argue that foreign economic policy played a decisive—if largely unrecognized—role in America's turn toward laissez-faire.

The overall right-wing tilt associated with these trends transformed both the Democratic and Republican Parties, which became much more responsive to the dictates of top income brackets, while the distribution of resources was dramatically skewed.[15] The trends deepened over time, and in 2018, the political scientists Benjamin Page and Martin Gilens concluded, "The wealthy, corporations, and organized interest groups have substantial influence" over the U.S. political process, while "ordinary citizens have little or no independent influence at all."[16] It was during the 1970s that these trends were set in motion.

The central theme of this study is that there was nothing inevitable about America's move toward wealth concentration and military buildup. Regarding the economic challenges of the period, a range of potential policies could have been pursued in response to inflation, including policies that would have been much more beneficial for wage earners. That policy makers opted for austerity and deregulation while disregarding alternatives reflected a political choice, not a necessity. And with regard to the right-wing turn in foreign policy, the additional military expenditure responded to an illusory security threat, not a real one. Overall, I argue that America's turn to the right resulted from elite political maneuvering, not inevitability.

When considered in retrospect, the 1970s may be viewed as a conjunctural decade, a fork in the road, when the old social order was breaking down and it was not immediately clear what would replace it. As a historical period, the 1970s most resembles the Great Depression of the 1930s, which also entailed a social crisis with an outcome that initially appeared uncertain. However, the two decades pursued very different trajectories in resolving their respective crises, with the 1930s producing a new order of greater equality in the form of the New Deal, while the crisis of the 1970s was resolved with precisely the opposite result: greater inequality. Explaining why the 1970s produced this strikingly inegalitarian outcome forms the task of this book.

DEEP LOBBYING

In assessing America's political turn, this study places special emphasis on "deep lobbying," which entails lobbying of elite and mass public opinion.[17] When most readers think of lobbying, they imagine corporate trade groups on K Street in Washington, DC, registered with the Department of Justice, whose agents contact members of Congress on behalf of interests they represent. The lobbyists then seek to pressure legislators with regard to specific policy issues. Deep lobbying, in contrast, seeks to influence the overarching ideologies of public officials and legislators and (where possible) the broader public. It traffics in the dissemination of ideas and aims at changing the climate of opinion. Deep lobbying has the advantage of appearing nonpartisan—as if it is not really lobbying at all—and its funding in most cases is tax exempt.

We will see that business interests engaged heavily in deep lobbying during the 1970s. Corporations lavishly funded such right-wing think tanks as the American Enterprise Institute, the Heritage Foundation, and Stanford University's Hoover Institution, among many others. These institutions experienced tremendous growth in both the scale of their operations and their overall clout in setting the agenda. In the context of prodigious growth, these think tanks hired top-tier academics and researchers whose ideological programs—heavily slanted toward militarism and laissez-faire economics—were circulated through the mass media, with high impact.

In addition to deep lobbying, this study will discuss traditional business lobby groups, such as the U.S. Chamber of Commerce, the National Association of Manufacturers, and the Business Roundtable. These groups also grew in size and political clout. I will argue, however, that deep lobbying by think tanks was ultimately the more effective form of influence. It is often said that in politics, "ideas matter";[18] and, indeed, the experience of the 1970s bears this out. Accordingly, business executives invested heavily in the development of ideas that advanced their interests, and also in the diffusion of those ideas, through deep lobbying. The effects were impressive, as we shall see, influencing both U.S. and also global economic policy.

Consistent with the idea of deep lobbying, this study will stress the role of academics and intellectuals, who served as agents of vested interests while teaching at universities—often with discreet corporate funding—or as affiliates at corporate-run think tanks. Business executives actively sought out academics to act as policy advocates and then bankrolled their research. Academics were especially prized due to their aura of prestige and objectivity, combined with the widespread view of faculty as independent actors. They were far more credible than professional lobbyists.

Several separate academic networks became influential during the 1970s, working in a range of policy areas, including foreign policy. In particular, a network of neoconservative intellectuals associated with the Committee on the Present Danger proved highly influential in arguing for raised military spending while obtaining generous support from military contractors and other interested parties. In arguing for these objectives, the neoconservatives advanced a strongly anticommunist worldview as a point of ideological principle.

We also will explore the conservative economists associated with the Mont Pèlerin Society, the most important member being Milton Friedman. Their core ideology was a celebration of the free market, and they advocated policies that aimed at reducing or eliminating government regulations from the New Deal and Progressive eras. Based on this ideology, Friedman and his MPS colleagues received heavy funding and support from some of the most powerful business interests in the country representing multiple sectors. Business support helped augment the standing of the MPS within the economics profession, enhancing its credibility with high-level policy makers and the general public. While the names of Friedman and other MPS economists will appear repeatedly in this study, it is important to bear in mind the powerful interests that quietly funded them.[19]

Although Friedman never held any official government position of consequence,[20] he was nevertheless a pivotal figure in America's turn to the right. Friedman proved to be a skilled public speaker and advocate, as well as a talented economist.[21] He was the deep lobbyist par excellence. Let me add that I have long been acquainted with Friedman's economics and began reading his work at age seventeen, when I was introduced to *Capitalism and Freedom* and was well aware that he was prominent in elite power circles. Yet, when I began research for this book and started studying the private papers of this period, I was startled by the extent of Friedman's influence, which was considerably greater than I had suspected.

During the 1970s, Friedman influenced such diverse areas as monetary policy, international economic policy, and educational reform. Most importantly, he was an effective advocate for austerity policies as a remedy for inflation. There has already been considerable research on the political influence of the Mont Pèlerin Society;[22] my study builds on this previous work to show how lobbying by MPS economists—and their corporate backers—successfully established a new era of laissez-faire economic policy during the 1970s. It is also worth noting that U.S. segregationists appreciated MPS's plans for privatizing education as a means of circumventing racial integration.[23] The twin goals of laissez-faire and segregation were thus intertwined. We will see that, in general, right-wing activists became experts in connecting economic and noneconomic issues to produce broad coalitions, with considerable impact.

Some may find it surprising that academics played a probusiness role, given the widespread stereotype of professors as left-wing critics of business. However, there is a long tradition of university faculty acting as advocates for vested interests—especially business—in the United States as well as other countries. From Germany, the sociologist Max Weber lamented the professor "who speaks for the dominant interests" and gains, as a result, "better opportunities for ascent due to the influence which these have on the political powers that be."[24] No doubt affiliation with the rich and powerful can be advantageous to one's academic career; clearly this was Weber's view.

Writing along similar lines, the journalist Upton Sinclair published a 1923 study of corporate control over U.S. universities, which was evidently considerable at the time. The University of Chicago, for example, was termed "The University of Standard Oil," while the University of Pittsburgh was "The University of the Steel Trust" and University of Oregon was "The University of the Lumber Trust."[25] Corporate influence extended to Harvard, where the banker Thomas Lamont participated directly in the promotion of faculty, as revealed in private correspondence.[26] And when, in 1961, Dwight D. Eisenhower warned about the military-industrial complex in his famous farewell address, he also warned about "the power of money" as a potentially corrupting influence on America's universities, and this development was "gravely to be regarded."[27] More recent research has documented the growing sway of Charles Koch of Koch Industries over U.S. higher education across numerous campuses.[28]

The field of economics has been especially susceptible to external influences, including moneyed interests. From Columbia University,

Jagdish Bhagwati expressed concern that "economists are 'corrupted' by consulting contracts, seats on corporate boards, and joint appointments with business schools—all of which require professors to be 'acceptable to business.'"[29] The view of economists as handmaids of the powerful was echoed by Paul Krugman, then at Princeton, who stated that whatever "the top 1 percent wants becomes what economic science says we must do."[30]

During the crises of the 1970s, corporate America made extensive use of economists as political advocates, enabling them to assume instrumental roles in engineering a rightward turn. The leading theories of the 1970s—monetarism and rational expectations—were used to justify policies that further enriched the already well to do. At the operational level, economic analysis was incorporated into virtually all areas of governmental policy making in the United States (and to some extent worldwide), while "economic style" influenced the whole of the social sciences, thus transforming academic debate.[31] Economics was "emerging as an imperial discipline,"[32] with considerable standing among the wealthy and powerful.

When beginning this research, I expected to find that right-wing victory in this period resulted from massive investments of funds in the political process, based on the straightforward assumption that money buys influence. But I have come to modify this judgment and accept that there was another, equally important reason for this victory, which was excellence of strategy. We will see that right-wing business interests—and intellectuals who assisted them—planned their campaigns with the utmost care and forethought. They engaged politics as an extended chess game, anticipating moves and countermoves by their opponents while planning how to respond to countermoves. Some executives viewed business and politics as extensions of warfare, based on such military classics as Sun Tzu's *The Art of War* and Carl von Clausewitz's *On War*,[33] reinforcing the strategic approach of the right. There was also a clear determination to build majority coalitions and win political battles. Impressively, there was a capacity to self-correct: when right-wing activists deployed strategies that proved ineffective, they would nimbly move to different strategies with greater effectiveness. In contrast, their liberal and leftist opponents responded to this offensive in piecemeal fashion with little sense of strategic focus.

That business ultimately prevailed in the ensuing battles owed as much to its superior strategy as it did to its funding and resources. One of the most significant elements of its strategy was clever use of crises as ideal moments to impose hidden agendas.[34] The 1970s was truly a decade of crises in both the domestic and foreign policy arenas; deep lobbyists at the Heritage Foundation and other corporate-funded think tanks viewed these crises as opportunities to impose their visions for the future—moving American politics radically rightward.

BOOK OVERVIEW

The main sources of information for this study are archival collections pertaining to major business figures, right-wing activists, and government officials who played key roles in U.S. politics in this period. More than eighty archival collections were consulted at forty-one locations throughout the United States (and one in Switzerland), as well as materials from digitized archives. I have also surveyed the vast number of oral histories, diaries, memoirs, public speeches, and other accounts by individuals who participated in the events described. Finally, I have made extensive use of periodical sources, with a particular focus on the business and financial press.

Following this introduction, chapters will proceed as follows. Chapter 1, "The Rich Accept a Compromise," discusses the social reforms established during the 1930s and 1940s, and the evolution of these reforms during the post–World War II era.[35] It demonstrates that there was indeed a measure of compromise between the interests of labor and capital, with a significant narrowing in the distribution of wealth and income; that the class compromise was gradually accepted by major corporations and both political parties; and that it became the cornerstone of American politics during the early postwar period. The chapter concludes with the late 1960s, when the compromise began to unravel, with declining rates of profit, rising inflation, and growing business anxiety leading to a mobilization of the wealthy classes.

Chapter 2, "The Rich Revolt," explores the beginning of the business-led rebellion against the class compromise during the Nixon administration and directly encouraged by the president himself. Here, I analyze the dense infrastructure of think tanks and lobby groups formed to protect elite interests. The chapter concludes that the Watergate scandal tainted the public reputation of business as well as the Republican Party and thus constituted a setback for the conservative policy agenda—though only a temporary one.

Chapter 3, "Building a Mass Base," presents public responses to the business-led mobilization. I describe how business interests discreetly bolstered socially conservative political organizations—notably those associated with evangelical Christianity, which evolved into the largest and most successful mass movement of the era—as well as libertarianism. The purpose of these mobilization efforts was to build a mass following for an overarching conservative movement, one that would be led by business interests.

Chapter 4, "Selling a New Cold War," looks at the extraordinary scope of America's political turn, which extended to foreign and military policy. I recount efforts by the Committee on the Present Danger and other corporate-funded lobby groups to increase military spending and foreign intervention to compensate for the lowered weapons procurement that resulted from the Vietnam debacle. The mobilization of militarists during this period helped enlarge the overall conservative movement, thus contributing to the rightist strategy of building coalitions, which aimed at achieving majority support. The New Right's majoritarian strategy—known as "fusionism"—became the key to its later success in transforming society.

Chapter 5, "The Rich Go Global," discusses the rightward turn in international economic policy, which began during the Nixon presidency and laid the groundwork for deregulating the global financial system and, later, for full financialization of the domestic economy. It examines the deregulation of international exchange rates, the global politics of oil, the increasingly intimate connections between the oil and financial sectors, and how these international economic trends helped skew the distribution of income and wealth in the United States. And finally, chapter 5 discusses how the United States became a launching point for the projection of laissez-faire economics around the world.

Chapter 6, "The Triumph of Laissez-Faire," explores the dramatic move to the right that took place during the presidency of Jimmy Carter, when the free market agenda was implemented on a large scale. Though President Carter began with relatively moderate programs, he would gradually comply with growing demands from business-driven think tanks and lobby groups. By the end of his presidency, Carter would implement conservative, antilabor polices through industrial and financial deregulation, regressive changes to federal taxation, and an austerity program aimed at controlling inflation through heightened unemployment.

The concluding chapter traces long-term effects of America's conservative shift, examining how it played out after the election of President Reagan. The political realignment that took place during the late 1970s set the United States on a course that would endure for many decades, well into the twenty-first century. It now appears, in retrospect, that the Carter presidency marked a basic inflection point in U.S. history from which there would be no going back.

A NOTE ON TERMINOLOGY

Throughout this book, I have taken special effort to write accessibly for the general reader and avoid academic jargon. The latter has become, in my view, a serious impediment to understanding the real world of U.S. politics. Accordingly, I use the well-understood phrases "conservative" and "right wing" to reference policies that advance economic deregulation and wealth concentration at the domestic level, militarism and military interventions overseas, and "traditional values" with regard to social and cultural issues. I realize that some elements on the right have come to question militarism and wealth concentration, but that is a trend of recent vintage; such questioning did not occur during the 1970s. I will avoid the confusing word "neoliberal," which is often used as a synonym for conservative economic policies, and the equally confusing "classical liberal," which is essentially a synonym for "libertarian." The term "liberal" will denote slightly left of center, consistent with common usage, while a "leftist" stands further left on the political continuum. "Class compromise" references the regulated capitalism and labor-friendly policies that emerged from the New Deal. Readers who wish to argue hair-splitting distinctions among different categories of words should consult a different book.

CHAPTER ONE

The Rich Accept a Compromise

The century on which we are entering . . . can and must be
the century of the common man.
—VICE-PRESIDENT HENRY A. WALLACE, 1942

The post-World War II era began with a conciliation among the social classes in the United States. Economic elites ceded some of their privileges, and a sizable union movement acted as a check on corporate power, while a federal welfare state was created, funded through progressive taxation. Fiscal and monetary policies boosted employment and controlled inflation. The gap between rich and poor was narrowed to a considerable degree, with a "Great Compression"[1] in the distribution of wealth and income. At the level of ideas, the notion of laissez-faire economics was largely discredited and replaced by state-regulated capitalism. Above all, the postwar period was one of economic success, with rapidly improved standards of living for virtually every segment of the population, high profit rates, and stable growth. It was the era of a historic compromise between labor and capital, the class compromise.

This chapter explores the evolution of the class compromise and how the business community acted strategically to limit its impact. Even as they accepted greater equality in principle, business groups and wealthy individuals funded a network of highly conservative think tanks, lobby groups, and religious organizations. These groups functioned as a check on liberalism and ensured that reform would remain within certain bounds. Business was retaining the right to veto the class compromise and repeal its most threatening features. We will see in later chapters that a repeal campaign was indeed launched beginning in the early 1970s, with far-reaching consequences. In this chapter, we will show that the groundwork for the repeal campaign had already been set in motion several decades in advance.

FORGING A CLASS COMPROMISE

It is our duty now to begin to lay the plans . . . [for] an American standard of living, higher than ever known before.
—FRANKLIN DELANO ROOSEVELT, 1944[2]

The contours of the postwar social order were established during the late 1940s, following the twin traumas of depression and world war, when many innovative ideas were given a hearing. One of the most significant proposals was guaranteed full employment, to be established as a matter of national policy and law. Some of the leading public figures of the era believed that permanent full employment was feasible and desirable, and it was explicitly advocated in John Maynard Keynes's classic, *The General Theory of Employment, Interest, and Money*,[3] the most influential economic treatise of the era. President Roosevelt endorsed the idea of full employment in his 1944 State of the Union address.[4]

In his address, Roosevelt advocated "a second Bill of Rights," which would provide economic opportunities for all Americans "regardless of station, race, or creed," and these included the following.

The right to a useful and remunerative job in the industries or shops or farms or mines of the nation;
The right to earn enough to provide adequate food and clothing and recreation;
The right of every farmer to raise and sell his products at a return which will give him and his family a decent living;
The right of every businessman, large and small, to trade in an atmosphere of freedom from unfair competition and domination by monopolies at home or abroad;
The right of every family to a decent home;
The right to adequate medical care and the opportunity to achieve and enjoy good health;

The right to adequate protection from the economic fears of old age, sickness, accident, and unemployment;
The right to a good education.[5]

Among the most salient of these proposals was the right to a "useful and remunerative job," which was presented as a fundamental right, comparable to the right to freedom of speech and religion, protected by the original Bill of Rights. Guaranteed employment was so widely accepted that even some leading Republicans, such as New York Governor Thomas E. Dewey, initially endorsed it in principle.[6] Full employment was to be an integral component of what the president termed "an American standard of living."

The idea of full employment was strongly influenced by the experience of World War II, when jobs became plentiful. Massive government spending associated with the war effort definitively ended the Great Depression far more effectively than the tepid level of state intervention during the New Deal.[7] This was achieved without any sacrifice of efficient production, as measured by total factor productivity (TFP). In fact, there were impressive gains in TFP, according to research by the economist Robert Gordon. The rate of TFP growth during the period 1940–1950 was by far the highest of any decade in history, from 1900 until 2014. With regard to productivity growth rates, "The singularity of the 1940–50 decade leaps off the page," according to Gordon, who adds that TFP growth "soared during World War II."[8] Overall, World War II may be viewed as an experiment on the efficacy of economic planning and full employment—with extremely positive results.

The main issue was whether the federal government would continue the economic successes that had been achieved during World War II and establish these conditions as a permanent state of affairs. The millions of soldiers returning from theaters of war expected a better future for themselves, and public pressure was a spur to the idea of full employment. The result was the Full Employment Act, introduced to Congress in 1945, which in its original formulation sought a permanent state of full employment.[9] The objective was to stimulate job creation by redirecting investment into the development of infrastructure and other civilian works. The danger of unemployment was to be abolished by act of Congress.[10]

A second goal on the national agenda was the expansion of union rights. From the standpoint of America's burgeoning labor movement, full employment by itself was insufficient; it also was important to increase wages and living standards through organizing and strategic agitation. By 1945, approximately 35 percent of the nonagricultural workforce was unionized (the highest in U.S. history up to that time),[11] but the majority of workers were not protected by unions. The Southeast, especially the states of the former Confederacy, had a particularly low level of union membership. The most dynamic and militant of the major unions, the Congress of Industrial Organizations (CIO), planned an aggressive organizing effort to expand membership in the South. "Operation Dixie," as the project was named, commenced in 1946 as hundreds of CIO activists were dispatched to begin organizing drives. Many of the CIO organizers were committed to not only extending union rights but also terminating the Jim Crow system of racial discrimination. The two objectives—furthering union rights and racial equality—were seen as interconnected and pursued simultaneously.[12]

Such an effort faced the obstacle of entrenched southern racism, which divided Black and white workers, an overarching issue that had long dominated regional politics and impeded past unionization efforts.[13] And yet, the CIO's 1946 campaign was not as quixotic or unrealistic as it may appear in retrospect. In fact, there was some precedent for interracial cooperation, most notably during the Populist movement of the late nineteenth century. A Populist leader from Georgia presented the following appeal to the two races of the South in 1892: " 'You are made to hate each other because upon that hatred is rested the keystone of the arch of financial despotism which enslaves you both. You are deceived and blinded that you may not see how this race antagonism perpetuates a monetary system which beggars you both.' . . . The accident of color can make no possible difference in the interests of farmers, croppers, and laborers."[14] And in more recent times, such politicians as Huey Long of Louisiana and "Big Jim" Folsom of Alabama deemphasized racism to some degree, which was viewed as a distraction from the central objectives of economic transformation and wealth redistribution.[15] In a memorable 1949 speech, Governor Folsom declared, "As long as the Negroes are held down by deprivation and lack of opportunity, the other poor people will be held down alongside them."[16] There was also a tradition of socialism in certain parts of the South, especially in the Ozarks region, and this tendency was antiracist.[17]

With Operation Dixie, in 1946, the CIO sought to build on this tradition of multiracialism and to unionize the South,[18] thus nationalizing the union movement for the first time. Had Dixie succeeded, the effects would have been far reaching. Unionization of the South could have produced a basic power shift in favor of the working class at the expense of business; while in the South itself, multiracial unions would have fatally weakened the Jim Crow system of oppression.

A third goal on the nation's agenda was government-directed control of inflation. During World War II, the federal government created the Office of Price Administration (OPA) to administer wholesale and consumer prices.[19] The massive and sudden augmentation of federal spending produced by wartime procurement ran the risk of triggering inflation, a prospect that was to be averted by the OPA price control system, which in effect administered a form of rationing. The OPA called forth the volunteer services of hundreds of thousands of (mostly female) consumers, who monitored local merchants for price gouging or other abuses and reported to federal officials.[20] The mobilization of volunteers not only reduced administrative expenses but also helped forge a mass political base for federal regulation of prices, empowering consumers as a counterweight to business. Mass public engagement in the OPA's operation served as an effective barrier against the possibility of "regulatory capture" by vested interests, which otherwise may have corrupted the agency's functioning. After the war, the OPA was often portrayed as a wartime necessity, reluctantly accepted by the mass public;[21] in reality, it was overwhelmingly popular throughout the war, a point confirmed by public opinion polls at the time, with support for OPA especially high among women.[22]

With the ending of war in 1945, the OPA continued to operate, helping stabilize the economy during the transition away from weapons production. The ongoing OPA system, with its mass base of volunteers and high public support, raised the possibility that some form of government-regulated prices might become a permanent feature of the political economy. On the one hand, such a system would have violated norms of market-based pricing, which undergirded classical ideas of economic rationality. On the other hand, companies in the oligopolistic

sectors of the economy were already violating market norms by practicing collusion and administered pricing, yielding high rates of profit.[23]
Some degree of federal price controls could have restrained oligopolistic practices and profiteering while offering protection against inflation.
In addition, the OPA's engagement with working-class consumers as a
means of directing price controls advanced the idea of popular democracy, now projected into the economic sphere. And finally, state-directed
price controls dovetailed with the proposed Full Employment Act by
ensuring that future full employment policies would not be undermined
by destabilizing inflation.

The prospect of a full employment economy would have entailed a
degree of state-directed planning as a basic feature of the overall system,
to channel investment toward employment-generating sectors, especially when the private sector was unable or unwilling to fulfill this role.
The need for an enlarged state planning and investment function was
recognized among economists of the era, led by Keynes himself. In *The
General Theory*, Keynes called for a "somewhat comprehensive social-
ization of investment," which would prove "the only means of securing
an approximation of full employment." And state-directed investment
would usurp the role of private capital markets, thus leading to a decline
of the financial sector more generally; or—as Keynes stated in a colorful
turn of phrase—planning would entail "euthanasia of the rentier, of the
functionless investor."[24] Note that Keynes did not advocate the nationalization of production, which he felt should be left mostly in private
hands. Nor did he advocate shooting or persecuting bankers; he simply
wanted the financial sector to gradually die a natural death, in the figu-
rative sense of the term, as its function declined.

Such a state-directed economy would have considerably weakened
the private sector. The CIO's program of intensified unionization
would likely have squeezed corporate profits, leading over time to a
less skewed distribution of wealth. These conditions would have been
enhanced by the existence of price controls, which could have prevented corporations—especially those in the oligopolistic sector—
from passing wage increases on to the consumer in the form of higher
prices, further reducing the rate of profit. However, economic theory
of this period tended to justify the idea of reduced profits and redistribution more generally as being consistent with economic rationality

as well as social justice. Progressive economists did not, in most cases, wish to do away with profitability and economic incentives altogether, which were regarded as necessary to stimulate innovation and risk taking. Keynes himself accepted the need for economic incentives— but he also stated emphatically that reduced incentives would be sufficient. ("Much lower stakes will serve the purpose equally well."[25]) Moderate levels of profitability would sustain the private sector.

This package of proposed reforms, had they been implemented, would have had an important political effect by reducing the influence of business interests on the policy process. The U.S. state has long adopted business-friendly policies as a means of coaxing private investment and thereby increasing employment levels; this need was especially acute during recessions and depressions. With the advent of state-directed investment, however, there would be less need to mollify business and cajole private investment. The perennial necessity of establishing business confidence would no longer be required—thus reducing the power of business to shape policy. The economist Paul Krugman recognized the inherent advantage of state-directed investment, which might "mean that politicians would no longer have to abase themselves before businessmen in the name of preserving confidence."[26]

The overall Keynesian program would have reduced the power of the wealthy classes through the redistribution of wealth. The upper classes had long been able to use their accumulated financial reserves to fund large-scale lobbying efforts to achieve political objectives by acting outside the democratic process. A more equal distribution of wealth would have lessened the ability of the rich to gain disproportionate influence while minimizing their capacity to repeal social reforms in future. And whatever residual power the rich might still possess would be counterbalanced by a large and nationally organized union movement, simultaneously being pushed by the CIO.

In recent years, the United States has been portrayed as deeply conservative, well behind other industrialized countries with regard to social protections and working-class political mobilization. But that was not always true. For a brief period after World War II, America was widely respected for some of the world's most dynamic working-class movements. A young Olof Palme—later serving as the left-leaning prime minister of Sweden—traveled through the Midwest and was deeply impressed by what he saw of American labor organizations. As a student at Kenyon College, he wrote his 1948 senior thesis on the United Auto Workers based in part on interviews conducted in Detroit with UAW President Walter Reuther. In later years, Palme insisted that he was not "repelled by what he found" in American society; he "was inspired by it." Indeed, it was Palme's visit to the United States that "made him a socialist," according to one account.[27]

Looking back at the policy proposals of the late 1940s gives one a sense of history as it might have been, of possibilities that existed for a time but then slipped away. The program of economic reforms noted earlier held promise for fundamentally altering the U.S. social structure and doing so in ways that would have been difficult to reverse. The prospect of a unionized South, as sought by labor activists, might have prevented or at least reduced the incentive of businesses to relocate in nonunionized regions, since such regions would have effectively disappeared, minimizing the danger of capital flight and deindustrialization while also breaking the racial caste system. And the package of domestic transformations was to be combined with similar changes to the system of international economic relations, aimed at restricting capital flight and establishing greater equality on a global level.[28] Such reforms would have affected a basic and probably permanent shift in the balance of political power away from capital.

A BUSINESS BACKLASH

The reform program elicited mobilization of business interests, which sought to defeat it. The most important target of business lobbying was the pending Full Employment Act, legislated during 1945–46. Broad coalitions of business interests came out against the proposal, led by the Merchants and Manufacturers Association, whose spokesman stated that "Full employment is akin to slavery," as well as the National Association of Manufacturers (NAM) and the U.S. Chamber of Commerce.[29] From the Senate, Republican leader Robert Taft presented vociferous opposition.[30] Public opinion likely remained supportive of the act, but in the end, mass enthusiasm would not drive the outcome.

Business also mobilized against the OPA and any postwar price controls, in this case spearheaded by the NAM and food distributors.[31]

Senator Taft denounced the OPA because it was "dominated by New Deal economists who want a continued regulation of profits." The office's very existence amounted to "an appeasement of labor."[32] And with regard to the CIO's unionization efforts, the southern business establishment mobilized, making common cause with segregationist groups and conservative Protestant ministers, all seeking to block the spread of unions, especially multiracial unions.[33]

In all these issue areas, business lobbying was largely successful. The Employment Act of 1946 was passed by Congress and signed into law by President Truman,[34] but its requirement of full employment was removed. Instead, the act merely encouraged the government to seek full employment; it was not to be a legal requirement. And significantly, the final version of the act was renamed the "Employment Act," rather than the original "Full Employment Act."

The OPA's authority was reduced considerably in 1946,[35] and it was abolished in 1947, when all price controls were lifted. In the future (during the Korean War, for instance) federal price controls were sometimes used,[36] but they never had anywhere near the authority of those undertaken by the OPA. And the OPA's unique idea of using large numbers of consumer volunteers to help administer price controls— and also to create political support for controls—was never revived. In the South, Operation Dixie was effectively defeated by the end of 1946, when the CIO began to reduce its commitment to the program and withdrew many of its organizers.[37]

A key factor in explaining these defeats was the president, Harry S. Truman. In public, Truman presented himself as heir to the legacy of Roosevelt and the New Deal; at a personal level, he was widely viewed as the incarnation of the common man in the White House, with a Midwestern background and a modest manner. In reality, the president retained long-standing ties to some of the most powerful business interests in the country: "Truman had been able to govern the country with the cooperation of a relatively small number of Wall Street lawyers and bankers," according to the Harvard political scientist Samuel Huntington.[38] And the military—an emerging power center during this period—established close ties to corporate interests, as exemplified by the career of General George C. Marshall, who served in President Truman's cabinet. According to one insider account, General Marshall "was one of the very many military men who got all their knowledge and thinking on economics from big business."[39] And at the level of policy, Truman was far more concerned with laying the foundations of American international hegemony and fighting the Cold War than he was with domestic reform, which appeared as more of an afterthought.

With regard to the specific reform programs just discussed, President Truman showed no sustained interest. In his public speeches, he barely mentioned full employment legislation. In one of the few instances when Truman did comment on the legislation in response to a question from the press, the strongest support he could muster was that he favored "some sort of [employment] bill," a very tepid endorsement indeed. And crucially, Truman declined to support the bill's proposal of full employment that was to be guaranteed and legally mandated.[40]

With regard to the CIO's efforts to unionize the South, I was unable to find any evidence of presidential support or interest whatsoever. Truman probably made his strongest efforts to preserve the OPA during the early postwar period. But even in this case, the Truman administration declined to use the full weight of the presidency and the executive branch to support the agency and oppose the business juggernaut arrayed against it, as Truman would later acknowledge in his memoirs.[41]

The complex politics of 1946 conspired to further undermine the power of organized labor. The immediate postwar era brought a brief recession, owing to the circumstances of economic conversion associated with the move away from military production. There was also a surge of price inflation associated with the weakening of the OPA and the relaxing of price controls. Finally, labor unions launched an extended wave of industrial strikes.[42]

These turbulent economic conditions—combined with Truman's own lack of charisma—led to a Republican sweep in the congressional elections of 1946, giving the Republicans control of both houses of Congress for the first time in sixteen years. The new Republican-controlled Congress immediately drafted the Taft-Hartley Act, a landmark piece of antilabor legislation, which passed by a two-thirds majority in 1947, overriding a presidential veto and thus becoming law.[43]

The Taft-Hartley Act introduced a series of constraints against any further expansion of the labor movement,[44] the most important of which was advancing "right-to-work" laws.[45] Under the right-to-work concept, states could pass legislation that allowed workers to refuse membership in a union even if the union was officially recognized. Proponents presented Taft-Hartley as proworker, since it allowed freedom of choice, but it was in reality a cleverly disguised effort to weaken unions. The basic problem was that right-to-work enabled workers to procure some of the benefits that unions offered without paying any dues, thus giving them an incentive to act as "free riders" and not join unions at all. There is widespread agreement in economic theory that under free-rider conditions, unionization will become difficult or impossible; most workers will naturally prefer to free ride, thus decimating membership and undercutting organizing drives.[46]

Taft-Hartley had a considerable impact. By 1958, some eighteen states had enacted right-to-work laws, including all but one of the states of the former Confederacy, affirming the status of the South as hostile toward unions.[47] Taft-Hartley became one of the principal constraints on the postwar class compromise, and it ensured that the union movement would never become truly national in scope, limiting its influence. Lawrence Richards emphasizes the psychological and symbolic significance of Taft-Hartley: it was detrimental to union organizing partly because "of the message it conveyed about the place of unions in American society."[48] It implanted the idea that unionization constrained freedom of choice, thus weakening the unions' moral authority and public popularity. At the level of rhetoric, the ability of right-wing activists to coin simple, powerful phrases such as "right to work"—and to subtly endow them with an ideological message—was impressive.

The rigors of postwar economic transition had darkened President Truman's reelection prospects in 1948. Facing an invigorated Republican Party—as well as third-party insurgencies from both the segregationist governor of South Carolina, Strom Thurmond, and former Vice President Henry Wallace[49]—Truman tacked left. He now promised to deepen the New Deal with additional reforms, which included national health care and a revived full employment program, combined with repeal of Taft-Hartley.[50] How seriously President Truman intended these campaign promises is open to question, since he would abandon them almost as soon as he was reelected. But at the time, the president seemed sincere enough. He struck a populist tone in his speeches, lambasting Republicans for their pandering to big business, as well as the wealthy classes for their greed and callousness. In one campaign speech, Truman denounced the rich "in their dining cars, in country clubs and [in] fashionable resorts" who take the view that "'labor must be kept in its place.'" He insisted that the working man must stand "side by side with the businessman and the farmer, and not one degree lower."[51]

The 1948 election would constitute the last time during the Cold War era that class-based rhetoric would appear to any significant extent in national-level politics. After 1948, references to the working class and class conflict would become taboo, and this taboo would endure through the remainder of the twentieth century (and well into the twenty-first). Class would remain a forbidden issue in American elections for almost seventy years, until 2016, with the arrival of the Bernie Sanders presidential campaign.

A CONSERVATIVE CLASS COMPROMISE TAKES SHAPE

With his new radical-sounding style, President Truman managed to defy the odds and win reelection. But almost immediately after the election, he pivoted away from the Fair Deal domestic reforms he had promised, instead focusing on the emerging Cold War with the Soviets, which probably had been his main interest all along. Truman orchestrated the crafting of the North Atlantic Treaty in 1949, which led to formation of the NATO alliance with Europe; and he laid the groundwork for a massive increase in military spending,[52] tied to his approval of the seminal National Security Council memorandum, NSC-68.[53] After June 1950, Truman directed U.S. and allied intervention in the Korean War. In pursuing these objectives, Truman needed some degree of assent from congressional Republicans (especially for the North Atlantic Treaty, which required a two-thirds majority in the Senate). This would prove difficult given partisan bitterness at the time, combined with continuing isolationism within the Republican Party.

In light of these circumstances, President Truman arranged what amounted to a far-reaching deal with congressional Republicans, as described by the political scientist Benjamin Fordham. In essence, the Republican Party decided to go along with Truman's globalist and Cold War agendas, thus breaking definitively with isolationism, and the president gave up most of his proposed domestic reform program.

He also acquiesced in the emerging antileftist purge of the federal bureaucracy and union movement directed by the Federal Bureau of Investigation and its zealous director, J. Edgar Hoover.[54] In private, President Truman complained about Hoover's unethical conduct, his investigations of people's sex lives, and his use of political blackmail. He added, "We want no Gestapo or Secret Police. FBI is tending in that direction."[55] Despite his reservations, Truman recognized the political benefits of working hand in hand with the bureau and orchestrating a purge of leftists. And expediency aside, these moves dovetailed nicely with the president's own anticommunist proclivities.[56]

The Korean War ended any possibility of new social reforms, while the political purges brought fundamental change to the labor movement,[57] removing some of the most effective and committed CIO organizers and strengthening the American Federation of Labor (AFL), the CIO's long-time rival. The purges further hobbled Operation Dixie, which was finally laid to rest in 1953; this proved a decisive setback for the CIO. With the defeat of Dixie, the CIO saw no option but to establish a common front with the AFL. The two unions set aside differences and merged in 1955 to form the AFL-CIO.[58] The new, combined union became the largest in the country and dominated U.S. labor politics for many decades.

The AFL-CIO was conceived on very conservative terms as an institutional reaction against leftist strains within the labor movement. One of the organization's most important activities became covert collaboration with the Central Intelligence Agency, with which the union worked to establish anticommunist labor unions around the world.[59] The AFL-CIO's usefulness in fighting communism, both domestically and globally, was appreciated by U.S. elites in both the government and the private sector. This arrangement helped legitimize the union as a player of importance in national politics, contributing to the overall class compromise. For their part, the AFL-CIO's leaders were gratified by their sense of prominence in the worldwide crusade against communism. Later, when the union began a steady decline, its leaders would fall back to an even greater degree on their foreign policy function, perhaps to reassure themselves that they still had an important role to play even as their mass membership gradually fell away.[60]

The increasingly conservative cast of the class compromise affected the character of economic theory as well. Keynesian ideas still remained influential, having been integrated into policy making through the Council of Economic Advisers, established in 1946 as part of the Employment Act, thus incorporating the idea of state-directed fiscal and monetary policy. The emerging economic orthodoxy was nevertheless different from the one advocated by Keynes himself. The modernized version had dropped altogether Keynes's ideas of permanent full employment and state-directed investment. The new formulation of Keynesian economics instead emphasized the dangers of full employment as a potential trigger of inflation. There was an associated assumption that inflation resulted from excessive consumption by the working classes; accordingly, the solution was to restrain working-class consumption through the imposition of austerity measures and augmented unemployment.

The shift in economic thinking was fundamental. The original version of Keynesian thought suggested that full employment was inherently desirable and also compatible with price stability. If policy makers sought to control inflation, there existed a range of possible solutions. In 1943, for example, the economist Michal Kalecki had proposed an "annual capital tax" as a means of reducing the national debt and thus restraining prices.[61] If overconsumption was the problem, it could be corrected by curtailing consumption by the wealthy through a capital tax, rather than shifting the burden on to the working class through unemployment. Another potential solution was state-directed price controls based on the wartime experience of the Office of Price Administration. However, these potential responses to inflation were being deemphasized by the late 1940s and largely removed from consideration.

The rightward turn in economic thinking was implemented through the 1951 "Treasury-Fed Accord,"[62] a discreet agreement among executive branch personnel, established without fanfare or major press coverage. It demarcated lines of authority between the two financial policy agencies—the Treasury Department and the Federal Reserve System—granting the leading role to the Fed on matters of price stability. There was a strong implication in the accord that fighting inflation would assume priority over full employment,[63] with a further implication that austerity through heightened unemployment would be the principal means of fighting inflation. The Treasury-Fed Accord no doubt gratified financial elites, who traditionally feared inflation and favored stable prices. Though finance had lost some of its earlier prominence, due to the 1929 crash and the Depression, it remained influential.[64] The financial sector was thus a key player in structuring—and limiting—the postwar class compromise.

From university economics departments, researchers accommodated themselves to the conservative policy shift. In fact, they helped promote it with the newly developed Phillips curve, which formalized the trade-off between inflation and unemployment.[65] The renowned MIT economist Paul Samuelson popularized the Phillips curve through his long series of economics textbooks, taught to generations of college freshmen (including this author) over many decades. Samuelson would later comment, "I don't care who writes a nation's laws—or crafts its advanced treatises—if I can write its economics textbooks. The first lick is the privileged one."[66] The imprimatur of Samuelson and other prominent figures ensured that the shift away from full employment would become a permanent feature of mainstream thinking. In the meantime, a corporate-funded organization, the Committee for Economic Development, recommended a target unemployment rate of 4 percent; this quickly became the consensus view of what would constitute "full" employment in the new, more conservative social order that was gradually taking shape.[67]

Keynes himself died suddenly in 1946 and was thus unable to comment on the evolution of economic theory associated with the advent of the Phillips curve. But there can be little doubt that what was now termed "Keynesian economics" was different from the original as set forth in *The General Theory*. A small number of traditionalists criticized the new orthodoxy as a corruption of Keynes's views, terming it "bastard Keynesianism," a phrase coined by the Cambridge economist Joan Robinson.[68] These dissidents aside, the economics profession coalesced around the idea that fighting inflation was more important than achieving full employment, and the two goals were viewed as mutually antagonistic to some degree. Alternative policies that sought to achieve both objectives simultaneously—associated with the earlier versions of Keynesian economics—were disregarded. The updated rendering of Keynesian thought meshed with the increasingly conservative politics of the early Cold War and the associated Red Scare.[69]

The Phillips curve would prove especially useful as an ever-present justification for austerity, which was viewed as a periodic necessity.

During the early years of the class compromise in the 1950s, that was not a major problem, as inflation remained low and austerity—at least in its more draconian forms—was not needed. However, the idea of austerity was now legitimated in principle, and it was embedded in the policy-making process through the anti-inflation Treasury-Fed Accord. In later chapters, we will see that during the 1970s, inflationary conditions would present a perfect pretext for implementing a conservative realignment—especially during the presidency of Jimmy Carter[70]—which entailed severe austerity and a breakdown of the class compromise.

A WORKER'S PARADISE?

Despite its conservative cast, there is no doubt that the postwar social order produced real benefits for working people. After some initial tur-moil and instability, the economy began a period of sustained growth in 1950, continuing into the early 1970s, when the good times essentially ended. The more than twenty years of prosperity were nevertheless impressive, with an average annual growth rate of almost 4 percent per year during the period 1948–1973. For most of the early period, wages and salaries actually grew faster than profits, leveling the distribution of income and wealth.[71] Overall, researchers have found "'extraordinary' wage compression by education, job experience, and occupation from 1940 to 1970." There were also indications that "segments of the work-force that were hardest hit in the Great Depression thrived, relatively, in the post-war period."[72] At a cultural level, the working classes were given prominence, especially in cinema, in such films as *Marty* and *Carousel*. In 1957, *Edge of the City* became one of the first films to address racism and racist violence, and it did so in a blue-collar setting. Working-class life was becoming integral to mainstream American life.

The popular culture of the era reflected an overall social leveling, which was occurring simultaneously at the level of federal legislation. In 1944, Congress legislated the Servicemen's Readjustment Act, the "GI Bill,"[73] which provided free university education to returning veterans, along with support for purchasing houses and starting small businesses.[74] The GI Bill had the effect of raising working-class incomes and educa-tional levels, thereby redistributing income and increasing productiv-ity across a broad range of sectors. The working-class prosperity that resulted from these conditions raised effective demand, fueling continued growth. Progressive taxation also played a role in leveling the distribution of wealth, with nominal tax rates for the highest incomes officially at 90 percent.[75] While actual rates were not so confiscatory in practice, taxation did reduce concentrated wealth to a considerable degree. Economic historians conclude that such high tax rates also held symbolic importance, as they "sent a signal that high incomes were unacceptable"[76]—or at least they were less acceptable than in previous periods.

Among the main factors that drove growth was the Cold War. While presidents were reluctant to undertake investment in purely civilian sectors, which were viewed as unacceptably socialistic, such objections did not apply to investment in weapons procurement, which was considered patriotic and therefore admissible. The idea of "military Keynesianism" was born, creating the ideal justification for federal spending and management of the economy while establishing the United States as a superpower. The economic benefits of military spending were emphasized in landmark foreign policy documents of the period, including NSC-68, which advocated a massive spike in such spending. In the view of the document's authors, "The economic effects of the [military spending] program might be to increase the gross national product."[77] Military spending has proven an inefficient method of creating jobs, less effective than spending in the civilian sector.[78] But given the conservatism of the U.S. business class, along with tensions of the Red Scare, military procurement was probably the only way to achieve state investment and economic planning.

Military Keynesianism became so popular that it was used to justify spending programs that were not really military in character. In 1956, President Dwight D. Eisenhower created the Interstate Highway System, and it was justified as a military necessity, as a means of integrating regional defense networks.[79] And in 1958, the administration authorized increased federal aid to science education through the National Defense Education Act,[80] which was also justified for military purposes.

The overarching salience of national defense became a pervasive feature of American political life during the early Cold War. At the same time, these new federal programs had important economic implications. Funding for education produced more competent work forces and contributed to rising productivity, while the federal highway program created high-paying construction jobs over an extended period. The resulting highway system lowered the cost of ground transportation, raising productivity even further. And the new highways encouraged automobile sales, which soon became a household necessity. The widespread adoption of the car helped reconfigure America's residential geography away from urban centers and toward the suburbs; and this process of reconfiguration further stimulated the economy, contributing to the postwar boom.[81] Automobiles became a leading economic sector, driving overall growth (even as they would later prove disastrous from an environmental standpoint).

Labor unions achieved significant success during this period, "boosting real wages," according to Gordon. Union wage benefits also may have "spilled over" into nonunionized sectors as well,[82] producing a more general working-class prosperity. In addition, political attitudes toward unions were shifting, symbolized by the 1950 "Treaty of Detroit," an agreement between General Motors, the world's largest car manufacturer, and the United Auto Workers. Under the terms of this agreement, workers' wages were to be indexed to the rate of labor productivity; as assembly-line efficiency improved over time, so did wages. The treaty also established a range of worker benefits, including guaranteed pensions and health care. The treaty at GM factories produced similar agreements at Ford and Chrysler plants, eventually becoming a model for labor-management accord that was widely imitated across industrial sectors.[83] These agreements ensured that workers would benefit from the rapid growth in efficient production and that they would have an incentive to support continued growth in efficiency.

The Treaty of Detroit led to a widespread availability of health insurance for workers, provided by private companies. The treaty was a mixed blessing, however, since it reduced political pressure for a state-directed system of health care of the type emerging in Western Europe.[84] President Truman's promise to establish federalized health care—a core feature of his Fair Deal—was now viewed as an unnecessary complication, a distraction from the all-important contest with global communism. The Treaty of Detroit contained other deficiencies: it left large numbers of nonunionized workers with little or no health coverage, many of whom would remain without coverage. Some of the later failings of U.S. health care—notably its lack of universal coverage—can be traced back to these events. At the time, however, the Treaty of Detroit appeared as a major advance for working people, with the prospect of even better conditions in the future. In 1955, AFL-CIO President George Meany declared: "American labor has never had it so good."[85]

Clearly, not all workers benefited equally from the emerging prosperity. The advancement of African Americans was held back by the pervasive racism of the period, especially in the South but in all regions of the country to varying degrees and also in some nominally integrationist labor unions.[86] Many of the New Deal reforms, including the GI Bill, were applied with a measure of racial discrimination. The economic condition of Blacks was further complicated by the mechanization of southern agriculture, which fueled the Great Migration to industrial cities of the upper Midwest.[87] The migration occurred under difficult circumstances, often straining social and family stability. And yet, African Americans were not altogether excluded from the class compromise, as some found employment among the unionized Pullman Porters, who serviced overnight trains.[88] This was a traditionally Black profession and a long-standing source of mobility, later memorialized by the songwriter Steve Goodman ("And the sons of Pullman Porters and the sons of engineers ride their fathers' magic carpets made of steel"). Others found work at plants in Detroit, Chicago, Cleveland, and other manufacturing centers, gaining relatively high salaries and benefits as well as social standing.

Federal policy was beginning to change as well, with President Truman's 1948 Executive Order to desegregate the military.[89] The U.S. Supreme Court produced important antidiscrimination rulings, including the 1948 *Shelley v. Kraemer* decision and the 1954 *Brown v. the Board of Education of Topeka* decision, which began the processes of housing and school desegregation.[90] Overall, there was a dramatic improvement in the wages of Black workers during the period 1940–1970, combined with a significant narrowing of the "racial wage gap" that had long separated Black and white workers.[91]

Major elements of business gradually acquiesced to the class compromise, which was regarded as irreversible. In fact, the compromise worked out well for business, given steady growth rates and high profit margins. During the 1950s, support for the compromise emanated from the Committee for Economic Development (CED), which received funding from leading U,S, corporate interests. The CED was instrumental in establishing a degree of consensus in favor of moderately prolabor policies among corporate executives. The liberalism of the CED gained broad support indeed: in 1948, its Board of Trustees included representatives of Colgate-Palmolive, Goldman Sachs, Procter & Gamble, General Electric, Coca-Cola, and Ford, among others.[92] And from Washington, DC, the Brookings Institution emerged as another proponent of relatively liberal economic policies, with heavy corporate support.[93] Leading business interests openly favored continuation of the welfare state and union protections, now viewed as a positive force according to a 1956 article in the *Wall Street Journal*: "The majority [of business executives] now realize that welfare programs help store up purchasing power in the hands of the consumer." The article quoted a Chicago banker: "I think social security is good. I think unions are good."[94]

President Eisenhower played a prominent role in legitimizing the idea of the class compromise. To be sure, he remained skeptical of Keynesian economics, especially with regard to deficit spending, and he made few efforts to expand the New Deal. On the other hand, he made no serious attempt to repeal New Deal reforms. And President Eisenhower tolerated the burgeoning union movement. Indeed, union membership reached a postwar peak during his tenure, representing 35 percent of the workforce in 1954.[95]

Overall, the Eisenhower presidency ensured that the class compromise was in essence a bipartisan project, endorsed by the mainstreams of both parties as well as major elements of business. The president held contempt for ultraconservatives who opposed the class compromise: "Only a fool would try to deprive working men and women of the right to join the union of their choice."[96] In private correspondence, he observed that opposition to the New Deal reforms was confined to only a "tiny splinter group. . . . Their number is negligible and they are stupid."[97] This is probably an exaggeration— business opposition was more than just "a tiny splinter group"—but Eisenhower's general point reflected a new reality: the class compromise had become mainstream.

Despite the equalizing tendencies just noted, wealth concentration remained a basic feature of American society (though the fortunes were certainly smaller, as a percentage of GDP, than in previous periods). Many of the older fortunes remained from the earlier Gilded Age, while new ones were created after the war in such rising sectors as aerospace technology, microelectronics, household appliances, office equipment, and automobiles.[98] The phenomenon of concentrated wealth ensured that the power of money remained a factor in U.S. politics, always ready to influence policy makers and public opinion. And business interests never lost their clout. In his classic study of this period, published in 1960, the political scientist E. E. Schattschneider emphasized the marked "dominance of business groups in the pressure system." He also stated that "the pressure system has an upper-class bias. . . . Even nonbusiness organizations reflect an upper-class tendency."[99] Capital retained its advantage.

With regard to attitude, business interests were diverse. While many executives had come to terms with the New Deal reforms, others refused to do so. Business retained its share of reactionaries. The eccentric oilmen H. L. Hunt and J. Howard Pew lavishly funded right-wing causes through much of the early postwar period. They were joined by Robert Wood of the Sears-Roebuck mail order company; Fred Koch, who founded an oil services and engineering firm; Harold Luhnow, a prominent furniture merchant; and Jasper Crane of the DuPont Chemical company. Also among this group were owners of small and medium-size businesses, some of whom were moderately rich. Business hardliners bankrolled such long-standing stalwarts of private enterprise as the U.S. Chamber of Commerce and the National Association of Manufacturers, as well as conservative think tanks and foundations, including the American Enterprise Institute, the Foundation for Economic Education (FEE), and the William Volker Fund.[100] In some cases, business executives favored conspiracy-minded groups, such as the movements surrounding Senator Joseph McCarthy[101] and the John Birch Society,[102] which veered even further to the right.

Collectively, these conservative institutions were less influential than the Keynesian-oriented CED or the Brookings Institution. But the conservatives gained some clout among certain (mostly Republican) members of Congress and were thus able to influence national legislation, at least at the margins. The hardliners were particularly successful in dampening the influence of organized labor. During the late 1950s, NAM supported congressional investigations into corruption in the unions, which gained broad publicity and stained the reputation of labor.[103] These investigations dovetailed with negative portrayals of unions in popular culture, notably Elia Kazan's award-winning film *On the Waterfront*.[104]

Efforts by labor to counter these moves were feeble and inadequately funded. And undeniably, the leadership of some unions— which had been weakened by the Red Scare—allowed such practices as featherbedding and graft to flourish, which of course played right into the conservatives' strategy of discrediting them. The corruption of the International Brotherhood of Teamsters was especially noteworthy. In 1959, conservatives scored a victory when Congress passed the Landrum-Griffin Act, further restricting union activity (and functioning as a follow-on to the earlier Taft-Hartley Act).[105]

Meanwhile, NAM and the Chamber of Commerce sought to mold school and university-level curricula to infuse it with a free enterprise bent. A series of teacher seminars and student internships were established implicitly projecting an antiunion message; they were financed by business interests and business-oriented lobby groups. Efforts were also made to influence the writing of textbooks. While these activities certainly did not destroy labor unions, they contributed to the gradual weakening of public support for unions, a trend that began during the late 1950s and gradually accelerated.[106]

A second area of activity for conservatives was the funding of evangelical Christian groups. Business leaders worried about the growth of left-leaning religious tendencies, including such ideas as the "social gospel," popular among liberal Protestants, and the Catholic Worker movement, led by Dorothy Day.[107] The doctrine of Christian conservatism emerged in part as a backlash against such liberal ideas and was strongly supported by business interests. The conservative religious thrust was led by the Reverend James W. Fifield, Jr., a California-based preacher who launched Spiritual Mobilization during the 1930s, a mass campaign that combined both Christian and free market themes.

The corporate funding for the campaign was spearheaded by NAM, whose president sought to establish "patriotism and religious faith" as a probusiness bulwark. The advisory committee to Spiritual Mobilization at one point included "three past presidents of the U.S. Chamber of Commerce, a leading Wall Street analyst, a prominent economist at the American Banking Association, [and] the founder of the National Small Business Association." With his formidable support, Fifeld sought to popularize laissez-faire ideology, which he actively promoted among the faithful.[108]

Another rising Christian leader of the postwar era was the charismatic southerner Billy Graham, who held mass revivals throughout the country, gaining national prominence from the late 1940s. His sermons invoked conservative political themes, often antiunion in character. At one point, Graham declared that in the Garden of Eden there were "no union dues, no labor leaders, no snakes, no disease."[109] He attracted considerable corporate support. According to one biography, "Graham enjoyed numerous long-standing relationships with men of great wealth," who avidly funded the pastor.[110]

Overall, these religious activities added an important "spiritual" dimension to the business campaign, as well as a mass base of Christian voters. In time, Christian conservatism would become a major national force with vast influence, a point we will discuss in later chapters.

THE CHICAGO BOYS

During the post-1945 era, a network of conservative U.S. and European economists rose to prominence. These economists explicitly rejected the prevailing Keynesian framework of state-managed economic growth and sought a return to the antistatist doctrine of an earlier era, that of laissez-faire. Their network included a core group of émigré Austrian aristocrats, which included Friedrich von Hayek, Ludwig Von Mises, and Gottfried Haberler, as well as a coterie of American-born followers, which included Milton Friedman. Financial support for this group emanated from such business-backed sources as the Volker Fund, Foundation for Economic Education, and Schweizerische Kreditanstalt (later known as Credit Suisse), which promoted their conferences and research activities. The International Chamber of Commerce also provided support. The Volker Fund and the FEE were especially helpful in establishing the conservatives at the University of Chicago, whose economics department became a leading center for the incubation of right-wing ideas. The Volker Fund was even allowed to pay for von Hayek's salary for a period of ten years while he taught as a Chicago faculty member. The FEE helped arrange the hiring of George Stigler, another exponent of laissez-faire economics. FEE also assisted Von Mises in securing an appointment at New York University, thus broadening the conservatives' scope of influence.[111] And in the South, white elites enthusiastically supported Friedman's plans for school vouchers as a means of circumventing racial integration.[112]

Another conservative institution was the Mont Pèlerin Society (MPS), named after the Swiss resort where it was founded in 1947. The MPS was an international networking organization for the propagation of free market ideas. Membership in the Mont Pèlerin group overlapped with the Chicago School affiliates, and the two were closely interlinked.[113] We will see in later chapters that the MPS and its members gradually gained funding from some of the largest and most powerful corporate interests in the United States, and their influence would increase accordingly.

The Chicago economists—the "Chicago Boys" as they were later termed—adopted a celebratory view of the free market as the locus of inherent efficiency, fairness, and excellence. The rougher edges of their economics were gradually smoothed and mainstreamed, making them more accessible to a broad corporate audience. The tendency of the Chicago School economists to mainstream their views is especially evident in their evolving analyses of monopoly power. In their original formulation, Chicago School economists were highly critical of monopolies, which were regarded as significant dangers requiring governmental action to maintain competitive conditions and prevent firms from achieving market power. In 1947, even Friedman held that "large corporations and monopolies posed a serious social problem that had to be addressed by public policy," while his colleague Henry Simons went further, declaring monopoly a "great enemy of democracy."[114]

During the 1950s, however, the Chicago economists began to reevaluate monopoly power, dismissing the whole issue as virtually a nonproblem, one that would be corrected under market conditions.

The principal enduring evils, in their view, were government-sponsored monopolies and labor unions, both of which constituted anticompetitive pathologies corrupting market efficiency.[115] In altering their stance on monopoly, the Chicago economists were conforming to the views and practices of their business supporters, some of which (United States Steel, for example) operated under nonmarket conditions and practiced administered pricing.[116]

The reconceptualization of monopoly also reinforced the Chicago School's preexisting bias against labor unions, and this feature appealed to such antiunion businesses as General Electric (an additional source of support for free market economics).[117] In the view of one historian of the Chicago economists, the new perspective on monopoly "amounted to an apologetic 'corporations can do no wrong' perspective."[118] The Chicago School's research agenda fit well with the interests of corporate America, and the relationship between the two sectors—the intellectual and the corporate—gradually became more intimate.

The conservative Chicago perspective was an outlier for an extended period, dissenting from the prevailing economic consensus, which remained loyal to Keynesianism for the most part.[119] Over time, the conservatives would come to dominate economic thinking, gradually displacing Keynesian thought during the upheavals of the 1970s. We will see that some of the major policy trends of that decade—including deregulation of industry, money supply targeting by the Federal Reserve, weakened labor unions, reduced antitrust enforcement, and floating exchange rates—had long been favored by Milton Friedman and his colleagues.[120]

Overall, conservative business interests established a range of institutions during the early postwar period that eventually enabled an assault on the class compromise. Such an assault did not begin in earnest until after 1970, but the groundwork was laid much earlier. Business support for conservative groups was sufficiently extensive that some analysts question whether the class compromise really existed at all.[121] This is surely an overstatement, as it elides the strong business support that clearly did exist in favor of the compromise; support for the class compromise was the dominant perspective.

One way to view business backing for conservative causes during this period is that such activity constituted an insurance policy for business against the possibility that it might eventually be in their interests to repeal the class compromise. Perhaps business was simply hedging its bets. Whatever the motive, this much is clear: Corporate America had at its disposal a series of interlinked institutions that would eventually enable a full-fledged campaign against labor unions and the welfare state, to be unleashed during the economic upheavals of the 1970s.

THE COMPROMISE BEGINS TO UNRAVEL

The gradual unraveling of the class compromise began during the late 1950s and especially after the 1957–1958 recession, the worst downturn of the decade. In retrospect, it appears that the spurt of economic dynamism unleashed after 1945 was already beginning to lose steam. The origin of the recession lay with a decision by the Federal Reserve to tighten monetary policy by raising interest rates as a means of constraining inflation and thereby restoring business confidence.[122] And the recession was probably intensified by the disruption of a worldwide influenza pandemic, the so-called Asian flu, which took place simultaneously.[123]

The downturn very likely accelerated capital flight, whereby hard-pressed industries migrated away from the unionized states of the northeast and upper Midwest and moved to the Sunbelt states of the South and Southwest, most of which had right-to-work laws, limited union influence, and low wages. State governments in the Sunbelt advertised their low wages and "business friendly" climates to lure investment away from other states as an integral part of an extended zero-sum game that would play out among various regions of the United States.[124] The long-term effects of the Taft-Hartley Act and other antilabor legislation, combined with the failure of Operation Dixie—its inability to achieve truly national labor unions—were now becoming apparent. As a result of these conditions, the level of union membership began a gradual decline, continuing over a period of several decades from its historic high point in the middle 1950s, coinciding with declining populations in industrial cities of the Northeast and Midwest. One often thinks of deindustrialization and union decay as phenomena of the 1970s and 1980s, but in reality, the process had commenced much earlier. The unionization of large portions of the labor force—the crowning achievement of the postwar social order—was already starting to disintegrate.

The economic sluggishness of this period weakened the credibility of the Republican Party. During the course of the 1960 presidential campaign, there was yet another downturn, which proved advantageous to the Democrats.[125] The result was the narrow election of a Democratic president, John F. Kennedy, who won on the slogan "Get America moving again"—an implicit promise of renewing postwar prosperity.[126] Kennedy's method was to use Keynesian-style fiscal stimulus, focusing on military spending.

The new president had criticized the Eisenhower administration for having placed too much emphasis on nuclear weapons and massive retaliation, a method of fighting communism on the cheap, neglecting conventional weapons and power projection. Kennedy was determined to overcome this problem by expanding ground forces, particularly mobile expeditionary forces and counterinsurgency units, enhancing the military's flexibility in response to international crises. At the same time, Kennedy did not overlook strategic nuclear forces, and he increased production of both silo-based and submarine-based missile systems, at considerable expense.[127] There was also expansion of the space program based on the president's decision to prepare for a moon mission.

The augmented federal spending on military equipment and space exploration did indeed produce a fiscal stimulus, generating high levels of growth, more than had occurred during the Eisenhower presidency. And Kennedy sought to open up new trade and investment opportunities overseas, especially in sub-Saharan Africa.[128] Military Keynesianism was working, at least in the short term.[129]

PRESIDENT KENNEDY CONFRONTS BIG BUSINESS

Another aspect to the Democratic strategy was a tax cut, using deficit spending to enhance the stimulus. Before undertaking the tax cut, however, Kennedy sought to prevent an inflationary spurt (an inherent risk in his expansionary policy). He was especially concerned about the price of steel, a leading sector at the time. It was also a sector that was heavily concentrated, with most steel being produced by eight companies operating on nonmarket principles through the familiar process of administered pricing.[130] From the labor side, the United Steelworkers negotiated regular pay increases for its members, which companies were able to pass on to consumers in the form of higher prices. In 1962, Kennedy pressured both steel companies and the union to restrain price and wage increases and achieved a good-faith agreement on price stability. Then one of the companies, United States Steel, raised prices in violation of the agreement. When Kennedy pressed U.S. Steel executives to rescind the price increase, they refused.[131]

The price increase precipitated a brief but illuminating crisis, revealing the extent to which business remained a privileged group. Kennedy used the resources of the executive branch to retaliate against U.S. Steel by withdrawing federal contracts and redirecting them to competitors who had cooperated with the price agreement. He also threatened antitrust prosecutions. In private, the president reportedly stated that his father had told him that "steel men were sons of bitches, but I never realized till now how right he was."[132] The comment was quickly leaked to the press (perhaps intentionally), eliciting considerable notice, especially in corporate circles. In response to these pressures, U.S. Steel finally backed down and rescinded the price hike, but the whole affair left a feeling of acrimony. The business press became highly critical. Kennedy's actions had dealt "a heavy blow to the confidence upon which the prosperity of Main Street as well as Wall Street depends," according to an editorial in *Barron's* financial weekly. The editorial added—with a hint of threat—that the president's challenge to U.S. Steel would "cost the nation dear."[133] It might cost the president dear as well.

Kennedy had won the battle with the steel industry, but in the end, he could not win the war. The feud produced a sudden loss of business confidence that appears to have been broadly based. It was widely believed that the president's confrontational stance toward U.S. Steel contributed to a generalized decline in stock prices.[134] It seemed that the business community was striking back against President Kennedy, who was shaken by these events. Any further loss of confidence risked a more generalized collapse of investment, which would undermine his strategy for sustained growth.

Overall, the steel controversy offered a clear lesson for future presidents: Business retained its ability to retaliate against uncooperative politicians—including those like President Kennedy, whose public popularity was consistently high[135]—thus acting outside the democratic process. As president, Kennedy possessed the ability to discipline business through selective contract allocation and the possibility of public denunciation. But in the final analysis, it was business that held the upper hand.

Following this loss of confidence, Kennedy made special efforts to propitiate business interests and the upper classes. The Kennedy tax cut that followed was legislated on conservative terms, disproportionately favoring the wealthy. Maximum rates were reduced from 90 percent, as had been established during the New Deal, to a new maximum rate of only 70 percent, generating a windfall for those with high incomes. The episode set a more generalized precedent of reducing taxes for the wealthy as a means to spur growth. The Kennedy precedent would be invoked repeatedly by both politicians and lobbyists during the 1970s and 1980s, often citing this experience as a justification for further and even more aggressive reductions in taxation rates in favor of the wealthy.[136] The Kennedy-era tax cut helped undermine the principle of progressive taxation in general and contributed to reversing the Great Compression, the postwar redistribution of wealth and income.

A FOOL'S PARADISE?

The tax cut was concluded after Kennedy's assassination, officially signed into law by President Lyndon Baines Johnson in early 1964.[137] In general, Johnson proved a far more astute politician than his predecessor and was especially capable in managing Congress. Proposals that Kennedy had only talked about were legislated by President Johnson. The earthy Johnson once said that for all their Harvard degrees, the Kennedy cabinet knew very little about passing legislation, no more "than an old maid does about fucking."[138]

With his political skills, President Johnson enacted breakthrough programs, including federally funded health care, through the newly established Medicare and Medicaid programs, environmental protection, and a host of new and expanded antipoverty projects associated with an overall "War on Poverty." Johnson also passed major civil rights protections, including the Twenty-Fourth Amendment to the Constitution, which guaranteed the voting rights of African Americans, and banned such practices as the poll tax, which restricted suffrage in the South.[139] Federal policy enabled Blacks to enter the mainstream of American life for the first time on a large scale, including as consumers. This combined package of domestic programs enhanced the fiscal stimulus. In addition, Johnson was not averse to using military Keynesianism, especially after his massive escalation of the Vietnam War, which began in 1965.

The immediate result of the Kennedy-Johnson program was improved economic performance, with no recessions during the period 1961–1969, accompanied by strong GDP growth.[140] With this apparent success to his credit, Johnson was easily reelected in 1964, defeating his ultraconservative opponent, Barry Goldwater, by one of the largest margins of popular vote in history. At the time of reelection, the Johnson presidency seemed the apex of achievement. Business was satisfied with record high profits,[141] while unions had easy access to a labor-friendly administration. To be sure, union membership had already passed its high point and was experiencing long-term deterioration, but it was easy to forget this detail amid a climate that appeared strongly favorable to workers. Professional economists expressed complacency with what seemed like idyllic conditions, a view shared by economic journalists. A 1964 *New York Times* article asked rhetorically, "Are Recessions a Thing of the Past?"[142] Even as late as 1970, Paul Samuelson spoke of the business cycle as a possibly obsolete concept, supplanted by a permanent state of stability accompanied by an overarching technocratic wisdom.[143]

Such optimism was unfounded, since the U.S. economy was about to enter a new era of turbulence, to be discussed more fully in later chapters. For now, we will note one basic indicator of growing turbulence: a rising and unchecked inflation. The inflationary spurt began in the late 1960s and then gradually accelerated, the result of overspending by the Johnson administration, which was simultaneously fighting the War on Poverty and another war in Vietnam.[144] And Johnson sought to do all this without a tax increase.[145] At the time, it was possible to dismiss price instability as a temporary difficulty; but in retrospect, it is clear that inflation had become a long-term feature of the economy and a source of political conflict. The standard remedy for inflation—austerity and recession—would not be implemented by

President Johnson,[146] who was too labor friendly for such measures. By the end of the 1970s, however, a particularly harsh version of austerity was finally imposed, at high social cost, a point to which we will return later in this study. The dysfunction of inflation would serve to legitimize a later austerity policy.

A second dysfunction was a secular decline in corporate profits. Beginning in the late 1960s, the rate of return on the capital stock for U.S. manufacturers dropped precipitously.[147] Given the twin threats of inflation and low profits, the stage was set for a business mobilization in defense of its interests. Clearly, the placid years of the postwar boom were drawing to a close as American capitalism entered a turbulent phase.

The post–World War II class compromise was a historic achievement, raising living standards for a large portion of the American working class. At the same time, this achievement was built on an unstable foundation, one that ultimately collapsed. The class compromise seemed as though it might last forever, but in the end, it proved relatively brief.

The compromise contained two main deficiencies. First, it left intact a sizable portion of the great fortunes that had long been a source of influence for business interests and wealthy individuals. With these accumulated funds, U.S. elites created a series of institutions—including lobby groups, think tanks, religious organizations, and academic networks—that allowed them to sway policy makers, enabling elites to act outside democratic norms. Second, private investors remained the main source of economic dynamism, and politicians of both parties would seek to placate them. The need for policy makers to maintain business confidence—and to do so on a continuous basis—furnished elites with another source of influence, which once again circumvented democratic processes. These two undemocratic features were not inevitable but resulted from specific decisions that were made during the late 1940s, when the proposed system of state-directed investment was undercut. The political order that resulted favored the upper classes.

Despite their inherent advantages, America's elites tolerated the class compromise—at least for a time—since it promoted stability and suited their interests. Their support was in fact essential to the whole arrangement, enabling it to function smoothly through the late 1960s.

With the rise of inflation and diminished profitability, however, elite interests gradually shifted away from compromise and moved toward confrontation. Unionized labor, the welfare state, progressive taxation, and economic regulation were increasingly seen as unacceptable burdens.

Stated simply, America's elites always retained a veto over the postwar social order, and during the 1970s, they began exercising that veto; it was an elite revolt. In later chapters, we will see how this revolt produced a sharp turn to the right in U.S. politics, combined with a rupture of the class compromise. The "Century of the Common Man" that Henry Wallace had heralded in 1942 would last for just three decades before it vanished.

CHAPTER TWO

The Rich Revolt

Perhaps the most downtrodden and persecuted of all American
minorities [is] corporate enterprise. . . . Isn't it about
time that investors began to fight back?

—ROBERT M. BLEIBERG, *BARRON'S*

The post–New Deal class compromise began to unravel during the
late 1960s due to an accumulation of stresses brought on by deteriorating economic performance. By the early 1970s, these stresses had
generated a backlash against the compromise, combined with a political mobilization seeking to move U.S. politics toward the right. This
chapter will show that the conservative mobilization of this period
was largely an elitist affair; it was dominated by corporate interests
and wealthy individuals, who furnished lavish funding for a range of
political groups. While many studies of the 1970s emphasize cultural
changes as the main force driving the rise of conservatism, we will see
that behind these cultural changes was massive financing by business
interests. President Richard Nixon played an especially pivotal role in
orchestrating this business campaign. These trends would transform
the climate of discussion in the United States, producing a basic shift
in public policy in a laissez-faire direction. With regard to motive, we
will see that corporate activism was motivated by a striking decline in
the rate of profit, especially after 1970. While little recognized in the
historical literature, the decline of corporate profitability counts as a
central factor in America's right turn.

A key development during this period was the rise of conservative economists associated with the Mont Pèlerin Society (MPS), the most influential of whom was the University of Chicago professor Milton Friedman, who became president of the MPS in 1970. While the topic of Mont Pèlerin economics is obviously complex, its objectives may be distilled as follows: MPS opposed fiscal and monetary policies that sought to raise employment levels as being inconsistent with market principles, which it venerated. MPS members were also hostile toward labor unions, which were viewed as interfering with market mechanisms. Above all, they sought to repeal the regulatory capitalism established during the New Deal in favor of free market capitalism.[1] These principles gradually evolved into the policy agenda behind the rightward transformation of U.S. politics, consistent with the interests of corporate executives who bankrolled the MPS.

Their sudden appearance in the limelight signaled a historic change. Previously, MPS economists had played a marginal role in public debates. They were long considered "lunatic fringe . . . far right, out there."[2] Their most important achievement initially was to advise the presidential campaign of Barry Goldwater in 1964,[3] which proved a disastrous failure. After this debacle, MPS members experienced a rapid ascent in both academic prestige and political power. Simultaneously, their base of business support expanded, and by the mid-1960s, the MPS organization and its individual members had received financial backing from some of the most prominent enterprises of the era, including Ford Motor Company, United Fruit, General Electric, DuPont Chemical, Shell Oil, and United States Steel.[4] And such corporate-funded think tanks as the American Enterprise Institute and the Hoover Institution later hosted MPS members.[5]

The Mont Pèlerin ideology was especially attractive to the financial sector. Friedman himself developed close ties to prominent banking interests, which evidently appreciated his theory of "monetarism," with its associated recommendation of rigorously controlling the money supply. The doctrines of tight monetary policy and low inflation are ideas of long-standing appeal to bankers. Accordingly, Friedman cultivated a personal friendship with Walter Wriston, CEO of Citibank, then emerging as a premier American financial institution. Wriston "worshipped at the shrine of University of Chicago economist Milton Friedman," according to one biography.[6] Both men became forceful advocates for the deregulation of finance.[7] From outside the United States, conservative interests connected to the Riksbank, Sweden's central bank, established the Nobel Prize in Economic Science, which was awarded to Friedrich von Hayek in 1974, to Friedman in 1976, and, later, to other MPS members. While centrists and Keynesians were also awarded Nobel Prizes, the most important achievement of this new prize was to confer legitimacy on the laissez-faire doctrines of the MPS.[8] The creation of the economics prize elevated the status of a profession that was rapidly moving rightward.

Through the course of the 1970s, Mont Pèlerin economists transformed not only academic research but also public discussion. Popularizations of MPS economics—notably von Hayek's *The Road to Serfdom* and Friedman's *Capitalism and Freedom*—became bestsellers with broad readerships. Their growing fame was likely aided by corporate backing, as well as the efforts of the New York public relations firm Hill & Knowlton, the MPS publicity agent.[9] The *Readers Digest*—long associated with the very conservative interests of DeWitt Wallace—ran articles by Friedman and his colleagues during the 1970s,[10] having previously published a condensed version of *The Road to Serfdom*. In addition, Friedman published regular articles in *Newsweek*. Laissez-faire was moving toward the center of public discussion. And with the inauguration of Richard Nixon as president in 1969, conservative economists would, for the first time, gain access to the White House.

PRESIDENT NIXON AS AN IDEOLOGICAL CONSERVATIVE

Seminal events in America's rightward turn took place during the Nixon presidency with direct presidential support. Readers may be surprised by this point, given the widespread perception of Nixon as an amoral chameleon rather than an authentic conservative. It appeared that Nixon had "no ideas, only methods," according to *Time* magazine.[11] In public policy terms, his presidency appears—at first glance—to have been remarkably liberal; in some respects, it was one of the most liberal of the post–World War II era. It was President Nixon who inaugurated landmark environmental protection and workplace safety legislation, including the creation of the Environmental Protection Agency as well as the Occupational Safety and Health Administration.[12] Under Nixon's tenure, the Department of Labor initiated federal support for job training to assist unemployed and underemployed workers.[13]

The scale of federal regulation increased significantly. Nixon implemented wage and price controls, while deploying classic Keynesian methods to stimulate economic growth, just prior to his 1972 reelection campaign. At one point, the president pronounced, "I am now a Keynesian in economics."[14] He cultivated friendly relations with at least some labor unions while resisting calls to undermine unions. "Under no circumstances should we assume an anti-labor posture," noted a White House document from 1971, reflecting an overarching strategy.[15] Affirmative action was initiated to advance hiring of African Americans (even as the president simultaneously appealed to white resentments, often using coded racist language in his speeches).[16] Movement conservatives such as William Rusher openly distrusted Nixon, and they pondered the possibility of third-party challenges against him.[17] But above all, Nixon is remembered as a *Zelig*-like figure who accommodated himself to the prevailing liberalism while holding no consistent principles of his own.

More recent evidence suggests that the foregoing interpretation is incomplete and that Nixon was also an ideological president who quietly sought to advance a conservative agenda, consistent with the direction of MPS economists, whom the president admired. That was apparently the view of Friedman, who, in his memoirs offered this perspective on Nixon: "Few presidents have come closer to expressing a philosophy compatible with my own." While Friedman disagreed with some of Nixon's specific policies (especially wage and price controls), he was nevertheless effusive in his overall assessment of the ex-president: "He was highly intelligent, an intellectual in the sense that he was interested in discussing abstract ideas, extremely knowledgeable." And Nixon was equally effusive in his assessment of Friedman. During the 1968 presidential campaign, he claimed to "have great respect . . . for Milton Friedman."[18] Though he never held any official position in the administration, Friedman served as "an unofficial advisor to the President."[19] It was under Nixon that the MPS ideas would move away from the right-wing fringe and into the mainstream.

Throughout the course of the Nixon presidency, Mont Pèlerin economics was a continuous presence, especially in the Department of the Treasury. One of the most influential figures was the MPS member George Shultz, who served in the Nixon administration as Treasury secretary, Labor secretary, and director of the Office of Management and Budget. Before entering the administration, he had been an economics professor at the University of Chicago as well as "a close friend, admirer, and disciple of Milton Friedman," according to one insider account.[20] Two other important figures were John Connally and William Simon, who also served as Treasury secretaries under Nixon; both were influenced by Mont Pèlerin economists, including Friedman and Shultz, as they would later acknowledge in memoirs.[21]

The first chairman of the administration's Council of Economic Advisers was Paul McCracken, who was yet another follower of Friedman. At the time of his death, an obituary noted that "McCracken described his economic philosophy as 'Friedmanesque,' after noted economist Milton Friedman."[22] His replacement as CEA chair was Herbert Stein, who had been appointed on "the recommendation of Milton Friedman."[23] Another significant figure was Nixon's Agriculture secretary, Earl Butz, who had been a Purdue University academic with close connections to Ralston-Purina and other agribusiness companies. He, too, was influenced by the laissez-faire economics of the MPS, as revealed in Butz's private correspondence with Friedman.[24]

Robert Bork, a former Chicago corporate lawyer, was appointed as chief litigator in the Department of Justice, the solicitor-general. Bork was yet another MPS member; his views on antitrust policy closely aligned with the Friedmanite perspective that monopoly was not a serious problem in a free market economy.[25] The Mont Pèlerin economists Gottfried Haberler and Fritz Matchlup served as economic consultants to the administration.[26] With regard to the president himself, in 1972, one official wrote in his diary, "My, how he [Nixon] has been taken in by the monetarist talk of Friedman and Shultz!"[27]

Throughout the Nixon presidency, MPS economists exerted a subtle influence on policy formulation, while their close association with the presidency enhanced their overall prestige, thus ensuring that their influence would endure long after Nixon left office. The clout of the MPS would carry over to Nixon's presidential successor,

Gerald Ford, who stated that Friedman's research on inflation formed "one of the foundations of this administration's economic policy."[28] During the course of the 1970s, the MPS network advanced a laissez-faire agenda with presidents from both political parties, including Jimmy Carter; and its ideas laid the groundwork for the deregulation of agriculture, air travel, trucking, rail transportation, international finance, and, finally, domestic finance. We will see in a later chapter that Friedman's monetarism would offer an ideal pretext for implementation of an austerity program—involving the intentional lowering of living standards—dealing a decisive blow against the New Deal class compromise.

NIXON MOBILIZES THE PRIVATE SECTOR

An important element of President Nixon's agenda was galvanizing corporate interests to fund right-wing think tanks, as counterweights against centrist think tanks and institutions—notably the Committee on Economic Development, Brookings Institution, Ford Foundation, and Council on Foreign Relations—collectively known as the "Eastern Establishment," to use Nixon's derisive phrase. Papers at his Presidential Library reveal that Nixon was acting strategically to craft a conservative intellectual network as an alternative to the Eastern Establishment, an endeavor engaging some of the president's top aides.[29]

Preparation for this campaign began in late December 1969, when White House staff began circulating strategy papers lamenting the power of Brookings and the lack of a powerful right-wing think tank. The goal of these strategy papers was to build up a conservative counterpart to Brookings to advocate for the administration's positions and advance "a conservative influence on future administrations."[30] Evidently, White House aides were planning a political transformation for the long term to continue well after Nixon himself left the presidency.

The focus of Nixon's efforts was the American Enterprise Institute (AEI), a small Washington, DC, think tank founded in 1938, then headed by William Baroody. Initially, it had only limited funding and influence. AEI researchers produced reports that argued against labor unions, federal spending on social programs, and state regulation of the private sector.[31] Its basic ideology was closely aligned with the views of Friedman, who had long served on the AEI Board of Trustees.[32] It received relatively modest subventions from corporate interests[33] but had nowhere near the funding or influence of its principal rival, the Brookings Institution. At an electoral level, AEI had long been affiliated with the Goldwater wing of the Republican Party.[34] Positioned well to the right of the mainstream consensus, especially on economic policy, the institute seemed confined to the margins of political respectability. But that would soon change.

In early 1971, White House personnel were working methodically to build AEI into a Washington powerhouse, as discussed in numerous documents. These endeavors were led by the presidential aides Bryce Harlow and Charles Colson. The president himself played a direct role. According to a document written by Colson, "The President a year ago met with John Swearingen [from Standard Oil of Indiana] and me. He gave the charge to Swearingen to raise funds necessary [for AEI] and told him . . . that if he ever needed any help, *the President would be happy to provide it if he could.*"[35]

White House efforts to generate support and funding for AEI were wide-ranging. Business executives and business-funded foundations were contacted in multiple sectors, eliciting contributions to AEI from the Lilly Endowment (funded by Eli Lilly pharmaceuticals), J. Howard Pew (Sun Oil), and the very wealthy Scaife family, as well as Indiana-Standard.[36] In the view of White House staff, corporate executives remained overly passive and resistant to the idea of challenging the centrist establishment; they required external encouragement and orchestration.[37] The president was pleased to furnish this orchestration, as he leaned on executives to finance a new and more rightist counterestablishment centered on the American Enterprise Institute. Nixon established a close personal relationship with AEI director Baroody.[38]

Nixon's campaign produced impressive results. In 1971, Colson noted with satisfaction that "we have over the year made great strides in obtaining funds for AEI. We have now more than doubled their operating budget; they are taking on a number of assignments that are very important to us."[39] The administration seemed especially pleased that AEI was able to support large numbers of conservative academics, who would be useful in influencing policy debates while serving as counterweights to liberal academics, whom the president despised. In addition,

AEI was encouraged to "get very active in the publishing business."[40] AEI personnel used its expanded funding to generate high-profile policy papers, press interviews, and policy conferences to advance their ideology and inject it into Washington discussions. Over time, the institute moved from the fringes of the D.C. establishment to the center, as the laissez-faire viewpoint it advocated gradually became the new mainstream.

While building up AEI, the Nixon administration also sought to undermine centrist institutions, especially the Brookings Institution, against which the president held a special animus.[41] One document noted White House efforts to "discourage contributions to Brookings,"[42] a strategy that Nixon strongly supported. When speaking with his aides about Brookings in 1971, the president's tone turned vindictive, as revealed in transcripts of presidential conversations: "We're up against an enemy, a conspiracy. They're using any means. We are going to use any means. Is that clear?" And then the president queried, "Did they get the Brookings Institute raided last night? No? Get it done, I want it done. I want the Brookings Institute safe cleaned out."[43] Nixon was thus advocating burglary against his political enemies at the Brookings Institution (though at least in this case, there is no evidence the proposed break-in was carried out). Other agencies of the Eastern Establishment, such as the Ford Foundation, also elicited caustic comments.[44] And he said with regard to the Council on Foreign Relations, "I'm going to get that Council [on] Foreign Relations. I'm going to chop those bastards off right at the neck. That's all there is to it."[45]

In these conversations, the president sounds like a character in a gangster film or perhaps an episode of *The Sopranos*. With regard to motive, Nixon's feud with establishment institutions has long been viewed as revenge against these institutions' (especially Brookings's) association with critics of the president's Vietnam policy. In memoirs, Nixon himself advanced this interpretation.[46] However, private papers from the Nixon Library suggest there was an additional reason for his vendetta against Brookings: It was part of an overarching strategy to establish a new—and much more right-wing—counterestablishment.

For the most part, the White House strategy of building a counterestablishment was conducted in secret. But from time to time, administration officials spelled out their objectives in public speeches. In 1971,

Vice President Spiro Agnew harangued executives that they needed to launch a massive campaign to combat "adversaries of our free enterprise system." The vice president also noted "the imperative need to begin mustering in the media and in the Nation's educational institutions" as part of this free enterprise effort.[47] With the building up of the American Enterprise Institute, the administration took specific actions to achieve the mustering of the media and the educational system while subtly moving U.S. politics to the right.

THE HISTORICAL SIGNIFICANCE OF THE WATERGATE SCANDAL

The principal significance of Watergate is that it prevented Nixon from implementing the conservative policy agenda that he likely had been planning for his second presidential term. But before discussing this scandal in detail, let us consider the larger context. In early 1973, the president formulated an ambitious legislative package entailing dramatic reductions to a broad range of federal antipoverty programs. The planned reductions "aimed to starve the welfare state," according to the presidential scholar Allen Matusow; these were to go well beyond routine budget cutting. It also appears that Nixon intended to undermine the post–New Deal system of economic regulations, beginning with the crucial energy sector,[48] in line with the antiregulatory messages emanating from AEI and the Mont Pèlerin economists whom he cultivated. The president was capitalizing on his landslide victory over the Democrats in the 1972 election to advance his agenda.

In memoirs, Nixon emphasized the ideological character of his second-term program: "Now [after re-election], I planned to give expression to the more conservative values and beliefs of the New Majority throughout the country and use my power to put some teeth into my New American Revolution." Nixon acknowledged that his conservative ambitions were opposed by "Congress, the bureaucracy, and the media" as well as "the Eastern Establishment," who were committed to the "the New Deal, the New Frontier, the Great Society," which he would now contest. Overall, President Nixon hoped his second term would prove "quite a shock for the establishment."[49] In a January 1973 interview, one White House official succinctly stated the Nixonian strategy:

"During the first term, we stopped [the Democrats'] revolution. *Now we can move forward with our own.*"[50]

The American Enterprise Institute—which Nixon had carefully built up—was to play a role in advancing this revolution. A key White House figure was William Baroody, Jr., son of the AEI head, who was hired in early 1973 as director of the White House Office of Public Liaison. From this post, Baroody helped generate support for the president's agenda from the National Association of Manufacturers (NAM), the U.S. Chamber of Commerce, and major corporate trade groups,[51] which would no doubt have proven helpful in moving the administration's agenda through Congress. Nixon placed special emphasis on NAM, where he exercised considerable sway: "The NAM is totally in our pocket politically," according to one presidential aide.[52]

Nixon also sought to lay the groundwork for an authentic Republican electoral majority through "Operation Switchover." The purpose of Switchover was to lure conservative Democrats in Congress—and Democratic voters—to join the Republican Party. There was a special focus on converting southern Democrats to the Republican cause as part of the president's overarching "Southern strategy."[53] Race and religion probably would have been deployed as wedge issues to operationalize the strategy, just as Nixon had done throughout his first term.[54] When viewed in retrospect, however, we cannot fully assess the president's agenda, in terms of either his electoral tactics or his policy program, since he did not have sufficient time to develop them in detail. But based on his memoirs, Nixon's second-term agenda was to be bold, ambitious, and right-wing.

All the president's plans were thwarted by the Watergate scandal, which engulfed his administration shortly after inauguration in January 1973. The nineteen months remaining in his presidency were consumed by scandal, making it impossible for Nixon to launch any new initiatives. The break-in at the Democratic headquarters at Washington's Watergate Hotel had initially been dismissed as a "third rate burglary" conducted by low-level White House zealots without higher-level guidance—but this explanation soon proved untenable. And after the initial break-in, Nixon memorably sought to cover up the crime, which opened the president to charges that he had obstructed justice and abused power.

Even some of Nixon's strongest supporters in Congress were genuinely shocked by his actions, as revealed in congressional hearings.[55] And from academia, the neoconservative Professor Daniel Bell wrote to a colleague that Watergate revealed "a myopia and moral blindness on a vast scale" in the Nixon White House. It represented a "carry over [of] the mentality and tactics of the international 'black' tactics and propaganda, reminiscent of the silent war between the CIA and KGB into domestic politics."[56] On August 9, 1974, Nixon resigned in the face of near certain impeachment and removal from office.

The Watergate scandal proved a setback for business interests, one that at least momentarily seemed serious. At the height of the scandal, one executive lamented to a *Business Week* reporter that "business will suffer from Watergate because it will lower public confidence in business as well as in the political system." Another warily noted a "deterioration of [public] confidence in the business community."[57] Watergate constituted a setback for the conservative movement as well, since its main electoral vehicle, the Republican Party, was tainted by its association with the Nixon administration. And there were further setbacks following Nixon's resignation. The November 1974 midterm congressional elections produced victory for the Democrats, who would now hold overwhelming majorities in both houses of Congress. The Democratic Party—especially its liberal wing—was thus emboldened. The midterm elections also strengthened the position of organized labor, which supported and financed many Democratic candidates. The U.S. Chamber of Commerce expressed grave concern about a rising labor tide stemming from the election.[58] The Democrats were well placed to block corporate efforts aimed at advancing antilabor and laissez-faire agendas—at least for a few years.

In short, Watergate's main contribution to history is that it delayed America's rightward turn in federal policy. Had the scandal not occurred, Nixon likely would have commenced this turn during his second presidential term, but he was stopped by Watergate. In the end, corporate America would recover from these setbacks, and it would impose a rightward policy turn, mainly during the latter portion of the Carter presidency. For a brief period at mid-decade, however, it seemed that the right's march to power had stalled.

THE PRIVATE SECTOR MOBILIZES

Despite Nixon's departure from office, the conservative movement managed to forge ahead. The task of sustaining the movement now fell to business executives themselves, who orchestrated and funded a dense network of ideological think tanks and associated lobby groups. Former White House aides eagerly lent assistance in establishing this network, thus maintaining continuity with the now defunct Nixon administration.

The centerpiece of the growing right-wing network remained the American Enterprise Institute.[59] AEI's Board of Trustees included executives from General Electric, Metropolitan Life, Rockwell International, Mobil Oil, and Eli Lilly, while its roster of financial contributors included a range of enterprises representing a cross section of corporate America.[60] In 1977, the *Washington Post* marveled at AEI's prodigious growth: "Two decades ago the American Enterprise Institute . . . was an $80,000-a-year right-wing propaganda mill, operating out of a hole-in-the-wall. . . . Today its well-appointed offices are spread over four floors of a modern building and its annual budget is $5 million."[61]

With this increased funding, the institute was able to massively expand its staff while, at the qualitative level, it was able to attract researchers with high public profiles. Its personnel featured former officials from the Nixon administration, including Herbert Stein, Paul McCracken, Melvin Laird, William Ruckelshaus, and Bryce Harlow, all of whom connected with AEI after departing federal government positions. Nixon's successor, Gerald Ford, also established close ties with AEI. After leaving the presidency in 1977, Ford join the institute's staff, becoming a "sort of traveling salesman for AEI's ideas," according to *Human Events.*[62] Other influential hires were the Harvard economist Haberler, who had previously worked as a consultant with the Nixon-era Treasury Department,[63] and the famous New York essayist Irving Kristol, a leading figure in the "neoconservative" movement, which was rapidly gaining favor among intellectuals.

The most influential of AEI's activities was its Center for the Study of Government Regulation, which sought to discredit the regulatory system established during the New Deal and replace it with a laissez-faire system. It was assisted by the Washington University economist Murray

Weidenbaum, an adjunct scholar at AEI who lent both academic prestige and ideological fervor to the project. Weidenbaum was widely regarded as "one of the leaders in criticizing regulation, especially by the U.S. federal government."[64]

In 1977, AEI began publishing *Regulation* magazine, helping propagate its antiregulation political agenda. AEI's studies were widely disseminated to congressional staff of both parties and to personnel in the executive branch. In addition to its academic reports and policy analyses, AEI also sought a mass audience, with a special focus on college students. "AEI is increasingly becoming a household word on an increasing number of campuses, where it sponsors forums or supports adjunct scholars." The institute's ideas were disseminated through a Public Affairs series, which was carried on seven hundred radio and television channels throughout the country.[65]

For public purposes, AEI projected a facade of scholarly detachment, which served as an effective media strategy. Moreover, it would sometimes invite Democrats and even liberals to its public forums to establish an image of political balance.[66] But there is no doubt that the institute remained a deeply ideological organization whose viewpoints were extensions of the corporate interests that funded it, a point recognized by the funders themselves. The president of the SmithKline Corporation wrote to a colleague in 1975, "I look upon support of the American Enterprise Institute as a long-term investment in the preservation of our business system. . . . I can think of nothing that will bring greater dividends to the business community" than support for AEI.[67] According to the president of Potlatch Corporation, AEI acts in "support of the free enterprise system."[68]

With its massive funding combined with influential personnel, AEI was becoming a Washington power center, a point that was widely noted. One observer offered this assessment in the *New York Times*: "The sheer volume of their [AEI] publications has maximized their press coverage. The radio and television work they do is very good, and expensive. They've used network professionals. I don't know anyone who has done it with more skill than AEI."[69] Conservatism was no longer a voice in the wilderness.

AEI played an instrumental role in helping build up additional conservative think tanks, which served as ideological allies and bolstered the institute's overall message. The most important of these allied groups was the Hoover Institution in Palo Alto, California, affiliated with Stanford University. Founded in 1956, Hoover initially functioned as a conservative backwater—though that would change. As a think tank, it was similar to the AEI both in its conservative, free market ideology and its close connections with the business community. The two think tanks forged close ties, with a series of jointly run programs.[70] They were formally linked as well, with AEI director William Baroody holding a seat on Hoover's Board of Overseers.[71] Hoover raised money from some of the same enterprises as AEI, but with an additional "emphasis on Sunbelt entrepreneurs," according to *Business Week*.[72] Like AEI, Hoover saw impressive growth through the 1970s, in both its funding and academic clout, attracting Friedman, who left the University of Chicago in 1977 and permanently relocated to the Hoover Institution, where he was a resident fellow. Hoover also drew the Harvard sociologist Seymour Martin Lipset, a respected neoconservative with influence in academia and the mass media.

Among rightist funders, a central figure was Richard Mellon Scaife, heir to the Mellon banking fortune. Like many wealthy activists during this period, Scaife began as a supporter of Richard Nixon, becoming the president's second largest contributor in the 1972 election campaign.[73] When Nixon's star began to fade due to the Watergate scandal, Scaife himself assumed a leadership role among corporate conservatives, seeking to galvanize his colleagues in raising funds for the cause. He gradually established full control over the Sarah Scaife Foundation and its vast reservoir of funds; Mr. Scaife then became "the leading financial supporter of the [right-wing] movement that reshaped American politics," according to the *Washington Post*.[74]

A full discussion of Scaife's role would be difficult, since he left no collection of personal papers and issued few public statements. Highly secretive, Scaife sometimes spoke abusively to investigative journalists. In 1981, a female reporter from *Columbia Journalism Review* suddenly queried Scaife, producing the following exchange:

QUESTION: "Mr. Scaife, could you explain why you give so much money to the New Right?"
SCAIFE: "You fucking communist cunt, get out of here."[75]

Despite his lack of personal charm, Scaife emerged as a central figure in rightist politics during this period. Often working with the beer magnate Joseph Coors, he raised a prodigious amount funds for AEI, Hoover, and numerous other conservative institutions, as well as direct support for a rapidly ascending Friedman.[76] Scaife and Coors were seeking to buy their way into the world of ideas on behalf of a laissez-faire ideology.

Perhaps the most important contribution of Scaife and Coors was their help in launching the Heritage Foundation, a Washington, DC, think tank, created in 1973. Heritage later drew support from a range of companies in retail, oil, construction, and chemical manufacture, establishing a sizable endowment.[77] Whereas most conservative think tanks projected a veneer of detached objectivity, Heritage assumed an openly partisan image, as "a committed rightist organization."[78] It would quickly emerge as a rival to AEI, with the two think tanks competing for funding.[79] But at an operational level, they worked on a complimentary basis; AEI produced lengthy studies on the merits of laissez-faire economics to move elite opinion over the long term, while Heritage produced shorter policy papers of more immediate use to conservative activists.

Another Heritage specialty was building up evangelical Christians and other social traditionalists into a coherent interest group and then forging linkages between social and religious conservatives on the one hand and business interests on the other. It also stoked white racial resentments, especially with regard to the "busing" of school children across district lines to achieve integration.[80] The overarching goal was to establish a broad conservative coalition as a mass base for the burgeoning right wing.

Heritage, Hoover, and American Enterprise Institute emerged as the leading conservative institutions of the era, but they were assisted by a cluster of second-tier think tanks and research institutes backed once again by corporate funding. The National Bureau of Economic Research (NBER) in Cambridge, Massachusetts, turned in a sharply rightist direction during the late 1970s and began emphasizing research on the negative effects of federal government taxation and, by implication, governmentally run social programs funded through taxation. NBER thus became one of "the most prestigious of the institutions that have helped to push the economic debate to the right" while gathering financial support from IBM, Exxon, and ATT, as well as from the Scaife Foundation.[81]

From the University of Miami, the Law and Economics Center sought to inject conservative economic ideas into the legal profession, especially among law faculty and members of the judiciary. In a private letter, Henry Manne, the director of the Miami program, casually noted, "We have traditionally received funding from large corporations." The program obtained grants from Procter & Gamble, General Motors, IBM, and Exxon.[82] And the ideological thrust was clear: Jurists who participated in the Miami program often found that "their instructors almost to a man were drawn from the free market school of economics," according to *Fortune* magazine.[83]

Georgetown University hosted the Center for Strategic and International Studies, which advocated a right-wing turn in foreign policy and forged close ties with the military-industrial complex.[84] Virginia Tech supported the Center for the Study of Public Choice, headed by the Mont Pèlerin economist James Buchanan, with grants from the Olin Foundation (associated with Olin Corporation), General Electric Foundation, Scaife Foundation, and Texaco.[85] Numerous additional institutions across the United States helped add to the growing atmosphere of right-wing intellectual resurgence—made possible by funding from top corporate interests.[86]

Clearly, large portions of corporate America were drifting rightward during the early and mid-1970s, but this drift was far from universal. There remained a coterie of executives who affiliated with the more centrist, even liberal-leaning think tanks. And some interests leaned further left, such as the General Motors heir Stewart Mott III, who helped finance George McGovern's run for president, and Samuel Rubin of Fabergé perfumes, who funded the left-leaning Institute for Policy Studies.[87] Many other wealthy individuals simply went along with the prevailing consensus—which, at least through the middle of the 1970s, continued to favor the New Deal class compromise.

The rising business conservatives viewed their liberal and centrist colleagues with deep frustration, even contempt, and this was expressed repeatedly during the 1970s in both public statements and private correspondence. According to Robert Malott of the FMC Corporation, business executives needed to stop supporting liberal causes, since "self-interest should guide corporate giving." Executives had to be "shaken out of their complacency."[88] A common complaint was that executives failed to "present a unified front" in defense of their interests, as stated by the U.S. Steel executive William Whyte.[89] A former presidential aide, Bryce Harlow, later with Procter & Gamble, echoed this view: "Most of us in business are almost compulsively inept and clumsy. . . . Business is not a cohesive community at all."[90]

Clearly, executives needed to professionalize their lobbying activities to improve their game; above all, they had to work together to advance their interests. Corporate-funded intellectuals made similar points. Friedman complained that "businessmen support their enemies. They support people who are undermining the basis of the free enterprise system."[91] From the American Enterprise Institute, director Baroody condemned " 'the abdication of the corporate class,' " which "threatens to strangle business and . . . the free society itself."[92]

Corporate moderates were thus "encouraged" to fall in line behind the emerging agenda of laissez-faire. To shock their colleagues into action, conservatives emphasized the dire nature of the threats they faced. In 1974, *Nation's Business* ran an editorial that evoked the memory of Franklin Roosevelt's New Deal, which was increasingly despised in corporate circles. The editorial concluded, "Business is as much under attack now as it was in 1936 [under Roosevelt]—or more so."[93] *Barron's* warned readers that "corporate enterprise and its owners have been living in a climate increasingly hostile to their interests" and that "Washington is rigging the market against investors."[94] The president of Castle & Cooke declared that corporate successes "are under siege and in greater danger today than at any time since the industrial revolution. . . . The time for corporate timidity is over."[95] A speech before a meeting of the Business Council predicted that "the American electorate will largely dismantle the free enterprise system in the next ten years if we businessmen continue to stand mute. . . . Gentlemen . . . we know this territory. . . . We built it and we command it. For once in our lives let's pull ourselves together and present it effectively to the American public."[96]

Following from the growing consensus among colleagues, some corporate interests terminated their support for liberal and centrist institutions.[97] The Committee for Economic Development (CED) was targeted for defunding due to its long-standing support for Keynesian economic policies, which many now viewed with disfavor. Some of the committee's most stalwart supporters, notably Goodyear Tire, which had funded the group for decades—and whose executives had served on the CED board—suddenly ended their support. In 1975, a Goodyear executive wrote, "We have been increasingly concerned that sometimes the views and reports of CED are not representative of the business community," while some committee researchers "have not been the truest supporters of the private enterprise system." Accordingly, "we decided to terminate our support to the CED," while "the funds normally given to CED will be contributed to the American Enterprise Institute"—the CED's long-standing rival.

Other liberal think tanks opportunistically shifted their political stance in accord with changing political winds, presumably to avoid defunding. Researchers at the Brookings Institution pivoted away from the regulated capitalism with which they had long been associated—toward a newly fashionable antiregulation stance, thus echoing positions from their challengers at AEI. A journalist summed up the changed climate at the Washington think tank: "Economists of virtually every political cast these days agree that there ought to be less regulation in air travel, shipping, and pollution control."[98] And the traditionally liberal Ford Foundation began channeling funds directly into AEI while gradually abandoning the progressive groups that it had long funded.[99] By the end of the decade, even Chase Manhattan Bank—long associated with the centrist Rockefeller family—was also contributing to AEI.[100] If Ford, Brookings, Chase, and other pillars of the Eastern Establishment could not beat the conservatives, they would join them.

THE RENAISSANCE OF CORPORATE LOBBYING

While the business mobilization of this period placed special emphasis on think tanks as a means of fighting the "war of ideas," it did not ignore more conventional methods of combat, including direct lobbying. An important development during this period was the creation of the Business Roundtable in 1972, representing a major advance for corporate power. The Federal Reserve chair Arthur Burns and the former Treasury secretary John Connally helped mobilize business interests behind the new roundtable, linking this endeavor once again to the Nixon presidency.[101]

The purpose of the roundtable was to bring together CEOs from the largest enterprises across a broad range of sectors to achieve the unified front that had long been sought. Its membership included General Motors, Exxon, Citibank, TWA, Prudential, Bechtel, and IBM, among many other top-tier companies. It was now time for corporate America to fight back against the forces of economic liberalism, and the Business Roundtable aimed to lead that fight. Through the remainder of the 1970s, the roundtable would stand at the forefront of corporate lobbying, advocating cuts in spending on social programs, limiting the power of labor unions, and deregulating the economy.

Individual businesses greatly accelerated their own lobbying efforts. In 1978, *Fortune* summed up the situation: "Ten years ago, only about 100 companies had Washington representatives; now the city is crawling with over 500 of them. Everybody also employs a lobbying firm: lobbying is the country's great growth industry."[102] And to advance the cause of antiunionism, business supported the National Right-to-Work Committee, which also grew prodigiously during the 1970s.[103] That was accompanied by the growth of antiunion consulting firms that assisted individual companies in breaking unions.[104]

Lobby groups were established at every level of the government. To lobby for conservative policies at the state level, the American Legislative Exchange Council (ALEC) was founded, which received funding from Joseph Coors and Richard Scaife and was closely connected to the Heritage Foundation.[105] ALEC sent brochures to legislators around the country advocating detailed conservative programs at the levels of both economic and social policy, advancing the cause in every state legislature.[106] Although it initially began on a relatively small scale, ALEC gradually evolved into a major force at the state level.

Another trend was the reinvigoration of older lobby groups, including the National Association of Manufacturers and the U.S. Chamber of Commerce.[107] For much of the post–New Deal period, these business federations were regarded as backwaters and seemed a throwback to an earlier era of lobbying. During the course of the 1970s, however, NAM and the Chamber of Commerce were transformed through a professionalization of their staff and a much bolder approach to lobbying. Meanwhile, NAM gradually moved beyond its base among small and medium-size companies and attracted support from such prominent enterprises as Allied Chemical, Campbell Soup, U.S. Steel, 3M, and the Bendix Corporation.[108] The chamber appears to have been even more dynamic, and it experienced massive growth in membership and funding while connecting with Raytheon, Bristol-Myers, Armco Steel, Marriott Hotels, and the Amway Corporation.[109]

In building this dense network of lobby groups, corporate America was acting on the basis of an overarching strategy, one that was distilled in a 1971 document for the U.S. Chamber of Commerce presented by Lewis Powell, a Virginia corporate lawyer. Throughout his career Powell had close ties to the tobacco industry through the Tobacco Institute and had served on numerous corporate boards.[110] His analysis flowed from extensive corporate connections. The thirty-four-page "Powell Memorandum" that resulted was based on the assumption that "the American economic system is under broad attack" from both liberals and the New Left, and that executives needed to fight back against these dangers with a massive influence campaign aimed at Congress, state legislatures, and courts. His memorandum also advocated lobbying the general public by disseminating procapitalist publicity through television and the mass media, as well as the educational system, at both the high school and college levels. Overall, Powell called for a probusiness campaign that would be "far more aggressive than in the past," to be backed by "generous financial support from American corporations."[111]

The Powell Memorandum was leaked to the *Washington Post* columnist Jack Anderson, who published portions in an exposé.[112] The exposé had the effect of spreading Powell's message among executives across the country, thus accelerating a private-sector mobilization that already was well under way. References to the Powell Memorandum appeared repeatedly in private correspondence and corporate files throughout the early and mid-1970s, always with a strongly positive tone.[113] President Nixon was evidently impressed, and he nominated Powell for a seat on the U.S. Supreme Court. In early 1972, Powell became a Supreme Court associate justice, a position he held for fifteen years.

The Powell Memorandum likely inspired the creation of a conservative legal infrastructure funded by corporate interests. In 1973, the California Chamber of Commerce helped launch the Pacific Legal Foundation,[114] whose board of directors included representatives from the Fluor Corporation, South Pacific Corporation, Santa Fe Railroad,

Copley Press, Title Insurance, and Coors Breweries. The foundation was especially active in filing legal briefs against environmental regulations. The corporate sector appreciated the foundation's efforts, which were "on the right side . . . doing yeoman work," in the words of *Barron's* financial weekly.[115] The success of the Pacific Foundation led to the creation of an interconnected series of conservative legal centers throughout the United States, including its D.C.-based counterpart, the National Legal Center for the Public Interest, all heavily funded.[116]

In addition to direct lobbying, companies supported political activist groups, including the Conservative Caucus, the Committee for the Survival of a Free Congress, and an extensive series of right-wing Christian organizations. These newly formed conservative groups—the "New Right," as they were collectively known—constituted a rising force in electoral politics, especially within the Republican Party. Observing the role of company executives in this overall network, the Republican activist John Saloma offered this assessment: "Among those attending the 'private' New Right strategy conference . . . in May 1979 were a vice president of the Chase Manhattan, an executive vice president of Adolph Coors Brewery, a group vice president of public affairs for Dart Industries, a vice president for government affairs of Georgia Pacific Corporation, and the director of governmental affairs for the National Association of Manufacturers."[117]

Rapid growth of right-wing political action committees occurred, which funded candidates, led by the National Conservative Political Action Committee, or NCPAC. And once again, it was business interests that provided the backing. In 1977, the National Association of Manufacturers "started a monthly publication specifically tailored to corporate PACs . . . and is cosponsoring a series of 'PAC workshops' with the National Association of Business PACs."[118]

EDUCATING AMERICA

A key recommendation in the Powell Memorandum was the need to educate the public on the merits of free enterprise. That idea was avidly pursued by a range of corporate interests and corporate-funded organizations, which began presenting school course materials with an overtly political focus. The politicization of these courses was widely recognized in the business press. In 1977, an article in *Fortune* observed that hundreds of companies were "spending tens of millions of dollars in . . . something called 'economic education.' . . . *They are programs of indirect advocacy, and their purpose is political persuasion.* 'Don't quote me,' says the director of one economic education program, 'but we're propagandizing, we're selling.'"[119] And *Business Week* noted, "More than ever before, corporations are moving into the education business, producing and distributing films, charts, and even comic books for school children. According to one count, nearly 3,000 corporations . . . now are distributing educational materials. And classroom teachers, squeezed by shrinking budgets, welcome the free materials."[120]

The U.S. Chamber of Commerce launched the "Economics for Young Americans Project" aimed at high schools and community colleges. The chamber's program sought to "promote the truth about business" to "show our youth the benefits of the free enterprise system."[121] ALEC sent brochures to state legislatures advocating a "Free Enterprise Education Act" to encourage the production of probusiness courses and educational materials.[122] ALEC's proposals included "a good free enterprise course as a prerequisite for high school graduation."[123] Phillips Petroleum financed the creation of a film series on "American Enterprise," which received wide circulation in public schools, especially in New York state.[124] Houston Natural Gas produced teaching materials for Texas high schools focusing on economics education.[125]

Corporate interests also sought to transform the mass media, which was considered excessively liberal. Mobil Oil took the lead in this effort. Beginning in 1971, Mobil's publicity department began placing both opinion articles and paid advertisements in 103 newspapers, including the *New York Times, Washington Post, Boston Globe, Los Angeles Times, Wall Street Journal,* and *Chicago Tribune.* Appearing throughout the 1970s on a regular basis, these journalistic pieces advanced Mobil's political interests—such as opposition to proposals for the breakup of oil companies—and the overall cause of private enterprise.[126]

In addition, Mobil financed nonpolitical television shows, notably the high-toned *Masterpiece Theater* through the Public Broadcasting Service. The purpose of the PBS funding was to establish "a goodwill umbrella" and "to build enough [public] acceptance to allow us to get tough on the substantive issues," according to a Mobil public relations specialist, who added, "Public broadcasting is the keystone" of Mobil's publicity efforts.[127] By 1979, Mobil had become "the 'nice guy' oil company, the 'classy' oil company, the 'public service oriented' oil company," in the view of the *Washington Post*.[128] Thus inspired, the other major oil companies joined the publicity effort, with assistance from the American Petroleum Institute, all financed on a lavish scale.[129] Exxon became especially active in funding probusiness television advertisements, building on Mobil's example.[130]

Beyond oil, companies in several economic sectors also used the media to advance their agenda. The U.S. Chamber of Commerce began hosting publicity training seminars for corporate executives.[131] Richard Scaife purchased 50 percent shares in sixteen California newspapers, presumably as a means of projecting his conservative views.[132] From the military sector, United Technologies became a major player in advocacy advertising, inserting conservative viewpoints into *The Atlantic, Harper's,* and *Washington Report*; this effort was spearheaded by the company president, Alexander Haig, former chief of staff to President Nixon.[133]

A particularly ambitious project was to publicize the ideas of Milton Friedman through the Public Broadcasting Service. The result was the *Free to Choose* series on PBS, which showcased Friedman's economics, presented in simplified format for the lay viewer and broadcast to a national audience in ten episodes beginning in 1980. In the words of *Reason* magazine, "*Free to Choose* talked about capitalism in upbeat, positive terms, stressing how it helped individuals rather than exploited them and how it brought about cooperation in a way that benefitted the poor most of all."[134] The series thus projected a populist tone while receiving funds from Getty Oil, National Presto Industries, the Bechtel Foundation, the Sarah Scaife Foundation, and the Reader's Digest Association. The editors at *Reader's Digest* magazine thoughtfully provided a positive review of the program.[135] *Free to Choose* elevated the influence of Mont Pèlerin economics, which aligned with the general direction of business mobilization that the MPS helped justify.

In addition to influencing the mainstream, there was also an effort to build up a distinctively conservative media through such publications as *Conservative Digest, Human Events*, and *Policy Review*. Perhaps the most important conservative publication of this period was William F. Buckley's *National Review*, which moved from the political margins to the center of policy debates during the 1970s. Its rapid ascent was aided by Buckley's close connection to elite corporate executives, who were actively cultivated. According to one of his associates, it became "Bill Buckley's pleasant custom in his capacity as editor of *National Review* to hold very occasional and very select luncheons . . . [for] a small number of America's top-ranking businessmen," presumably to build support for his publication. These *National Review* luncheons were attended by representatives from ITT, Exxon, Continental Can, Lorillard Tobacco, IBM, and Standard Oil of Indiana.[136]

While much of the publicity effort aimed at friendly relationships with the media, another thrust sought to intimidate journalists who were deemed excessively liberal or hostile toward corporate interests. To monitor and fight against alleged antibusiness press coverage, the media watchdogs Accuracy in Media and the Media Institute were created, with funding from the oil industry and the Scaife Foundation.[137]

To be sure, conservative media efforts were not always successful. The former presidential aide Roger Ailes helped establish a new conservative-leaning media company, Television News Inc., with funding from Coors, but it folded in 1975, achieving little impact.[138] For the most part, however, corporate efforts aimed at influencing the climate of opinion were highly effective. By the end of the 1970s, mass media had adopted a more conservative cast than previously, especially at America's leading newspaper, the *New York Times*. In 1984, even the Heritage-affiliated *Policy Review* acknowledged the change of tone: "The *New York Times* . . . is reaffirming its greatness by retreating from the radicalism of the past two decades and again taking up responsible journalism. It is the first liberal institution to identify the excesses of liberalism . . . and to correct them."[139] Just as the Brookings Institution and Ford Foundation accommodated themselves to the rightward turn in political culture, so did the *Times*. Apparently, the vast sums of corporate funding had not gone to waste.

WHY DID BUSINESS MOBILIZE?

In reading through the business literature and private papers of this period, one is struck by the widespread tone of fear when discussing a growing anticorporate culture among America's youth associated with environmentalism, the New Left, and organizations founded by Ralph Nader.[140] Certainly, these left-leaning tendencies presented new challenges to corporate America—yet this was not their main challenge. Their real enemy was simply this: During the 1970s, average rates of profit were falling, reaching historically low levels. The need to compensate for declining profits constitutes the main impetus for the "revolt of the rich" that forms the central theme of this book.

A study by Martin Feldstein, Lawrence Summers, and Michael Wachter documents this decline: "Between 1969 and 1970 *there was an unprecedented drop in the net rate of profit* from 10.2 percent to 8.1 percent, at that time *the lowest rate in the postwar period.*" The authors also conclude, "The year 1970 appears in the statistics to mark *the beginning of this new 'low return' period.*"[141] To further document this drop, let us consider the data in table 2.1.

The most important statistic is the final number, for rates of return during 1970–1976, which averaged only 7.9 percent—well below long-term historical averages. Later research has documented that profit rates remained low for the remainder of the decade and continued for many years.[142] It seemed that the spurt of economic dynamism unleashed by recovery from the Great Depression and World War II had run out of steam.

TABLE 2.1
Average annual rates of return on nonfinancial corporate capital, 1950–1976

Period	Average annual rates of return
1950–1959	11.1
1959–1965	10.9
1960–1969	11.7
1948–1969	11.5
1970–1976	7.9

Source: Martin Feldstein, Lawrence Summers, and Michael Wachter, "Is the Rate of Profit Falling?," *Brookings Papers on Economic Activity* no. 1 (1977): 216.

Note: These are figures for net rates of return.

A detailed discussion of why profit rates were falling goes beyond the scope of this study. But in brief, recent research suggests that the overall decline in economic performance derived from reduced federal spending on infrastructure during the 1970s, especially the decline in spending on transportation infrastructure.[143] Another significant source of stagnation was high oil prices, the "energy crisis" that constituted a major source of economic dislocation throughout the decade.[144]

Whatever the cause, falling rates of profit constituted a basic fact of life for corporate America during the 1970s.[145] The shrill tone of business complaint that followed appears readily comprehensible. It is no wonder that businesspeople felt they were "the most downtrodden and persecuted of all American minorities," as *Barron's* lamented in the opening quote to this chapter. The source of business anguish was clear, and low profits were surely one of the major factors behind the business mobilization that defined the era.

Another danger was inflation, which rose relentlessly through the course of the 1970s and eroded the value of accumulated wealth. This, too, proved a vexing problem for America's upper classes. A comprehensive study on the distributional effects of inflation was conducted by the Brookings specialist Joseph Minarik and published in a report to Congress. One of its main conclusions was that "the wealthy have no safe and profitable store of value in times of inflation."[146] Stocks and bonds became unreliable stores of wealth, while alternative investments such as gold were risky and complicated to manage.

Inflation thus constituted an additional source of corporate grievance: While business enterprises themselves were losing money due to low profit rates, their executives and stockholders were losing a second time due to inflation. And during the 1970s, the rate of inflation was considerable, far higher than in previous decades, as indicated in table 2.2.

Also note that inflation accelerated over the period 1971–1980, reaching double digits by the end of the decade, intensifying the stress on America's richest citizens. The rising rate of inflation was thus an additional motive for mobilization by the wealthy classes, who aimed to tilt governmental policy in their favor as a means of compensating for declining fortunes. The corporate political activism of this period—the revolt of the rich—must be seen in context of the twin threats emanating from low profits and inflation, both of which impacted the rich.

TABLE 2.2

U.S. mean annual rates of inflation, 1961–1980

Period	Annual rates of inflation (%)
1961–1970	2.8
1971–1980	7.9

Source: Data aggregated from "Inflation, Consumer Prices for the United States," 1960–present, FRED Economic Data, Federal Reserve Bank of St. Louis, accessed October 17, 2023, https://fred.stlouisfed.org/series/FPCPITOTLZGUSA.

THE POLITICS OF INFLATION

It is important to emphasize that inflation was more of a problem for the affluent than it was for middle- or low-income groups, a point that was emphasized in a 1979 study published in *Review of Income and Wealth*. The study concluded that during the period 1969–1975, "the poor and middle class gained relatively to the rich from this inflation" and that "inflation acted like a progressive tax"—effectively redistributing funds from the rich to the poor and middle classes.[147]

Contrary to popular misperception, the majority of Americans were not so severely impacted by inflation, because in the 1970s, wages generally rose in tandem with prices, a process termed the "wage-price spiral."[148] This spiral moderated the effects of inflation on overall living standards. In addition, middle-class homeowners benefited from rising house values, a trend that coincided with inflation, while the real value of their mortgages declined. Low-income families who were heavily indebted usually gained from inflation, since rising prices reduced the value of debts.

One nonelite group was severely impacted by inflation, notably segments of the elderly population who depended primarily on private pensions for income. Pension benefits tended to be fixed, and rising prices eroded their real value. Even in this case, the elderly were partly compensated by Social Security payments, whose benefits were indexed, according to Minarik: "The notion of the Social Security recipient as the chief loser in inflation is largely incorrect; the Social Security benefit keeps up with inflation."[149] And elderly families that held significant debt benefited from inflation as well. Even Herbert Stein, who served as Nixon's top economic adviser, acknowledged that inflation was more of a problem for the affluent.[150] Also note that the high inflation years of the 1970s coincided with some of the lowest levels of income inequality in American history, according to data presented by the economist Thomas Piketty.[151]

The inflation of the 1970s took place in what was in essence a decade of crises. Clearly, a multitude of challenges needed to be addressed, including growing unemployment, deindustrialization, declining union membership, decaying cities, deteriorating productivity, growing international competition, and macroeconomic instability. Inflation was only one problem among many, but it gradually became *the* national problem, the focus of attention. And the nature of inflation was often misrepresented as being a burden for all Americans that was shared more or less equally by both rich and poor. This misrepresentation began with President Nixon, who stated in 1971, "Inflation robs every American, every one of you."[152] Some public figures went further and claimed that inflation targeted the working classes and the poor.[153] The fact that inflation was more of a problem for the rich received little notice.

The dangers of inflation were especially exaggerated and sensationalized by economists associated with the Mont Pèlerin Society. When receiving his Nobel Prize in 1976, Friedman darkly raised the possibility that inflation could transform into hyperinflation,[154] whereby money loses virtually all value, on the model of contemporary Argentina (or possibly Weimar Republic Germany). This possibility seems far-fetched, however, since hyperinflation has occurred only in underdeveloped countries with immature financial systems and in advanced countries, such as Germany in the 1920s, that had experienced defeat in war and major social upheaval.[155] There is no instance in economic history of an advanced, industrialized country like the United States experiencing hyperinflation.

Other MPS economists would present even more extravagant claims. In a coauthored essay, James Buchanan stated that rising prices contributed to "increasingly liberalized attitudes toward sexual activities."[156] He thus implied—in all seriousness—that inflation caused sexual promiscuity. Evidently, it was a menace to the social order.

The economic crisis of the 1970s was effectively redefined as a crisis of inflation. And this redefinition was highly significant, since combating inflation served as a useful pretext for ushering in a conservative policy program. Mont Pèlerin economists had long advocated using crises strategically as opportunities to impose hidden agendas. Friedman stated the matter succinctly: "Only a crisis . . . produces real change. When a crisis occurs, the actions that are taken [by policy makers] depend on the ideas that are lying around. That, I believe, is our basic function: To develop alternatives to existing policies, to keep them alive and available until the politically impossible becomes the politically inevitable."[157]

Inflation would thus present the crisis that Friedman and his MPS colleagues were waiting for, and the widespread perception of crisis would enable them—and their corporate sponsors—to impose on the country their laissez-faire vision for the future. Inflation would be invoked again and again as an all-purpose justification for such measures as economic deregulation and cuts in social spending. Inflation would later justify austerity programs designed to reduce working-class living standards.[158] The crisis of inflation would transform American society at every level, leading to a rupture of the social contract and an upward redistribution of wealth.

AN EXPERIMENT IN AUSTERITY

The 1973–1975 recession proved a major challenge for the presidency of Gerald R. Ford while also presenting an opportunity to deploy austerity for the first time on a large scale. Within the administration, the principal figure behind this policy was Treasury secretary William Simon, who was determined to use austerity as a means of shattering the old order of class compromise in favor of laissez-faire. He enjoyed excellent relations with the business community. During his tenure, Simon traveled around the country delivering campaign-style speeches to business groups and trade associations that advocated "a fundamental shift in our economic priorities," with a rightward push. One of Simon's main objectives was to establish "greater profits" for business through deregulation combined with cuts in consumer and governmental spending ("a shift *away* from the consumer and government expenditures that have dominated our economy").[159] Simon's speeches were enthusiastically received by business audiences, who repeatedly gave him standing ovations.[160] With a firm political base among executives, Simon was able to consolidate his influence over economic policy making within the Ford cabinet.

The rigors of recession generated financial stresses throughout the country, with an especially pronounced impact on New York City, which experienced a major fiscal crisis. by February 1975, the New York City government was unable to meet payments on accumulated debts, raising the possibility of outright default. In an atmosphere of desperation, city officials appealed to the federal government for emergency financial support.[161] At first, Secretary Simon seems to have opposed federal support as punishment for perceived profligacy. However, major elements of the U.S. business community feared that default risked destabilizing financial markets. Even so conservative a figure as Walter Wriston of Citibank advocated federal aid to New York on an emergency basis to prevent default. Based on such pressure, the administration "concluded—reluctantly—that it would be appropriate for the federal government to intervene in the city's problems, but only with tight strings attached," as Simon later described in his memoirs.[162] Federal aid was conditioned on austerity measures to be implemented by the New York City government.

Austerity produced immediate results. Public hospitals were closed and social services were curtailed, while the City University of New York began charging tuition, breaking with its tradition of free college education for all qualified residents. Cutbacks fell especially hard on African American communities.[163] The powerful New York municipal unions were restrained as city personnel were laid off; wages and benefits were reduced. Many of the changes from this period would prove permanent and transform the lives of New York residents by increasing the skew in the distribution of income. The overall rationale for these cutbacks was to save money and balance the city budget over the long term, preventing the need for federal bailouts in the future. The Ford administration was especially eager to reduce spending on municipal bailouts as a means of restraining inflation.[164] President Ford had already declared that "inflation [is] public enemy number one."[165]

Curbing government spending in New York and elsewhere would help defeat this enemy. The New York fiscal crisis was thus integrated into a growing national crusade against inflation.

There was never any doubt that the administration was using the New York case to set a precedent, with far-reaching implications. As Simon emphatically stated in congressional hearings, the federal demands were deliberately "made so punitive [and] the overall experience so painful that no city . . . would ever be tempted to go down the same road" of high social spending, as New York had done.[166] The former presidential aide Patrick Buchanan later observed, "Simon wants to use the example of New York City . . . to shake up a nation."[167] Similar views were echoed by Jude Wanniski of the *Wall Street Journal*, who favored using the New York experience as a basis for reducing government spending across the country.[168] Austerity was an idea whose time had come.

The logic behind austerity is open to question, however, since cutbacks in spending run the risk of worsening social problems, which can be very costly indeed. In 2006, an article in the *American Journal of Public Health* underscored the enormous long-term costs that resulted from the New York City episode:

> Budget and policy decisions designed to alleviate the [1975 New York] fiscal crisis contributed to the subsequent epidemics of tuberculosis, human immunodeficiency virus (HIV) infection, and homicide. . . . Cuts in services; the dismantling of health, public safety, and social service infrastructures; and the deterioration of living conditions for vulnerable populations contributed to the amplification of these health conditions. . . . We conclude that the costs incurred in controlling these epidemics exceeded $50 billion (in 2004 dollars); in contrast, the overall budgetary savings during the fiscal crisis was $10 billion.[169]

It appears ironic that spending cuts ended up costing the city five times more than was saved when viewed over the long run. Whatever the merits of these policies in financial terms, this much is clear: The New York City fiscal crisis functioned as a proving ground for austerity, helping legitimate the idea. New York's status as America's leading city and a center of media and communications—as well as a worldwide symbol of capitalism—guaranteed that the precedent would be widely noticed.

We have seen that during the 1970s, corporate executives experienced new challenges emanating from low rates of profitability and rising inflation. As a result of these challenges, they resolved to set aside their earlier acceptance of the New Deal class compromise and mounted an assault against it. The result was one of the most orchestrated, carefully planned, and well-financed political campaigns in history, with the creation of new lobbying institutions such as the Business Roundtable and Heritage Foundation, as well as the reinvigoration of older institutions. Their lobbying was directed at both government officials and the general public. In mounting this campaign, business interests were able to set aside their parochial differences and gradually come together as a reasonably unified social class,[170] advancing their collective interests with an ideological objective. And soon, the New York fiscal crisis offered conservatives their first opportunity to implement an austerity policy through reduced government spending at the municipal level. Austerity would not be fully applied on a national scale until the end of the Carter presidency; but the groundwork had been laid in New York City.

CHAPTER THREE

Building a Mass Base

Neither current events nor history show that the majority rules or ever
did rule. The contrary I think is true.

—JEFFERSON DAVIS, 1864

So far, this book has focused on elite mobilization and efforts aimed
at shifting government policy rightward while neglecting popular
responses to this mobilization. In this chapter, I will consider the popular response in detail. In many ways, the story of America's shift to
the right seems extraordinary, since it entailed an initiative to reduce
living standards of the majority in favor of already wealthy individuals
and business executives. These facts seem surprising, given the forces
arrayed against elites: labor unions represented a significant portion of
the workforce, at 27 percent in 1970, down from the height of labor
power in the early postwar period but still formidable.[1] America's youth
had organized large-scale social movements around such issues as
women's rights, racial equality, and environmentalism, generally operating outside unions and political parties but tilted toward the political
left. The Democratic Party—the party of Franklin Delano Roosevelt and
the New Deal—still controlled large majorities in both houses of Congress. Public opinion polls showed consistent support for social welfare
programs, employment-generating policies, and the overall project of
class compromise.[2] Given this strength of opposition, how was it possible for business to prevail?

We will see that advocates for right-wing, probusiness policies strate-
gized to divide opposition forces along lines of religion, race, and culture,

thus creating a series of "wedge issues," fragmenting the public and distracting them from the process of wealth concentration. The mobilization of religion was central to this strategy. Rather than emphasizing such unpopular measures as economic austerity and militarism, business-funded activists extolled "morality," "family values," and "patriotism," helping forge a mass movement of immense size and influence. Right-wing activists showed great facility in using simple, powerful words and phrases to influence these movements while subtly shifting the meaning to advance a strategy of divide and conquer. America's upper classes eagerly funded these endeavors, fueling their effectiveness.

POLITICAL MANIPULATION IN THEORY

The challenge of winning over the public engaged some of the most talented conservative thinkers of the era. The Nixon presidency served as a prime incubator for conservative strategists, and others emerged from Washington think tanks, notably the American Enterprise Institute and the Heritage Foundation. One of the most important of these new conservative intellectuals was Paul Weyrich of Heritage, who came to play a central role in planning and orchestrating wedge issues.[3] It is instructive to consider Weyrich's corporate backers. He had collaborated with the beer merchant Joseph Coors and the Mellon heir Richard Scaife to create the Heritage Foundation in 1973. Heritage became a magnet for corporate funds from a range of sources extending well beyond the Coors and Scaife families, and these funds enhanced the foundation's Washington power base.[4]

Viewed in retrospect, Weyrich appears as a political strategist of great ability and imagination with an overriding determination to win political battles. His approach stressed the mobilization of cultural conservatives and religious voters. Learning from the historical experience of the left, Weyrich understood the importance of a mass base in achieving power, and he sought to cultivate such a base for the right.[5] He also recognized the right's long-standing weakness in this area: "The conservative movement . . . had some very powerful thinkers, but it didn't have many troops. And as Stalin said of the Pope, 'Where are his divisions?' Well, we [conservatives] didn't have many divisions." Fortunately for Weyrich and other right-wing activists, organized religion came to the rescue: "When these [religious] folks became active, all of a sudden, the conservative movement had lots of divisions. We were able to move literally millions of people, and this is something we had no ability to do prior to that time."[6]

Weyrich's model of social conservatism flowed from a popular reaction against the cultural changes of the 1960s, including the anti-war movement on college campuses and such seemingly radical ideas as feminism, gay rights, and alternative lifestyles. The "silent majority," to use Richard Nixon's famous phrase, objected to what many considered the immorality associated with these social changes.[7] In 1973, the director of the Society for the Christian Commonwealth lamented, "Evidence of moral decay is everywhere. . . . Families are disintegrating. Motherhood is becoming a 'dirty word.' Immorality and pornography are disgustingly popular. . . . Where are our Christian leaders? . . . Where are our 'soldiers of Christ?'"[8] This statement nicely distilled the atmosphere of cultural backlash that would soon generate the hoped-for soldiers of Christ, while New Right activists such as Weyrich helped orchestrate the divisions and armies that resulted. Clearly, Weyrich and his colleagues did not create this backlash, but they were ready to manipulate it for their own purposes, advancing the conservative policy agenda of the business interests that funded them.[9]

From the White House, President Nixon—who was very much an ideological conservative—echoed these views. Nixon understood that the Republican "program had little to offer voters in 'blue collar suburbs.'" Nixon stated that Republicans must "get beyond material things. . . . If they're thinking economics, we lose."[10] He strongly emphasized social class: "We should aim our strategy primarily at disaffected Democrats, at blue collar workers, and at working class white ethnics."[11] The emphasis on white ethnics suggested a tinge of racism, consistent with the administration's "Southern strategy."[12] In later interviews, the former presidential aide John Ehrlichman confirmed that the president was deploying a subtly racist approach, seeking to grow his support among southern whites through coded language.[13]

The ultimate objective was to divide the public, cleaving away an important segment of Democratic voters, to be claimed by Republicans, with a special focus on states of the former Confederacy. The divisive character of the administration's method was frankly acknowledged by

Vice President Spiro T. Agnew, who stated in 1971 that "dividing the American people has been my main contribution to the national political scene. . . . I not only plead guilty to this charge, but I am somewhat flattered by it."[14]

In promoting this wedge strategy, conservative thinkers acknowledged that their image had been tainted by overly public association with corporate interests. In the view of Weyrich, "In the past, we conservatives paraded all those Chamber of Commerce candidates with the Mobil Oil billboards strapped to their backs. It doesn't work in middle class neighborhoods."[15] Weyrich and his colleagues understood the value of tactical flexibility, recognizing past operational errors and self-correcting. Accordingly, conservative activists learned to be discreet about their corporate ties and to emphasize instead the more popular social and cultural issues that had the potential of broad appeal. With regard to the latter, the ever-cynical Weyrich conceded, "Yes, they're emotional issues, but better than talking about capital formation."[16]

Overall, Weyrich and other New Right activists emphasized the drawing together of disparate political groups to form broad coalitions, an idea known as "fusionism," assembling both business interests and cultural conservatives.[17] Ultimately, it was business interests that dominated these coalitions and bankrolled their operations; while cultural conservatives benefited to some degree, they remained junior partners. This strategy would transform the political landscape by the end of the 1970s and engineer a historic break with the New Deal class compromise.

POLITICAL MANIPULATION IN PRACTICE

The 1970s was a decade of religious mobilization, with major growth in evangelical Protestant sects outside the more established churches. This mobilization played a key role in Weyrich's political strategy. For purposes of this chapter, "evangelical Protestant" will denote groups that emphasize literal readings of the New Testament, personalized relationships between individual Christians and Jesus Christ, and the salience of life-transforming "born again" experiences. This mobilization was accelerated by evangelical-oriented radio, television, and media. The "televangelist" who preached to huge television audiences came into prominence during the 1970s. Christian publishing also saw considerable success, with books about Armageddon, "end times," and the second coming doing especially well (and with Hal Lindsay's apocalyptic *The Late Great Planet Earth* emerging as one of the best-selling books of the decade).[18]

The growth of evangelicalism was impressive. In 1976, one third of the U.S. adult population reported that they had experienced being born again. At the same time, more mainstream congregations, such as the Episcopalians, Lutherans, Methodists, and the United Church of Christ (as well as the Catholic Church), all saw significant declines in membership, consistent with the more generalized loss of public confidence in established institutions that became one of the hallmarks of public opinion. Among the more mainstream churches, the one that did manage to expand during this period was the Southern Baptist Convention; and, fittingly, Southern Baptists were among the most evangelical of all the purportedly mainstream Protestant groups.[19]

The mobilization of this socially conservative, Christian wave began during the Nixon presidency, with the president himself actively involved in the effort, assisted by his aides Patrick Buchanan and Charles Colson.[20] More generally, Nixon sought to activate the "Social Issue, in order to get the Democrats on the defensive," as he later noted in his memoirs.[21] The most important element in Nixon's strategy was his alliance with the Baptist pastor Billy Graham, who held mass rallies that were widely televised. These rallies combined emotional commitment to scripture with subtle gestures of support for President Nixon and his political agenda.[22] From the president's standpoint, affiliation with the Baptist preacher was a clever move, as it added to the populist veneer to his administration. It also generated political backing for Nixon from among Graham's numerous admirers, many of whom were working-class southerners, who traditionally voted Democratic. While Graham himself opposed segregation, that was not the case with many of his white followers, for whom Christian identity entailed an element of bigotry.[23] All of these trends meshed well with Nixon's electoral strategy, which emphasized the strategic use of wedge issues.

Despite his populist image, Reverend Graham also had impressive connections to corporate interests, which no doubt increased his value to the Republican Party. Graham's base of support included such prominent oilmen as H. L. Hunt, Clint Murchison, Sid Richardson, and J. Howard Pew, as well as the hotel magnate J. W. Marriott.[24] He appears to have been especially close to Pew of the Sun Oil fortune, who became one of his main funders. Specifically, Pew financed *Christianity Today*, a Graham-affiliated magazine that became one of the leading publications of the evangelical movement. In 1971, one of the founders of *Christianity Today* wrote to a colleague that Pew was a "great benefactor" of the publication as well as "one of the most wonderful men I have ever known."[25] Graham's business connections were no doubt gratifying to President Nixon, who sought to recruit not only Christian voters but also Christian business executives. At one point, the president directed an aide to "develop a list of rich people with strong religious interest to be invited to the White House church services."[26]

In addition, Nixon associated with socially conservative strains in popular culture, most notably country music. The country star Merle Haggard performed at the White House, pointedly playing *Okie from Muskogee*, with these lyrics:

We don't smoke marijuana in Muskogee.
We don't take our trips on LSD.
We don't burn our draft cards down on main street.
Cause we like livin' right and free.[27]

While *Okie from Muskogee* did not directly reference religion, it resonated with socially conservative themes being advanced by evangelicals, and it fit nicely with the overarching White House strategy: President Nixon was presenting himself as a man of the people, defending the Silent Majority against haughty cultural elites.[28]

The president's alignment with social conservatives paid rich dividends during his 1972 reelection campaign. The Republicans' religious pitch proved to be especially effective in light of the Democratic Party's move in a secular direction. The election saw a large swing of evangelical voters away from the Democrats; these trends contributed to Nixon's landslide victory over the Democratic nominee, George McGovern. Nixon's support among white southerners who attended church regularly reached 86 percent—in a constituency that had traditionally voted Democratic.[29] In addition, Republican affiliation with

Reverend Graham enabled Nixon to further cement his ties to corporate America.

In the end, the Nixon presidency collapsed in disgrace with the Watergate scandal and the president's resignation from office in August 1974—events that threatened to undo the religious-business alliance. For his part, Billy Graham was so embarrassed by the scandal that he effectively retired from politics, refocusing his energy on religious matters.[30] For right-wing activists like Weyrich, prospects had darkened considerably.

THY WILL BE DONE

Although Nixon's resignation constituted a setback for social conservatives, just as it did for business conservatives, both groups relentlessly continued their efforts. Such activists as Richard Viguerie, Howard Phillips, and Weyrich were charting a course for the conservative movement, emphasizing the remobilization of evangelicals with corporate funding.[31] Spearheading this effort was the evangelical Bill Bright, who, in 1975, founded the Christian Embassy in Washington, which sought to "evangelize members of Congress, the military, the judiciary, and the diplomatic service," as well as the "Here's Life, America" organization, which sought to evangelize the general public.[32] Bright's endeavors attracted massive financial support from the Coors, the Hunts (of Hunt Oil), Mobil Oil, Pepsico, and Coca-Cola, among many others. Bright also founded a Christian publishing company, Third Century Publishers, which distributed copies of conservative tracts combining religious piety with praise of free markets. Third Century's editor-in-chief, Rus Walton, also served as a director at the National Association of Manufacturers.[33]

The evangelical Fellowship Foundation "tapped wealthy businessmen," and with these funds, they organized prayer groups among members of Congress and other high government officials.[34] From Southern California, the evangelical leader Demos Shakarian "continued to recruit the Sunbelt's merchants and financiers" into his church, while he advanced "pro-capitalist politics."[35] From Texas, the pastor James Robison gained a large following for his overtly political sermons, receiving funds from wealthy donors including H. L. Hunt, the owner of the Texas Rangers baseball team, and a Houston banker.[36] Robison denounced "the radicals, and the perverts and the liberals and the leftists and the communists."[37] Secular liberals scoffed at such crude rhetoric, as well as the New Right's affiliation with this tendency. What liberals often missed, however, was that religious mobilization was an extremely effective strategy.

Perhaps the most important evangelical leader of the 1970s was Jerry Falwell, who led a congregation in Lynchburg, Virginia, and whose radio and television show, *The Old Time Gospel Hour*, had a national audience. Reverend Falwell also established Liberty University to provide a Christian college experience for the faithful. He preached against the "wave of immorality in this country," which included such evils as homosexuality, abortion rights, and pornography.[38] Falwell was also a strong believer in capitalism: he quoted from the increasingly popular Milton Friedman while affirming that "the free enterprise system is clearly outlined in the Book of Proverbs."[39] One researcher dryly observed that Falwell's position "coincides with the interest of local business owners and managers far better than it does with those of most people in his own congregation."[40] With his fervently probusiness positions, Falwell attracted many wealthy benefactors. He would also develop close connections with the burgeoning New Right and its wide range of corporate funders, who would prove instrumental in transforming Falwell's ministry into a major political force.[41]

At least some wealthy funders were acting on the basis of cynical realpolitik rather than religious commitment. One prominent supporter of evangelical causes was the Hunt Oil patriarch H. L. Hunt; he was only a "nominal believer, who had a regular mistress and a healthy gambling habit."[42] For some, religion was simply a useful vehicle for advancing the conservative ideology that many business figures supported instinctively as a matter of self-interest. But that was not always the case. There also emerged during the 1970s a group of Christian business interests that combined an authentic religious zeal with revenue-generating activity, including such prominent enterprises as the Amway Corporation, Days Inn, Chick-Fil-A, and Mary Kay Cosmetics. The market for Christian music produced several highly profitable companies run by managers who were themselves fervent evangelicals. All these interests become ready sources of political support for Christian causes.[43]

In other instances, the business world sensed a growing evangelical bandwagon and saw the benefits of climbing aboard. Such was the case with the Walmart retail chain, which began as a regional enterprise serving the Ozarks before expanding nationally and globally.[44] Walmart was founded and run by the relatively secular Sam Walton, who was a practicing Presbyterian, not a fundamentalist or evangelical. As charismatic Christianity ascended during the 1970s, however, Walmart managers gradually recognized the popularity of Jesus-themed products as well as the growing religiosity of their customers. Accordingly, Walmart began catering to its Christian clientele, initially as a sales tactic, but over time this tactic helped transform the corporation into a quintessential Christian enterprise. Such Christianization was also beneficial in establishing an atmosphere of obedience and submission among Walmart's vast workforce, who generally resisted unionization. These benefits were especially prized by company executives, as their traditionally low wage scales translated into high profitability. No doubt Walmart managers wished to sustain the climate of employee submissiveness, and evangelical Christianity aided them in doing so.[45]

Widespread Christianization also proved valuable for New Right activists, who readily engaged the culture wars sweeping through the country in mid-decade. One of the first major flare-ups began in 1974 in Kanawha County, West Virginia, where evangelicals protested against public school textbooks that contained excerpts from Mark Twain, Bernard Malamud, Eldridge Cleaver, and James Baldwin. Protests continued over a period of months and involved repeated acts of violence, bombings, and shootings. Local Christian ministers led the protests, which gradually evolved into a more generalized revolt against "short skirts, long hair, civil rights, nudity, dirty movies"—a standard litany of morality issues that resonated with Christian conservatives across the country.[46] In this case, the culture wars assumed an overtly racist character: the Ku Klux Klan staged rallies against the despised books, working in tandem with at least some of the local protesters.[47] The Heritage Foundation immediately saw an opportunity to curry favor with evangelicals. Accordingly, Heritage personnel directly supported the protesters, offering free legal and public relations assistance.[48] The Heritage engagement helped nationalize the West Virginia protests and magnify their importance.

The culture and morality wars continued throughout the decade, playing out around issues of school curriculum, affirmative action, homosexuality, feminism, abortion rights, crime, gun control, and drug addiction. They were often led by right-wing female activists such as Phyllis Schlafly, Anita Bryant, and Connie Marshner.[49] Schlalfy had long been connected with corporate power circles and had begun her career at the American Enterprise Institute.[50] During the 1970s, the Coors family helped bankroll Schlafly's activities, notably her crusade against the Equal Rights Amendment to the Constitution, which proposed equality of the sexes. She also developed close ties to the Amway Corporation.[51] Her work was promoted by the business-funded American Legislative Exchange Council (ALEC), which listed Schlafly among its "National Issue Experts."[52] Marshner was backed by the impressive financial and political resources of the Heritage Foundation, her employer.[53]

Meanwhile, AEI worked with the Nixon administration to promote crime as a wedge issue—with, once again, a subtle appeal to racial prejudice—while Heritage worked closed with antiabortion activists.[54] The National Pro-Life Political Action Committee also received backing from ALEC, as did a series of New Right organizations that were themselves heavily backed by corporate interests.[55] The conservative movement extended its reach beyond the evangelical Protestants who were at its core and also engaged some socially conservative Catholics[56] and Jews.[57] And as Nixon had intended, the culture wars held special appeal among working-class whites,[58] who were readily distracted from the developing economic turmoil of the period.[59]

The growing social and religious movements were integrated into the broader conservative movement, forming a broad coalition. The culture wars thus helped mobilize the "divisions" of which Weyrich spoke. And these mobilization efforts produced a basic shift in the political orientation of evangelicals, who became far more engaged in politics than previously. This shift began around the middle of the decade, as described by the political scientist Robert Putnam: "Prior to 1974 . . . most studies found evangelicals less disposed to political participation than other Americans—less likely to vote, to join political groups, to write to public officials, and to favor religious movements in politics. After 1974, in contrast, most studies have found them *more* involved politically than other Americans."[60] Conservatives were forging a popular base for their programs, including laissez-faire economic policy, with widespread support.

THE BIG RIG

A second motivating force for the New Right was libertarian ideology, which wielded significant influence by the end of the decade, especially among youth. The Libertarian Party was founded in 1971, outside the regular party structure, and gradually gathered popular support from a small (but growing) number of disaffected voters. Its free-market radicalism and opposition to taxation attracted support, as did the libertarians' tolerance for diverse lifestyles, including diverse sexual lifestyles. The libertarian idea fit well with the antiauthoritarian atmosphere that was widespread in popular culture and originally pioneered by the New Left. Libertarians also proved adept in manipulating language by redefining such words as "liberty" and "freedom," which now became property of the political right, consistent with laissez-faire economics.

Despite its grassroots image, the libertarian movement was heavily intertwined with elite business interests, notably the influential brothers Charles and David Koch, whose wealth derived from their oil services firm Koch Industries. Charles Koch "reportedly contributed up to $15,000,000" to the fledgling Libertarian Party in 1979, while David became the party nominee for president in 1980.[61] An authoritative source on Koch funding is *Radicals for Capitalism* by Brian Doherty. This work is an insider account—basically a memoir—written by the editor of the libertarian-leaning *Reason* magazine. But it is far from a whitewash. Writing with candor, Doherty describes the massive influx of Koch money into the movement during the 1970s: "This sudden injection of enormous wealth into a small movement [produced a] bizarre gravitational shifting as Planet Koch adjusted everyone's orbits. . . . Many in the movement came to treat Charles Koch as a walking wallet." The influx alienated at least some dissident members of the libertarian movement, who coined the term "Kochtopus"[62] as a derisive description of the Koch family's expanding influence. The Kochs' objective was to use money as a means of controlling the movement and its members, as David Koch would later acknowledge: "If we're going to give a lot of money, we'll make darn sure they spend it in a way that goes along with our intent. . . . We do exert that kind of control."[63] The image of libertarianism as a purely populist phenomenon—which remains widespread—amounts to a distortion of facts.

The Kochs presented themselves as political purists, disdaining opportunism Accordingly, they displayed contempt for conventional conservatives, including their business supporters. A 1974 pamphlet written by Charles described U.S. business interests as sellouts to the collectivist establishment. Even Lewis Powell of the U.S. Chamber of Commerce, whose earlier manifesto had galvanized business, was viewed negatively as being insufficiently committed to laissez-faire principles.[64] In addition, secular libertarians had little in common with the evangelicals and cultural conservatives, who were becoming pillars of the mainstream right.

To advance their own vision for the future, the Koch brothers financed a series of think tanks, including the Institute for Humane Studies (IHS), the Center for the Study of Market Processes (later the Mercatus Center), and the Cato Institute, all of which helped propagate the libertarian perspective among intellectuals and graduate students. It appeared that the Kochs were buying their way into the world of ideas, and this was especially apparent at the IHS, where they created an atmosphere of political surveillance. According to Jane Mayer, Charles Koch "reportedly demanded better metrics with which to *monitor students' political views*. . . . Applicants' essays [at IHS] had to be run through computers in order to count the number of times they mentioned the free-market icons Ayn Rand and Milton Friedman."[65]

At the level of a mass movement, libertarianism was especially influential among middle-class college students, among whom it competed for members with mainstream conservative groups. One competing group was the Young Americans for Freedom (YAF), which was integrated into the conservative mainstream, notably the *National Review* network. YAF members often experienced adversarial interactions with libertarians, who cherished their role as political outsiders.[66] No doubt the outsider image of libertarianism was a useful selling point in attracting idealistic youth.

The libertarian appeal extended well beyond college campuses. During the late 1970s, truck drivers who were alienated from the highly corrupt Teamsters union—and from the liberal mainstream more generally—became sympathetic toward libertarianism. The trade publication of independent truckers, *Overdrive*, became a forum for discussion of libertarian viewpoints. At one point, *Overdrive* introduced its blue-collar readers to the ideas of Friedman, who conducted an interview with the magazine in which he extolled the virtues of deregulation.[67] Thus inspired by Friedman, truck drivers lobbied for the deregulation of the trucking industry during the administration of President Jimmy Carter.

We will see that when President Carter finally did deregulate trucking, in line with the libertarian agenda, it produced disastrous consequences for truckers, generating a collapse in their living standards. It is a testament to the political skills of libertarian strategists that they were able to persuade truckers to advocate policies that were destructive to their own interests. A recent study of the trucking deregulation fiasco is entitled *The Big Rig*—an apt metaphor indeed.[68]

The influence of libertarian ideas also extended to education policy. Libertarians had long derided the evils of mandatory taxation, combined with tax-funded and governmental-run school systems, which were viewed as public monopolies. This was a particular topic of interest to Friedman. In fact, Friedman wished to eliminate public support for education altogether. In a 1959 letter, he stated, "In principle, the full burden of education should be borne by the parents of the children."[69] The implication was that children of low-income families might receive no education at all. At the same time, Friedman understood that such a program was politically unworkable, and so his views on education gradually evolved—at least for public purposes. In his popular 1962 book, *Capitalism and Freedom*, Friedman conceded that government had a role in subsidizing education but should do so by issuing school vouchers to parents; they could use the vouchers for whatever public or private schools they wished, thus breaking the public school "monopoly."[70] Libertarian activism helped popularize the idea, and in 1973, the Nixon administration began supporting school voucher programs in several localities.[71]

The program gradually proved popular with important segments of the public. Through vouchers, citizens could choose schools for their children while still receiving state support to defray some of the cost. They were "free to choose," as Friedman liked to say. In addition, the program offered advantages to specific subgroups. Vouchers effectively subsidized religious schools, a detail that was appreciated by the growing evangelical movement. They also enabled parents to bypass racially integrated public schools, magnifying a major wedge issue of great benefit to the right. Finally, vouchers undermined public school teachers, who were heavily unionized, while building up private schools, which were typically nonunionized, thus deactivating a potential source of opposition.

When viewed in retrospect, school vouchers did little to improve the quality of education, and they exacerbated social inequality, effectively transmitting it across generations.[72] Despite a lack of substantive merit, school vouchers proved highly effective in advancing the agenda of the right, as well as interest groups affiliated with the right.

Superficially, the rambunctious libertarians appeared as challengers to the New Right and to conservative orthodoxy more generally. But these tensions should not be overstated. In reality, the two camps—libertarians and conventional rightists—sought similar objectives. Both promoted programs associated with market economics, deregulation, and reduced taxation.[73] Although libertarians pushed these programs more vigorously and uncompromisingly than most conservatives and operated outside the conservative mainstream, they nevertheless served to advance the substantive agenda of the mainstream, whether or not they intended to do so. And by remaining outside the mainstream, libertarians were better able to reach youthful audiences by appearing rebellious and countercultural. Milton Friedman helped bridge the two camps, since he was popular in both. In the end, the rise of libertarianism would prove advantageous to the New Right.

Another ideological bridge was the football star Jack Kemp, who was elected to Congress as a Republican in 1971. While in Congress, Kemp adopted a libertarian style, emphasizing his long-standing fascination with Ayn Rand and Friedrich von Hayek, becoming a major public figure in the process.[74] At the same time, Kemp cultivated a public image of altruism and compassion, a "bleeding heart conservative," as his supporters liked to say. The congressman seemed sufficiently impressive that he was discreetly mentored and coached by

Irving Kristol of the American Enterprise Institute, who introduced Kemp to his vast network of corporate backers. Kristol had high hopes for Kemp, as suggested in the following 1978 letter: "I had a very interesting conversation with Laurence Tisch, the head of Loews Corporation. . . . Larry is a Republican and he was moaning about the absence of emerging new leaders for the party. . . . I told Larry he should invite you [Kemp] down [to meet Republican donors] and he said he was interested in doing so."[75] Kristol stated that a sizable number of corporate "fat cats" would attend the meeting, with the implication that they could fund Kemp's future political campaigns. Shortly after, Kristol wrote a second letter to Kemp: "I spoke to Larry Tisch this morning and he said you were 'terrific,'"[76] suggesting that the funders were duly impressed with the legislator. With this heavy corporate backing, Kemp helped normalize libertarian ideas within the Republican mainstream as he ascended the party hierarchy.

The overarching goal of the New Right was to knit together various elements of conservatism into a broad alliance. To the extent that some libertarians remained outside this coalition and operated independently, they were a unique case. Libertarians aside, the New Right sought to meld the objectives of corporate conservatives with those of social conservatives and evangelicals through its strategy of fusionism. Heritage founder Paul Weyrich strongly promoted this coalition-building strategy, while Phyllis Schlafly's organization had "an extraordinary ability to unite in a coalition" with other conservative groups.[77] The overall approach was distilled by Ronald Reagan in a 1977 speech before the Conservative Political Action Committee: "The time has come to see if it is possible to present a program of action . . . that can attract those interested in the so-called 'social' issues and those interested in 'economic' issues. In short, isn't it possible to combine the two major segments of contemporary American conservatism into one politically effective whole?"[78]

The eagerness to build broad coalitions—and to do so as a long-term strategy—accounts for much of the conservatives' success in this era, just as much as the massive amounts of money that undergirded that success. Another factor in their success was the lack of any effective opposition.

THE OPPOSITION

The most important source of opposition to the business-led mobilization—at least potentially—was organized labor. In previous periods of U.S. history, labor unions had been at the forefront of progressive change. During the 1970s, however, labor was hobbled by exceptionally feeble leadership, a product of the earlier Red Scare, which denuded unions of their most talented organizers. The resulting weakness was especially evident in the American Federation of Labor-Congress of Industrial Organizations (AFL-CIO), the nation's largest union, led by president George Meany and his heir apparent, Lane Kirkland. Under their direction, the AFL-CIO presented no alternative economic programs of any consequence and no vision for the future. While the Mont Pèlerin economists, New Right activists, and associated think tanks were busily advancing concrete programs to weaken unions and erode worker rights, Meany and his colleagues made surprisingly few efforts to counter these moves. They adopted a fundamentally reactive approach, responding to antilabor initiatives in piecemeal fashion.[79] It should be noted that there were more progressive unions—notably the United Auto Workers—which did put forward broadly based programs of economic reform combined with aggressive efforts to protect worker rights. There was also a growing coterie of younger workers who loosely associated with the New Left and advocated radical social changes.[80] But these dissenting voices could not compensate for the overwhelming conservatism that prevailed within the AFL-CIO, which remained America's most influential union.

The AFL-CIO leadership failed to stem diminishing union membership, as a percentage of the total labor force, which had been in decline since the late 1950s. Insofar as the record shows, the leadership had little interest in this problem at all. President Meany's own lack of interest was dramatically displayed in a 1972 interview with *U.S. News and World Report*:

QUESTION: "Why is the total membership [of the union movement] not growing as fast as the country's labor force?"
MEANY: "*I don't know, I don't care. . . .* I used to worry about the membership, about the size of the membership. But quite a few years ago,

I just stopped worrying about it, because to me it doesn't make any difference."[81]

While there were some significant unionization drives during the 1970s, especially in the public sector and "pink-collar" jobs typically held by women, these efforts could not compensate for the general decline, which worsened over time.[82] The dwindling labor clout that resulted from this state of affairs constrained any possibility for opposing the agenda of the New Right.

The lassitude of Meany and Kirkland was also evident at the policy level in their response to the globalization of production. While they often complained about the effect that globalization was having on U.S. jobs, they made no serious effort to counter the trend.[83] In 1975, unions in several countries sought to establish procedures for transnational collective bargaining—to advance worker rights on a global scale—but they received little support from the AFL-CIO, which hampered the effort. The union "held aloof from the transnational [union] bargaining effort," according to *Nation's Business*.[84] In interviews, American trade officials noted the AFL-CIO's indifference to globalization and its effects on workers.[85]

If there was one issue that did energize the AFL-CIO leadership, it was U.S. foreign policy,[86] especially their support for anticommunist labor unions around the world, an effort that was spearheaded by Kirkland and strongly favored by Meany.[87] As a result of this Cold War orientation, union leaders were vociferously supportive of the Vietnam War while hostile toward opponents of that war. Meany had long viewed antiwar critics as "victims of communist propaganda."[88] And in 1976, the AFL-CIO played an instrumental role in organizing the Committee on the Present Danger, which aimed at reinvigorating U.S. militarism after its failures in Southeast Asia.[89]

The hawkish foreign policy views of Meany and Kirkland triggered a rupture between the union on the one hand and the antiwar movement and the New Left on the other. After the Democratic Party's nomination of George McGovern, labor became estranged from a large portion of mainstream liberalism as well, introducing a basic rift within the American left, militating against any broad-based progressive front.[90] At the 1972 Democratic convention in Miami Beach, Meany lamented that "there were no steelworkers, no pipefitters . . . no plumbers."[91] The complaint that the Democratic Party had moved away from the working class was perfectly valid, but this was a problem that Meany himself had done much to create.

Let us pause to consider the counterfactual. In a different historical context, the antiwar movement and the unions might have operated as allies rather than adversaries. Such an alliance would have raised the political striking power of both groups. An antiwar-labor coalition also would have been well placed to advance a range of progressive goals in both foreign and domestic issue areas, while the connection to organized labor could have anchored the youthful antiwar activists, giving them a greater sense of direction and purpose. In the real world of American politics during the 1970s, however, the AFL-CIO's enthusiasm for the Vietnam War blocked any possibility of alliance. The two groups—labor unions and antiwar activists—became the bitterest of enemies, and the resulting divide would poison left-wing politics for years to come.

Overall, the New Right's method of drawing together disparate groups for unified action had no counterpart on the left, which remained fragmented throughout the decade, a problem that began with the split between labor and the antiwar movement. Once it became fully established, organizational fragmentation became the order of the day. The fragmentation problem was evident within the antiwar movement itself, which eschewed national organization. Antiwar activism flowed from localized peace groups based on college campuses, with only limited coordination among groups. Lacking structure, the movement proved incapable of advancing its activism into issue areas beyond the Vietnam War. Once the U.S. combat role in Vietnam ended in early 1973, along with the draft, the antiwar movement effectively ceased to exist; it had no staying power. Writing from Harvard in November 1973, Seymour Martin Lipset marveled that the once powerful antiwar movement "had almost disappeared."[92] By the time the Committee on the Present Danger mobilized to increase military spending and interventionism later in the decade, it met little opposition.

With the collapse of the antiwar movement, activism fragmented further, establishing separate groups—and separate agendas—for women, gays, Blacks, Chicanos, and Native Americans.[93] The growing environmental movement operated independently from other progressive groups for the most part, with a single-issue focus. And within these groups, there was further fragmentation. In the women's movement, for example, there was a schism between the National Organization for Women and a series of smaller and more radical groups, such as the Combahee River Collective.[94] The environmental movement was split between advocates of "deep ecology" and more mainstream groups, such as the Sierra Club, as well as those focused on specific environmental issues, such as protesters against the nuclear power industry. During the 1970s, the left seemed to reject the very idea of majoritarian politics almost as a matter of principle. Most initiatives to form broad coalitions foundered on issues of gender and racial identity. Within certain Protestant groups, for example, there were efforts to form a progressive alternative to the growing Christian right, but such efforts largely failed due to divisions between African American and white members.[95] The women's movement contributed to the breakup of the New Left, with female activists establishing their own organizations.[96] Indeed, it is difficult to even speak of the left as a distinct tendency given the organizational fragmentation that played out, though I will continue to use the word "left" as a convenient shorthand for the collection of social movements from this era.

The most noteworthy characteristic of social movements during the 1970s was the lack of strategic vision or long-term planning or any recognition that these things were even important.[97] While the New Right and its corporate/evangelical allies were pursuing fusion in their quest to undermine the class compromise, their opponents on the left were moving in the opposite direction, dividing themselves into multiple factions that were unable to present a common front in defense of their collective interests. If the right was seeking to divide and conquer, then the left naively played into this strategy. There was also an asymmetry of political skill, with the best political strategists appearing on the right and almost none on the left. To be sure, the 1970s produced a new coterie of left-leaning theorists, who invigorated academic research. Marxist ideas influenced several fields of study, while in the humanities, deconstruction and postmodernism were beginning to make their presence felt. But the left produced no one with the practical skills or strategic vision of Nixon, Weyrich, or Friedman. These strategists planned out their moves over extended periods—acting with discipline and focus—but their opponents on the left showed little interest in planning or collaborating, much less building mass coalitions. And the left's emphasis on social issues left the economic realm largely uncontested.

While the new social movements of this era did achieve well-known successes, including landmark environmental legislation and major changes in societal attitudes regarding the roles of women and gays, their distinctive tendency to fragment limited their effectiveness, especially over the long term. Stated simply, the social movements of the left were no match for their counterparts among the New Right. In 1980, a *New Republic* journalist reflected on the success of the Heritage Foundation in drawing together disparate conservative tendencies and added, "It would be difficult to form a similar alliance of disparate liberal interest groups, since *cohesion among them does not exist."*[98]

THE WORKING CLASS

The rising social movements of the left made few efforts to organize the working class. Indeed, there was some tendency to disparage working people—especially working-class whites—who were seen as supporters of Meany's hidebound labor movement and Nixon's Silent Majority. The widely publicized image of hardhat-clad construction workers attacking peace demonstrators in New York in 1970 served to underscore the antiworker stereotype.[99] Many on the left were inclined to write off the white proletariat as unreachable and perhaps not worth reaching. The loss of blue-collar support that resulted from these biases hobbled the American left through the remainder of the decade and for many decades to come.

To be sure, this negative image of the proletariat did not always match the facts. Survey data from the era show that adults of lower educational levels were more progressive in some respects than the well-educated, as noted in correspondence by Lipset, who served as coeditor of the *Public Opinion Quarterly*. With regard to the Vietnam War, "A majority of the public felt that intervention in Vietnam was a mistake long before their [highly educated] betters did." While Lipset acknowledged that the majority of the public tended to be conservative on "social and noneconomic issues," they were in fact "more liberal than the better educated on economic and class-related matter, e.g., government action to reduce unemployment, minimum wages, progressive tax policies, old age pensions, [and] measures to increase opportunity for the poor." There was also a strong inclination to express "hostility to big business."[100]

The unfavorable stereotype of working people persisted nonetheless, and it was reflected in popular culture, especially cinema. A particularly noteworthy film was *Joe*, which premiered in the summer of 1970 and focused on the fictional white factory worker Joe Curran. We first meet Joe at the American Bar and Grill, and he is ranting.

> Why work? You tell me. Why the fuck work when you can screw, have babies, and get paid for it. Welfare, they get all that welfare money. . . . I sweat my balls off forty hours a week in front of a fucking furnace. They get as much money as I do, for nothing. . . . All you gotta do is act Black and the money rolls in. . . . Ah, the liberals, 42 percent of all liberals are queer. That's a fact. . . . The white kids, the rich, white kids—the worst. Hippies! Sugar tit all the way. Cars, the best colleges, vacations, orgies. . . . They're all going the same God-damned, screw America way! . . . Sex, drugs, pissing on America, fucking up the music. I'd like to kill one of them.[101]

Joe is shown mispronouncing the word "orgies," with a hard G, underscoring the character's low intelligence. The film ends with Joe instigating a mass killing of hippies at a commune. When viewed in retrospect, *Joe* appears crudely directed and sensationalist; it has not aged well. At the time, however, the film was widely influential and positively reviewed.[102]

The image of working-class and rural whites as violent, racist, and ignorant became commonplace, appearing in such films as *Easy Rider*, *Billy Jack*, *Deliverance*, *Taxi Driver*, and *Saturday Night Fever*. Some films presented working people in a more sympathetic light, such as *Norma Rae*, but they constituted exceptions to an overall trend that was becoming strongly negative. The popular television program *All in the Family*, debuting in 1971, featured Archie Bunker, a blue-collar character who was probably based on Joe Curran.[103] Like Joe, Archie was presented as inarticulate; his mispronunciations and verbal miscues were basic sources of humor for the show. In some episodes, Archie was also portrayed as kind-hearted—but with an overarching tone of class con-descension, which came to define *All in the Family*.

The contrast with earlier periods of political activism is striking. During the 1930s and 1940s, popular culture celebrated the lives of working people in the giant murals of San Francisco's Coit Tower and Aaron Copeland's orchestral composition *Fanfare for the Common Man*. By the 1970s, the common man was being presented with a tone of suspicion and even contempt. There was little fanfare.

Progressive organizing campaigns tended to bypass working people. That was true among both the liberal establishment and the remnants of the New Left, in which "postmaterialist" ideas became dominant. The only major exception to this tendency was the Congressional Black Caucus, which systematically sought to build bridges to low-income whites. But it was a unique exception; most progressive groups of the era tended to ignore class issues. Environmental activists often spoke of limiting economic growth, or even doing away with growth altogether—though without much thought of how such policies would affect employment levels among workers who depended on growth for their livelihoods.[104] Environmentalists later recognized that a sustainable economy would require greater growth and more employment to enable a reconfiguring of infrastructure, but that was not widely appreciated in the 1970s.[105] The image of an antigrowth environmental movement was guaranteed to alienate working people.

The women's movement, in contrast, began with an emphasis on issues relating to working women, especially in its push for govern-mentally funded childcare in 1971, but that working-class focus quickly faded.[106] By the middle of the decade, mainstream feminism appealed mostly to an educated, professional constituency, a trend that was evident in *Ms.* magazine, cofounded by Gloria Steinem. A survey of *Ms.* from the 1970s reveals an emphasis on feminist culture, style, and sexuality—with a pronounced upscale tone.[107] Analyses of female abortion rights activists found that they were predominantly affluent and well educated.[108] The antiwar movement, too, began with a significant blue-collar base among disgruntled Vietnam veterans, many of whom became peace activists.[109] But when the movement disappeared after the 1973 Paris Peace Accords, antiwar veterans were demobilized and never remobilized around any new issues. A more imaginative New Left leadership might have used this base to break into new issue areas, such as the limited economic opportunities available to veterans and working people more generally. In addition, the New Left could have made common cause with reformist elements within the AFL-CIO, against the lassitude of President Meany, in favor of more robust defense of worker rights. But such efforts were never undertaken to any significant extent. Clearly, antiwar activists lacked the tactical flexibility that was one of the hallmarks of the New Right.

There was a further problem of style. Leftist activists deployed a vocabulary that was abstract, jargon-ridden, and inaccessible to working people, in sharp contrast to the populist style of the right. Progressive causes often showcased elite celebrities, such as Leonard Bernstein, Jane Fonda, and Shirley MacLaine.[110] From academia, Herbert Marcuse and Charles Reich wrote dismissively of the working classes, who were viewed as relics of the past.[111] While Republicans were enlarging their political base, Democrats and the activist left were shrinking their own base, casting off working-class supporters. There were some dissenting voices, such as the journalist Jack Newfield, who advocated a populist approach emphasizing protecting living standards, breaking up monopolies, and activating the proletariat.[112] But these ideas gained little traction in a left culture that was already committed to an identitarian agenda based on an affluent and well-educated constituency.

The left was opening itself up to a backlash, which was led by Vice President Agnew.[113] In a thinly veiled attack on liberals, the vice president denounced "snobs who characterize themselves as intellectuals."[114] That set the stage for many further denunciations of alleged elitism and snobbery, which became a standard rhetorical technique for the right long after Agnew's resignation from office.[115] Progressives bristled at the resort to demagoguery, especially the cutting accusations of snobbery, but they missed the key point that such accusations contained a kernel of truth. The image of the liberal snob would prove an important wedge issue that was immensely advantageous to the right, while the resulting loss of working-class support became an enduring handicap for liberals.

The most divisive wedge issue of all was race, especially with regard to the integration of schools. During the 1970s, federal courts ordered new rounds of school integration, which met fierce resistance from many whites, underscoring the fact that racism remained a potent force in American society. One of the most notable flare-ups took place in Boston, where District Judge Arthur Garrity ordered desegregation of several public school systems beginning in 1974. Despite its liberal reputation, Boston was highly segregated[116] due to the long-standing practice of "redlining," whereby banks refused to grant mortgages to Black families seeking access to traditionally white neighborhoods.[117] Segregation was also enforced by local white residents, who angrily resisted all efforts at integration. Judge Garrity was determined to remedy this problem through mandatory busing of students across district lines, sending them to newly integrated schools outside their own residential areas.

The court order led to an explosion of racialized anger and violence centered on the white neighborhood of South Boston, whose residents sought to keep Black children out of local schools. The protests were led by the politician Louise Day Hicks, who claimed that Black militants "tyrannize our schools." She added for good measure that white women "can no longer walk the streets safely," while the justice system conferred "special privileges for the Black man and the criminal."[118] The South Boston protests quickly achieved national prominence. From Alabama, Governor George Wallace expressed solidarity with the white protesters, as did groups even further to the right, including the American Nazi Party and the Ku Klux Klan.[119] From the opposite standpoint, prominent civil rights leaders spoke out in favor of Garrity's desegregation order. Coretta Scott King stated (plausibly enough) that "racism, not busing [is] the real issue."[120]

The Boston controversy included an important economic dimension: both the white and African American neighborhoods affected by the desegregation order were among the poorest in the city, with high rates of unemployment and growing deindustrialization. Desegregation coincided with a major recession, which no doubt contributed to the tension. One study of the Boston controversy notes evidence of "a direct connection between unemployment and anti-busing activity," with the most impoverished white communities showing the greatest resistance to busing. There were additional grievances: South Boston residents complained that the court order made no effort to desegregate affluent communities while focusing on low-income communities. In addition, protesters criticized Judge Garrity for his perceived elitism and Harvard education. To many South Boston residents, Garrity epitomized the image of the liberal snob, and one critic summed up his court order as "the Harvard plan for the working-class man."[121] All these features intensified public anger, especially among whites. Mandatory integration of Boston schools may well have been the only realistic solution to entrenched segregation—just as it was in the South during the 1950s and 1960s—but this solution proved extremely contentious.

Conflicts over busing played out in cities across the country, and New Right activists sensed yet another opportunity to build support.[122] The Heritage Foundation publicized a proposed constitutional amendment to ban busing,[123] while ALEC organized against busing at the state level.[124] The right was once again playing the populist card, fomenting a particularly potent wedge issue—racism—with considerable effect.

Evidently, wedge issues were separating poor and working-class people along the lines of race, gender, religion, sexuality, and lifestyle, with growing intensity. The main beneficiary of the culture and race wars that resulted was the New Right and its wealthy backers. The Boston controversy thus raised a fundamental question of strategy: perhaps what progressives needed was a new approach to draw working people together around common interests, possibly overcoming or at least attenuating the animosities that were dividing them, working toward a program of class solidarity. Such an initiative was, in fact, launched—by the Black community.

THE BLACK CAUCUS PROPOSES FULL EMPLOYMENT

In 1975, the issue of full employment was thrust into public discussion with the introduction of the Full Employment and Balanced Growth Act, or Humphrey-Hawkins Act, cosponsored by Senator Hubert Humphrey and Representative Augustus Hawkins.[125] The bill mandated that all citizens had a right to employment as a basic human right, to be guaranteed by the federal government. Unemployment was to be abolished by law. Humphrey's association with the bill elevated its national profile, but the real originator was the Congressional Black Caucus, chaired by Hawkins, as well leaders within the civil rights movement associated with the Reverend Jesse Jackson.[126] The Black community was advancing a clear political objective: they sought to establish common ground with working-class whites. Rep. Hawkins himself emphasized the politically unifying character of full employment, which had the potential to draw in broad segments of the population "regardless of race, creed, color."[127]

In advocating full employment, the Black Caucus was not ceding ground on school integration, which remained a basic objective. Rather, it recognized the need to couple civil rights activism with an overarching economic program. Certainly, the Humphrey-Hawkins bill would have benefited African Americans, who suffered from much higher rates of unemployment than the population at large. At the same time, the legislation had the potential to benefit a wide range of groups and gain majority support. But within the Black community, this interracial approach was controversial. Some Black academics had been advancing a race-specific tactic of reparation payments as compensation for a past history of slavery, as well as post-slavery violence and discrimination under the Jim Crow system.[128] The Black Caucus and the civil rights leadership opted instead for a multiracial agenda. In advocating Humphrey-Hawkins, Jackson argued that "the struggle for economic well-being of poor whites and poor Blacks has begun."[129]

The Humphrey-Hawkins full employment bill is a largely forgotten chapter in U.S. political history, and at the time, the whole idea of full employment was widely dismissed as impractical. But this negative judgment is open to question, since it ignores the sensational success of full employment when it was implemented during World War II, which not only ended the Great Depression but also achieved some of the highest rates of productivity growth ever recorded. The idea of full employment was a central feature of Keynesian economics during the 1930s and 1940s and was advocated by John Maynard Keynes himself in *The General Theory*.[130] From the standpoint of its supporters, the Humphrey-Hawkins bill sought to revive the full employment doctrine of classical Keynesianism, in order to protect living standards amidst growing economic insecurity and deindustrialization.[131] When viewed in retrospect, the bill appears as the only serious effort by the political left to craft a solution to the crisis of the 1970s. It constituted the sole attempt to present an authentic working-class program with a multiracial, class-based appeal.

The proposed full employment program militated against the economic orthodoxy of the period, which was predicated on the assumption that unemployment was a vital instrument for restraining overconsumption by low-income groups, which in turn helped control inflation. By the 1970s, full employment was viewed as inherently inflationary and therefore unacceptable. Critics of Humphrey-Hawkins repeatedly emphasized the inflationary character of the bill,[132] and its supporters never offered an adequate response to these criticisms, weakening their public credibility.[133] In reality, there were solutions to inflation that were compatible with full employment. Specifically, the federal government could have raised taxes on the wealthy, as originally proposed by the economist Michal Kalecki in 1943.[134] If overconsumption was a cause of inflation, one solution was to reduce consumption at the top income brackets rather than among the working classes. Recall from previous chapters that inflation was primarily a problem for the affluent; it had less impact on people with low and moderate incomes. Statistical studies of inflation show that its main effect was to redistribute wealth from rich to poor.

The Humphrey-Hawkins program almost certainly would have produced a major redistribution of income and wealth in favor of the lower income brackets, through either a Kaleckian program of progressive taxation or continued inflation. It also seems likely that full employment would have raised wages and encouraged unionization by creating a permanently tight labor market, further redistributing resources in favor of labor. Thus, it should come as no surprise that the Business Roundtable, the National Association of Manufacturers, and the U.S. Chamber of Commerce all lobbied against the bill.[135] There also was strong resistance from the mainstream media, as well as the leaders of both political parties.

The success of Humphrey-Hawkins would have required the formation of a mass political movement to overcome such formidable opposition, but that proved impossible given the political fragmentation on the left that was one of the defining features of the era. The entire logic of identity politics and postmaterialism worked against the notion of a far-reaching economic program such as the Humphrey-Hawkins Act. Accordingly, the new social movements of this period—including the women's movement and environmentalism—offered only minimal support, at best.[136] Among labor unions, the very conservative AFL-CIO initially opposed the bill altogether, presumably because of fears that federally funded employment programs would detract from the all-important military budget. It eventually did endorse the bill, but only after the full employment guarantee was substantially weakened.[137]

Beyond the Black Caucus, the only groups that enthusiastically supported the bill were some second-tier unions, notably the United Auto Workers and the Machinists Union.[138] The Black Caucus and other supporters made their share of mistakes, holding no mass rallies for the legislation.[139] They underestimated the momentous effort that was required to gain acceptance for the full employment program. And as noted, supporters did not adequately address the issue of inflation in their public presentations.

The Democratic leadership was eager to bury the whole idea of full employment, which it deemed far too radical, but to do so in a way that would not risk offending the Black Caucus or the African American community more generally.[140] As the bill gradually moved through the legislative process during 1975–78, its contents were watered down, leaving little of substance. When President Carter finally signed the act into law in 1978, it merely encouraged the government to seek full employment rather than making it a legal requirement.[141] The legislation amounted to a "grab bag of symbolic gestures," according to the *Wall Street Journal*,[142] while the *Hartford Courant* called the legislation a "defanged version" of the original Humphrey-Hawkins bill.[143] In the words of the economist Herbert Stein, the legislation was "forgotten as soon as enacted."[144] With the failure of Humphrey-Hawkins, the Democratic Party and the activist left had no economic program of any consequence; they presented no real solutions to the extended economic crisis. The momentum for change moved sharply toward the New Right—which clearly did have a program. And increasingly, it was developing a popular base of its own.

Even after the death of Humphrey-Hawkins, there were still intermittent efforts by Black activists to establish coalitions with poor whites around the idea of economic reform. A particularly striking case was the presidential campaign of Jesse Jackson in 1987–88, which assembled significant support among white workers and farmers, as well as Blacks, as described in the following *Rolling Stone* interview:

JACKSON: I walked down the streets of Cudahy, Wisconsin, with 6,000 workers. On some porches there were American flags, Confederate flags, and Jesse Jackson pictures.

QUESTION: What was your gut-level reaction to seeing the Confederate flag side by side with your picture?

JACKSON: A sense of gratification, a sense of vindication. A sense of joy. . . . Many people think they'll find security in the Confederate flag, or a sense of defiance. But, apart from these symbols, we still have the most in common at the plant gate they're closing when the workers have gotten notice, the most in common at the hospital where people died because they couldn't get the yellow card you need to go upstairs where there's a bed waiting for the rich to get sick. To make progress, we have to forgive each other, redeem each other, and focus on common ground.[145]

Evidently, there was potential for interracial coalitions during this period. If this potential was never fully realized, it represented a failure by the left.

Some of the most influential movements of the 1970s—notably evangelical Christianity and libertarianism—were influenced by well-funded corporate campaigns, and the cumulative effect of these campaigns was to create a popular base for the New Right. It is important to emphasize that these movements did not constitute a pretend form of populism; this was not mere "Astroturfing." What was emerging was an authentic mass movement of the right, with millions of enthusiastic supporters. At the same time, the agendas of these grassroots movements were subtly molded—behind the scenes—by their corporate paymasters. Through the doctrine of fusionism, social conservatives were integrated with economic conservatives to form an unbeatable coalition. Finally, the success of these fused conservative movements was facilitated by the weakness of the American left, which mostly failed to present any credible alternative or even to work together for common objectives. By the end of the decade, the energy and initiative had shifted overwhelmingly to the right, setting the stage for their later victory in the 1980 election.

CHAPTER FOUR

Selling a New Cold War

Fishmongers sell fish; warmongers sell war.

—SIR RODRIC BRAITHWAITE, UK INTELLIGENCE OFFICIAL

The rightward shift of the 1970s was remarkably broad in scope, affecting a variety of issue areas. In this chapter, we examine its consequences for foreign and military policy. The decade began with relatively restrained foreign policy initiatives, reflecting reduced U.S. willingness to intervene in overseas conflicts, improved relations with Communist adversaries, and significantly lowered military spending. This restraint elicited a backlash, however, which aimed at much greater military assertiveness combined with heightened arms acquisition. We will see that this backlash was led by business interests, especially those in the military sector.

Throughout this chapter, I stress the same political forces that have been discussed throughout this study—the mobilization of corporate interest groups, the substantial investment of resources to support their activities, and the integration of business into a coalition that included organized labor and religious organizations—and how these mobilized forces were able to influence the political process. In addition, I show that by the end of the decade, this conservative mobilization proved highly successful in effecting basic changes in foreign policy, resulting in a new and more intense phase of superpower confrontation. This chapter will once again emphasize the central importance of Richard Nixon, though in a different role from what we have seen previously. In earlier chapters, we noted that the Nixon White House was instrumental in orchestrating the rightward shift, including its business support. With regard to foreign and military policy, however, the shift was orchestrated largely in opposition to President Nixon's policies. The rightist forces that he had done so much to assemble and mobilize turned against the president in the specific case of foreign and military policy.

And finally, the move toward a militarist policy eventually would help undermine the class compromise by directing money away from social programs in favor of weapons production, thus heightening economic austerity at the domestic level and reducing living standards for low-income groups. At the same time, the enrichment of weapons-producing companies would benefit the wealthy. Overall, the turn to a more militant foreign policy contributed significantly to the overall rightward turn in U.S. politics that took place during the 1970s.

THE VIETNAM SYNDROME

The decade began with a general reduction in U.S. interventionism. While this policy was implemented by President Richard Nixon and his chief foreign policy adviser, Henry Kissinger, it was ultimately driven by public disdain for military stalemate in the Vietnam War, as well as widespread opposition to the prospect of any more overseas adventures. The military services were losing credibility due to their lackluster performance in Vietnam combined with disturbing stories of brutal behavior. The notorious 1968 My Lai massacre, where American troops killed hundreds of Vietnamese women and children—and photographed the whole affair—stained the military's reputation.[1]

A new era of cynicism pervaded mainstream institutions. Newspaper reporters no longer accepted official pronouncements about overseas activity as willingly as they had in the past; they questioned and contradicted official sources, often undercutting government disinformation. This critical attitude first appeared during the late 1960s, especially after the Tet Offensive in Vietnam, and continued well into the 1970s. Newspaper editors, too, became critical. In 1971, the *New York Times* and *Washington Post* both published excerpts from the secret Pentagon Papers study of the Vietnam War, which had been illegally leaked by the military analyst Daniel Ellsberg.[2] For many, the Pentagon Papers confirmed that the war had been predicated on official lying all along. As Ellsberg stated the matter, "Truman lied from 1950 on, on the nature and purposes of the French involvement, the colonial reconquest of Vietnam that we were financing. . . . Eisenhower lied about the reasons for and the nature of our involvement with [South Vietnamese President Ngo Dinh] Diem. . . . Kennedy lied about the type of involvement we were doing there, our own combat involvement. . . . Johnson of course lied and lied and lied."[3]

The idea that presidents would intentionally lie to the public became generally accepted,[4] even if this was a new and startling realization for many. Allegations of misdeeds by the Central Intelligence Agency were widely circulated, including agency involvement in overseas coups, attempted assassinations, propaganda dissemination, and generalized illegality. These allegations were later confirmed by a 1975 investigation directed by Senator Frank Church.[5] Within academia, left-wing perspectives began to reshape the study of U.S. diplomacy. Such anti-interventionist scholars as William Appleman Williams, Gabriel Kolko, and Marilyn Young became highly influential and helped transform academic understanding of the Cold War, recasting America's global role in a far less positive perspective.[6]

At the cultural level, an attitude of antimilitarism pervaded, especially among the very young; it was reflected in such popular movies as *Mash*, *Catch-22*, and *Slaughterhouse Five*, which presented U.S. conduct in previous wars with a critical light; they were now seen through the lens of Vietnam. Mainstream political and corporate life was viewed as merely another form of criminality, an attitude nicely distilled in Francis Ford Coppola's *Godfather* series. Consider the following dialogue from *The Godfather, Part II*, in which the rising criminal boss Michael Corleone conferred with a highly corrupt Senator Patrick Geary:

SENATOR GEARY: I don't like your kind of people. I don't like to see you come out to this clean country in oily hair, dressed up in those silk suits and try to pass yourselves off as decent Americans. . . . I despise your masquerade, the dishonest way you pose yourself . . .
MICHAEL CORLEONE: *Senator, we're both part of the same hypocrisy.*[7]

At the end of the day, there was little to distinguish between the methods of the Mafia gangsters, on the one hand, and the supposedly respectable senator, on the other. The public's taste in film tracked widespread suspicion about the political system, which was beginning to look quite dark indeed.

The root cause of this growing cynicism was the faltering war effort in Vietnam. Polling data from this period registered widespread dissatisfaction with the war and high levels of military spending more generally.[8] Such attitudes extended beyond college campuses. In 1969, the Gallup poll found that 52 percent of the public felt the government was spending "too much" on the military, while only 8 percent felt they were spending "too little."[9] In memoirs, Kissinger frankly acknowledged the public mood: "The passionate critique of the war in Vietnam spread to an attack on the defense establishment as a whole."[10] This antiwar milieu forms the backdrop to foreign policy debates of the 1970s.

THE NIXON DOCTRINE

When Richard Nixon was inaugurated in January 1969, he remained committed to the basic assumptions of the Cold War and the associated expectations for U.S. "leadership" in that struggle, while recognizing the need to accommodate public opinion in favor of reduced militarism. And members of Congress from both political parties began demanding withdrawal from Vietnam. The result of these combined pressures was a full reassessment of U.S. strategy, known as the Nixon Doctrine.

The core feature of this doctrine was to avoid deploying regular military forces in any new international conflicts and instead to rely on other countries in protecting U.S. overseas interests.[11] The idea was that the United States would select allies in key regions, supply them with arms and military training, and encourage them to act as surrogates for American power. When direct military intervention was required, the United States would act through these surrogate forces; any resulting combat casualties would not be American citizens. Official policies could thus evade public condemnation. Another aspect of the Nixon Doctrine was to emphasize operations by the CIA undertaken in secret—an especially prized feature for the secrecy-obsessed Nixon administration.

Based on the doctrine, the administration built up the military capabilities of allied states across the globe, including Brazil, Japan,

Pakistan, the Congo/Zaïre, and South Africa.[12] Two particularly critical allies were Israel and Iran in the volatile Middle East region,[13] which were focal points for the Nixon Doctrine, receiving extensive supplies of the latest fighter planes and other advanced weapons. Toward the end of the Nixon presidency, Saudi Arabia would be added to the list of top-tier allies. While Iran and Saudi Arabia paid for their weapons on a commercial basis, due to prodigious oil exports, the United States subsidized Israel's arms acquisitions; these subsidies grew over time, becoming one of the largest foreign aid programs in history.[14] With regard to the Vietnam War, Nixon commenced a policy of "Vietnamizing" the war, which entailed a gradual draw-down of ground forces combined with intensified reliance on South Vietnamese soldiers, who would assume the combat burden on their own.

President Nixon also sought to reduce the tempo of contention with America's Communist adversaries, most notably the Soviet Union, through the strategy of *détente*, one of the hallmarks of the Nixon-Kissinger foreign policy.[15] The administration established commercial, cultural, and scientific ties with the Soviets, including plans for a joint space mission (undertaken in 1975). Détente produced a series of arms limitation agreements, including the 1972 Strategic Arms Limitation Treaty, which established mutual ceilings on numbers of strategic nuclear weapons, and the Anti-Ballistic Missile Treaty, which limited defensive systems.[16] Simultaneously, Nixon established de facto U.S. recognition of the People's Republic of China, thus reversing decades of policy that aimed at isolating China. The recognition policy began with a series of table tennis matches between American and Chinese teams held in China in 1971, which served as an early confidence-building measure.[17] Then, "ping-pong diplomacy" led to a triumphal visit by President Nixon to Beijing in 1972, where he met with Chairman Mao Zedong and other Communist leaders amid considerable fanfare, thus fundamentally altering the international relations of Asia.[18] This new U.S.-China relationship elicited enthusiasm on both sides. "I voted for you during your election," a light-hearted Chairman Mao told Nixon, adding, "I like rightists."[19]

At an economic level, the administration loosened controls on sales of computers and other high-technology products, opening opportunities for U.S. exporters in Communist states. And the United States became a major supplier of grain to the USSR. Financing for this East-West trade was furnished by both private banks and official government agencies, notably the Export-Import Bank. These commercial opportunities included a political dimension: Such powerful interests as International Business Machines, Bank of America, PepsiCo, and Brown Brothers Harriman & Co. lobbied for continued and improved relations with the USSR; and they helped create the American Committee on U.S.-Soviet Relations, which promoted détente to the public. These efforts were supported by the New York public relations firm Burson-Marsteller, which cultivated favorable press coverage for the committee.[20] One government figure observed that U.S. "lending policy to the Soviet Union has to be closely related to the economic benefits we can get out of it."[21] No doubt this corporate support for détente helped reduce criticism of the whole endeavor—at least for a time.[22]

The Nixonian foreign policy contained an important offensive dimension, sometimes undertaken through covert means. Several of the operations that resulted—notably the CIA-directed overthrow of the elected Chilean government of Salvador Allende and support for a Kurdish insurgency in Iraq—entailed considerable violence and destabilization. They were implemented with a tone of moral callousness: "Covert operations should not be confused with missionary work," Kissinger once said with regard to the Iraq operation.[23] And there was regular military action as well. In Vietnam, U.S. troops engaged in extended combat within South Vietnam, generating tens of thousands of American deaths[24] and vastly higher numbers of Vietnamese casualties. While détente produced some relaxation of Cold War tensions, it certainly did not imply termination of these tensions.

Bear in mind that these offensive actions took place within the context of overall restraint in the overseas use of military force that was the core of the Nixon Doctrine. Perhaps the most significant feature of the Nixonian strategy was a considerable reduction in military expenditure, as a percentage of gross domestic product, to its lowest level of the Cold War up to that time, as indicated in table 4.1.

The uniformed services were losing their traditional share of the federal budget, reversing the sustained growth in military spending of previous periods. The magnitude of the military cut was considerable, in the view of Paul McCracken, then chairman of the Council of Economic

TABLE 4.1

U.S. military expenditures, 1968–1978

Year	Spending in millions of U.S. dollars at constant 1973 prices	As a percentage of GDP
1968	$103.077	9.3
1969	$98,698	8.7
1970	$89,065	7.9
1971	$82,111	7.1
1972	$82,469	6.6
1973	$78,358	6.0
1974	$77,383	6.1
1975	$75,068	6.0
1976	$71,022	5.4
1977	$73,966	5.3
1978	$71,475	5.1

Source: Stockholm International Peace Research Institute, *SIPRI Yearbook, 1979* (London: Taylor & Francis, 1979), 35, 37; and *SIPRI Yearbook, 1983* (London: Taylor & Francis, 1983), 171.

Advisers: "The economy is making a far more major adjustment away from reliance on defense spending than people realize."[25] By the end of Nixon's first term, the Pentagon was enduring an "Era of Austerity," according to *Fortune* magazine.[26] While it was Nixon who initiated this reduction, it was maintained by his successor, President Ford, who continued moderated levels of military spending.

A MILITARIST BACKLASH

The restrained policies of the Nixon Doctrine soon provoked a backlash, orchestrated by vested interests that favored a more hawkish policy. The backlash was led by Senator Henry Jackson, Democrat of Washington state, or "Scoop" Jackson, as he was universally known. Though Jackson was never able to achieve his goal of becoming president, lacking the charisma to win a national election, he nevertheless came to dominate foreign policy debates during this period; and ultimately, he won those debates. In retrospect, it was Jackson's politics that prevailed, and his views maintained prominence for many decades to come.

The story of Scoop Jackson is to some degree the story of his home state as it existed at that time. Washington would eventually develop a highly diversified economy, and its leading city, Seattle, would become renowned for its sophisticated lifestyle. But in the 1970s, the state was far less dynamic. Seattle appeared as "an isolated and insulated backwater." It was "an Omaha that happened to be situated on the Pacific Coast," as one former resident acidly observed.[27] In those simpler times, aircraft manufacturing was one of the state's leading industries, and the Boeing Corporation (based in Seattle) was a political power center. Senator Jackson was highly attentive to his Boeing constituents, as one might expect, and this connection influenced the senator's long-standing enthusiasm for the military-industrial complex, of which Boeing was a crucial component. Indeed, Jackson had long been known as "the Senator from Boeing,"[28] as well as strongly promilitary. It seemed natural that Senator Jackson would lead the crusade for greater military spending.

Another feature of Washington was a strong union presence. The state was "one of the most powerful bastions of organized labor for much of the post–World War II era," according to one study;[29] and, this, too influenced Jackson, who was proudly prolabor.[30] He was especially close to the nation's largest union, the American Federation of Labor-Congress of Industrial Organizations, the AFL-CIO. This connection reinforced Jackson's hawkish orientation, since the American labor movement that had survived the Red Scare of the early Cold War was fervently anti-Communist and favorable toward military intervention.[31] The union leadership expressed greater enthusiasm for fighting communism overseas than for the apparently boring task of organizing and defending workers in the United States. Given this context, it should come as no surprise that the AFL-CIO supported Jackson's call for renewed confrontation with the USSR, along with greater spending on the military. Labor emerged as one of the stalwart interests that mobilized against détente.

Whether viewed from the standpoint of his personal opinions or his self-interest, Jackson was strongly inclined to support expanding the military budget. With regard to foreign and military policy, he stood well to the right of Richard Nixon. Publicly, Nixon administration officials displayed respect for Jackson, even as the senator became the leading congressional critic of détente. In his memoirs, however, Henry Kissinger stated caustically that Jackson possessed "one of the ablest—and most ruthless staffs" of any figure in Washington.[32] And in private, Kissinger called Jackson "a menace" for the senator's promilitary extremism.[33]

Senator Jackson thus emerged as a leader of the backlash against détente and moderation in the Cold War. Behind him stood a range of powerful and interconnected interests, of which Boeing was only one element; all those interests were threatened by the policies of the Nixon Doctrine and the public disdain for overseas interventionism. The first aggrieved interest group was the uniformed military itself, which had to deal with greatly diminished prestige, a circumstance that inevitably attended military failure in Southeast Asia, as well as reduced access to personnel, which became especially pressing in 1973, when the draft was officially abolished.[34] Another aggrieved group was private-sector arms producers, whose profit margins were squeezed by the low levels of federal procurement associated with reduced military expenditure—a direct result of Nixon's policy.

American arms producers were also losing ground in overseas sales. During the 1970s, France became a major arms exporter, and French equipment—notably the Dassault corporation's Mirage fighter plane—offered stiff competition,[35] especially after the sensational success of the jets when they were used by Israeli pilots during the 1967 Six Day War. Clever use of air power had been the key to Israel's victory in that war, and its air force was mostly French built, with the Mirage its leading plane. In light of that, weapons purchasers around the world often turned to the French for their fighter planes instead of U.S. suppliers, which were seen as tainted by growing failure in Vietnam. This move away from American equipment was especially marked in Latin America, which had long been a special zone of influence. In 1972, U.S. companies accounted for only 20 percent of Latin American arms imports, well below previous years.[36] Armaments manufacturers became increasingly anxious about this newly competitive environment, which was viewed as a product of U.S. weakness overseas stemming from the Vietnam fiasco.

In response to these perceived threats, various elements of the military-industrial complex intensified their lobbying, aiming to swing policy back toward unrestrained militarism. The effort was initially led by the American Security Council (ASC), which had long-standing ties to weapons companies. Backed by retired generals and admirals, the ASC had effectively acted as the military-industrial complex's representative in Washington, DC.[37] In the words of Elbridge Durbrow, who served as vice chairman of the ASC during this period, "If our military and industry can't get together how are we going to defend our country?" Durbrow added, "The military-industrial complex is a very healthy thing."[38] Wealthy benefactors stepped up their fund-raising. The ASC increased its contributions from $910,000 in 1972 to $1,650,000 in 1977. Another promilitary lobby, the National Strategy Information Center (NSIC), also saw its funding increase, from $620,000 in 1971 to $1,100,000 in 1976.[39] These lobby groups were backed by Georgetown University's on-campus think tank, the Center for Strategic and International Studies, which enjoyed close ties to the American Enterprise Institute.[40]

The promilitary lobbies found ready support in Congress from a series of hawkish legislators from both parties, led by the redoubtable Scoop Jackson. While at first these groups emphasized their opposition to the peace movement and more dovish members of Congress, such as George McGovern, they increasingly turned against the Nixon administration as well. It may seem ironic that Nixon—who had always positioned himself as a man of the right—would eventually be out-flanked by groups that were even further to his right, but that is in effect what was happening, especially toward the end of his presidency.

Despite their prodigious funding, military pressure groups were hobbled by their crude style of presentation, a throwback to an earlier era. The retired officers and Cold Warriors associated with the ASC and the NSIC were simply not up to the task of moving public opinion in the era of Vietnam and the growing antiwar sentiment, especially given the formidable support in favor of détente.[41] In time, however, the older-style lobbyists would be joined by some of the most talented writers and intellectuals in the country, who would enthusiastically support the campaign for increased military spending.

FOREIGN INVESTORS JOIN THE BACKLASH

While the military-industrial complex was the strongest voice against the Nixon Doctrine and détente, it was joined by a sizable bloc of multinational corporate interests, including firms not directly associated with weapons manufacture. By the middle of the 1970s, overseas investors would gradually come to support the promilitary position. A broad elite coalition was beginning to form.

Overseas investors had traditionally sought support from the military and the CIA, which were useful in intimidating and, when necessary, destabilizing regimes that were perceived as unfriendly toward corporate interests, an overall state of affairs that has been well documented by researchers.[42] In the 1970s, the U.S. military role in protecting investments was called into question due to its failures in the Vietnam War, as well as public doubts about projecting military force that arose in its aftermath. The same was true of the CIA, which also lost credibility during this period.[43] At the same time, foreign investments were rapidly growing as corporations took advantage of high rates of profitability that existed overseas,[44] while banks lent considerable sums to Third World governments.[45] The problem: these investments were often situated in unstable regions. Periodic bouts of instability flared up in Nigeria, South Africa, Saudi Arabia, and South Korea, and these incidents were major concerns to multinational business executives, who worried over the security of their capital stock. The 1979 Iranian Revolution proved especially disruptive to business interests. All this occurred at a time when U.S. military power was weakening, leaving overseas investors exposed and vulnerable.

And there were additional worries. Third World economic nationalists demanded that foreign corporations pay fees, share technology with indigenous companies, and restructure their investments in ways that contributed to local industrialization. There was also a wave of nationalization of oil and natural resources.[46] It appeared that the era when multinational corporations could invest with few restrictions had come to an end, much to the chagrin of investors.[47]

American military weakness was once again seen as the source of the problem. Executives expressed concern about "Washington risk," which included the danger of not receiving adequate federal government support.[48] These mounting concerns led to criticism of official policy. In 1979, *Business Week* ran a special issue dedicated to lamenting "the decline of U.S. power," which noted the following:

> The U.S. has been buffeted by an unnerving series of shocks that signal an accelerating erosion of power and influence. . . . "As I travel the world, there is no question that U.S. prestige is being openly questioned and challenged," says Otto Schoeppler, chairman of Chase Manhattan Ltd. in London. . . . "There is also a parallel decline in standing and prestige of U.S. companies in international markets." . . . And S. A. Constance, managing director of Manufacturers Hanover Ltd in London, goes even further: "The most talked about subject in the world" is the erosion of American power, "and nothing could epitomize it more than the spectacle of the Mexican President lecturing the President of the U.S."[49]

It appeared that Third World states were no longer awed by U.S. power.

An additional issue for corporate America was energy insecurity. In 1973, the Organization of the Petroleum Exporting Countries (OPEC) spiked the worldwide price of oil, with damaging effects on the domestic economy.[50] The "energy crisis" that resulted from the OPEC price hike— and the inability of the federal government to alleviate the problem through military action[51]—was yet another justification for an interventionist shift in policy. Overall, the idea of a military buildup to protect U.S. economic interests was becoming popular among American executives. All these promilitary business figures would soon be bolstered by the Israel lobby.

THE ISRAEL LOBBY MOVES AGAINST DÉTENTE

During the 1970s, the American Jewish community developed an intense identification with the state of Israel. Support for Israel gradually transformed Jewish life at every level, as described by the historian Peter Novick: "Popular Jewish attitudes underwent a profound 'Israelization.' The hallmark of the good Jew became the depth of his or her commitment to Israel."[52] In addition, American Jews gradually cast aside their traditional antimilitarism as they came to admire and identify with the accomplishments of the Israel Defense Forces, especially after its victory in the 1967 Six Day War. Consistent with this Israelization, American Jews began to invest considerable time and money in lobbying the U.S. government in favor of pro-Israeli policies, conducted through the American Jewish Committee, American Jewish Congress, Anti-Defamation League, and, most notably, the America-Israel Public Affairs Committee (AIPAC), which grew into a major Washington powerhouse during this time. AIPAC would serve as a model for other ethnic lobbies, notably anti-Communist Cubans.[53]

The pro-Israel lobby soon developed hostility toward the Soviet Union, a prominent opponent of Israel (the USSR had severed diplomatic relations in 1967), as well as an arms supplier for Israel's adversaries. Vehemently anti-Soviet attitudes began to emanate from the American Jewish Committee, which was becoming increasingly conservative and hawkish, openly expressed in the organization's influential monthly publication, *Commentary*, as well as in private reports.[54] These anti-Soviet attitudes hardened during and after the 1973 Yom Kippur War, when Syrian and Egyptian forces, with Soviet support, unexpectedly attacked the Israelis.[55] The pro-Israel lobby was now ready for a full assault against détente—which was viewed as emboldening the increasingly despised Soviet Union—and looked to Senator Jackson as their champion.[56]

As a special point of focus, Senator Jackson began criticizing Soviet restrictions on the emigration of Jews, many of whom were planning to settle in Israel. Jackson teamed up with Congressman Charles Vanik of Ohio to introduce the Jackson-Vanik Amendment, which passed both houses of Congress and was later signed into law in 1975 by the newly installed President Ford.[57] The amendment required the president to restrict trade with the Soviet Union—thus undermining one of the main economic features of détente—until the Soviets lifted Jewish immigration restrictions. Given the circumstances, it appears likely that the Jackson-Vanik legislation was intended as a means of damaging détente.

The successful passage of Jackson-Vanik strengthened Jackson's already high standing among many Jews and anti-Soviet voters more generally. At the level of outcome, however, the Jackson-Vanik Amendment resulted in greatly reduced levels of Jewish emigration, as the Soviets reacted with defiance against what they viewed as an affront to their sovereignty,[58] producing a major setback from a human rights standpoint. However, the amendment was highly successful in demonizing the idea of détente. It helped solidify the growing unity between supporters of Israel and Jewish causes, on the one hand, and supporters of an intensified Cold War and an end to détente, on the other.

A particularly striking development of this period was the advent of "Christian Zionism" among evangelical Protestants, who, by one estimate, constituted one-third of the U.S. adult population.[59] Christian Zionism was predicated on biblical prophecy that the founding of the Jewish state anticipated Armageddon and the Second Coming of Jesus Christ; therefore, the modern-day state of Israel deserved support as a fulfillment of God's will. On the Arab-Israeli conflict, the evangelicals were unequivocal: "God is . . . on the side of the Jews as against the Arabs," one of the pro-Zionist ministers affirmed.[60] Jewish organizations actively sought to mobilize Christian support. In 1978, an AJC document noted, "We have been doing exceedingly well in the mobilization of Christian public opinion in support of Israel."[61] The rationale for this mobilization was clear: Established Jewish groups recognized the limits of their own influence given their relatively small numbers, constituting only 3 percent of the total U.S. population at the time. Outside New York and a handful of other states, Jews held little electoral clout. The blossoming alliance with evangelicals, however, enabled the Israel lobby to reach a far larger constituency, thus enhancing its power.[62]

The emerging Jewish-evangelical alliance had implications for U.S. foreign policy more generally, apart from the specific issue of Israel. In time, the Christian groups would advocate strongly militarist and interventionist positions—acting in concert with their increasingly hawkish Jewish allies—while once again justifying their stance in theological terms. According to Rev. Jerry Falwell, a rising evangelical leader, "Jesus was not a pacifist. He was not a sissy."[63] Clearly, evangelical Christianity had joined the campaign for a new Cold War.

THE RISE OF NEOCONSERVATISM

Yet another group that joined the foreign policy backlash were liberal intellectuals, a sizable number of whom began to move rightward during the early 1970s, thus assuming the term "neoconservative" or "neocon," as they are sometimes known. This group included prominent academics, public intellectuals, and writers, including Irving Kristol, Richard Pipes, Edward Teller, Norman Podhoretz, Richard Perle, Paul Wolfowitz, Eugene Rostow, Jeane Kirkpatrick, Carl Gershman, Daniel Patrick Moynihan, and Albert Wohlstetter. They worked closely with long-standing Cold Warriors and military figures, such as Paul Nitze and Admiral Elmo Zumwalt, whose connections enhanced their impact. Neoconservative writing was characterized by a fiery anticommunism and combative style. One of the signature neoconservative stances— among both Jewish and gentile neocons—was strong support for the cause of Israel, and their political positions often tracked those of AIPAC and other pro-Israel lobby groups.[64]

To the extent that the neocons had a formal organizational structure, they initially operated through the Coalition for a Democratic Majority (CDM), a pressure group within the Democratic Party that sought to move the party in a more conservative direction after the 1972 electoral defeat. The CDM operated with close ties to organized labor (its principal funders) and the ever-present Senator Jackson.[65]

Neoconservatives have been widely seen as men and women of ideas who were concerned with moral principle, a view that is accepted by even some of their harshest critics.[66] However, we must also consider the element of self-interest in their activities. Some neocons sought to parlay their public standing into avenues for making money. In 1980, Perle established himself as a consultant to military contractors after having worked as a top aide to Senator Jackson. In doing so, he relied on the very well-connected Nitze, who thoughtfully introduced him to prospective clients, including the TRW Corporation and Raytheon.[67] Later in his career, during the War on Terror, Perle pursued lucrative ventures in the security and antiterrorism business.[68] Wolfowitz became a consultant to Northrop Grumman and a trustee for Dreyfus Funds,[69] while Wohlstetter joined Continental Telephone, where he served as chairman of the Board of Directors.[70] And Kristol (the "godfather of neoconservatism") offered his services to a wide range of corporate interests, discussed at length in his personal papers.[71]

In time, military contractors and other businesses would bankroll the neocons' political agenda and their quest for power, a topic we will address shortly. The neoconservatives liked to present themselves as intellectual outsiders who argued fearlessly against the conventional wisdom[72]—even as they became intertwined with the corporate establishment and the military-industrial complex.

Whatever their motives, the neoconservatives became a highly important addition to the growing backlash against détente, furnishing intellectual prestige and national fame. Many of the neocons were gifted writers and added a measure of literary flair to the overall effort aimed at moving U.S. policy and public opinion toward renewed interventionism and augmented military spending. And, finally, the neocons infused their discourse with a tone of morality and moral urgency, which elevated the impact of their arguments.

THE HUMAN RIGHTS AGENDA

My personal hunch is that human rights is our secret weapon.
—DANIEL PATRICK MOYNIHAN[73]

An important development during the 1970s was the growth of a grassroots movement for the promotion of human rights, which, in its American incarnation, was associated with such groups as Amnesty International, USA, and, later, the Congressional Human Rights Caucus. This movement was to some extent a reaction against the cynical tone that had accompanied the Vietnam War and the numerous human rights violations that attended that war. Revelations of CIA support for dictatorial regimes, as shown by the Church Committee investigations, would add further weight to the movement's credibility.

Ultimately, the human rights agenda was hijacked by the neoconservatives, who turned it into an argument for renewed interventionism. It must be emphasized, however, that at first, the human rights movement assumed a strongly anti-interventionist slant predicated on the assumption that past U.S. interventions had often caused abuses. The moral case for a noninterventionist policy was succinctly stated by Senator J. William Fulbright in a 1973 speech: "Nonintervention in the internal affairs of other countries is one of the cardinal rules of international law and relations." Fulbright emphasized that external interventions were justified only in rare instances: "Much more often than not, however, nonintervention is more likely to advance justice than to detract from it. As we Americans discovered in Vietnam, outsiders are seldom wise enough, just enough, or disinterested enough to advance the morality or welfare of a society not their own."[74]

An implicit assumption of the early human rights movement was that American activists had a special obligation to publicize abuses resulting from past U.S. interventions as a matter of the utmost urgency. Accordingly, activists cast a spotlight on such allies as South Vietnam, Iran, the Philippines, South Korea, Greece, and several states in the southern cone of Latin America, where dictatorial regimes used political repression, torture, rape, and targeted killings to maintain their grip on power—often with direct U.S. support. It should be noted that activists initially paid somewhat less attention to human rights abuses perpetrated by America's adversaries, such as the Soviet Union, which seemed to constitute a clear form of bias, even a moral double standard.[75] On reflection, this bias appears justifiable given the context: The federal government had repeatedly helped bring oppressive regimes to power and then furnished them with military aid; in some instances, U.S. officials actively assisted dictators in oppressing their own populations by training their security forces. Human rights activists based in the United States believed that as American citizens, they had a duty to correct problems that their own government had helped create, so these cases should take precedence over equally oppressive regimes—in the Communist bloc, for example—that the United States had not created and whose forces the government had not trained.

The activists' stance was based on solid evidence that American officials had indeed been complicit in the perpetration of brutality. Such complicity is dramatically illustrated by the following transcript taken from a 1974 interview conducted by a U.S. academic with Amir Abbas Hoveyda, who served as Iranian prime minister during the reign of the shah:

QUESTION: Mr. Hoveyda, the Shah in an interview in *Le Monde* a few days ago indicated that torture was being used in the prisons of Iran.
HOVEYDA: I don't believe he said that.
QUESTION: Yes, he said exactly that . . .
HOVEYDA: No, I believe he said that Iran only did what other nations of the world do.

QUESTION: He said that other nations tortured psychologically, and that Iran was now beginning to use this kind of torture as well, implying that Iran had been practicing physical torture all along. Mr. Prime Minister, is torture going on in the prisons of Iran?

HOVEYDA: [*Weak laugh*] You mean like pulling out nails and breaking fingers . . . that kind of torture? No [*laugh*] of course not.

QUESTION: What would you say if I told you I know of individuals personally who had been tortured in Iranian prisons, friends who had been whipped, beaten, and had their fingernails pulled out.

HOVEYDA: Perhaps. But that is not our business. This is police business. I have nothing to do with their activities . . .

QUESTION: Well, I find this torture business depressing.

HOVEYDA: [*Shouting*] Well you taught us how! You trained us! You Americans and British![76]

Note that the shah's regime was itself the product of past intervention, notably the 1953 coup that had brought him to power after the overthrow of a parliamentary system with CIA support. True, Iran was hardly the only country in the world with human rights abuses, which also existed in Communist states; but in the latter cases, there was no evidence of official U.S. complicity, unlike in Iran, where the United States was deeply complicit.

Overall, the tendency of human rights activists to pay special attention to abuses by U.S. allies seems entirely defensible when viewed in retrospect. Nevertheless, the propensity to emphasize these cases and concomitantly to place less emphasis on abuses by U.S. adversaries—however justified in principle—left the movement vulnerable to criticism. Neoconservatives did not fail to exploit this vulnerability, and in the process, they took control of the discussion. They appropriated the human rights agenda as their own, and in doing so, they acquired a powerful new argument in favor of resurgent military intervention and against détente.

THE WEAPONIZATION OF HUMAN RIGHTS

Initially, many neoconservatives viewed the human rights movement negatively, as a source of embarrassment for the cause of U.S.

interventionism, which the neocons promoted.[77] By the middle of the decade, however, they had changed their perspective and began to actively appropriate human rights rhetoric in articles for *Commentary* magazine.[78] And from the Senate floor, Scoop Jackson often invoked human rights when presenting his case for free Jewish emigration. Among politicians of the era, it was initially Jackson who led the way on the issue. According to Barbara Keys, "In the first half of the [1976 election] year, Jackson was the only Democratic candidate with what was seen as a human rights program. When Common Cause prepared a detailed analysis of six major candidates' foreign policy positions, in April 1976, for example, the only one associated with human rights was Jackson."[79] At first, the neoconservatives' adoption of a human rights stance appears to have been tactical, aimed at improving their public standing, but over time there is no doubt that they internalized the idea and came to believe in it as a basic feature of their ideology.

In showcasing their commitment to human rights, the neoconservatives naturally emphasized abuses by the Soviet Union and its allies. They celebrated the heroism of Soviet dissidents, most notably the exiled writer Aleksandr Solzhenitsyn, who had written about political oppression during the Stalinist era and had won the Nobel Prize in Literature.[80] Increasingly, the whole logic of détente was presented as antithetical to human rights, since it promoted trade and negotiations with an oppressive state; it amounted to "an 'accommodation' with 'totalitarian communism,'" in the view of Moynihan.[81] And neocons sought to extend their argument. Widespread evidence of mass killings by the Khmer Rouge in Cambodia, which seized power in 1975, as well as growing repression in a reunified Vietnam, served to sustain the neoconservatives' long-standing conviction that the Vietnam War had been morally justified all along.[82] The war was increasingly presented as a noble, if unsuccessful, effort to prevent brutality, of a sort that occurred in any case after the United States withdrew. These facts were used to argue in favor of greater military spending and willingness to use force overseas as a means of preventing the rise of new incarnations of the Khmer Rouge, which might generate further killings. By the end of the decade, the neoconservative right had gone a long way toward transforming the human rights discourse as a new and powerful justification for militarism.

Under scrutiny, the neoconservative case for human rights is open to question, especially with regard to the Vietnam War. If one reads the Pentagon Papers, it is clear that U.S. intervention after 1954 was the principal cause of the war, which produced appalling brutality and loss of human life.[83] And in Cambodia, it was the secret U.S. bombing campaign after 1970 that destabilized the country and led to the rise of the Khmer Rouge, as William Shawcross persuasively argued.[84]

Neocons underestimated the way that military interventions and wars—even those undertaken with the best of intentions—typically worsen human rights abuses. Their stance was riddled with inconsistencies. In 1975, U.S.–allied Indonesia invaded East Timor and wiped out a large percentage of the population—eliciting no condemnation and little notice from neoconservatives.[85] They tended to ignore abuses committed by China, which neocons now viewed as a prospective partner in the struggle against the Soviet Union and therefore largely immune from criticism.[86] After 1979, neoconservatives extended uncritical support to extremist Islamist groups in Afghanistan who battled against Soviet forces; the Islamist guerrillas used vicious methods to achieve their aims—once again eliciting no comment from the neocons, who backed them.[87]

Whatever their intellectual merits, neoconservatives effectively transformed the human rights discourse, moving it away from anti-interventionism—which had been the original idea—in favor of a new prointerventionist agenda. In the process, they were able to assume the moral high ground as protectors of the innocent, while Senator Jackson was able to clean up his image, recasting himself as the quintessential human rights candidate, a man of principle. He was no longer the "Senator from Boeing." Even the stalwart antiwar activist Joan Baez began to question her previous positions on Vietnam while developing friendly relations with the neoconservative Max Kampelman.[88]

Those who challenged the neocons could be dismissed as amoral cynics, insensitive to human suffering in Communist states—or even as apologists for communism—and this rhetorical strategy proved effective as a means of circumscribing debate and silencing opposition. Human rights did indeed prove to be the neoconservatives' secret weapon, perhaps to a greater degree than even Moynihan himself could have foreseen. Humanitarianism was now enlisted into the overall crusade to generate a new phase of Cold War conflict and to sell this idea to the public.

THE COMMITTEE ON THE PRESENT DANGER

In November 1976, the Committee on the Present Danger (CPD) was officially launched, after months of preparation, "to sound the alarm to the American public about what they consider dangerous Soviet policies," according to the *Washington Post*.[89] The Board of Directors for the new committee comprised a long list of prestigious former government officials, ambassadors, generals, business executives, and elite academics; they represented a sizable segment of the American establishment. The committee soon became a prominent player in foreign policy debates.

The purpose in forming the committee was clear: It was time to knit together the various groups that sought a rightward move in foreign policy into a unified organizational structure. While the CPD was created from the initiative of neoconservative intellectuals led by Eugene Rostow of Yale Law School, they brought together a diverse group of personalities, including some who had not previously been part of the neocon network. The formation of the CPD represented a major advance over previous organizing efforts. Unlike narrowly promilitary groups, such as the American Security Council, the CPD included top-notch writers and publicists who were capable of reaching broader audiences. And in contrast with the Coalition for a Democratic Majority, which worked within the Jackson wing of the Democratic Party, the CPD directed appeals to both parties.[90] While individuals within the group continued to emphasize the human rights benefits of invigorated militarism, the main thrust of CPD's pronouncements was advancing U.S. security in response to the perceived menace posed by the Soviet Union.

The committee had excellent connections to the corporate world. The CPD leadership[91] included Cochairman David Packard, a founder of the Hewlett-Packard Corporation; Packard had also served as head of the Business Council, which comprised "many of the largest corporations in the nation."[92] A second cochairman was Henry H. Fowler, a partner in Goldman Sachs and former Treasury secretary. The CPD's treasurer was Charls Walker, a top Washington lobbyist who represented "General Motors, Gulf Oil, Alcoa, and several major airlines."[93] Walker stated that he would engage directly in the committee's lobbying efforts and would "approach this task pretty much as our firm goes about representing close to 200 business corporations."[94] The CPD received support from a range of corporate interests, corporate-affiliated foundations, and wealthy individuals. The Scaife interests were especially generous.[95]

And CPD militarists established close connections with the free marketeers of the American Enterprise Institute, forging an alliance with advocates of economic conservatism. The two organizations had overlapping memberships and shared compatible objectives. In addition, the militarists established ties to the antifeminist crusader Phyllis Schlafly, thus building bridges to social conservatism.[96] The agenda of the CPD was integrated into the overarching rightist agenda, linking both domestic and foreign policy.

Some CPD members worried about accepting donations from military contractors, since the committee championed positions that would benefit these contractors, raising conflict-of-interest concerns. Its leadership did not want to be "labeled an arm of the military-industrial complex."[97] To allay this concern, the CPD officially refused contributions from companies that derived more than 15 percent of their income from military contracting. Among researchers covering the group, the "15 percent" restriction was often accepted at face value without dispute. The influential study by Justin Vaïsse, for example, accepts the restriction as authentic.[98] In reality, the 15 percent rule was likely bogus; in private correspondence, one member of the Board of Directors suspected that "a substantially larger portion [of CPD funding] actually comes from defense money" than the organization was willing to admit, and he implied that significant military funding was being concealed from the public.[99] The CPD gained additional support from within the uniformed military, who no doubt appreciated the group's demand for increased military spending.[100]

Committee members emphasized the dire nature of the security threats Americans faced, and these threats were emphasized in both public statements and private correspondence. The Soviets had achieved military superiority, especially in the area of strategic nuclear weapons, while the United States had "engaged in a form of unilateral disarmament," in the view of Kampelman.[101] Another CPD member believed that "The Russians are virtually on a 'war footing.'"[102] In 1979, committee members promoted the documentary *First Strike*, which argued that the USSR could effectively wipe out America's nuclear deterrent in a surprise attack, possibly forcing a surrender.[103]

In general, worldwide events were viewed as an onward march of Soviet power, to America's detriment. In keeping with this narrative, the Islamic Revolution in Iran was said to have resulted from Soviet meddling. Jay Lovestone wrote that as he observed revolutionary developments in Iran, "I see the meticulous care that has gone into preparations . . . by Moscow's best minds," who were apparently orchestrating the upheaval.[104] Clare Boothe Luce speculated that the Soviets were seeking a pretext to invade and take over the country, similar to the way the Nazis used "the burning of the Reichstag" to take over Germany.[105] In retrospect, even friendly accounts of the committee acknowledge that its claims were often exaggerations at best.[106]

Initially, the press treated the CPD as a highly partisan right-wing organization, but the press attitude gradually softened. According to one assessment, when the CPD was initially formed, "it was identified as 'hawkish,' and its members as 'cold warriors' or 'representatives of the military-industrial (or intellectual) complex.' Six months later, the Committee was described as 'nonpartisan,' a 'study group,' and 'a group of nationally prominent individuals, including Democrats, Republicans, labor leaders, liberals, conservatives.'"[107] To be sure, the committee and its associated lobby groups still encountered opposition, most notably from business interests who favored détente associated with the American Committee on East-West Accord. However, by the end of the decade, the CPD and other antidétente lobby groups were outspending their prodétente adversaries by a vast margin.[108]

All the lobbying activity began to generate concrete results in terms of changing public opinion. One survey found that in 1978–79, there was a growing public perception that the Soviet Union was gaining the upper hand. Some 66 percent believed that the United States "was falling behind the Soviet Union in power and influence."[109] No doubt Rostow and other CPD members were gratified by these results. What was really needed was some sensational event to fundamentally change the climate of opinion. In 1977, Rostow paraphrased the views of his wife, who worked in the field of psychotherapy: "So far as the nightmare of war is concerned . . . it takes Pearl Harbor to wake us up."[110] Rostow and his CPD colleagues were deploying the time-honored strategy of waiting for a crisis to justify a radical turn in policy. Two years later, the "Pearl Harbor" event would finally arrive in the form of the Soviet invasion of Afghanistan.

PRESIDENT FORD JOINS THE BACKLASH

Initially, President Gerald Ford followed the course charted by Nixon, including détente with the Soviets and reduced levels of military spending. The architect of the Nixonian policy, Henry Kissinger, stayed on as secretary of state and national security advisor, ensuring continuity of policy. Ford and Kissinger acted to deepen détente, holding summit meetings with Soviet officials in Vladivostok and Helsinki to enhance the commercial, cultural, and scientific ties between the two super-powers. They also began laying the groundwork for a new and more comprehensive treaty on strategic nuclear weapons as a follow up to the Strategic Arms Limitation Treaty.[111] Then in 1975, President Ford signed the Biological Weapons Convention, which established a ban on the production and use of bioweapons for both superpowers.[112] Within the federal bureaucracy, the CIA's National Intelligence Estimates (NIE) affirmed that the Soviets were acting with restraint, consistent with the overarching goals of détente.[113]

Almost immediately following inauguration, Ford encountered resistance from a series of well-funded interest groups led by neoconservatives who aimed to undermine his polices. A special focus of the neocon lobbying effort was to influence the CIA's intelligence reporting.[114] These efforts resulted in what has been termed the "Team B" affair, a key turning point in the foreign policy of the Ford presidency.

The idea of a Team B began to take shape in 1975, when neoconservatives criticized the CIA reports from their perch at the President's Foreign Intelligence Advisory Board; this appointed body included Edward Teller, soon to become a prominent member of the Committee on the Present Danger. These critics demanded the appointment of a special group—to be designated Team B—that would be given access to the same classified information that CIA analysts had used to prepare the National Intelligence Estimates; and then Team B members would present their own, alarmist findings. Given the increasing influence of the antidétente movement within the Republican Party, President Ford assented to the Team B evaluation, which took place in 1976, during the final months of the Ford presidency.[115] The team concluded that the Soviet leadership "regarded nuclear weapons as tools of war whose proper employment . . . promised victory," not just deterrence.[116]

There can be little doubt that the whole evaluation process was designed at the outset to produce a negative judgment on Soviet conduct while casting the overall strategic situation in the harshest light. Team B itself had a heavily neoconservative complexion, including the Harvard Professor Richard Pipes, who chaired the team, as well as other hardliners, such as Paul Nitze. The membership was markedly one-sided, with a pronounced hawkish orientation. Other experts who might have presented more restrained views—such as George Kennan or Averell Harriman[117]—were not invited to participate. From Brookings, Raymond Garthoff observed that since Team B's whole purpose was to present an ominous view of the strategic situation, "it is not surprising it came up with more ominous results."[118]

According to Pipes's own account, the evaluation process overwhelmed CIA personnel, mostly "young analysts, some of them barely out of graduate school" who were "intimidated by senior government officials, general officers, and university professors." One of the agency analysts had "barely begun his criticism of Team B's effort . . . when a member of Team B fired a question that reduced him to a state of catatonic immobility."[119]

Team B members selectively leaked information to the press, underscoring the politicized character of the whole exercise.[120] Documentary information that has become available since the end of the Cold War disconfirms many of Team B's principal allegations,[121] which nevertheless had a major impact on intelligence reporting through the 1980s. The main implication of the Team B exercise was this: A growing segment of the U.S. foreign policy establishment was moving against détente; disconfirming intelligence would not be allowed to stand in the way of what was essentially a political decision.

The Team B affair coincided with a generalized foreign policy shift over the course of the Ford administration. Prominent Republicans, such as Clare Boothe Luce, were privately counseling the president to scrap the policy and the word "détente," both of which were viewed as unacceptable to the party base.[122] The leading proponent of détente within the administration, Kissinger, was effectively demoted, losing his role as national security advisor (though he remained as secretary of state). As the presidential campaign began, in 1976, Ford was challenged by the much more conservative Ronald Reagan, who almost won the nomination, before being defeated by the incumbent Ford. And during the course of the general election, Ford no longer used the word "détente" at all[123] but instead presented the slogan, "peace through strength," with its more martial sound.[124]

In April 1976, *Fortune* magazine observed that "Détente is in trouble. For a policy associated with the idea of world peace, it has remarkably few advocates these days."[125] By the time Ford left office in January 1977, the United States was on track for substantially increased levels of military spending, combined with a new level of Cold War confrontation. The viewpoints of the neoconservatives and the CPD would soon become the official view.

THE VICTORY OF NEOCONSERVATISM

The newly elected President Jimmy Carter initially continued the policy of accommodation, consistent with the principles of détente. Carter sought to build on Nixon's Strategic Arms Limitation Treaty with a new treaty, SALT II,[126] which proposed further limits on the strategic nuclear arsenals held by both superpowers. And in 1979, he deepened America's engagement with the People's Republic of China (PRC), establishing full diplomatic relations for the first time, with exchange of ambassadors. Carter also terminated U.S. recognition of Taiwan, noting, according to an official statement, "The Government of the United States of America acknowledges the Chinese [PRC] position that there is but one China, and Taiwan is part of China."[127] There was a strong rhetorical emphasis on the promotion of human rights (although in practice, the administration continued to support long-standing allies, such as Shah Mohammad Reza Pahlavi of Iran, who had a record of repression).[128]

Overall, the Carter administration operated from "the premise that military policies are less important than economic policies," as later noted in *Euromoney* magazine.[129] And the president believed that U.S.-Soviet conflict was winding down, as he implied in a 1977 speech at the University of Notre Dame: "We are now free of that inordinate fear of communism."[130] For a brief period, it seemed that that United States was moving away from its long-standing fixation on the Cold War.

Evidently, Carter had underestimated the forces that were arrayed against him led by the newly formed Committee on the Present Danger, which began a concerted campaign to discredit the president. In an entry in his presidential diary from August 1977, Carter noted that when he had conferred with members of the CPD, "it was an unpleasant meeting, where they insinuated that we were on the verge of catastrophe, inferior to the Soviets, and that I and previous presidents had betrayed the nation's interests." In another entry, Carter added that from the Senate, Scoop Jackson led "the most vitriolic anti-Soviet forces."[131] And these forces were formidable indeed. By 1979, the CPD and its political allies were outspending groups that supported détente by a ratio of fifteen to one, with a massive lobbying and public relations campaign.[132]

The neocons adopted an adversarial stance toward the Carter administration, but they did have one potential point of access: The national security adviser, Zbigniew Brzezinski, held an instinctive distrust of communism and the Soviet Union and functioned as the administration's in-house hardliner.[133] While the neoconservatives pressured Carter from outside the administration in favor of a more militarized policy, Brzezinski lobbied from the inside as well. Over time, these combined forces began to have an impact on the president, who had no prior experience in foreign policy.

In January 1979, Carter reversed course and opted for elevated military expenditure, the first major increase of the decade. The president called for a 3 percent (inflation-adjusted) increase in military spending, to be sustained over several years. This increase was especially significant given that the overall federal budget emphasized austerity for major domestic programs; the military was one of the few areas that was exempted from austerity and saw a raise in funding. One constituency that benefited from these policies was military contractors. According to the *Washington Post*, "Business is booming for most of the defense contractors of this country and will stay that way. . . . This is the view from the executive suites of the aerospace industry as well as from the cubicles of the Commerce Department where analysts have been going over the sales figures on planes, ships, missiles, and tanks. . . . 'Business hasn't been as good as this since the late 1950s and early 1960s' . . . said James W. Beggs, executive vice president of General Dynamics."[134]

Carter commenced a new series of foreign interventions in several regions of the world, sometimes in league with the PRC.[135] America's relationship with China was now taking on the character of a de facto political alliance directed against the common enemy of both states: the Soviet Union. In essence, Carter was moving in the confrontational direction advocated by Nitze and other CPD members. He was acceding to their pressures, or, as the *Washington Post* described the situation, "In order to 'beat' Paul Nitze, the Carter administration has had to join him."[136]

President Carter was moving toward a full-fledged return to earlier Cold War policies based on high military spending and unapologetic willingness to project force overseas. In the achievement of these objectives, the main problem remained the American public, which was not yet sold on the idea. The main issue was cost. A January 1979 poll found that only 34 percent favored elevated military spending.[137] A subsequent poll in June found the public overwhelmingly concerned with domestic economic problems, notably the high cost of living; only 5 percent listed "International Problems, Foreign Policy" as a major concern.[138]

What was needed was some sensational event to shock the electorate into accepting the idea of rearmament and military assertiveness, which might assuage public concerns about the financial costs of militarism and lingering memories of the Vietnam fiasco. The required sensational event arrived in December 1979, when the Soviet Union invaded Afghanistan. It was widely claimed that Afghanistan was a country of exceptionally great strategic importance and that the Soviet invasion was an effort to use that country as a staging area for a planned invasion of the Persian Gulf region, or possibly the Indian Ocean coastline. In his January 1980 State of the Union Address, President Carter declared that the invasion "could pose the most serious threat to the peace since the Second World War."[139]

THE INVASION OF AFGHANISTAN

In this chapter, I have argued that President Carter's policy shift resulted from lobbying by vested interests who expected to benefit from increased military spending, while I have downplayed the possibility of any heightened threat emanating from the Soviet Union. The alleged "Soviet threat," I argue, served as a pretext to justify the policy shift. Some readers may suspect that I overstate my case by ignoring genuinely menacing actions undertaken by the USSR during this period. The 1979 invasion of Afghanistan stands out as a particularly striking example of Soviet aggression, so the argument goes, in addition to numerous other threatening actions in multiple regions. Perhaps Carter altered his policy in response to an authentic security threat rather than because of anything the CPD was doing. It would go beyond the scope of this book to analyze in detail the Soviet Union's worldwide interventions. Instead, I will focus on its most significant intervention, the Afghanistan invasion.

Fortunately, we have an exceptionally complete record of documentation on this issue, comprising both U.S. and Soviet materials from the highest governmental levels. These records clearly show that the invasion presented no significant threat to the United States and its allies. Claims to the contrary—which were widespread at the time—are incorrect. First, Afghanistan did not hold any real importance to Western security, due to its exceptionally rugged geography, as well as its lack of modern infrastructure. It was not close to the Persian Gulf. A 1950 study by the U.S. Joint Chiefs of Staff, for example, stated the matter succinctly: "Afghanistan is of little or no strategic value to the United States."[140] This view was restated many times by multiple officials throughout the early Cold War, with only occasional dissents.[141]

Soviet officials, by contrast, did display some interest in Afghanistan, since it bordered their country. Accordingly, the Soviet government established large-scale economic and military aid programs beginning in 1954. It appears the purpose of this aid was to ensure that the country would retain its officially neutral position during the Cold War and not pose a threat to the USSR's southern frontier.

Declassified U.S. documents present no evidence that the USSR was seeking to subvert or destabilize Afghanistan. On the contrary, it appears that the Soviets sought a politically stable Afghanistan, one that would pose no security danger. A small Afghan Communist Party elicited only limited interest from Soviet officials.[142] A 1967 study by Marshall Goldman concluded, "Soviet aid to Afghanistan has been immensely successful. . . . Even American officials are hard pressed to find major flaws."[143] In 1973, a correspondent for the *Wall Street Journal* asked, "Do the Soviets Covet Afghanistan? If So, It's Hard to Figure Why." Afghanistan appeared as a "vast expanse of desert waste" of no real importance, in the view of the reporter.[144] During his long career as a Columbia University political scientist, Brzezinski published extensively on international relations—but a search of his writings reveals no significant interest in Afghanistan,[145] which was viewed as a backwater. Later claims that Afghanistan was vital to Western security do not hold up to scrutiny.

In April 1978, the People's Democratic Party of Afghanistan (PDPA), the local communists, suddenly seized power in a coup d'état, which had been launched in response to efforts by the Afghan government to repress the party. The new PDPA-led government announced that its takeover inaugurated the "Saur Revolution," designed to transform Afghan society with a program of land reform, a literacy campaign, and equality of the sexes. While these reforms may have been laudable in principle, the implementation was disorganized and chaotic, and the communist cadres who directed implementation were widely resented. The result was a mass rebellion against the communists led by a series of Islamist groups collectively referred to as the Mujahidin.[146] In the civil war that followed, the PDPA received arms and military training from the Soviet Union, which sought to block a Mujahidin victory. Military aid led to the December 1979 decision by the Soviets to send their own forces into Afghanistan, effectively invading the country and then occupying it with a force of one hundred thousand troops.

At the time, it was widely believed that the Soviets had orchestrated the 1978 communist takeover, laying the groundwork for a later occupation. In fact, information gleaned from Soviet sources since the end of the Cold War contradict this view, presenting little evidence of direct Soviet involvement.[147] USSR officials had long distrusted the Afghan communists, whom they regarded as impulsive and politically inept; they believed that Afghanistan was too underdeveloped to be ready for socialism. From Moscow, one official stated at the time, "If there is one country in the developing world we would *not* want to try scientific socialism, it is Afghanistan."[148]

Once the PDPA was firmly established in power, however, the Soviets set aside these reservations and furnished military aid to the new government, but they did so with a measure of caution. Declassified Soviet records show repeated requests by the Afghan government that the Soviets should send their own troops as a replacement for

Afghan forces, who were viewed as ineffective; Soviet officials repeatedly refused these requests for troops.[149]

High-level documents that have become available since the end of the Cold War confirm Soviet restraint. At a March 1979 Politburo meeting, Foreign Minister Andrei Gromyko spoke out against the idea of using regular Soviet forces, expressing the consensus view of the Politburo: "[We must] rule out such a measure as the deployment of our troops into Afghanistan. The [Afghan] army there is unreliable. Thus, our army when it arrives in Afghanistan, will be the aggressor. . . . What would we gain? Afghanistan with its present government, with a backward economy, with inconsequential weight in international affairs. On the other side, we must keep in mind that from a legal point of view too we would not be justified in sending troops."[150] Thus, Afghanistan, with its "backward economy" and "inconsequential weight in international affairs," was not viewed as a strategic prize. In the available Soviet documents, there is no mention of using Afghanistan as a springboard for attacking the Persian Gulf or other regional objectives.

In late 1979, the Soviet perspective began to change, in favor of invasion. One factor in this changed perspective was the Carter administration's decision, in July 1979, to provide nonlethal aid to the Mujahidin guerrillas,[151] an action that likely increased Soviet paranoia about American intentions. At the Politburo, Soviet officials feared that Afghanistan was becoming a "new hotbed of military threat on the southern borders,"[152] a menace to their security. These concerns, combined with long-standing fears about the fragility of the Afghan state and the PDPA, caused the Politburo to set aside its previous caution and opt for direct intervention.[153] The overall record of evidence suggests the following conclusion: The 1979 Soviet invasion was undertaken with reluctance, and it presented no serious danger to Western security. Afghanistan remained the "vast expanse of desert waste"—to use the *Wall Street Journal*'s colorful phrasing—that it always had been.

The political turmoil that followed the invasion was nevertheless advantageous to the Carter administration, enabling full implementation of the president's promilitary program. Immediately after the invasion, he presented what became known as the Carter Doctrine,[154] which threatened the Soviet Union with war if it were to engage in further aggression in the Middle East region. Détente was definitively terminated as the president imposed a series of economic sanctions against the USSR as punishment for the invasion, including an embargo on the sale of grain, and U.S. athletic teams withdrew from the upcoming 1980 Moscow Olympics. In addition, Carter disowned the SALT II Treaty, which he had recently negotiated with the Soviets, removing it from consideration by the Senate.[155]

A U.S. military buildup commenced. President Carter authorized an elevated level of military spending, which entailed a 5 percent annual increase, significantly greater than the 3 percent increase that had been announced the previous year.[156] At the president's direction, the new Rapid Deployment Joint Task Force was established in the Persian Gulf/ Indian Ocean region, which constituted the first major projection of direct military power into the area.[157] While administration officials voiced shock at the Soviet invasion, some also displayed a measure of satisfaction. In the *Christian Science Monitor*, an unnamed administration official stated, "I think the Soviets have done us a big favor" by invading Afghanistan.[158] When National Security Advisor Brzezinski heard that the Soviets invaded, he exclaimed, "They have taken the bait!"[159] And in his memoirs, Brzezinski once again expressed satisfaction that the Soviets had invaded.[160]

Vested interests outside the administration also had reason to be pleased. "Very good times are indeed around the corner for defense contractors," noted a *Washington Post* article in response to the president's decision to raise military spending.[161] With its traditionally close ties to the aerospace industry, *Air Force Magazine* expressed optimism that the invasion would set U.S. foreign policy "on the road to renewed credibility." The magazine noted an important historical precedent: "North Korea's invasion of the south in 1950 triggered U.S. rearmament," with the hopeful implication that the Afghan invasion might trigger another round of rearmament and heightened military spending. The editorial concluded that by invading Afghanistan, "The Soviets, once again, may inadvertently save us from ourselves."[162]

The general turn to the right that took place during the 1970s had a marked impact on foreign policy. The turn began with a large-scale mobilization led by weapons procurement companies, anticommunist labor unions, and neoconservative intellectuals, all of whom sought to raise military spending and generate intensified confrontation with the Soviet Union. These militaristic objectives were finally achieved during the period 1979–1980, at the end of the Carter presidency, producing a heightened level of Cold War tensions. These changes also enriched weapons procurement companies (and their stockholders), which had lobbied for such policies.

At the level of collective action, the rise of militarism enlarged the overall conservative coalition in the United States. While economic and social conservatives had initiated the political mobilization, they were now joined by militarist conservatives, and the combined movement that resulted would soon transform U.S. politics.

CHAPTER FIVE

The Rich Go Global

The left has been complaining for years that the rich have
too much power. They ain't seen nothing yet.
—CHARLES MURRAY, AMERICAN ENTERPRISE INSTITUTE

It has become fashionable to view globalization as an inevitable process, a natural state of affairs, one that privileges markets while it undercuts efforts to regulate them.[1] When working people are harmed, they have no option but to accept their fate and adapt. Often overlooked is that globalization was created by intentional actions orchestrated by economic elites, governmental officials, and academic economists, who worked in unison to advance a free market agenda, a process that began in earnest during the Nixon presidency. I argue that there was nothing inevitable about any of it. Other policies that might have led to different outcomes, including ones that would have proven more consistent with the interests of working people, were excluded from consideration, and such exclusion constituted a political choice, not passive acceptance of the inevitable. Policy makers thus established a very conservative form of globalization, which undermined the class compromise while opening new vistas for capital, especially banking.

Another theme of this chapter is the dismantling of New Deal financial regulations, setting the stage for a conservative global order. The Nixon administration began the process by deregulating exchange rates, which established the value of the dollar when measured against other currencies. And this new policy became the world standard, helping to globalize finance. The deregulation of exchange rates generated a cascading series of secondary and tertiary effects, moving business activity away from manufacturing and toward financial speculation. The deindustrialization that resulted from these developments eliminated entire classes of high-paying jobs, dealing a major and largely irreversible blow to the living standards of working people while fundamentally altering the long-term distribution of wealth and power. The United States gradually changed from an industrial superpower to a financial superpower.[2]

A final theme is the international politics of oil, specifically the massive increases in oil prices orchestrated by the Organization of the Petroleum Exporting Countries (OPEC). We will see that the U.S. government and private companies worked closely with oil-producing states and were complicit in price increases. The oil price spikes that resulted played key roles in propping up the dollar following the deregulation of finance, and these events contributed to the intensification of economic inequality, which defined the era and became an integral component of globalization. Oil policy played a central role in facilitating America's transition to a postindustrial low-wage economy.

In presenting this chapter, I fear some readers will be frightened by the technical character of international economics, which is often viewed as the province of experts. Rest assured that I have taken special effort to discuss the material in an accessible manner. And we should not imagine that the obscure nature of international economics—as well as the dense language used to describe it—means that the public is unaffected by its workings. On the contrary, we will see that it constituted a critical policy arena, one that reconfigured the country's social structure at every level. The shift in foreign economic policy during the 1970s was a seminal event in the unraveling of America's class compromise.

A REGULATED INTERNATIONAL CAPITALISM

Before proceeding with the deregulation of the international economy, let us begin with the regulated version, which was forged at the United Nations Monetary and Economic Conference at Bretton Woods, New Hampshire, during the summer of 1944, toward the end of World War II. This agreement formed the basis of international economic relations through the early 1970s, when the regulated system was terminated and replaced by a market-based model.[3] The Bretton Woods agreement constituted an extension of President Roosevelt's New Deal, now to encompass foreign economic policy. We will emphasize several principal features of the agreement.

First, currency exchange rates were to be controlled by a new organization, the International Monetary Fund (IMF), which was to be staffed by professional economists and serve as the locus of a regulated international economic order. If any country wished to raise or lower the value of its currency against other currencies by more than a 1 percent, it would need advance permission from IMF economists.[4] The "fixed exchange rate" system, as it was known, anchored the Bretton Woods agreement. Its objective was to provide public oversight for the international economy, consonant with the New Deal notion of a regulated capitalism.[5]

Second, the new system assigned a privileged role to the United States. Accordingly, the key currency was the dollar, to become the mainstay of international activity, especially for the trading of goods and services. In addition, the dollar was to function as the reserve currency held by central banks across the globe, further cementing its primacy. The newly created IMF was placed under effective U.S. political control and located in Washington, DC.

Gold continued to hold a nominal function under the new system. The dollar was to be fixed at $35 to the ounce of gold, and central banks of all foreign states were free to exchange any dollars they held for gold. The linking of the dollar to gold was a polite bow to the defunct gold standard of an earlier era.[6] The new international system was very much a dollar standard, however, with gold playing a secondary role. And the emerging dollar standard played a central role in the Cold War as an instrument of U.S. power.

Third, Bretton Woods limited the role of private finance, whose prestige had been stained by the widespread perception—confirmed by academic research—that banks had been a significant cause of the Great Depression.[7] While bankers were not excluded altogether from the new system, their influence was circumscribed by public institutions, led by the IMF. And the system of fixed exchange rates (that the IMF managed) served to limit the role of private traders in determining the value of currencies. Within the United States, bankers were additionally restrained by a cluster of New Deal regulations, notably the Banking Act of 1933, the "Glass-Steagall Act," which separated investment and commercial banking,[8] and the Federal Reserve's Regulation Q, also enacted in 1933, which regulated interest rates.[9] The banking regulations of this era were consistent with Keynesian principles, which presented a somewhat negative view of finance; recall that Keynes had favored "euthanasia of the rentier." The main focus of economic policy was to be the manufacture of goods, since manufacturing employed large labor forces and held the potential for establishing high wages and mass unionization, consistent with the class compromise.

In the early postwar period, bankers faced limited prospects. Large corporations were mostly self-financing due to stable growth and high profit rates, and for the most part, they did not require regular bank loans.[10] The stock market remained in a state of depression long after the Great Depression officially ended; the Dow Jones Industrial Average did not return to its pre-Depression levels until 1959.[11] In this context, it seemed that bankers had little to do. A common joke of the era was that they operated on the "3-6-3" principle: Pay 3 percent interest on deposits, lend out to borrowers at 6 percent, and then proceed to the golf course no later than 3:00 p.m.[12] Meanwhile, the real economy boomed through the 1950s and 1960s, raising living standards to unprecedented levels for virtually all social classes. In short, the early postwar period proved unfavorable for bankers, given the extensive system of domestic and international regulations, as well as an unfavorable political environment inherited from the Depression.

The controlled system established at Bretton Woods would gradually break down, however, leading to a deregulated free market system. To escape domestic regulations, U.S. bankers began migrating overseas in the late 1950s, where they participated in the growing practice of currency trading and speculation.[13] The center of these speculative activities was the City of London, where the British had deregulated domestic banking as a means of returning the city to its former glory.[14] British deregulation led to the formation of what was termed the "Eurocurrency market," or Euromarket for short. On the Euromarket, private traders took advantage of lax regulation to speculate against various currencies, in essence placing bets on the likelihood that their values would change. And U.S.

traders based in London did not need to worry about Regulation Q or other New Deal restrictions.

Among speculators of all nationalities, there was a widespread tendency to attack the U.S. dollar by trading off dollars in favor of stronger currencies, notably Deutsch marks and Swiss francs, as well as gold. The dollar was weakening during this period due to American overspending on the Cold War, which worsened after the 1965 escalation of the Vietnam intervention.[15] U.S. profligacy had the effect of spiking global inflation, thus reducing international confidence in American financial leadership. As a result, Euromarket attacks on the dollar increased toward the end of the 1960s. U.S. traders who were based overseas showed no compunctions about attacking their own country's currency: "If a foreign exchange trader gets patriotic, he's an idiot," one trader later observed.[16]

As Euromarket speculation continued to undermine the dollar,[17] American companies moved their operations overseas at an accelerating rate, diversifying their assets as a hedge against the dollar's continued instability. And the outward migration affected not only finance but also manufacturing. In response, the federal government imposed a series of new regulations as a means of reducing capital flight, most notably the Interest Equalization Tax (IET) of 1964[18] and the Foreign Direct Investment Program (FDIP) of 1968.[19]. These regulations were generally ineffective—being unenforceable beyond U.S. borders—as capital flight continued unabated.[20]

The rise of unregulated finance soon produced an echo at the level of popular culture, with a new genre of writing—the "financial thriller"—which combined the styling of James Bond spy novels with the additional feature of private-sector intrigue. The genre was established by Paul Erdman, a banker-turned-novelist, whose bestseller *The Crash of '79* set the literary standard.[21] Despite its sensationalized features, *The Crash of '79* was praised for its accurate portrayal of a newly globalized financial order—in which private bankers rivaled state officials for influence and power—that was beginning to emerge. International finance was indeed becoming untethered from government control.

In responding to these myriad challenges, U.S. officials faced two possible courses of action: They could update the Bretton Woods system through enhanced regulation aimed at reining in currency speculation and capital flight at a global level—which was a perfectly feasible option[22]—or they could give up on the whole idea of regulation and move toward laissez-faire. In the end, they opted for laissez-faire, as we will soon see. A new era of deregulated international finance emerged, setting the stage for a later deregulation of the domestic economy as well.

A LOBBY FOR DEREGULATION

In the context of incipient globalization spawned by the Euromarket, U.S. banks began pushing for an end to regulation. Bankers resented the new constraints on their overseas activities imposed by the Kennedy and Johnson administrations—notably the IET and FDIP—and also the long-standing banking regulations left over from the New Deal. Above all, they felt that the Bretton Woods system of fixed exchange rates hindered their currency trading. A major figure during this period was Walter Wriston, CEO of Citibank, who emerged as the personification of a newly internationalized financial sector and a public advocate for the deregulation of exchange rates, as well as for free markets more generally.[23] According to the *Washington Post*, Wriston "battered down the regulatory walls" and "spoke out for laissez-faire capitalism," while the *New York Times* termed him "the man who freed the banks."[24] Wriston's antiregulation viewpoint was widely shared among his financial colleagues.[25]

In arguing for deregulation, the banks were joined by manufacturers, whose activities were also becoming globalized in the form of the multinational corporation. As multinationals grew, they financed operations on the Euromarket; multinational managers developed interests similar to those of the bankers who financed them, and both sectors—finance and manufacturing—favored reduced regulation.[26] Reflecting an increasingly globalized perspective, the National Association of Manufacturers would soon endorse deregulation of global finance.[27]

A third interest group was a network of conservative economists associated with the Mont Pèlerin Society, most notably Gottfried Haberler, Milton Friedman, George Shultz, and Ludwig von Mises. As we saw in previous chapters, MPS members were ideologically hostile toward virtually all forms of government regulation as a point of principle.

The conservative economists accordingly opposed the fixed exchange rate system, which constituted a straightforward case of regulation. As early as 1953, Friedman had argued against fixed rates in his widely read essay, "The Case for Flexible Exchange Rates."[28]

Other Mont Pèlerin economists, notably Haberler, advanced similar arguments[29] predicated on a strongly ideological worldview. It was widely believed among MPS economists that unrestrained capital mobility was a positive force that would discipline individual governments, dissuading them from pursuing redistributionist policies. And capital mobility had a political advantage, since it would achieve antiredistributionist objectives in ways that would seem automatic and apolitical and therefore more acceptable to the public. Market discipline would appear as an inevitable force of nature. Some members of the group—most notably von Mises—went so far as to argue that capital mobility constituted a moral necessity; the right to move capital was a foundational feature of human freedom, apparently on par with such rights as freedom of speech and religion.[30] Recall that the Mont Pèlerin economists were closely connected with business interests, which funded MPS activities from the time the group was formed in 1947; their business backing became much closer over time. These backers included prominent financial figures—notably Wriston of Citibank, who was closely connected to Friedman.[31]

With the election of Richard Nixon in November 1968, Mont Pèlerin academics were well placed to begin implementing their vision for the future. Shortly after the election, Friedman met with Nixon and urged the president-elect to "set the dollar free" by abolishing regulations.[32] For his part, MPS member Haberler chaired Nixon's Task Force on U.S. Balance of Payments Policies which advised the presidential transition team in the period before inauguration. The resulting task force report contained ideological language worthy of its MPS imprimatur. It criticized the regulated system of fixed exchange rates while calling for terminating controls on capital flight that "undermine our free enterprise system." The report noted, with a hopeful tone, "Ultimately, there will be a 'one world of finance.'"[33] The document implied a deregulated globalized economy. And as Treasury secretary, MPS member Shultz was destined to play a particularly important role as a champion of deregulation. The brakes on international finance that had been imposed during the New Deal would soon be dismantled.

THE NIXON SHOCK

By most accounts, President Nixon was ill informed about international economics, lacking training or background in the area.[34] His main focus was managing the strategic relationship between the United States and its communist adversaries through détente, winding down the Vietnam War, and building up a conservative counterestablishment over the long term. But above all, Nixon was interested in his own political success, especially in the upcoming 1972 election campaign. While Nixon sympathized with the laissez-faire ideas of the Mont Pèlerin economists, whom he promoted, the president would not allow ideological considerations to stand in the way of his reelection.[35] As a consequence, MPS economists and their business supporters maneuvered around Nixon's obsession with reelection to advance their free market agenda. They patiently waited for a crisis to justify their position before acting.

The drama began in early 1971, when Nixon resolved to raise the level of economic growth to improve his public standing ahead of the 1972 election.[36] According to one account, the president "bludgeoned Fed chairman Arthur Burns into cutting interest rates" to generate consumer spending and growth.[37] A strategy of low interest rates soon commenced. This strategy worked splendidly from the standpoint of Nixon's reelection campaign, which he won by historic margins. However, low interest rates also triggered renewed instability for the dollar, which had come to be viewed as a less reliable investment. Euromarket traders began attacking the dollar, while foreign governments exchanged their dollars for gold, reflecting a loss of confidence in U.S. financial leadership. Even British officials set aside their traditional fealty to the United States and sought gold.[38] Nixon had clearly exacerbated the dollar's underlying weakness. Continued capital flight was an additional concern, as noted in reports from the Treasury Department.[39] These problems were compounded by deterioration in the U.S. merchandise trade balance, producing the first year-long deficit of the twentieth century.[40]

Overall, "the situation is ripe for an international monetary crisis . . . based on the growing conviction that the present status of the dollar is untenable," said the Treasury official Robert Solomon in early 1971.[41] The hour of crisis had arrived, creating an opening for Friedman and his Mont Pèlerin colleagues, who gradually took control of the situation.

The person most responsible for addressing the crisis was Treasury Secretary John Connally,[42] who was sympathetic to the deregulatory agenda of MPS economists, as he later revealed in memoirs.[43] The specific program that Nixon and Connally devised to address the crisis—termed the "Nixon Shock" by journalists—was announced in a national address on August 15, 1971.[44] The main consequence of the shock was establishing that the dollar would no longer be exchanged for gold, thus terminating one of the foundational features of the international financial system, setting it on a path toward full deregulation, consistent with the MPS's agenda.

Nixon's speech also announced a new import "tax," really a tariff.[45] In reality, the import tax proved a temporary measure meant to allay public anger regarding foreign competition, but it was terminated at the end of the year.[46] Several months before the Nixon Shock, David Rockefeller was quietly reassured that "the President is at bottom a free trader,"[47] which was likely true despite the momentary lapse into protectionism. Finally, the president's economic package unveiled a series of wage and price controls as a means to subdue inflationary pressures, but these controls were gradually abandoned.[48] This package was presented to the public with demagogic condemnation of "international money speculators,"[49] but the rhetoric was just for show. We will see that Nixon's policies enriched the hated speculators.

The real centerpiece of the shock—its most enduring feature—was discarding the link between the dollar and gold, dealing a fatal blow to the 1944 Bretton Woods agreement and the regulated system it represented. The "Bretton Woods system has ended," one official stated in private several days after Nixon's speech.[50] The stage was set for the deregulation of exchange rates and, later, for a generalized deregulation of the whole financial sector. The dollar-gold link had been emblematic of the 1944 agreement, and now that this emblem had collapsed, the rest of the agreement would soon collapse, too.

From the private sector, Wriston was gratified by the new policy. In November 1971, he met with Treasury Secretary Connally and assured him that, soon, "the dollar is going to be floating"[51]—with its value to be determined by market forces. In his memoirs, Connally implied that he had favored floating rates all along.[52] The first step had been taken toward deregulation, in line with the conservative agenda advanced by Wriston. The broader business community reacted to Nixon Shock with elation, while Connally himself became "a hero in business circles," according to *Fortune* magazine.[53] When he spoke to a group of executives in early 1972, David Rockefeller described the speech: "I introduced him [Connally] and there were 120 top business executives, chief executive officers. And I've never seen such enthusiasm as they had for him. They gave him three standing ovations, and I've never seen anything like it."[54] As a long-standing advocate of deregulation, Friedman was also pleased, and he congratulated Secretary Connally in a private letter.[55] Meanwhile, Wriston began to mobilize his banking colleagues to support the emerging policy of floating rates.[56]

Now that the first steps had been taken against Bretton Woods, the free marketeers moved to settle the matter once and for all. Connally himself stepped down from the administration in 1972 to resume his lucrative practice in corporate law and lay the groundwork for a later presidential run. His replacement as Treasury secretary was George Shultz, who had been a professor of economics at the University of Chicago with a clear vision for turning the international economic order in a conservative direction. The new secretary was, according to a recent study, "a strong proponent of floating rates, courtesy of Milton Friedman."[57] This is confirmed by Shultz's memoirs, where he acknowledges that the idea of moving toward a floating system "emerged out of a conversation with Milton Friedman."[58] In advancing this free market agenda, the secretary had to proceed with a measure of caution, since some European officials were reluctant to abandon fixed rates altogether. But the diplomatic Shultz "did not have to wait too long to get what he truly wanted," which was elimination of the whole fixed-rate system.[59]

In March 1973, the fixed exchange rate system definitively ended, establishing a new global standard.[60] Thereafter, exchange rates moved to a floating system based on trading in private currency markets.[61] And in early 1974, the Treasury Department swept away the capital controls that had been established by the Kennedy and Johnson administrations— including the Interest Equalization Tax and Foreign Direct Investment Program—to "restore Americans' freedom to invest their money as they choose."[62] "Freedom to invest" became a basic theme of this period, along with an emphasis on market forces to achieve policy objectives.

The fundamentally laissez-faire logic of the new policy was distilled in a 1976 document: "The Treasury's central commitment in international economic policy is to the implementation of market-oriented policies." And the Treasury sought "full acceptance of an exchange rate system in which currencies are given value by market forces"[63]—based on the deregulated system of floating rates.

We will see shortly that deregulation would play a major role in undermining heavy industry in the United States, as well as the labor forces who depended on industry for their livelihoods. Financial interests nevertheless were pleased with the outcome.[64] Even David Rockefeller—a relative political moderate[65]—supported the new policy, stating, "It is very encouraging to note that . . . the United States ended several major controls over the movement of dollars abroad. Hopefully this will be an enduring step toward the elimination of *all* barriers to the free flow of capital funds across national boundaries. . . . The highest priority must be given to encouraging unimpeded access to capital globally."[66] Freed from regulation, finance was well on its way to becoming a leading sector.

At first glance, it seems easy to conclude that deregulation resulted from a series of ad hoc decisions and historical accidents rather than any coherent plan. The historian Daniel Sargent summed up this perspective: The move toward floating exchange rates "did not mark a self-conscious choice. . . . The ascent of finance and the retreat of state power was the work of unintended consequences, not intelligent design."[67] This view is untenable, since it neglects the role of the Mont Pèlerin academics, especially Haberler and Friedman, who painstakingly laid the intellectual groundwork for deregulation over a period of decades and then worked to implement that goal. These economists clearly did have a consistent objective and an intelligent design. And their strategy of deregulation had a formidable constituency in the private sector, notably in finance and multinational enterprise.

At the level of impact, the move to floating rates failed to achieve monetary stability. The literature on international finance is in agreement that "exchange rates have been notoriously volatile since the switch to floating rates."[68] And the correction of the U.S. trade imbalance also proved temporary; imbalances soon returned with a vengeance, turning the United States into a net debtor country over an extended period. Indeed, the increased speculation—which deregulation served to unleash—would further undermine the dollar's viability as the key currency, thus worsening the problem. The persistent weakness of the dollar eventually led to the program of austerity and reduced living standards that unfolded during the Carter presidency.

The failures of the Nixon Shock were frankly acknowledged in the opening remarks to a 1980 conference sponsored by the American Enterprise Institute:

> One of the main shortcomings of the present system of widespread floating is said to be excessive volatility of exchange rates . . . which is said to put inflationary pressures on some countries. . . . [It has not] prevented, as it was supposed to, the emergence of stubborn balance of payments disequilibria. . . . It has failed to insulate countries from external shocks. . . . It did not, contrary to what has been claimed on its behalf, give national monetary authorities freedom to pursue independent monetary policies.[69]

If deregulation of exchange rates was supposed to bring economic stability,[70] it was an abject failure.

In addition, the new exchange regime failed to free the market from state support. Indeed, the new system inaugurated an era of government-directed bailouts. When speculative ventures went badly and bankers lost money, their losses were often socialized at taxpayer expense, on the principle that financial failures produced systemic risk for the whole economy. Such practices in turn set precedents that encouraged other banks to engage in risky speculation, confident in the assumption that federal officials would bail them out, thus presenting the familiar problem of "moral hazard." This scenario in fact played out in 1974, when the Franklin National Bank of New York took losses on its overseas currency trading and faced the prospect of collapse. Because Franklin was the twentieth largest bank in the country, the Federal Reserve determined that its demise would be destabilizing. As a result, the Fed extended an emergency loan to Franklin, bailing it out.[71]

The Franklin case constituted the first major bank bailout of the newly globalized era, to be followed by many more in the years to come. Conservative economists such as Friedman decried public bailouts as violations of free enterprise principle[72]—even while they advocated deregulatory policies that made such bailouts inevitable. Clearly, deregulation did not mean the federal government would stay out of finance altogether; rather, it would serve a new role, socializing private losses through the investment of public funds. The deregulation of finance would not be cost free.

Whatever its merits in policy terms, deregulation proved advantageous to the financial interests that had long been its principal advocates. The Euromarket boomed, and according to one informed account, this period witnessed a "meteoric rise in trading volumes," mainly due to "the move to floating exchange rates."[73] The international speculators that Nixon had condemned profited handsomely from his policies while they remained confident of public bailouts when they sustained excessive losses. Although the burgeoning speculation took place mainly in London, much of the resulting profits spilled over into the United States, since major U.S. banks operated on the Euromarket through their foreign branches. By 1979, "The most dynamic element [in international finance] has been the US banking system both at home and in the offshore centres," according to a report by the Bank for International Settlements.[74] It was clear that banking had recovered from its post-Depression timidity. In addition, overseas speculation created political pressures for the deregulation of U.S. domestic finance, to begin later in the decade, offering further windfalls for the financial sector.

The move to floating exchange rates was a highly disruptive event for both the U.S. and the world economy, eroding living standards over the long term. Floating rates did not improve performance in the real economy, which remained sluggish throughout the decade.[75] However, we will pause our discussion of finance and move to a new topic: the energy crisis of 1973–74, which produced equally momentous results. The crisis affected every part of the economy, and it was the triggering cause of the mid-decade recession, the worst downturn since the Great Depression.[76]

THE ENERGY CRISIS

The basic facts of the crisis are well known. World oil prices escalated relentlessly through the early 1970s, and these price increases were led by OPEC, which was composed mostly (though not exclusively) of Arab- and Moslem-majority states.[77] The main triggering event was the October 1973 Arab-Israeli War, when OPEC implemented a series of sudden, massive price increases. Initially, Arab states led by Saudi Arabia used oil as a political weapon designed to punish the United States with an oil embargo for its support of Israel during the October war. After several months, however, the anti-Israel initiative evolved into a generalized effort to raise global oil prices as much as possible, with the new objective of simply maximizing revenues. These secondary price increases attracted much broader participation, including oil exporters such as Iran, which had no strong interest in the Arab-Israeli dispute; it simply wanted to make money.[78] For the United States, the energy crisis became an all-encompassing obsession of policy makers, as described in the memoirs of Herbert Stein, who served as chairman of the Council of Economic Advisers. Stein observed that "we all became energy experts" during this period. He added, dryly, "An energy expert was a person who knew that Abu Dhabi was a place and [Muammar] Gaddafi was a person."[79]

The energy crisis of the mid-1970s has long been presented as a fortuitous event, a matter of bad luck from the U.S. standpoint.[80] Officials in the Nixon administration sought to cope with the crisis as well as they could.[81] To the extent that the crisis was orchestrated, the orchestration emanated from the OPEC states themselves, not from the U.S. government. In this section, we will see that this benign interpretation of American policy amounts to a myth. In reality, the Nixon administration actively encouraged oil price increases, thus establishing a measure of complicity with the OPEC states. The complicity of the U.S. government in the crisis constitutes a disturbing topic, given that the crisis devastated large sectors of the economy. But the official complicity is well established, based on multiple sources of information.

One of the central players in the energy crisis was the government of Iran, led by Shah Mohammed Reza Pahlavi, who ruled until his overthrow in 1979; he was a key U.S. ally, backed by both President Nixon and Secretary of State Henry Kissinger. While the shah played no major role in orchestrating the initial oil embargo against the United States of October 1973, he proved a central figure in the second-phase price increases. Indeed, Iran was a "ringleader" among the states that sought higher prices, in the view of William Simon, who became Treasury secretary in 1974.[82] In seeking price increases, the shah had been encouraged by President Nixon himself. In a 1970 meeting, for example, Nixon stated to the Iranian Foreign Minister Ardeshir Zahedi, "Tell the Shah you can push [us] as much as you want [on oil prices]," as Zahedi recalled in a later interview.[83] Support for the shah's oil policy formed a consistent theme throughout the Nixon presidency; this support extended into the presidency of Gerald Ford.[84] One dissenter was Treasury Secretary Simon, who favored pressuring the shah to lower prices. But on this issue, Simon received little encouragement from Nixon, as noted in the following conversation from July 1974:

SECRETARY SIMON: Is it possible to put pressure on the Shah [to lower oil prices]?
PRESIDENT NIXON: *You are not going there.* . . . He is our best friend. Any pressure probably would have to come from me.[85]

Nixon never applied significant pressure on the shah. Simon would lament, "To my knowledge . . . the US has never indicated to any member of OPEC that their relations with the US would be affected by their behavior with respect to oil prices."[86] In a 1974 meeting with the president, Simon stated candidly, "The Shah has us. No one will confront him."[87]

President Nixon effectively blocked efforts to lower prices, which had emanated from the government of Saudi Arabia in 1974. The Saudis offered to restrain OPEC price increases and communicated this to the Nixon administration—which rebuffed the offer. Writing in the *Washington Post*, Jack Anderson described the situation: "In secret messages to Washington, the Saudis offered to block the price rise, if the Nixon administration would bring pressure on the Shah to hold oil prices down. They [the Saudis] pleaded that they couldn't stand alone against their fellow oil producers. . . . But Nixon and Kissinger did nothing."[88] The lack of U.S. interest in this proposal evidently surprised the Saudi petroleum minister, Ahmed Zaki Yamani, who later wrote a delicately worded letter to Simon: "There are those amongst us [Saudi officials] who think that the U.S. administration does not really object to an increase in oil prices. There are even those who think that you encourage it."[89]

U.S. support for price increases was widely noted by informed observers both inside and outside the administration. A contemporary investigation published in *Foreign Policy* concluded, "The United States has encouraged Middle East oil producing states to raise the price of oil and keep it up." The article was based on interviews with U.S. officials, including the former ambassador to Saudi Arabia, James Akins, and it was piquantly subtitled "We Pushed Them."[90]

At the level of motive, American support for higher oil prices stemmed from the perception that the shah was a critically important ally, designated by the Nixon administration as the guardian of Western interests in the Persian Gulf region. Another factor was the shah's formidable political clout, carefully cultivated over an extended period. From Washington, the Iranian Embassy curried favor with the U.S. press corps. Iranian diplomats dispensed tins of top-quality caviar and other expensive gifts to hundreds of journalists and media executives, which included Barbara Walters and Joseph Kraft, who in turn produced positive, often fawning, coverage of the shah and his government.[91] The Iranians hired as a publicist Marian Javits, the wife of Senator Jacob Javits, who served as a senior member of the Senate Foreign Relations Committee.[92]

In addition, the U.S. corporate sector profited from the shah's policies, and this further cemented the U.S.-Iranian partnership. Iranian arms purchases proved a special bonanza for Northrop, Grumman, and Bell Helicopter, which gained lucrative sales contracts; these benefits were made possible by the energy crisis, which fueled Iranian imports.[93] The major oil companies also benefited from the energy crisis, which elevated their profits.[94] And from Tehran in 1974, U.S. Ambassador Richard Helms noted with pleasure, "The number of American businessmen not to mention those of other nations keeps the hotels full to overflowing and keeps this Embassy hopping to help as best we can. . . . U.S. business is getting more than its share of the action here, I am glad to say."[95] The partnership was further bolstered by corporate social networks, including the influential Rockefeller family, who had long been friendly with the Pahlavis.[96] These connections advanced the cause of U.S.-Iranian alliance, as well as discreet American support for oil price augmentations—favored by the Iranians.

The turmoil that resulted from this state of affairs destabilized the world economy, exacerbating inequalities between oil-exporting and oil-importing countries. Non-oil-producing Third World countries were most severely affected, and they suffered from widespread trade imbalances and financial predicaments, erasing years of social progress in some cases.[97] Several countries secured loans on international capital markets to alleviate distress, producing multiple rounds of debt crises when countries were unable to repay the loans. In the post–Bretton Woods era, the IMF developed a new function: to impose and manage austerity programs in countries that were negatively affected by the growing instability. In time, numerous countries would undergo IMF-directed "structural adjustment" programs, often conducted in close cooperation with private finance.[98] Even among oil exporters, which were beneficiaries of the new economic order, many states wasted their revenues on arms purchases, prestige projects, and generalized corruption. This was especially true of Iran, where official misuse of oil funds was a major factor in the Iranian Revolution of 1979.[99]

In the United States, the energy crisis generated nationwide gas shortages, with long lines at service stations, leading to mass protests and public anger. The Nixonian policy of supporting the shah's oil price hike was costly to the domestic economy, since it lowered living standards for most people, but Nixon was determined to pursue this policy and did not waver.

While Nixon and Kissinger focused on their geostrategic maneuvering, the problem of foreign debt festered due to a continuing deficit on America's trade balance and overspending on worldwide military adventures.[100] The United States was moving into the category of a permanent debtor state. Administration officials used the energy crisis as a means of financing this debt by drawing Middle Eastern "petrodollars" into U.S. Treasury bonds. Oil and finance would become integrated to some degree, and both would emerge as leading sectors of a new economic order—undergirded by the Saudi monarchy. America's relationship with Saudi Arabia would also impact the domestic economy by elevating the financial sector.

SAUDI ARABIA UNDERWRITES THE DOLLAR

In the story of international oil politics, the Kingdom of Saudi Arabia was a central player as the world's largest producer, holding huge reserves.

It also sustained a long-standing association with the United States beginning with the formation of the Arabian American Oil Company (ARAMCO) in 1933, led by Standard Oil of California, which forged a state-to-state bond that endured across multiple presidencies.[101] Despite this history, the Nixon administration initially experienced a tense relationship with the Saudi monarchy. A point of contention was Nixon's support for Israel, thus colliding with the Saudis' rejection of Zionism and the whole idea of a Jewish state in the Middle East. As a result, Saudi Arabia helped engineer the 1973 oil embargo against international supporters of Israel, especially the United States. While Nixon and Kissinger favored high oil prices in general, they deeply resented the Saudi-led embargo. The Saudi government also established adversarial relationships with the major oil companies, the "Seven Sisters," which dominated the world market; five of these were American owned.[102]

Notwithstanding this rocky start, the Nixon administration eventually settled its differences with Saudi Arabia, and, by 1974, the two governments had established a close alliance, which benefited both countries. From the U.S. standpoint, the Saudis' stores of financial reserves were very attractive, and they would be used to restore confidence in the dollar. The figure most responsible for forging the U.S.-Saudi collaboration was Treasury Secretary William Simon.

At first glance, Simon's role may seem surprising, since he was not a Middle East specialist or even a foreign policy specialist. His background was in finance; before entering the Nixon administration, he had worked as a bond trader with Salomon Brothers, rising to become president of the firm. Simon approached Middle East policy from the standpoint of an investment banker. He also was an enthusiastic advocate for free markets, widely considered the most ideological member in the cabinet. At Treasury, he began as a protégé of George Shultz, who in turn connected Simon with his conservative network in the Mont Pèlerin Society.[103]

The MPS economists were once again playing behind-the-scenes roles in shaping policy, as they did throughout the 1970s. Shultz later recalled, "One of the most important things I did for Bill [Simon] was to introduce him to Milton Friedman," of whom Simon became an admirer. In addition, he enjoyed close connections with Citibank's

Wriston—on his way to becoming America's leading financier—who had recommended Simon's appointment to the Treasury Department.[104] As Treasury secretary, Simon would prove a worthy understudy to the trio of Shultz, Friedman, and Wriston, and he would build on their initial accomplishment of deregulating exchange rates. He went on to play a key role in financializing the domestic economy and weakening the industrial base, thus establishing himself as a central figure in overturning the class compromise.

In July 1974, Simon flew to Jeddah, along the Red Sea coast, and achieved a far-reaching agreement with Saudi officials entailing their purchase of Treasury bonds in large quantities.[105] The idea was for the Treasury to establish a surplus on its capital account—made possible by Saudi money—thus compensating for weak exports and a deficit on the merchandise trade balance.[106] The consequence of this arrangement was a strengthened dollar. In return for their funds, the Saudi royal family gained U.S. military and political support, a coveted goal.[107] The decision to bolster the dollar was no doubt made easier by the fact that the Saudis' oil exports were priced mostly in dollars, and they had a vested interest in protecting its value. As part of the deal, the Saudi monarchy was expected to set aside its long-standing hostility toward the administration's pro-Israel policy, a sacrifice it was evidently willing to make.[108]

At the bureaucratic level, Simon established a close connection between the Treasury Department and the Saudi Arabian Monetary Authority.[109] While the U.S. pivot toward Saudi Arabia took place during the end of the Nixon presidency, it carried over to Nixon's successor, Gerald Ford. The Jeddah agreement was sufficiently sensitive that the details were classified for an extended period and have only recently come to light.

In essence, Simon persuaded the Saudis to underwrite U.S. financial hegemony. Other OPEC states quickly followed the Saudi lead,[110] and by 1978, the bulk of OPEC surpluses had been invested in Treasury bonds and other dollar-denominated assets.[111] From a U.S. standpoint, the prospect of Saudi and other OPEC funding was viewed as beneficial. Shortly after the Jeddah deal was concluded, the investment banker Robert Roosa noted, "We can pay for [imports] without straining our balance of payments . . . because more and more of the OPEC money is flowing in here."[112] Saudi funds generated additional benefits. The fact that the world's leading oil producer was investing in America's future signaled to central bankers and private investors around the world that the United States remained a safe haven for their surplus funds; this signal would stimulate mass flows of funds into the United States, as a supplement to the Saudi and OPEC petrodollars, further shoring up America's financial position for the long term.[113]

Following the Jeddah agreement, American officials accepted Saudi Arabia as a strategic partner, as a supplement to Iran, in protecting the Gulf, and both countries became the "twin pillars" of Western security in the region.[114] After the shah was overthrown in 1979, U.S. policy relied to an even greater extent on the Saudis. For its part, the United States helped modernize the Saudi air force through the sale of fighter planes and advanced electronic equipment, while Saudi intelligence was encouraged to intervene throughout the Middle East and Africa, acting as a proxy for U.S. power. The arrangement clearly satisfied the Saudi royals' desire for influence and prestige, made possible by their growing alliance with the United States.[115] Over time, they would build up a formidable lobbying and public relations presence within the United States, thus ensuring that the U.S.-Saudi alliance would be long lasting.[116] Any moralistic concerns regarding political repression and human rights violations in the kingdom were dismissed.[117]

From a commercial standpoint, the U.S. alliance with Saudi Arabia generated lucrative opportunities for arms merchants, who gained a new market,[118] as well as heavy engineering companies such as the Bechtel Group, which gained contracts for megaprojects, including the King Khalid International Airport in Riyadh. These deals were advanced by high-level political connections. In the Bechtel case, for example, a senior company executive was George Shultz, who had recently served as Treasury secretary.[119] His successor, William Simon, joined Olayan Investments, "a Liechtenstein-based company belonging to the Olayan family in Saudi Arabia."[120]

When assessing the U.S.-Saudi alliance, we should not overlook old-fashioned moneymaking as a significant motive, and such private sector *baksheesh* forms a long-standing tradition in U.S. diplomacy. But the most important feature of the alliance remained simple: The Saudis would prop up the dollar.

HOW THE SAUDI DEAL FORTIFIED
AMERICAN HEGEMONY

The deal presented major benefits in promoting the United States as a superpower, even though it produced negative consequences for the domestic economy and working classes. But first, let us consider the benefits. Within the Nixon and Ford administrations, the Saudi agreement to purchase Treasury bonds helped resolve dilemmas on how to retain the dollar as the world's primary currency at a time when the United States was gradually becoming a permanent debtor country with a deficit on its trade balance. Clearly, officials placed a high priority on remaining the issuer of the top currency, and the 1974 Saudi deal ensured that these advantages would endure.[121] As a result, the U.S. government influenced every facet of international economic activity. A 1975 report presented to the elite Bilderberg forum observed that "world monetary liquidity was *determined very largely by the monetary and exchange policies of the United States*," mainly due to "the predominant role of the U.S. dollar."[122] The central importance of the dollar thus contributed to America's global clout, especially control over the IMF and the other international institutions.[123] In addition, the influx of funds associated with the Saudi deal helped offset the vast expense of maintaining hundreds of overseas U.S. bases in allied states, further contributing to—and prolonging—the American Century.[124]

On the negative side of the ledger, the strategy of strengthening the dollar with Saudi funds undermined the industrial base, along with industrial work forces. Stated simply, the strong dollar policy artificially increased the importation of foreign-manufactured products while reducing exports, thus generating deterioration of the U.S. industrial sector.[125] It is important to emphasize that this policy reflected an intentional choice among various options.

An alternative policy would have been to favor industry, which was a viable possibility. In 1973, Under-Secretary of State for Economic Affairs William Casey observed that the United States might solve its problems through an "export-oriented business strategy, a devalued dollar, and U.S. government pressure on other countries to open their markets."[126] Continued devaluations would have risked undermining confidence in the dollar as the world's currency, but this was not an insuperable barrier. From the Council of Economic Advisers, Marina Whitman advocated simply abandoning the dollar's key currency status altogether.[127] Even so mainstream a figure as David Rockefeller contemplated a new international currency as a replacement for the dollar,[128] possibly based on an expansion of the IMF's program of special drawing rights.[129] Secretary Simon disregarded these alternatives, as he opted for a strategy of bolstering the dollar with foreign funds.

From Simon's standpoint, the influx of petrodollars accomplished two goals: while enhancing American power, the petrodollar inflow also supercharged the financial sector in which Simon had worked throughout his adult life. The inflow enabled the "financial sector to unleash itself," in the colorful phrase of one official.[130] The strategy of drawing in foreign capital would play out well into the twenty-first century, attracting investors from all over the world, who would be lured into Treasury bonds and private-sector capital markets, further strengthening the dollar.[131]

Through multiple presidencies, the Treasury Department facilitated this influx of foreign funds, pressuring governments around the world to deregulate their own financial systems to make more funds available to finance the U.S. debt.[132] As a result of this external funding, the United States was able to maintain its superpower status long after the 1974 Jeddah agreement. While American officials clearly appreciated the prestige that was associated with governing a superpower, this prestige was achieved at high cost to the domestic economy.

HOW GLOBALIZATION UNDERMINED THE NEW DEAL

Hot ladles and steel and men working. Then it was gone.
—RESIDENT OF YOUNGSTOWN, OHIO[133]

Over the long term, the trends discussed in this chapter would transform the economy, generating changes that proved fundamental and irreversible. First, the deregulation of international finance during the Nixon presidency set a precedent for future rounds of deregulation that played out over an extended period.[134] As one analyst stated the matter, "The deregulatory ball once pushed developed a momentum of its own."[135] Deregulation would occur in phases, gradually sweeping away the last vestiges of New Deal restrictions, producing a take-off in the financial sector. The take-off began with the 1971–1973 deregulation of international exchange rates and the resulting surge of the Euromarket; this financial surge was enhanced in 1980, when domestic interest rates were deregulated as well.[136] Following this take-off, finance would no longer exist as a support mechanism for industrial production—as originally intended by the framers of Bretton Woods—but would emerge as a leading sector in its own right, accounting for 44 percent of all corporate profits by 2002.[137]

The ascent of finance came to affect every facet of the domestic economy. It had an especially pronounced effect on manufacturing, which also began emphasizing financial activity; vehicle manufacturers, for example, would often look to their auto loan departments as their main profit centers.[138] At the same time, corporate executives pursued short-term stock gains for their companies, thus achieving "shareholder value," while avoiding long-term investments in capital equipment. The growth of finance thus played a significant role in promoting deindustrialization, a point that is widely recognized in both the academic literature and the business press.[139] According to *Forbes* magazine, "the financial industry has pursued short term financial returns over long-term goals such as technology and product development investments. . . . [These trends] have played a major role in the decline of manufacturing. . . . There was more profit in making money from money rather than in engineered products."[140] Stated plainly, the economy became geared toward financial speculation instead of manufacturing, promoting the effective dismantling of industry—in short, deindustrialization. The advent of deindustrialization inaugurated a historic shift. During World War II, it had been commonplace to extol the "immense potential of American industry," to quote Charles de Gaulle;[141] by the late 1970s, however, such ideas had come to seem quaint, as America's vaunted industrial base began to disappear. The high-paying jobs associated with this industrial base also disappeared.

A second aspect of industrial decline was the 1974 agreement with Saudi Arabia for the recycling of petrodollars, as well as the inflows of foreign capital that followed the agreement. With access to external funds, U.S. authorities no longer needed to promote exports to balance their international accounts. The result was an artificially strong dollar,[142] which contributed to America's great power status while accelerating the decline of industry. According to the Stanford economist Ronald MacKinnon, the influx of foreign funds "speeds up the pace of deindustrialization in the United States. . . . [It aggravates industrial decline] well beyond that experienced by other mature industrial countries."[143] And the influx of foreign funds that followed from the Saudi deal enhanced still further the ascendancy of finance within the domestic economy,[144] further intensifying financialization and the resulting industrial decay.

A third trend has been the globalization of manufacturing, which closely tracked the growth of the Euromarket and the globalization of finance following the Nixon Shock. As a result, U.S. manufacturing increasingly migrated overseas, often to low-wage countries that lacked union protections, minimum wage laws, and social safety nets. Manufactured products from these countries were then exported back to the United States, contributing still further to deindustrialization.[145] The New York financier Robert Johnson later remarked that "capital has wings. . . . [It] can deal with twenty labor markets at once and pick and choose among them. Labor is fixed in one place," presenting a systematic disadvantage for labor.[146] There also was an important psychological component to globalization: The mere threat that a company might move production overseas would often prove sufficient to frighten workers into accepting reduced pay, benefits, and job security while undermining unions, a strategy that business interests would use repeatedly with considerable effect.[147]

And beyond the United States, Mont Pèlerin economics spread around the world with massive private-sector backing, thus establishing *the* global model, widely copied in every region, on all continents.[148] The increasingly internationalized economics profession promoted these laissez-faire trends, giving clear direction to policy makers. Deregulation and fiscal austerity defined the new standards. In addition, MPS conferences propagated laissez-faire ideas in overtly ideological terms, especially in Latin America. According to a Guatemalan economist who attended a 1980 MPS gathering, "The meeting served as an intellectual weapon which we need to win the ideological war."[149]

University of Chicago–trained economists, *"los Chicos de Chicago,"* helped restructure the Chilean economy into one of the most deregulated in the world during the dictatorship of General Augusto Pinochet, thus establishing Chile as a free market beacon, inspiring conservatives throughout the region.[150] In 1979, Margaret Thatcher came to power in Great Britain with support from a series of business-funded think tanks (closely linked with counterparts in the United States), inaugurating a free market transformation while establishing yet another beacon.[151]

The phenomenon of deep lobbying was now playing out on a global scale, fighting the war of ideas with impressive results. The strategy that had worked so well in advancing free market ideology within the United States was now being projected outward. By the 1980s, even such communist states as Yugoslavia, Hungary, and Poland had begun adopting market mechanisms in line with the new orthodoxy, often accompanied by austerity and reductions in living standards.[152] These overall trends were encouraged and to some extent orchestrated by the U.S. Treasury Department—backed by the prestige of American hegemony—working in close cooperation with private-sector capital markets. Indeed, the Columbia University economist Jagdish Bhagwati later expressed alarm about the growing power of a "Wall Street-Treasury Complex,"[153] which was coaxing countries to deregulate their economies, setting them up for later financial crises. And international organizations, including the International Monetary Fund, advanced market-based programs among less developed countries, especially those experiencing economic distress.[154] This was truly "The Age of Milton Friedman,"[155] as his ideas expanded globally; it was the globalization of free market economics.

Contrary to popular misperception, however, the worldwide turn toward market mechanisms has not been associated with improved macroeconomic performance in terms of expansion of gross domestic product.[156] World Bank data in figure 5.1 show declining rates of GDP growth after 1973—during the period of global deregulation—and this reduced growth persisted over many decades. The widespread view that deregulation has coincided with exceptional worldwide dynamism is a myth. While some countries have benefited during this period, the average rate of global growth has been unimpressive. Overall, the Age of Milton Friedman has been one of diminished economic performance.

The process of globalization has clearly weakened the capacity of governments to regulate economic activity and ameliorate the

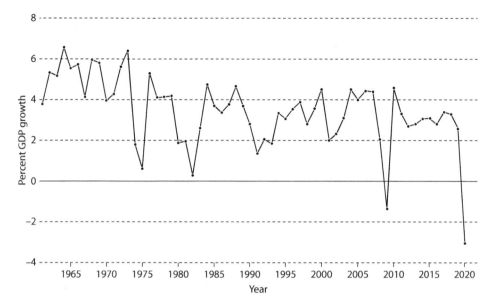

FIGURE 5.1 Global GDP growth, 1961–2020

Source: World Bank, World Bank National Accounts Data, and OECD National Accounts Data Files, "GDP Growth (Annual %)," worldwide data, 1961–2022, percentage growth per year, accessed November 6, 2023, https://data.worldbank.org/indicator/NY.GDP.MKTP .KD.ZG.

effects of stagnation, as well as the unemployment that results from stagnation. Specifically, the use of fiscal policy to raise employment levels and living standards has been complicated by the problem of "fiscal leakage,"[157] whereby the effect of government spending is dissipated as some of the funds leak out internationally, as a by-product of globalization. Similarly, the effects of austerity policies undertaken in other countries leak inward, further frustrating policy makers. And countries pursuing expansionary, employment-generating policies ran the risk of having their currencies attacked by Euromarket traders, undermining their efforts.

In the United States, speculative attacks proved to be major challenges for President Jimmy Carter, who responded by abandoning his policy of fiscal stimulus altogether.[158] Indeed, all over the world, states found it increasingly difficult to implement policies aimed at reducing unemployment or raising wages, or economic planning more generally. The new order of financial liberalization constrained policy makers' freedom of action and reduced their ability to depart from the free market consensus—just as the MPS economists had intended.

In addition, international tax havens in the Cayman Islands and elsewhere have undermined the ability of countries to tax assets and raise revenues and thus fund employment-generating domestic programs, while they have contributed to the growth of great fortunes and the concentration of wealth. The origin of such offshore havens can be traced back to the 1970s, and their growth closely tracked the deregulation of finance and the ascent of the Euromarket. According to the economist Susan Strange, the rise of such havens was encouraged by U.S. policy; their growth "could easily have been checked at any early stage" if policy makers had been interested in doing so.[159] Policy makers thus chose to enable the creation of tax havens, just as they chose to enable the globalization of finance more generally, which undergirded the tax havens.

The changes in U.S. foreign economic policy that occurred in the early 1970s assumed a character different from that of the issue areas discussed in the foregoing chapters. Previously, we saw that policy changes required massive public relations and lobbying efforts designed to rally elite and mass opinion in favor of a conservative turn. In the case of foreign economic policy, however, public lobbying proved unnecessary, given the abstruse nature of the topic. Hardly anyone outside professional economics circles understood the intricacies of exchange rate policy or the balance of payments. As a result, a handful of specialists, led by Milton Friedman and several other economists associated with the MPS, were able to achieve decisive influence, working behind the scenes without fanfare. The targets of their efforts were an equally small number of specialist policy makers, mostly in the Treasury Department. In advancing their lobbying campaign, MPS economists worked in tandem with financial and other corporate interests who sought to benefit from deregulation, notably Walter Wriston of Citibank.

Whether the American public realized it or not, the policy changes that resulted from this lobbying would have a major impact on their living standards. And at the international level, the rightward turn that began in U.S. economics departments and think tanks would soon drive a worldwide transformation of considerable proportions. America's right turn had gone global.

CHAPTER SIX

The Triumph of Laissez-Faire

The standard of living for the average American has to decline.
—PAUL VOLCKER, FEDERAL RESERVE CHAIR

[When] Volcker approached the podium at the American Bankers Assn. convention, the band broke into strains of "Mr. Wonderful."
—TOM REDBURN, *LOS ANGELES TIMES*

In the overall story of America's rightward shift, the conclusive stage occurred during the presidency of James Earl Carter, the topic of the current chapter. A key event in his presidency was the 1979 appointment of Paul Volcker to head the Federal Reserve, a decision that would prove instrumental in redistributing wealth and income toward the privileged classes at the expense of the less privileged. Carter also pioneered the use of deregulation as a means of restraining organized labor, with damaging effects on working-class living standards. While previous chapters discussed Carter's rightward move on foreign policy, this chapter emphasizes his simultaneous move on domestic policy. The Carter presidency marked a decisive historical turning point, when all the accumulated tensions of the decade came to a head. By the end of his presidency, business elites finally achieved their objective of ending the New Deal class compromise, thus restructuring the character of American politics.

JIMMY CARTER, CORPORATE DEMOCRAT

It seems easy to understand why the Democratic establishment accepted Jimmy Carter as its presidential nominee in 1976, since he appeared to resolve many of the dilemmas that had long vexed the party. As a southerner, he offered the possibility of regaining support from white voters in the former Confederacy, whose party loyalties had been strained by the civil rights movement. On the other hand, Carter presented himself as a new type of southern politician, one who was comfortable with integration and racial equality.[1] While serving as governor of Georgia from 1971 to 1975, he established positive relationships with the state's Black leaders, who became some of his most enthusiastic supporters when he ran for president.[2] Indeed, it was the African American vote that proved decisive in his later electoral success.

Furthermore, Carter was a born-again Christian who openly used religious language and taught Sunday School, thus gaining support from Protestant ministers and socially conservative voters while also holding moderately progressive views on women's rights and abortion. As a graduate of the U.S. Naval Academy, he could reclaim the mantle of patriotism for the Democrats, and his image as a simple peanut farmer from a small town projected a halo of populism. It seemed Carter would renew the New Deal coalition while overcoming the cultural and racial conflicts that were so debilitating for the Democratic Party and the country at large. Carter would surely find some middle ground, or so it seemed.

Carter offered another advantage for Democrats: his excellent business connections. These connections were forged during his single term as governor of Georgia through his chief of staff, Charles Kirbo,[3] who had previously served as a senior partner in the Atlanta law firm of King & Spalding. Kirbo "provided Carter with a crucial link to Georgia's key corporate interests," including the state's leading enterprise, the Coca-Cola company, one of King & Spalding's clients.[4] Coca-Cola's board chairman, J. Paul Austin, actively promoted Carter's image both statewide and nationally. Austin used his influence with *Time* magazine executives and urged them to showcase Carter's accomplishments.[5] As a result, Carter's face appeared on *Time*'s cover in 1971 in a lead story on southern governors, presenting him for the first time to a national audience. Carter was emerging as the avatar of a racially tolerant "new South."[6]

Carter also undertook a series of trips to Europe, Latin America, and the Middle East aimed at advancing the state of Georgia in international commercial circles (and perhaps burnishing his own credentials as a future presidential candidate). According to one study, Carter "had assistance on these junkets from Coca-Cola. . . . With its offices all over the world and with its resources and expertise, the soft drink firm resembles a private version of the State Department,"[7] proving useful to the ambitious governor.

Carter further advanced his standing when, in 1973, he had a dinner meeting with David Rockefeller, president of Chase Manhattan Bank and chairman of the Council on Foreign Relations. Rockefeller was in the process of forming a new international discussion and networking group, the Trilateral Commission, to comprise prestigious figures in government and the private sector from the United States, Western Europe, and Japan. The purpose of this new commission was to improve cooperation among the three international power blocs, which had been severely frayed by tensions associated with the Vietnam War. Rockefeller was sufficiently impressed with Carter that he invited the governor to participate in commission meetings,[8] enabling Carter to establish amicable relationships with some of the most powerful business figures in the world. The dinner with Rockefeller and the resulting Trilateral Commission membership helped elevate Carter from a parochial southern politician to a figure of national and international prominence.

It should come as no surprise that elite interests were solicitous of Carter, given his firmly procorporate outlook. Records of the Trilateral Commission from 1973, stored at the Rockefeller Archive Center, present these comments: "Governor Carter said that in ten countries he had recently visited, the personnel of U.S. MNCs [multinational corporations] were often better informed than the people in the U.S. embassies; he urged the [Trilateral Commission] to educate public opinion on how MNCs and governments can cooperate." Carter thus admired MNCs, and he added, "Ultimately governments should emulate the interlocking of the international business world."[9] Both publicly and privately, Carter presented himself as a probusiness politician.[10]

Coming from the South, Carter had little interest in labor unions. One of his closest aides would later observe, "There were no unions down there [in Georgia] when he was growing up. . . . [Labor unions] were alien to his background and style of governing. You didn't govern when you were Governor of Georgia by worrying about the AFL-CIO."[11] Though he never developed direct ties to Milton Friedman or the Mont Pèlerin Society economists in Friedman's orbit, Carter held reliably conservative views on economics, many of which were compatible with those of Friedman. Carter was especially keen on deregulating the economy, the need to "free" the market from governmental control. This objective was evident even before the presidential inauguration.

Carter's secretary of agriculture, Robert Bergland, later recalled his first interview with Carter after the 1976 election, in which the president-elect emphasized his predilection for deregulation: "[He] was very strong on letting the marketplace sort things out. . . . A Democrat could do these things that a Republican couldn't have done on matters like deregulation." With regard to the specific area of agriculture policy, Carter asked Bergland, "Would you be comfortable in getting rid of . . . a lot of these old 1930s vintage New Deal regulatory authorities[?]" And Carter opined, "I think we ought to get rid of all we can get rid of."[12] In reality, the Nixon administration had beaten Carter to the punch, having deregulated agriculture to a considerable degree.[13] But these statements underscore a basic fact: Carter was a true believer in deregulation. As president, he would become a champion of deregulation, setting aside New Deal regulatory structures, with reliably detrimental effects on workers.

Finally, at an ideological level, Carter was very much a conservative, especially on economic matters. During the 1976 campaign, he "ran to the right of his Democratic challengers for the Democratic nomination," in the view of White House aide Stuart Eizenstat.[14] According to another presidential staffer, "Carter would never use the word liberal in describing himself . . . [He] thought of himself as being conservative."[15] And in 1978, the president himself acknowledged, "In many cases I feel more at home with the conservative Democratic and Republican members of Congress" than with the liberals, even though "the liberals vote with me much more often."[16]

In appointments to his presidential cabinet, Carter selected impeccably mainstream figures while cementing close ties to the Business Roundtable, U.S. Chamber of Commerce, National Association of Manufacturers, and, of course, the Trilateral Commission.[17] The commission's director, Zbigniew Brzezinski, became Carter's national security adviser. The Carter administration appears to have had an especially close relationship with the Business Roundtable, according to *Fortune* magazine:

"The White House's favorite lobby was the Business Roundtable. Whenever the President wanted the counsel or the help of business, says an aide, 'They [the Roundtable] were the first group we'd turn to.'"[18] Carter also established ties to AT&T, General Electric, and Dupont, whose executives constituted an informal "corporate brain trust," to advise the new president on economic matters.[19] And the new president retained his long-standing connections to Coca-Cola executive Austin, who enjoyed "regular access to the Oval Office," according to a recent biography.[20] During the first two years of his administration, Carter's intimacy with the corporate sector was often noted in the press. An article in the *New York Times* stated, "Big business has the ear of Jimmy Carter, Democrat, to a greater degree than was true of Richard M. Nixon or Gerald R. Ford, Republicans, and some in the business establishment . . . say they are getting along better with Mr. Carter than they did with predecessors."[21] It is fair to conclude that the Carter presidency began as one of the most business friendly in recent history.[22]

President Carter liked to present himself as a fiscally prudent technocrat who, in close cooperation with the private sector, would manage the economy toward greater efficiency. Perhaps, in a different and more placid era, the president would have been reasonably effective in this capacity and even popular with the public. The 1970s were anything but placid, however, and Carter was thrust into the position of being not merely a conservative president but an austerity president, one who presided over a reduction of living standards for average Americans. And for a large part of the population, austerity would become a permanent way of life.

THE LAST GASP OF THE NEW DEAL

Despite his conservative bent, Carter was nevertheless a Democrat, and his party leaned somewhat more to the left on economic matters than the president himself. And however much Carter disliked unions, he nevertheless had to make some gestures of support to this key Democratic constituency. In 1977, sizable portions of the private sector remained tepidly receptive to the class compromise established by Franklin Roosevelt (although that would soon change). Based on all these considerations, Carter began his presidency with a burst of reform.

Given his instinctive conservatism, it remains open to question how positively he really viewed these reforms, especially in the area of economic policy. Whatever his personal reservations, President Carter began with the appearance of a traditional liberal.

The reform phase of the Carter presidency did achieve some successes, especially in environmental policy, with passage of the 1977 Surface Mining Control and Regulation Act, which regulated "strip mining" and reduced its environmental damage.[23] His energy program emphasized the importance of conservation and the development of renewable energy, including solar.[24] He later added solar panels to rooftops of the White House. In his appointments to the federal judiciary, Carter selected sizable numbers of African Americans, Hispanics, and women.[25] In foreign policy, too, he achieved significant successes, including the Panama Canal treaty, which terminated U.S. control over the canal zone and improved America's image in Latin America; and the Camp David accords between Israel and Egypt, which ended the long-standing state of war between the two countries. In 1979, President Carter formally recognized the People's Republic of China, going beyond the de facto recognition that had been established by President Nixon.

The centerpiece of Carter's economic program was a fiscal stimulus package, use of government spending to alleviate unemployment. The country was still recovering from the 1973–1975 recession, the worst since the Great Depression. Though the economy was officially in recovery mode when Carter assumed office, the rate of unemployment—7.5 percent in January 1977—remained stubbornly high (see table 6.1). White House staffers were well aware that high unemployment was one of the principal factors that had discredited Carter's predecessor, Gerald Ford, and enabled his electoral defeat. It should also be noted that deindustrialization continued to eliminate whole categories of high-paying jobs, a process that proceeded well into the Carter presidency. In 1977, the Youngstown Sheet and Tube company closed a major plant in northeast Ohio; this closure eliminated fifty thousand jobs over the next several years.[26]

However fiscally conservative President Carter may have been in principle, he recognized the imperative to raise employment levels. He signed into law a $20.1 billion stimulus package ($85.5 billion in 2020 dollars) that aimed to create jobs through federal spending, with

TABLE 6.1

U.S. unemployment rate, 1975–1982

Month	Unemployment rate (%)
May 1975	9.0
November 1976	7.8
January 1977	7.5
May 1977	7.0
December 1978	6.0
July 1979	5.7
December 1979	6.0
August 1980	7.7
November 1980	7.5
July 1981	7.2
November 1982	10.8

Source: U.S. "Unemployment Rate," by month, from January 1948, FRED Economic Data, Federal Reserve Bank of St. Louis, accessed November 3, 2023, https://fred.stlouisfed.org/series /UNRATE. Based on data from U.S. Bureau of Labor Statistics; figures are seasonally adjusted.

a special emphasis on the building of "libraries, municipal buildings, schools, sewage treatment plants." The May 1977 spending package was especially "targeted to areas hardest hit by unemployment."[27]

The effects of the stimulus were modest; the amount of federal spending was simply too small to have much effect. The unemployment rate did gradually drop through Carter's first years in office, finally reaching a nadir of 5.7 percent in July 1979. But unemployment had been dropping months before the stimulus began. Unemployment during the Carter presidency remained well above historical averages for the post–World War II era. And we will soon see that toward the end of Carter's term, unemployment rose again, permanently wiping out whole classes of blue-color jobs, and they would never return. The very limited nature of President Carter's stimulus program reflected his conservative ideology. The Congressional Black Caucus was advocating full employment as a permanent government policy, to be guaranteed in law, as embodied in early versions of the Humphrey-Hawkins bill.[28] But Carter rejected the idea of full employment as going against the need for fiscal restraint.

When viewed comparatively, Carter's first-year economic policies differed little from those of his Republican predecessor, Gerald Ford. In a later oral history, Ford's former adviser, Alan Greenspan noted that Carter's early policies "were not really very different from those Ford probably would have followed" had he been reelected.[29] In a similar vein, the MIT political scientist Walter Dean Burnham concluded, "Carter's essential economic policies were Republican policies."[30] And the fundamentally "Republican" character of Carter's presidency would become more pronounced over time.

THE END OF THE NEW DEAL

The policy of stimulus did not last long, as it was challenged by rising price levels. Inflation had been an entrenched problem since the late 1960s, and it began spiking toward the end of the decade (see table 6.2). The 1977 stimulus was widely viewed as a contributor to inflation, and it was accordingly abandoned.

The overall significance of inflation is open to debate. As we discussed at length in chapter 2, inflation posed a special danger for

TABLE 6.2
Average annual rates of inflation, 1975–1983

Year	Annual rate of inflation (%)
1975	9.1
1976	5.7
1977	6.5
1978	7.6
1979	11.3
1980	13.5
1981	10.3
1982	6.1
1983	3.2

Source: U.S. "Inflation, Consumer Prices in the United States," 1960–present, FRED Economic Data, Federal Reserve Bank of St. Louis, accessed November 3, 2023, https://fred.stlouisfed.org/series/FPCPITOTLZGUSA.

the affluent, since rising prices reduced the value of accumulated assets, held disproportionately by the highest income earners, a point acknowledged even by former Nixon's economic adviser, Herbert Stein.[31] In 1979, *Business Week* pronounced "the death of equities," because "inflation is destroying the stock market."[32] But contrary to popular misconception, inflation was somewhat less of a burden for most working- and middle-class Americans. The main effect of inflation was to redistribute resources from the wealthy to the less wealthy, according to a study of inflation during the period 1969–1976.[33] Similar results were produced by a Brookings Institution researcher, as published in a congressional report.[34]

Whatever the facts, there was a widespread assumption in the Carter White House that inflation was *the* most important economic challenge and that all other challenges—most notably unemployment—were secondary.[35] The crusade against inflation would evolve into a national obsession and a basic factor in President Carter's turn toward austerity. Anti-inflation also served to justify economic policies that favored the wealthy.

The president's January 1978 State of the Union address outlined "a lean and tight" federal budget[36]—in accord with his new anti-inflation objective—which presented no significant initiatives aimed at generating employment, raising incomes, or alleviating poverty.[37] An analysis in the *Wall Street Journal* observed that "the budget destroys some old Carter campaign promises" of enhanced social spending and urban revitalization. The budget was bound to anger "Blacks and big city mayors."[38] Significantly, military spending had been exempted from austerity in the new budget. And in 1979, Carter would initiate substantial increases in military spending,[39] effectively diverting money from domestic social programs.

President Carter was not yet ready to advocate policies that deliberately depressed employment and living standards as a formal objective—though that would soon be coming. Carter often claimed that in introducing budgetary austerity, he had no choice, being constrained by circumstances beyond his control, most notably the vexing problem of inflation. The phrase "no alternative" appeared multiple times in his speeches. In a 1978 speech in Tennessee, for example, the president declared, "As President, I have no alternative except to bring inflation under control,"[40] with the strong implication that austerity was a severe but unavoidable solution to inflation.

In reality, however, there were always alternative policies available to the president. He could have substantially raised taxes for high-income brackets.[41] If it was necessary to reduce consumption as a means of controlling inflation, he could have achieved that through progressive taxation of those who were most able to afford it. As one economist stated the matter, "Fighting inflation means squeezing somebody."[42] Accordingly, the administration could have squeezed the affluent. Another option was to restrain inflation through reduced military spending, thus opting for butter over guns. Yet a third option would have been to allow prices to continue rising, on the assumption that the main effect of inflation was to redistribute income, at least somewhat attenuating the burdens on the less privileged.

These alternative courses of action were never attempted or even given serious consideration. The fight against inflation would in fact rely on austerity at the expense of "the average American." Carter liked to believe that he was forced into a policy of austerity, but this constituted a political choice, not a necessity. And for most people, the cure of austerity would prove far worse than the disease of inflation.

Carter's budgetary conservatism was associated with a much more generalized shift, initiated in 1978, in all policy areas. This shift was evident at both the executive and congressional levels. Congress produced a series of highly regressive tax reforms that raised payroll contributions for Social Security—effectively raising the tax burden on lower-income groups—while cutting taxes for investors. Despite reservations, Carter signed the legislation into law.[43] In describing the new tax cuts, *Barron's* was full of praise: "The Revenue Act of 1978 looms as a fiscal landmark. . . . Investors especially have benefitted tangibly with a less onerous capital gains level. . . . Corporations also have shared in the largesse. Besides enjoying a hefty tax cut, they have won more liberal depreciation rules." *Barron's* concluded that the it was "the best piece of tax legislation to come down the pike in a long while."[44] The president dropped the idea of universal health care as too inflationary, thus reneging on a campaign promise.[45] He made half-hearted efforts to create a new consumer protection agency, but this proposal was defeated in Congress due to strong corporate lobbying spearheaded by the Business Roundtable.[46] The interests of organized labor were largely ignored:[47] *Fortune* magazine reported "Seething Impotence in the Labor Camp," partly due to a lack of presidential support.[48]

The president's relationship with labor worsened in 1979, when he bailed out the failing Chrysler Corporation with federal loan guarantees; the bailout was conditioned on extensive layoffs combined with cuts in pay and benefits for those who remained. The Chrysler austerity program had a far-reaching impact on the entire automobile industry, as described by the labor historian Nelson Lichtenstein: "As the company slashed its payroll and closed many of its older urban factories, Chrysler employment dropped by 50 percent. Deunionization swept the auto parts sector while pattern bargaining among the Big Three domestic [auto] producers was broken for a decade."[49] These working-class setbacks might have been counteracted by federal programs aimed at raising wages and boosting employment levels, as had been proposed by the Black Caucus in early versions of the Humphrey-Hawkins bill, but the president firmly rejected this possibility. Austerity would soon be imposed on every level of the economy.

DEREGULATING AMERICA

> I'd love to see the Teamsters to be worse off. I'd love to see the automobile workers to be worse off.
>
> —ALFRED KAHN, FORMER WHITE HOUSE ADVISER
> AND DEREGULATION ADVOCATE[50]

In 1978, the Carter administration began large-scale deregulation of the economy, starting with air travel and later extending into other sectors. The initiative was spearheaded by Alfred Kahn, a Cornell University economics professor appointed to head the Civil Aeronautics Board (CAB). The airline industry had been heavily regulated since the establishment of the CAB in 1938 as part of the overall New Deal regulatory program.[51] The board allocated routes to specific airlines, restricting access to the aviation market while protecting existing airlines and their unionized workforces, thus boosting both wages and profits.

At first glance, the CAB seemed an easy target for reform, since it produced monopoly rents for vested interests while increasing airfares and limiting productivity. From the standpoint of market economics, it looked like a straightforward case for deregulation, one that was sure to produce long-term benefits for the public[52]—although this assumption proved a complete delusion, as we shall see. Deregulation was also viewed as a simple way to reduce consumer prices in specific sectors, thus alleviating inflation.[53]

It appears likely that deregulation also aimed to lower wages in regulated sectors and more generally as well. This objective was strongly implied in Kahn's public statements (including his earlier quote). And in a speech before a group of securities analysts in New York City, Kahn stated, "The necessary sharing of resultant benefits between employees and the providers of capital is somewhat out of proportion today"[54]—a delicate way of saying that wages were too high and had to be lowered. He displayed compassion for corporate executives and the regulatory challenges they faced. In a letter to one executive, Kahn lamented that "companies you work for . . . did terribly badly during the entire first half of this decade, when they were more tightly regulated than ever in their history."[55] At the same time, Kahn emphasized that he was a political liberal—"I have all my life strongly believed in unions"[56]—which no doubt made it easier to sell antiunion policies to the public. Deregulation proved to be the opening salvo in an extended campaign against the U.S. working class, setting the stage for the even more intense assault that would come during the presidency of Ronald Reagan.

The doctrine of deregulation began as a right-wing idea among Milton Friedman and other Mont Pèlerin economists, later popularized by business-funded think tanks.[57] Certainly, Friedman and his colleagues were delighted by the prospect of removing regulatory structures inherited from the New Deal. Airline deregulation offered an early opportunity to achieve this objective. By 1978, the idea had gained broad elite support, including from the American Enterprise Institute[58] and the National Association of Manufacturers (although specific airline companies—notably Delta and Eastern—remained opposed[59]). There was a growing realization that deregulation was good for business, at least for most businesses. In addition, prominent liberals including Ralph Nader endorsed the idea, thus climbing aboard the bandwagon.[60] President Carter himself had long favored deregulation as a policy objective, and on October 24, 1978, he signed into law the Airline Deregulation Act.[61] Consistent with the act, the Civil Aeronautics Board was gradually phased out, closing down altogether in 1985.

In the end, the whole project would prove a failure, at least in terms of lowering prices. After deregulation was implemented, airlines consolidated and then used monopoly power to raise ticket prices. The consolidation might have been blocked by vigorous antitrust enforcement from the Justice Department and Federal Trade Commission, but antitrust had gone out of fashion after 1970, based on the increasingly popular Mont Pèlerin doctrine that monopoly was not a serious problem in a deregulated economy.[62] The results were less than stellar. In a retrospective analysis, the Northwestern University economist Robert Gordon concluded, *"There was no change in the real price of airline travel* in the decades after the 1978 deregulation act."[63] On the other hand, deregulation proved much more effective in depressing wages in the airline industry, which fell significantly, setting a precedent for reducing wages across multiple industries.[64]

Whatever its actual effects, airline deregulation was celebrated as a major accomplishment for the Carter administration, winning bipartisan praise.[65] In light of his achievements, Kahn was rewarded with a new appointment as presidential adviser on wage and price stability, in effect becoming the leading figure in the administration dedicated to tackling inflation. And over the longer term, Kahn was hailed by business-funded think tanks as a hero of deregulation. The Cato Institute and the Mercatus Center have been especially effusive in their praise of Kahn.[66] The case of airlines generated further rounds of deregulation, notably in the trucking and rail transport sectors, which were deregulated in 1980.[67] In addition, oil prices were decontrolled as a means of achieving energy conservation through market mechanisms.[68] The deregulation of trucking had an especially pronounced effect in cutting wages and worsening working conditions. After deregulation, trucking became the "sweatshops on wheels," according to one study of the industry.[69]

Perhaps the most important instance of deregulation was the Monetary Control Act of 1980, which terminated New Deal restrictions on bank lending.[70] Most notably, the act effectively repealed Regulation Q, which had capped interest rates since 1933.[71] Thereafter, banks faced no federal restrictions on interest rates, and they raised bank service fees for consumers and small businesses. The act also exempted mortgages from state usury laws, raising rates for new homeowners, thus increasing the burden of debt.[72] It seems fair to conclude that the Monetary Control Act was "a gift to the banking community," as noted in one study.[73] The overall result of financial deregulation was a sustained expansion of credit in the economy. In time, college students would also become heavily indebted through a new model of higher education that would be based on debt, while creating new markets for creditors.[74]

The Monetary Control Act was long in the making. The Nixon administration had deregulated finance at the international level, with the move to floating exchange rates in 1973,[75] and in 1980, President Carter deregulated finance at the domestic level, thus building on Nixon's achievement. The result was a "financialized" U.S. economy, one that became gradually more and more geared toward speculative investments in the financial sector instead of long-term improvements in manufacturing. For investors, deregulation of finance proved highly advantageous, as it opened up profitable arenas of activity with relatively quick returns; and there was the unstated assumption of a federal bailout in the event that investments went badly, especially for institutions that were "too big to fail." For America's working classes, however, financialization would prove less positive, as it would wipe out whole classes of industry[76] as well as the high-paying jobs that industry had long provided.

PROPOSITION 13

Let us pause our discussion of the Carter presidency to consider the larger context. During the late 1970s, both political parties began moving right on economic policy. For Democrats, there was a tendency to remain liberal on social issues, such as environmentalism and women's rights—which distinguished them from Republicans—while adopting increasingly conservative stances on economics. Nowhere was this tendency more evident than in California, with the 1974 election of Jerry Brown as governor. Youthful and telegenic, Governor Brown combined a quirky, New Age style with an antigovernment rhetoric reminiscent of the libertarian right. Although he was a Democrat, Brown's economic conservatism was sufficiently authentic that he impressed William F. Buckley[77] as well as Brown's predecessor, Ronald Reagan. According to an analysis by the *American Conservative*, "Governor Brown was much more of a fiscal conservative than Governor Reagan. . . . In Brown's first year in office, Reagan's director of programs and policies joked that his old boss 'thinks Jerry Brown has gone too far to the right.'"[78] Brown reduced government spending so quickly that he accumulated a massive surplus in the state budget. Though Brown was proud of this surplus, it had the unintended effect of fueling one of the largest and most success-ful anti-tax movements in U.S. history.

The move toward tax cuts began in California during 1977–1978 with the advent of Proposition 13, which proposed a major reduction in property taxes combined with a state constitutional amendment requiring a supermajority of two thirds of the legislature to pass any tax increases; it also proposed restrictions on new taxation by localities. The tax cut was presented as a reasonable response to conditions of fiscal surplus created by Governor Brown.

The placing of Proposition 13 on the ballot was directed by Howard Jarvis and Paul Gann, longtime conservative activists. Their campaign was backed by small- and medium-size enterprises, especially owners of apartment buildings and rental properties. The Apartment Association of Los Angeles County played an instrumental role in supporting and financing the campaign; Jarvis himself had once worked as executive director for the group. Local chambers of commerce endorsed it.[79] The proposition was also endorsed by *Libertarian Review* and the associated libertarian movement—which was in turn funded by the substantial resources of the brothers Charles and David Koch, with their oil-based wealth.[80] And the ubiquitous Milton Friedman—now at the Hoover Institution in Palo Alto—argued in favor of the proposition based on his long-standing hostility toward government taxation.[81] It seems likely that in arguing for Proposition 13, Friedman was reflecting the views of corporate executives who had long backed his activities.

At the same time, at least some of California's elite business estab-lishment was initially cool toward Proposition 13, especially with regard to the proposed supermajority for approving any future tax increases. The proposition risked constraining the state's response to future fiscal crises, and this was viewed as excessively risky, even destabilizing.

From San Francisco, the Bank of America publicly opposed the measure.[82] Friedman was incensed by this opposition: "Any business that comes out against [Proposition 13] is absolutely insane. Business seems to have this inclination toward self-destruction."[83] Much of the California political establishment also opposed the tax cut, including even Governor Brown, despite his antigovernment rhetoric.[84]

When assessing the California antitax movement, one must consider the overarching political atmosphere, which was becoming hostile toward government programs in general—fueled at least in part by years of campaigning by business interests, as well as business-funded intellectuals at the American Enterprise Institute (AEI), Heritage Foundation, and Hoover Institution. And Proposition 13 advocates held a decisive advantage: They showcased a program to raise living standards, thus protecting citizens from growing economic insecurity—or at least they projected the appearance of doing these things. Their opponents on the left seemed to have no program at all, especially after the failure of the Humphrey-Hawkins full employment bill. For ordinary people, it seemed that only the right had answers.

On June 6, 1978, the proposition passed with support from 63 percent of voters, with high turnout. This decisive victory served to energize right-wing activists throughout the country.[85] Whatever reservations big business initially may have had about Proposition 13 evaporated after its triumphant passage. *Barron's* applauded California's "taxpayer revolt," which was the "brightest hope for the future."[86] Antitax legislation was strongly supported by the National Tax Limitation Committee, whose sponsors included current and former executives of the Ford Motor Company and Chase Manhattan Bank, and such nationally prominent conservatives as Clare Boothe Luce—associated with the Time-Life fortune—as well as M. Stanton Evans and General Albert Wedemeyer.[87]

In California, a series of new follow-up tax cuts were proposed as a "Spirit of 13" campaign in 1979. The president of Chevron Oil helped coordinate fundraising for the new campaign.[88] From Washington, Congressman Jack Kemp—with long-standing backing from the AEI and a wide range of business interests[89]—proposed substantial tax cuts at the federal level. *Forbes* pronounced Kemp's tax bill a "national version of Proposition 13."[90] Meanwhile, the American Conservative

Union sought to use the growing tax revolt "to broaden our base and increase our membership."[91] Apparently, conservatives had found a winning issue.

It is tempting to view these developments as indicators of a basic change in public opinion in favor of the free market right, but the evidence for that view is negative. In fact, public opinion polls through the end of the 1970s showed relatively stable support for government programs aimed at reducing poverty and economic inequality.[92] It appears that the change in public opinion during this period was confined to the specific issue of tax reduction, which seemed like an easy way to raise income levels in the short term in an era of weak macroeconomic performance combined with high unemployment,[93] and when the Democratic establishment presented no serious alternative programs to address these concerns.

Whatever the situation with the general public, business was clearly moving rightward with an accelerating momentum. Increasingly, executives began turning toward the unbridled free market viewpoints of the investment banker William Simon, who had previously served as Treasury secretary. Simon assumed a leadership role among business conservatives during this period, and his influence was enhanced in 1978 with the publication of his best-selling book, *A Time for Truth*. It was a conservative manifesto, advancing a familiar list of complaints: "The government in the United States had grown too big, too bureaucratic, too wasteful, and too expensive; taxes are too high; . . . and unreasonable regulation is stifling productivity."[94] The book attacked President Carter in hyperbolic language. With regard to his energy conservation program, "Carter proposed a strangling economic dictatorship . . . an 'energy police state.' "[95]

Despite his lack of nuance, Simon had many powerful admirers, who helped publicize *A Time for Truth*. The textile magnate Roger Milliken, oil prospector Henry Salvatori, and retired Chase Manhattan president George Champion all financed the book's promotion,[96] while John M. Olin of the Olin Corporation joined the promotional campaign.[97] Frank Shakespeare of RKO General contacted more than three thousand Republican activists and urged them to read the book.[98] The publication of *A Time for Truth* helped galvanize the laissez-faire right, especially within the corporate sector.

In retrospect, the year 1978 represented an inflection point for U.S. business.[99] By the end of the year, many previously moderate voices were ready to set aside their moderation in favor of a free market revolution. No matter how conservative President Carter's actual policies were becoming—no matter how far he leaned in favor of business—executives had simply lost confidence in the president's leadership, especially on the key issue of inflation. The business press offered withering criticism: *Business Week* condemned the President's "deep-rooted ineptitude," while *Forbes* pronounced him to be "almost totally ineffectual."[100] The *Wall Street Journal* denounced Carter's policies while urging executives to cease cooperation with the White House.[101]

The turn in U.S. business during this period was amply demonstrated by the character of corporate contributions during the run-up to the November 1978 congressional elections. While business donations in 1976 had been evenly split between Democrats and Republicans, these interests moved in a sharply Republican direction only two years later: By 1978, donations from business-funded political action committees were going 62 percent to Republican candidates and only 37 percent to Democrats.[102]

With this asymmetrical funding, right-wingers were in a position to make significant gains, especially in the Senate, where such liberal incumbents as Dick Clark of Iowa, Floyd Haskell of Colorado, William Hathaway of Maine, Thomas McIntyre of New Hampshire, and Wendell Anderson of Minnesota were defeated for reelection, reinforcing a conservative trend that was well under way. Given the political changes in Congress, there would now be less pressure on President Carter to veer away from the rightward course that he seemed determined to pursue.[103] And the mass defections of Carter's business supporters likely intimidated the president and thus accelerated his policy turn to the right.

A GROWING SENSE OF CRISIS

The year 1979 proved a crisis period for the Carter presidency, as accumulated stresses reached a heightened level of intensity. The issue of inflation had already become the overriding focus for the administration, yet this problem was steadily growing worse. The overthrow of

America's long-standing ally Shah Mohammad Reza Pahlavi of Iran generated turmoil throughout the Persian Gulf region and a substantial rise in worldwide oil prices. The spike in oil prices raised the overall rate of inflation, which reached double digits for the first time of the Carter presidency, with a yearly average of 11.3 percent. Inflation was generating tensions at both the domestic and international levels.

From the City of London, Euromarket traders were again speculating against the dollar, signaling a loss of confidence in U.S. leadership.[104] Traders disposed of their dollars in favor of stronger and less inflation-prone currencies. Repeated efforts to control speculation had failed. At one point, Treasury Secretary Michael Blumenthal publicly reassured financial markets that the fundamentals of the U.S. economy remained sound, but with no effect: "The speculators just laughed."[105] Another concern was the Kingdom of Saudi Arabia, whose government was one of the world's largest purchasers of U.S. Treasury bonds. The Saudis were considered a strong point in favor of stabilizing the dollar, but by the late 1970s, they were running out of patience. Saudi officials worried that inflation was driving down the value of their dollar-denominated assets, and in private meetings with Treasury personnel, they communicated growing frustration.[106]

Inflation was thus threatening the credibility of the dollar as the world's reserve currency and the overall credibility of U.S. power and prestige. The timing was inauspicious, coming so soon after America's defeat in Vietnam and its humiliating departure from Saigon. And now, at the end of the decade, American power was facing new military challenges, notably in the Persian Gulf. It seemed that the country's status as a superpower was under threat at both the military and economic levels. Clearly, something drastic had to be done. The record of evidence suggests that in the middle of 1979, President Carter resolved to engineer a recession—which would prove the worst downturn since the Great Depression, even worse than the mid-decade recession of 1973–1975. Austerity through recession would reduce inflation at the domestic level, while the reduced inflation that resulted from austerity would restore confidence in the dollar at the international level.

The president probably believed that a deepened austerity was the only option open to him, that he had no alternative, as he stated repeatedly. But once again, alternative policies could have been pursued: Carter could have terminated the dollar's role as the international reserve currency, an idea that had been under discussion since the beginning of the decade in the most mainstream policy circles.[107] Within the State Department, Under Secretary for Economic Affairs Richard Cooper apparently favored this option.[108] And among professional economists, there has long been a body of opinion that the advantages of having the dollar as the international currency have been overestimated.[109] Discarding the dollar's special international status would have reduced the pressures in favor of austerity, but Carter evidently rejected that possibility, opting instead for recession and elevated unemployment. From the Treasury Department, officials grimly contemplated the prospects for lowering living standards, immiserating large portions of the population. They also sought to coordinate U.S. austerity policies with other governments. According to one Treasury document, "Countries are going to have to work together . . . to obtain the public support required for what will be *very unpopular policies*."[110]

In orchestrating these "very unpopular policies," President Carter used the Federal Reserve as his chosen instrument. He sought to install an anti-inflation hawk as head of its Board of Governors, who could then begin the process of raising unemployment—putting people out of work. Initially, Carter considered offering the job to David Rockefeller of Chase Manhattan, given the man's enormous credibility in financial circles, but Rockefeller declined. With characteristic understatement, Rockefeller explained his refusal this way: "As a wealthy Republican with a well-known name, and a banker to boot, it would have been extremely difficult for me to make the case for tight monetary policy and sell it to a skeptical Congress and an angry public."[111]

In the end, Carter appointed Paul Volcker, a Rockefeller protégé.[112] Having worked at Chase Manhattan, the Treasury Department, and the New York Federal Reserve, Volcker, too, enjoyed credibility among elite financial circles. And being less known to the general public than Rockefeller was an asset for Volcker.[113] A nominal Democrat, Volcker was nonetheless highly conservative on economic matters.[114] His appointment offered hope that the president could repair his relationship with the financial community and quiet its growing chorus of criticism. On August 6, 1979, Volcker became chair of the Board of Governors of the Federal Reserve System, opening a new chapter in U.S. economic history.

President Carter would later seek to distance himself from Volcker's actual policies,[115] given their manifest unpopularity, insisting that the Fed was acting independently. In retrospect, however, it seems likely that Volcker was doing exactly what the president wanted him to do. This was confirmed by Carter's top domestic policy adviser, Stuart Eizenstat, who later wrote in the *Financial Times* that Carter "appointed Mr. Volcker to chair the Fed knowing full well what he planned."[116]

The appointment signaled a radical change in policy, a change that was immediately recognized by economists. One recalled, "I remember sitting in the lounge at the National Bureau of Economic Research that day [Volcker was appointed] when *everyone*, both economists friendly to and opposed to the Carter Administration, understood what had happened. . . . Carter had finally caved to Wall Street's demand for an aggressive attack on inflation without regard for the social costs."[117]

"MILTON FRIEDMAN HAS FINALLY WON!"

As Federal Reserve chair, Volcker proceeded to raise interest rates to extraordinary levels as a means of slowing economic growth and restraining inflation. The prime rate charged by banks reached over 15 percent in 1980, the highest since 1929.[118] The prime would reach even higher levels in the early months of the Reagan presidency. Federal Reserve policies reverberated internationally, often stunning world leaders. German Chancellor Helmut Schmidt stated that interest rates were the highest "since the birth of Christ."[119] The new interest rate policies had the predictable—and no doubt intended—effect of driving the U.S. economy into a deep recession, beginning in January 1980 and continuing until November 1982. Unemployment eventually reached a peak of 10.8 percent.

In a technical sense, the 1980–1982 downturn was not one recession but two. The initial phase extended over the first six months of 1980, followed by a year of very weak recovery; and then the second phase began in 1981, which continued for an additional sixteen months. But these two recessions can more appropriately be viewed as a singular, integrated event, the classic "double-dip" recession.[120] This extended recession had the effect of transforming the political economy. The reduced consumption associated with recession extinguished high inflation rates during the mid-1980s while permanently resetting the distribution of wealth and resources—in an upward direction.[121] The international value of the dollar was finally stabilized, securing U.S. financial leadership and the prestige associated with it. Volcker himself would become a hero in elite financial circles, the first true "celebrity" central banker.[122]

For much of the population, however, the results were less positive due to exceptionally high rates of unemployment and lowered living standards. By August 1980, the unemployment rate had reached 7.7 percent,[123] with Black unemployment at 14.6 percent.[124] And these figures do not include the large number of workers who faced growing underemployment through reduced hours and wages.[125] The feeling of hard times among working-class Americans was nicely captured by the folk singer Bruce Springsteen. In 1980, he sang "The River," a tale of austerity, with the following lyrics:

> I got a job working construction for the Johnstown Company.
> But lately there ain't been much work on account of the economy.
> Now, all them things that seemed so important,
> Well Mister, they vanished right into the air.[126]

In addition, the Fed's high interest rate policies triggered bankruptcies among small businesses and family farms, which were highly dependent on credit. A prominent economist once asked Volcker "how he thought monetary policy worked to crush inflation. His answer surprised me: By causing bankruptcies."[127] No one can say that Volcker's methods were gentle.

The grain belt of the Midwest was especially hard hit by the Fed's policies, producing waves of farm foreclosures that would continue well into the Reagan presidency, shrinking populations of agricultural areas and small towns.[128] There was also a spike in rates of mental illness and suicide resulting from harsh economic conditions.[129] In response, dispossessed farmers organized new political groups and militias that advocated white supremacy, anti-Semitism, and antigovernment violence. Researchers at the Southern Poverty Law Center and American Jewish Committee later expressed apprehension as they tracked the rising extremism that emanated from rural America.[130]

In the story of austerity, it is important to emphasize the central role of Milton Friedman. Though Friedman once again held no formal position, his ideas had a deep effect in shaping government policies in response to inflation. In 1974, at a Washington economic conference, Friedman had advocated austerity as a cure for rising price levels.[131] At that early point, few were willing to explicitly favor austerity in public, but Friedman had no such compunctions. And the end-of-decade recession was, in a sense, Friedman's crowning achievement, since it was predicated on his theory of monetarism, which emphasized strict control over the money supply as the key to controlling inflation.

On October 6, 1979, Volcker officially announced that the Fed would adopt monetarism as its guiding economic principle.[132] After this announcement, the Fed would no longer focus on setting interest rates, as it had done in the past, but would instead work to control the money supply; it would use its regulatory powers to rein in the creation of money.

With the Fed's move toward monetarism, Friedman's own theory became the basis for U.S. economic policy. It was final proof that Mont Pèlerin economics had moved from the margins of respectability to the very center—during a Democratic administration, no less. The head of the Boston branch of the Federal Reserve would later exclaim in a private meeting, "Milton Friedman has finally won!"[133] In practice, however, Friedman's monetarism never lived up to its billing. Federal Reserve Board member Nancy Teeters would later state, "It turned out that the money supply had nothing to do with inflation. . . . We did what they [the monetarists] suggested and nothing happened."[134]

The soundness of monetarist theory as a cure for inflation is thus open to question. But the main contribution of monetarism was not theoretical; it was political. It enabled the Board of Governors to adopt a fashionable economic doctrine, which diverted attention away from the high interest rates and reduced living standards it was orchestrating. As a result of monetarism, Volcker could disassociate himself from escalating interest rates—he claimed he was just managing the money supply—while his policies clearly *were* raising rates to the highest levels in recent history, thus immiserating large parts of the population. There was thus an element of deception in Volcker's method. And the new doctrine offered an additional advantage: Hardly anyone outside specialized economic circles understood monetarism, which served to confuse the public and thus protect the Fed from criticism.

According to former Council of Economic Advisers chair Charles Schultze, the Fed's move toward monetarism was "political cover," which "allowed them to do what they could never have done"—which was to deliver high interest rates and the deepest recession since the 1930s. Schultze added, "They could never have done what had to be done if it looked as if they were the ones raising interest rates." But with monetarism, "they could just say 'Who us?'"[135] Volcker would still have his moments of candor,[136] as when he stated before Congress that standards of living for average Americans would drop, but for the most part deception was the order of the day.

The politics of recession thus amounted to an extended exercise in evading accountability—in essence, passing the buck. President Carter could deny any responsibility for high interest rates and their damaging effects, since this was being directed by the Federal Reserve. In a 1980 campaign speech, Carter stated, "The Federal Reserve Bank . . . is an absolutely independent agency. Under law, the President has no influence over the decisions made by the Federal Reserve Board."[137] The president was passing the buck to Federal Reserve Chair Paul Volcker, indirectly blaming him for historically high interest rates. For his part, Volcker implied that he had no control over interest rates, since the Fed was now managing the money supply in accordance with Friedman's doctrine of monetarism, passing the buck to Friedman. In response, Friedman—who held no public office—complained that the Fed was not correctly using monetarism,[138] thus passing the buck back to Volcker. Clearly, no one wanted to accept responsibility; no one was accountable. In retrospect, the person most responsible for the harsh economic conditions of this period was the man who had appointed Volcker to the Fed in the first place: the president of the United States, Jimmy Carter.

THINGS FALL APART

During his last two years in office, Carter made feeble efforts to regain public support, delivering a series of speeches aimed at creating an atmosphere of self-sacrifice. In a major address of July 15, 1979, Carter admonished Americans to be less concerned with their own material well-being while criticizing those who "worship self-indulgence and consumption" and showed excessive interest in "owning things and consuming things." His main conclusion was clear: "There is simply no way to avoid sacrifice."[139] Carter was appealing to the public that they should accept reduced living standards in the interest of the greater good—but this was hardly a winning message. By 1980, an climate of gloom had pervaded White House staff, and this is reflected in the documentary record. One presidential aide lamented that "our whole approach seems to be to push the country into a recession." He added, "A recession may be a comforting thought to the same economists who run those econometric models, but it hardly makes the public stand up and cheer."[140]

Evidently, economic policy would not prove President Carter's strong suit. On the other hand, the president did benefit from the foreign policy crises of this period, at least initially. The turmoil of the Iranian Revolution worked in Carter's favor, creating a wave of patriotic support for the president; he was gaining from the "rally round the flag" effect familiar to political scientists and pollsters. In November 1979, Iranian crowds stormed the U.S. embassy in Tehran, taking as hostages more than fifty American citizens. And then in December, the Soviet Union invaded neighboring Afghanistan, adding to the atmosphere of crisis. In response to these perceived threats, Carter could present himself as a resolute leader, defending the national interest. In private, National Security Adviser Brzezinski took a measure of satisfaction in the Afghan invasion, since it "represented an opportunity for [Carter] to demonstrate his genuine toughness," as he later recounted in his memoirs.[141] By January 1980, Carter's approval rating had climbed to 58 percent, the highest point of his last two years in the White House.[142] *Time* magazine came out with a flattering image of Carter on its cover, under the title "Taking Charge."[143]

The president's positive appearance did not last long. In April 1980, Carter launched Operation Eagle Claw, in which Delta Force and Ranger commandos were airlifted into Iran to rescue the hostages, but the operation proved a disastrous failure.[144] Eight U.S. military personnel were killed, and no hostages were rescued. The Eagle Claw fiasco ended President Carter's brief appearance as an effective military leader. His approval ratings gradually sank back into negative territory as his presidency unraveled.

During 1979–1980, Carter saw his popularity decline with core Democratic constituencies that had helped elect him in the first place, including African Americans, Jews, and feminists.[145] A particularly noteworthy development was Carter's loss of support among evangelical Christians, who had long been some of his strongest backers. Carter's relatively liberal views on social issues—especially abortion rights—proved unacceptable to evangelicals,[146] and the New Right sensed an organizing opportunity. In the summer of 1979, the Virginia preacher Jerry Falwell and Heritage founder Paul Weyrich worked together to create the Moral Majority, an umbrella group for Christian conservatives across the country.[147] The Moral Majority and its affiliated organizations held mass rallies and voter registration drives to amplify their electoral clout.[148]

Falwell's political endeavors attracted substantial financial support. According to one account, "Texas oil billionaire Nelson Bunker Hunt had given millions to the Moral Majority. . . . [Other contributors included] life insurance moguls Arthur Williams and Art DeMoss, cotton magnate Bo Adams, and a wealthy Pennsylvania poultry farmer, Don Hershey."[149] The beer merchant Joseph Coors also provided funds, while the president of the American Security Council (representing weapons manufacturers) developed close ties to one of the Moral Majority's affiliated groups, the Religious Roundtable.[150] And the dense network of New Right activist groups—heavily interconnected with corporate interests—lent organizational support to Christian conservatives.

The ideology of the Moral Majority mixed religious fervor, social conservatism, and free market economics,[151] consistent with the emerging Republican doctrine of "fusionism," which aimed at building broad ideological coalitions. Christian conservatism had become a major force in American politics, serving as a bulwark for the Republican Party during the 1980 election and for many years afterward. The results were no doubt gratifying for New Right strategists such as Weyrich. For President Carter, however, the loss of evangelical support constituted yet another nail in the coffin for his faltering election plans.

ELECTION IN A TIME OF AUSTERITY

When looking back at Carter's record, it seems surprising that he even bothered to run for reelection given prevailing conditions. The past precedents could not have been comforting. The last time a president ran for reelection in the midst of a serious economic crisis was 1932, when Herbert Hoover went down to a humiliating defeat. Now, in 1980, it seemed that Carter would run as a reincarnation of Hoover—though as a Democrat. The historical irony of the situation was striking.

Even before the general election, Carter faced a challenge for the Democratic nomination from Senator Edward Kennedy, representing the party's liberal wing. He ran with the piquant phrase, "Put a real Democrat in the White House"[152]—with a clear implication that Carter was a Republican in disguise. Kennedy pointedly criticized Carter for cutting social programs, as well as his costly military buildup.[153] Running to the left of Carter, Senator Kennedy gained traction among blue-collar voters in hard-pressed areas, building multiracial coalitions that included Blacks, Hispanics, and whites. At the campaign's high point, Kennedy won the key primary of New York.[154] Surely, Carter did not want to become the first sitting president of the twentieth century who failed to receive endorsement from his own party, and he proceeded to use all the powers of incumbency and the machinery of the Democratic Party—which he now controlled—to defeat Kennedy's insurgency. And Kennedy made his share of missteps, sometimes appearing unprepared and inarticulate during interviews.[155] Overall, Kennedy's campaign constituted the only real pushback against Carter's austerity policies that emanated from the political left, but it was too little, too late. At the Democrats' August convention in New York's Madison Square Garden, Carter was able to secure his party's nomination to run against the Republican nominee, Ronald Reagan.

In the course of the general election campaign, Reagan would hammer away at the austere economic conditions, especially for working people. His most memorable television advertisement displayed an unemployed worker walking forlornly through an abandoned factory, expressing grief at the decline of U.S. industry. At one point, he asked, "If the Democrats are good for working people, how come so many people aren't working?"[156] Reagan also emphasized Carter's alleged failures in foreign policy,[157] while he cultivated Christian conservatives and pitched coded racial appeals to white voters, especially in the South.[158] But overwhelmingly, his campaign focused on the economy. At the level of personal style, Reagan projected a sunny, upbeat tone while relentlessly attacking Carter's record. And the Carter campaign had no effective response. Presidential aide Eizenstat later commented, "We never developed a coherent and positive strategy against Reagan, except stoking fear against him. . . . The Democratic strategy was largely negative."[159]

In the last presidential debate, on October 28, one week before the election, Reagan underscored Carter's failures, especially "unemployment lines" that were so long they could "reach from New York City to Los Angeles." And perhaps Reagan's most effective statement of the debate—and indeed of the whole campaign—was the following: "Next Tuesday all of you will go to the polls. . . . It might be well if you would ask yourself: Are you better off than you were four years ago? Is it easier for you to go and buy things in the stores than it was four years ago? Is there more or less unemployment in the country than there was four years ago?"[160]

In the end, Carter lost the election in a landslide, by a margin of almost 10 percent in the popular vote, prevailing in just six states and the District of Columbia.[161] Even in Carter's traditional stronghold of the South, he won only his home state of Georgia, losing everywhere else. In addition, Democrats sustained major losses in both houses of Congress, ceding control of the Senate for the first time since 1954. Carter's loss was indeed the worst electoral performance of any incumbent president since Herbert Hoover.

ASSESSING CARTER AS A HISTORICAL FIGURE

In recounting the presidency of Jimmy Carter, this chapter has presented an unflattering image. Now, I would like to acknowledge that Carter has had a more meritorious role after he left the presidency, achieving numerous accomplishments, including the Nobel Peace Prize in 2002. As ex-president, Carter has mediated international conflicts throughout the world, helping reduce the scale of violence. He played a leading role in international efforts to contain Guinea-worm disease, formerly a scourge of the rural populations in Africa and the Middle East; it is now virtually eradicated, at least partly due to Carter's efforts. I suspect that many readers' perceptions of Carter have been shaped by his postpresidency accomplishments rather than what he did in office.[162]

An especially notable achievement of ex-president Carter is that he declined to profit financially from his political career, breaking with the tradition of soft corruption that has been a temptation for many former presidents, both Democratic and Republican.[163] To gain some perspective on Carter's personal integrity, it is worth considering the postpresidency of Dwight D. Eisenhower, which was marred by conflicts of interests, as described by a *Wall Street Journal* reporter:

> In 1961 . . . President Eisenhower retired to a 576-acre farm near Gettysburg, Pennsylvania. The farm, smaller then, had been bought by General and Mrs. Eisenhower in 1950 for $24,000, but by 1960 it was worth about $1 million. Most of the difference represented the *gifts of Texas oil executives connected to Rockefeller oil interests.* The oilmen acquired surrounding land for Eisenhower under dummy names, filled it with livestock and big, modern barns, paid for extensive renovations to the Eisenhower house, and even wrote out checks to pay for hired help.[164]

As president, Eisenhower had been deferential toward the Rockefeller family and the oil sector more generally, and then he benefited from their gifts. In contrast, Carter chose to live modestly on his federal pension, without ethically questionable subventions from vested interests. When viewing Carter's career in its entirety, one has the image of a well-intentioned figure.

Despite all these positive qualities, Carter also must be judged on his presidential record. He played a crucial role in engineering policy shifts in favor of the wealthy at the expense of the less privileged. In later years, Carter may well have regretted many of his presidential decisions. In public statements in 2017, he lamented the "disparity in income," which had "harmed decent, hardworking, middle-class people."[165] It appears ironic that as president, Carter helped generate this disparity, however much he may have regretted it later. In the class war that defined the 1970s, the rich had won.

We have seen that America's march rightward occurred in distinct phases. The first commenced during the early 1970s, when President Nixon mobilized business interests to create a right-wing counter-establishment focused on the American Enterprise Institute and the Mont Pèlerin Society. Then, after Nixon left office, the business community itself would develop a vast infrastructure of right-wing think tanks, lobby groups, and educational institutions, thus advancing the doctrine of laissez-faire. While intellectuals such as Milton Friedman and Friedrich von Hayek furnished the brains behind this effort, wealthy interests financed the dissemination of their ideas, thus setting the stage for a later policy transformation. The Carter presidency constituted the final phase of this long rightward march when government policy moved in a free market direction and the ship of state finally turned decisively.[166] While Carter had only a single term as president, his essentially Friedmanite program would be eagerly taken up by his successor, Ronald Reagan. In the view of popular mythology, it was Reagan who engineered America's right turn toward market economics and wealth concentration, but in reality, Reagan merely expanded on a right-wing policy agenda that had commenced earlier—during the presidency of Jimmy Carter.

Conclusion

There's class warfare, all right, but it's my class, the rich class,
that's making war, and we're winning.
— WARREN BUFFETT

The United States experienced an extended episode of social, economic, and international crises in the 1970s, which were finally resolved during the presidency of Jimmy Carter. The end result of these crises was a redistribution of wealth and income favoring the wealthy classes, combined with renewed use of military power projection overseas. The decade produced a fundamental shift away from the regulated capitalism associated with the New Deal toward a new order of laissez-faire.

The main agent generating this shift was elite business interests, which used their resources to launch a sustained campaign of influence directed simultaneously at politicians, policy makers, and the general public. In undertaking this campaign, business executives were able to achieve a remarkable degree of consensus about the need for a rightward turn, thus setting aside disagreements that in the past had strained their unity and limited their capacity to act as a cohesive social class.

One of the main conclusions of this study is the importance of human choices in driving outcomes. Thus, such conservative activists as William Baroody, Paul Weyrich, Phyllis Schlafly, Jerry Falwell, Milton Friedman, and President Richard Nixon made clever strategic choices, and such cleverness aided them in achieving their goal of moving the United States in a rightward direction. Certainly, conservative efforts were aided by the large quantities of funding they received, generously provided by corporate executives. But by itself, corporate funding was not sufficient. In the end, the conservatives' careful strategizing—and their willingness to adjust tactics in response to changing circumstances, their capacity to recognize and correct operational errors—accounts in no small measure for their success. The decision of corporate conservatives to fund and forge an alliance with evangelical Christians counts as a special stroke of brilliance, one that broadened their base of support.

Most importantly, conservatives acted on a majoritarian strategy, termed "fusionism," which sought to persuade a majority of Americans to join their side. Their strategy was highly effective in ending the New Deal and shifting policy in a free market direction. And, as shown in chapter 5, the American style of free market capitalism soon became the international standard, transforming policy making at a global level (with largely negative results in terms of economic performance).

Another finding is the salience of academic researchers who worked for vested interests while holding faculty appointments at universities. They used their academic prestige to promote free market and militarist ideas through such organizations as the Mont Pèlerin Society and Committee on the Present Danger, thus conferring legitimacy to those ideas. Professors are often viewed as fiercely independent dissidents, hostile toward the corporate establishment—but the reality is altogether different. One is reminded of the 1979 Bob Dylan song, "Gotta Serve Somebody":

Well, it may be the devil, or it may be the Lord.
But you're gonna have to serve somebody.[1]

Even esteemed scholars will end up serving somebody, often somebody with a large quantity of money and a political agenda. In our story of wealth concentration, universities played a central role in advancing the interests of the rich and powerful at the expense of the working class.

America's plutocratic turn was further facilitated by the lack of any significant opposition. The AFL-CIO was more interested in fighting communism overseas than in organizing workers to oppose the right-wing agenda in the United States. And the numerous progressive groups that emerged during this period made no sustained effort to develop a mass base or work together for common purpose. On the political left, there was a tendency to fragment along the lines of gender, race, and sexual identity; leftists showed little interest in adjusting their activities in response to past failures. And, critically, no group on the American left—with the sole exception of the Congressional Black Caucus—presented a practical program of any consequence to raise living standards for working people. As we have seen, the Black Caucus did propose guaranteed full employment in the Humphrey-Hawkins bill, but it received no significant support from the Democratic establishment, progressive activists, or the AFL-CIO.[2] Overall, these groups could have acted with greater strategic focus and organizational unity, as the right was doing, but they chose not to.

Finally, I have emphasized the centrality of choices made by public officials and presidents of the era, most notably Jimmy Carter. As we have seen, officials had a range of options to deal with economic and foreign policy challenges of the era. In the end, they chose deregulation, fiscal austerity, and military buildup while disregarding alternatives. And in making these choices, officials ensured that the extended crises of the 1970s were resolved by reducing living standards for America's working classes to the benefit of the wealthy. By 1980, U.S. politics had been transformed. In this conclusion, I will briefly sketch the trajectory of how this transformation played out over the long term.

FROM CARTER TO REAGAN

On January 20, 1981, Ronald Reagan was inaugurated as America's fortieth president, beginning what was widely portrayed as a conservative revolution of dramatic proportions,[3] offering a sharp contrast to the supposed centrism of his Democratic predecessor, Carter. This portrayal is misleading. In reality, there was a broad continuity of conservative policy from Carter to Reagan, and the two administrations had much in common. Both relied heavily on Federal Reserve Chair Paul Volcker, who was appointed by Carter in 1979 and stayed on during the Reagan presidency. President Reagan was sufficiently impressed that he nominated Volcker to serve a second term, and Volcker continued in that role until 1987. Through both presidencies, Volcker orchestrated a policy of austerity as a means of controlling inflation, producing exceptionally high unemployment rates combined with wage compression.[4] By the end of 1982, unemployment had reached 10.8 percent,[5] the highest level since 1940. Both presidents quietly supported these austerity policies[6] despite the mass unemployment that resulted.

The austerity regime directed by Volcker played a major role in reducing working-class incomes, which never fully recovered. In addition, Reagan shared Carter's enthusiasm for cutting government benefits and social programs, especially for low-income groups.[7] Another commonality was tax policy: beginning in 1981, Reagan undertook a major restructuring of the federal tax system, with massive cuts for high-income earners.[8] In doing so, he was building on the tax program of 1978—signed into law by Carter—which had eased the capital gains tax, to the advantage of the very wealthy.[9] Overall, the rightward changes in domestic policy were the product of both presidents, not just Reagan.

One of Reagan's most decisive victories was his 1981 suppression of a strike by Professional Air Traffic Controllers Organization, the PATCO union. In response, Reagan took the extraordinary measure of firing thousands of controllers and replacing them with nonunion personnel, effectively breaking the strike and the union as well (it was soon dissolved). The destruction of PATCO has been retrospectively viewed by historians as a turning point in U.S. labor history, which transformed labor relations. After PATCO's defeat, companies were far more willing than before to deal ruthlessly with their labor forces, crushing strikes with greater intensity than was previously acceptable. Reagan's actions helped permanently weaken union power across a wide range of sectors, dealing yet another blow to the New Deal class compromise.[10] The rate of union membership saw a decline after the PATCO defeat, with the percentage of U.S. employees who were union members dropping from 19 percent in 1981 to 14 percent in 1991; and then dropping still further in later years.[11]

The breaking of PATCO was the culmination of a bipartisan campaign against labor begun in earnest under Carter, who had appointed such antiunion economists as Volcker and Alfred Kahn to key positions. As we have seen, some of Carter's most important policies—including deregulation of trucking, the bailout of the Chrysler Corporation, and the overall program of austerity—were extremely damaging to the interests of labor. Kahn openly acknowledged his antilabor views. And from his perch at the Federal Reserve, Volcker was pleased by Reagan's suppression of the air traffic controllers, as he revealed in a later interview: "The significance [of Reagan's suppression of PATCO] was that someone finally took on an aggressive, well-organized union and said no."[12] Again, we see continuity from Carter to Reagan.

At the level of foreign policy, Reagan continued the military expansion begun under Carter in 1979, which gradually progressed into the largest peacetime expansion in history at that time. When adjusted for inflation (to 2012 dollars), military spending increased from $359 billion in 1978 to $554 billion in 1986, accounting in that year for 6.6 percent of the gross domestic product.[13] The military presence in the Persian Gulf/Indian Ocean area, established for the first time on a large scale under President Carter with the Rapid Deployment Joint Task Force in 1980, was enhanced under Reagan. During Reagan's tenure, the task force evolved into the U.S. Central Command,[14] which would eventually become the most important of the military's overseas command centers. The military expansion of this period is often remembered as a Reagan-era buildup, but in reality, it was a Carter/Reagan buildup, with, once again, continuity from one president to the next.

With regard to economic impact, increased spending on military equipment drained money from social programs, thus accelerating the overall trend of austerity, to the detriment of citizens who depended on government transfer payments. At the same time, the improved circumstances for military contractors that resulted from raised spending presented opportunities for investors, who benefited handsomely, thus contributing to the concentration of wealth.[15] And the new atmosphere of nationalism that attended the more confrontational foreign policy of this period distracted from the process of wealth concentration and austerity.

Throughout history, external threats have often been used to forge social cohesion, especially in times of economic stress. At a fictional level, this was a major theme of George Orwell's great novel *1984*, in which continuous wars generated public passivity and compliance while anathematizing all dissent. And so, during the Carter/Reagan period, perceived threats from the Soviet Union helped frighten the American public into submitting to reduced living standards; they grimly accepted that such sacrifices were required "in the national interest" as a patriotic duty.

There were, of course, some obvious differences between the two presidents. Certainly, Reagan was more conservative on social issues, such as abortion rights, than Carter had ever been; and he was also less supportive of civil rights and racial equality. In some instances, Reagan sought to increase his popularity with white voters by stoking racial fears: in a 1981 interview, for example, he told the story of a "welfare queen"—with a strong implication that she was a Black welfare queen— who profited from government largesse at taxpayer expense.[16] In doing so, he offered a contrast with his Democratic predecessor, Carter, who had sought to reduce racial tensions. And Reagan displayed far less enthusiasm for environmental regulations than his predecessor. While he made no serious effort to repeal the body of environmental legislation that was already in place—lacking votes in Congress to make this possible—there was a concerted effort to reduce enforcement of these laws, especially by such strongly ideological figures as James Watt, who served as secretary of the Interior.[17] The array of solar panels that Carter had installed on the White House roof were pointedly dismantled under Reagan, while the federal budget for renewable energy development was reduced.[18]

Reagan's most visible innovation was to introduce a proudly ideological style of leadership, a conservative style, delivered with a tone of certitude. From the American Enterprise Institute, Herbert Stein explained Reagan's distinctive stylistic contribution to U.S. politics: "The new birth of confidence was especially great with the transition from Carter to Reagan. . . . Carter was exuding uncertainty, ineptitude, and diffidence. We had come to think that Carter was the national problem. . . . Reagan on the other hand represented clarity and self-confidence."[19] More than any other single factor, it was President Reagan's ideological style that created the fable that it was Reagan— rather than Carter—who had commenced the rightward thrust in federal policy. Fables aside, it was indeed Carter who commenced this rightward thrust.

President Reagan proved highly successful in an electoral sense. Certainly, the president benefited from ending the 1980–1982 double-dip recession, which was definitively completed by the time he ran for reelection. The acceleration of federal spending on weapons procurement associated with the overall military buildup, combined with tax cuts, produced a Keynesian-style growth spurt.[20] As a result of this short-term improvement in economic conditions, Reagan was well positioned for his reelection campaign. In addition, previously high rates of inflation had been reduced to just 3.2 percent in 1983, its lowest rate in more than a decade.[21] Due to declining inflation, the Federal Reserve reduced interest rates,[22] effectively putting an end to its austerity policy, accelerating growth still further and raising employment levels. During the 1984 campaign, Reagan ran on the memorable slogan, "It's morning again in America," as a metaphor for an upward swing in the business cycle, and this resonated with voters. The television advertisement associated with the slogan laid out the case for Reagan's reelection in straightforward terms: "Today, more men and women will go to work than ever before in our country's history. With interest rates at about half the record highs of 1980, nearly 2,000 families today will buy new homes. . . . Why would we ever want to return to where we were, less than four short years ago?"[23]

In the end, President Reagan easily beat his Democratic opponent, Walter Mondale, winning in forty-nine of fifty states while retaining a Republican majority in the Senate. The immense scale of Reagan's 1984 victory no doubt enhanced his political stature and hence his ability to sell the conservative agenda to Congress. Any remaining doubters about the desirability of the move rightward, whether Republican or Democratic, could be pushed aside and marginalized. However, we should not overstate Reagan's popularity, at least with the general public: his average approval rating—52.8 percent, according to the Gallup poll—was only one-tenth of a percentage point above the average for the thirteen presidents who had served since World War II, from Harry Truman to Donald Trump.[24]

The notion that the Reagan presidency was exceptionally popular is a myth. And Reagan's laissez-faire ideology was not especially popular either. Public opinion surveys show remarkably stable support for

New Deal–style social programs based on polls extending from the 1970s into the twenty-first century.[25] On the other hand, there is no doubt that laissez-faire became exceptionally popular among corporate executives, who were always Reagan's core constituency. One of the main conclusions of this study is that it was elite business interests, not the general public, that were the main forces driving the political changes of this period.

At the level of public policy, the events of late 1970s and early 1980s heralded a true realignment of U.S. politics toward a new order of free market economics, wealth inequality, and military power projection, endorsed to varying degrees by most mainstream politicians of the era. And this right-wing program would, in turn, evolve into the new center of American politics based on a recalibration of the whole ideological spectrum. While Carter began the process of policy realignment, it was Reagan who succeeded in cementing it as a long-term feature of the political landscape. Reaganism thus became the new normal.

WINNERS AND LOSERS

In the course of America's turn toward free market economics during the Carter and Reagan presidencies, the principal winner was America's wealthier classes. The wealthy certainly benefited from reductions in the rate of inflation—associated with Volcker's austerity program—which protected the value of their accumulated assets; their asset values had previously been declining in real terms due to inflation.[26] The stock market once again became a reliable investment, in the context of the "Reagan bull market,"[27] after recovering from a long period of stagnation.[28]

In addition, investors faced significantly lowered levels of taxation due to regressive changes to the federal tax code that began in 1978, further adding to their income and wealth. Finally, salaries and bonuses for top corporate executives grew prodigiously, at a rate unrelated to firm-level productivity,[29] with no serious efforts by governmental regulators or Congress to rein in this growth. The Justice Department made few attempts to restrain the formation of monopolies and oligopolies, which became widespread during the Reagan era and contributed to the concentration of wealth.[30] Evidently, the vast sums of money that wealthy individuals had invested in political influence campaigns—the main theme of this book—had been highly effective.

Given these trends, it should come as no surprise that there has been a dramatic concentration of resources in the United States, as presented in table C.1. The data tell a straightforward story. During the first phase, 1948–1968, America had only a moderate degree of income inequality; then, in a second phase, in the 1970s, inequality fell to an even lower level. Indeed, by 1978, top incomes had fallen to one of the lowest levels of the post–World War II era (as a percentage of total income). And then, during the last phase, after 1978, top earners realized remarkable gains: the richest 1 percent of Americans saw their income proportions more than double over the next thirty years. Meanwhile, the top 0.1 percent—the top thousandth of the population—almost quadrupled their share, gaining over 10 percent of aggregate income.

While the wealthy sustained impressive increases, working people lost ground. The average rate of worker compensation peaked in 1978 and then fell significantly in real terms through the 1980s and 1990s—despite the decline in inflation. The disinflation of the 1980s appears to

TABLE C.1

U.S. income distribution, 1948–2008, selected sates (as percentage of total national income)

Year	Received by top 1 percent (%)	Received by top 0.1 percent (%)
1948	12.2	4.1
1958	10.2	3.2
1968	11.2	4.0
1978	9.0	2.7
1988	15.5	6.8
1998	19.1	9.0
2008	21.0	10.4

Source: Data from Table S8.2 in "Technical Appendix" for *Capital in the 21st Century*," Thomas Piketty, *Capital in the 21st Century* (Cambridge, MA: Belknap Press of Harvard University Press, 2014), http://piketty.pse.ens.fr/files/capital21c/en/Piketty2014 FiguresTablesSuppLinks.pdf.

have had no positive impact on working-class incomes. Workers did not regain their 1978 level of compensation until 2001, twenty-three years later; and even after that date, compensation grew more slowly than during the class compromise of the earlier postwar period.[31] And significant subgroups saw even worse outcomes; their living standards were permanently reduced, with no recovery, even after decades of growth. Thus, the median full-time, year-round male worker earned $54,000 in 1977 (inflation adjusted); forty years later, in 2017, his average salary had declined to only $52,000.[32] Some segments of the working class saw such dramatic declines in living standards that their life expectancy declined as well, in what has been termed "deaths of despair."[33]

The right turn in economic policy had an especially pronounced impact on African Americans, especially after 1980. Since that year, there has been little progress in closing the "racial wage gap" between Blacks and whites, as described in a 2000 study published in the *American Economic Review*: "In 1940, Black men's weekly wages were 48.4 percent of white men's wages. By 1990, this number had increased to 75 percent—an improvement of 60 percent over five decades, although *the improvement from 1980 to 1990 has been stationary*."[34] In other words, the period of the class compromise saw considerable advancement in Black incomes and a gradual closing of the racial wage gap—up to the year 1980, when advancements effectively ended. Later studies show that during the twenty-first century, the Black-white wage gap has increased, deepening the racial divide.[35]

In summary, following the crisis period of the 1970s, America experienced an extraordinary redistribution of resources, tilted in favor of the wealthiest at the expense of the lower income groups. And once this redistribution had been established, there would be no turning back. In the story of America's distribution of income and wealth, the late 1970s appears once again as a historical turning point toward a degree of wealth concentration that was reminiscent of the pre–New Deal period or, perhaps, the Robber Baron era of the late nineteenth century.

CLASS WARFARE AFTER REAGAN

After 1992, President William Clinton played an important role in establishing the durability of America's rightward shift, ensuring that it was not an aberration and that it was fully bipartisan. Clinton's historic role was parallel to that of Dwight D. Eisenhower in an earlier era: just as President Eisenhower confirmed the legitimacy of the New Deal, Clinton confirmed that the New Deal had definitively ended. Thus, it was President Clinton who restricted government transfer payments to indigent families, promising to "end welfare as we know it,"[36] in a major shift away from the Democrats' traditional support for the social safety net. And then, Clinton presided over effective repeal of the 1933 Banking Act, the Glass-Steagall Act, breaking with the New Deal system of bank regulation while invigorating the financial sector.[37] He was a strong supporter of the Democratic Leadership Council, which sought to institutionalize the party's right turn. In his 1996 State of the Union address, the president declared that "the era of big government is over."[38] So was the New Deal.

One of Clinton's top economic advisers was Lawrence Summers, an admirer of Milton Friedman—who had once represented economic thinking among the far-right wing of the Republican Party, the Barry Goldwater wing. Now, it seemed that both parties embraced Goldwater-style economics. Summers later wrote that "any honest Democrat will admit that we are now all Friedmanites."[39] And Summers frankly endorsed the growth of inequality as a positive development: "One of the reasons that inequality has probably gone up in our society is that people are being treated closer to the way they're supposed to be treated."[40] The Democratic establishment was sufficiently impressed by Summers that he was promoted to serve as Treasury secretary under Clinton and then as chairman of President Barack Obama's National Economic Council. For his part, Obama declared his policies were so mainstream that "in the 1980s, I would be considered a moderate Republican."[41] The process of wealth concentration continued to march forward.

In 2011, the Columbia University economist Joseph Stiglitz observed that U.S. politics had become government "of the 1 percent, by the 1 percent, for the 1 percent."[42] And this was during a Democratic presidency. At the electoral level, Democrats largely abandoned working-class voters—their traditional base—and did so openly. In 2016, the Democratic leader in the Senate, Charles Schumer, declared, "For every blue-collar Democrat we lose in western Pennsylvania, we will pick up two moderate Republicans in the suburbs in Philadelphia."[43]

The party was cultivating a new, more affluent voting base. Consistent with the values of their upscale base, Democrats developed an obsession with elite higher education, which is underscored by their nominations: from 1988 through 2016, every Democratic presidential nominee held a degree from either Harvard or Yale. But, as Stiglitz noted, the true base of both parties remains the very highest income bracket—the top 1 percent.[44] The Democrats still remain less enthusiastic about promoting inequality than their Republican counterparts,[45] but the difference is one of degree. Both parties had shifted radically rightward on economic policy, and that shift proved to be long lasting. If we date the post–New Deal realignment from 1980, we would see that realignment has already endured more than four decades.

One might imagine that such conditions of entrenched inequality would produce an opening for the political left, working outside the Democratic establishment. However, progressive groups have been hobbled by a jargon-ridden vocabulary, which speaks to the highly educated but holds little appeal for working people.[46] The jargony style projects an image of exclusivity. There is a long-standing tradition that political communication should be as clear and direct as possible—exemplified by such models of clarity as George Orwell and Noam Chomsky—but the American left has turned away from that tradition. As a result of these limitations, the left has failed to develop a working-class base on any significant scale. A 2018 survey found that citizens who held the most left-wing viewpoints (8 percent of the total population) had the highest incomes and educational levels of any ideological grouping.[47] Once again, I emphasize the element of choice: progressive activists have chosen to use inaccessible language and an exclusionary style, implicitly accepting the limitations that this language and style place on their effectiveness.

The political right, in contrast, has been highly effective in building a working-class base, especially through the manipulation of religion and "morality" issues, as well as appeals to racism. And they speak in simple, clear language that is readily accessible to a mass audience—while advancing policies that favor the highest income groups. The 2016 election of Donald Trump was certainly a startling development, which may herald a new realignment. Indeed, the economist Thomas Piketty writes, "In 2016, *for the first time in the history of the United States,* we find that the Democratic Party won more votes among the top 10 percent of U.S. earners than the Republican Party."[48] Trump, in contrast, presented himself as an antielitist man of the people. And yet, after the election, President Trump continued the Republican tradition of favoring the very rich despite his populist pretentions.[49] In sum, the most remarkable feature about America's turn toward Friedmanite economics is how durable this turn has been.

Could there be a democratic reversal of U.S. plutocracy, of government "by the 1 percent"? Reversing this trend would require a popular movement of vast size, including reinvigoration of labor activism,[50] with at least the potential of acquiring majority support. The impediments to forming such a movement would be formidable, including opposition by a corporate-funded right wing, as well as racial tensions that have long divided America's working class.[51] And to be effective, the movement would need to be more enduring than Senator Bernie Sanders's recent presidential campaigns. Despite all the obstacles, popular rebellions have emerged throughout history, often unexpectedly, and there is nothing in principle to preclude such a rebellion from emerging in twenty-first century America. Politics always involves choices, including personal choices, and the public still retains the option of using its power of numbers to demand social change.

Acknowledgments

Writing this book has been an intellectual departure for me, since in the past I have focused on topics outside U.S. borders, with previous books on the Democratic Republic of the Congo and the former Yugoslavia, as well as many articles on Afghanistan. However, I have always intended to gain a better understanding of my own country, and this volume is the result. In preparing for this topic, I was aided by having studied with Leo Ribuffo as an undergraduate at George Washington University, and then with Walter Dean Burnham and Thomas Ferguson as a graduate student in political science at MIT. Another influential figure during my early career has been Benjamin Page of Northwestern, who helped publish my first book. And I also would like to thank Noam Chomsky, who has long influenced my thinking from my time at MIT and is now an academic colleague at the University of Arizona, where he has relocated. All these figures helped disabuse me of the idea that American politics is inherently tedious and uninteresting.

In explaining America's rightward shift, the principal actors were elite corporate interests and right-wing intellectuals who served them; they collectively orchestrated the policy turn of the 1970s. But I also emphasize failures of the political left during this period, especially its ineffectiveness in countering the business-led mobilization. In addition, my book is critical of the libertarian movement, which aided the overall rightward turn. I offer these criticisms with mixed feelings, as I have come to respect some aspects of libertarians' thinking, especially their uncompromising defense of free expression and (more recently) anti-interventionist views on foreign policy. In many respects, libertarians have become the most stalwart defenders of free speech and antiwar positions. I have published articles in libertarian venues, and a positive review of my previous book has appeared on the website of the Cato Institute.[1] However, facts are facts, and I have no interest in whitewashing the compromised history of libertarianism, including its close association with powerful donors such as Charles and David Koch, whose interests libertarians often served.

I thank the following persons, both academics and nonacademics, who read chapters and provided various kinds of assistance during the course of research and writing: Noam Chomsky, Ronald Cox, Galina de Roeck, Patrick Diehl, William Gaston, Merryl Gibbs, Vilja Hulden, Edward Miller, James Nolt, Peter Ore, Jami Parrish, Henrik Petersen, Betts Putnam-Hidalgo, Claudia Riche, Paul Riche, Nathan Rix, Michael Schaller, Kathleen Schwartzman, Ragini Srinivasan, Latha Varadarjan, Jeremy Vetter, Douglas Weiner, David Wilkins, Shelly Wilkins, and Albert Woodward. And special thanks to my wife Diana Rix, who read the manuscript multiple times and has been my best critic.

It has been a pleasure to work with Stephen Wesley, my editor at Columbia University Press. Financial support was provided by the Gerald R. Ford Foundation, Earl H. Carroll Magellan Circle, and Social and Behavioral Sciences Research Institute of the University of Arizona. My participation in the multiyear Sawyer Seminar, "Neoliberalism at the Neopopulist Crossroads," funded by the Mellon Foundation, helped develop my ideas. Small portions of this book pertaining to religion and U.S. politics appeared as a chapter in Leerom Medovoi and Elizabeth Bentley, eds., *Religion, Secularism, and Political Belonging* (Durham, NC: Duke University Press, 2021).

This book is dedicated to my late mother, Sybil Rhoda Gibbs, who grew up in an era when being Jewish did not mean you were affluent or even particularly well educated. She was proud of her blue-collar background and her rough Bronx accent. Some of my earliest memories are of my mother telling me about her experiences during the Great Depression, as well as her appreciation for Franklin Delano Roosevelt's

New Deal. Recalling these early conversations has helped me realize how much working people have lost due to the business assault against the New Deal, which began during the 1970s. My mother connected me with an earlier era of American history, now long disappeared, when the political left was based on the working class rather than the highly educated.

Notes

INTRODUCTION

1. Data are for compensation (wages and benefits) of production/nonsupervisory workers in the private sector and net productivity of the total economy. "Net productivity" is the growth of output of goods and services less depreciation per hour worked. Compensation is calculated in terms of hourly compensation (including wages and benefits) for "production/nonsupervisory workers." For further discussion of this issue, see Michael Brill et al., "Understanding the Labor Productivity and Compensation Gap," *BLS Beyond the Numbers* 6, no. 6 (June 2017), https://www.bls.gov/opub/btn/volume-6/pdf/understanding-the-labor -productivity-and-compensation-gap.pdf; and Organisation for Economic Co-operation and Development, "Decoupling of Wages from Productivity: What Implications for Public Policy," in *OECD Economic Outlook 2018, Issue 2* (Paris: OECD, 2018), https://www.oecd.org/economy/outlook/Decoupling-of-wages-from -productivity-november-2018-OECD-economic-outlook-chapter.pdf.

2. Thomas Piketty, *Capital in the Twenty-First Century* (Cambridge, MA: Harvard/Belknap, 2014).

3. On polling, see Thomas Ferguson and Joel Rogers, "The Myth of America's Turn to the Right," *The Atlantic*, May 1986; and Benjamin I. Page and Lawrence R. Jacobs, *Class War: What Americans Really Think About Economic Inequality* (Chicago: University of Chicago, 2009).

4. John Carson-Parker, "The Options Ahead for the Debt Economy," *Business Week*, October 12, 1974.

5. I have borrowed this phrase from Mike Lofgren, "The Revolt of the Rich: Our Financial Elites Are the New Secessionists," *American Conservative*, August 27, 2012.

6. Regarding weak rates of productivity growth during the 1970s, see Bureau of Labor Statistics, "Productivity Change in the Nonfarm Business Sector, 1947 Q1 to 2023 Q1," accessed November 20, 2023, https://www.bls.gov/productivity /images/pfei.png.

7. Bruce J. Schulman, *The Seventies: The Great Shift in American Culture, Society, and Politics* (Cambridge, MA: Da Capo, 2001), 131. The literature on politics of the 1970s is considerable, though it tends to downplay the revolt of the rich as a driving factor, in contrast with the present study. See Thomas Borstelmann, *The 1970s: A New Global History from Civil Rights to Economic Inequality* (Princeton, NJ: Princeton University Press, 2012); Jefferson Cowie, *Stayin' Alive: The 1970s and the Last Days of the Working Class* (New York: New Press, 2010); Peter N. Carroll, *It Seemed Like Nothing Happened: America in the 1970s* (New Brunswick, NJ: Rutgers University Press, 1990); Laura Kalman, *Right Star Rising: A New Politics, 1974–1980* (New York: Norton: 2010); Edward D. Berkowitz, *Something Happened: A Political and Cultural Overview of the Seventies* (New York: Columbia University Press, 2006); Rick Perlstein, *Nixonland: The Rise of a President and the Fracturing of America* (New York: Scribner, 2008); Perlstein, *Reaganland: America's Right Turn, 1976–1980* (New York: Simon & Schuster, 2020); Meg Jacobs, *Panic at the Pump: The Energy Crisis and the Transformation of American Politics in the 1970s* (New York: Hill & Wang, 2016); Dominic Sandbrook, *Mad as Hell: The Crisis of the 1970s and the Rise of the Populist Right* (New York: Knopf, 2011); David Frum, *How We Got Here: The 70s—The Decade That Brought You Modern Life, for Better or Worse* (New York: Basic Books, 2000); and Judith Stein, *Pivotal Decade: How the United States Traded Factories for Finance in the Seventies* (New Haven, CT: Yale University Press, 2010).

8. Some commentators claimed that inflation had an especially severe impact on low-income groups. Jimmy Carter, "Atlanta Georgia, Remarks Accepting the Martin Luther King Jr. Nonviolent Peace Prize," January 14, 1979, in American Presidency Project, ed. Gerhard Peters and John T. Woolley (University of California, Santa Barbara), https://www.presidency.ucsb.edu/documents/atlanta -georgia-remarks-accepting-the-martin-luther-king-jr-nonviolent-peace-prize.

9. Herbert Stein, *Presidential Economics: The Making of Economic Policy from Roosevelt to Clinton* (Washington, DC: American Enterprise Institute for Public Policy Research, 1994), 219.

10. Edward N. Wolff, "The Distributional Effects of the 1969–1975 Inflation on Holdings of Household Wealth in the United States," *Review of Income and Wealth* 25, no. 2 (1979); Joseph J. Minarik, "The Size Distribution of Income During Inflation," *Review of Income and Wealth* 25, no. 4 (1979). In making his points about inflation, noted earlier, Herbert Stein references Minarik's research.

11. See data from table S8.2 in Piketty, "Technical Appendix of the Book *Capital in the 21st Century*," accessed November 20, 2023, http://piketty.pse.ens.fr/files /capital21c/en/Piketty2014FiguresTablesSuppLinks.pdf.

12. Martin Feldstein, Lawrence Summers, and Michael Wachter, "Is the Rate of Profit Falling?" *Brookings Papers on Economic Activity*, no. 1 (1977): 211–28.

13. Philip Jenkins, *Decade of Nightmares: The End of the Sixties and the Making of Eighties America* (New York: Oxford University Press, 2006), 173. On the foreign policy aspects of the 1970s, see also Daniel J. Sargent, *A Superpower Transformed: The Remaking of American Foreign Relations in the 1970s* (New York: Oxford University Press, 2015).

14. For example, Sargent, *A Superpower Transformed*, 108.

15. Data on inequality show a very rapid rise beginning in 1980, sustained over time. See U.S. Census Bureau, "Change in Income Inequality for Families: Percent Change in the Gini Coefficient Relative to 1967," 1948–1999, accessed November 20, 2023, https://www2.census.gov/programs-surveys/demo/visualizations/p60/204/fig1.gif.

16. Quote from Jared Bernstein, " 'Democracy in America?' An Interview with Authors Ben Page and Martin Gilens," *Washington Post*, January 23, 2018. These themes are further developed in Benjamin I. Page and Martin Gilens, *Democracy in America: What Went Wrong and What We Can Do About It* (Chicago: University of Chicago Press, 2017); and Benjamin I. Page, Jason Seawright, and Mathew J. Lacombe, *Billionaires and Stealth Politics* (Chicago: University of Chicago Press, 2019). For theoretical models of elite dominance, see Randall Bartlett, *Economic Foundations of Political Power* (New York: Free Press, 1973); and Thomas Ferguson, *The Investment Theory of Party Competition and the Logic of Money-Driven Political Systems* (Chicago: University of Chicago Press, 1995).

17. The term "deep lobbying" appears to have been first used in William Greider, *Who Will Tell the People: The Betrayal of American Democracy* (New York: Simon & Schuster, 2010), 42–45. Greider uses this term in a way that differs from the definition used in this book.

18. Dietrich Rueschemeyer, "Why and How Ideas Matter," in *Oxford Handbook of Contextual Political Analysis* (New York: Oxford University Press, 2006), ed. Robert E. Goodin and Charles Tilley; Richard M. Weaver, *Ideas Have Consequences* (Chicago: University of Chicago Press, 2013).

19. Friedman himself celebrated the idea that the wealthy would finance the production of ideas: "In capitalist society, it is only necessary to convince a few wealthy people to get funds to launch any idea, however strange." Milton Friedman, *Capitalism and Freedom* (Chicago: University of Chicago Press, 2002), 17.

20. The closest that Friedman came to any official government position was his service on a presidential commission that ultimately recommended for the abolition of mandatory military conscription, which led to the creation of an all-volunteer military in 1973. Bernard Rostker, *I Want You! The Evolution of the All-Volunteer Force* (Santa Monica, CA: Rand, 2006), 66, 748–49. During the 1930s and 1940s, Friedman held a number of relatively low-level jobs in the federal government. See Alan S. Blinder, *A Monetary and Fiscal History of the United States, 1961–2021* (Princeton, NJ: Princeton University Press, 2022), 40.

21. Friedman's most notable academic achievement, in my view, remains Milton Friedman and Anna Jacobson Schwartz, *A Monetary History of the United States: 1867–1960* (Princeton, NJ: Princeton University Press, 1963).

22. On the MPS movement and the business role in building up the right wing, see Philip Mirowski and Dieter Plehwe, eds., *The Road from Mont Pèlerin: The Making of a Neoliberal Thought Collective* (Cambridge, MA: Harvard University Press, 2009); G. William Domhoff, *The Myth of Liberal Ascendancy: Corporate Dominance from the Great Depression to the Great Recession* (Boulder, CO: Paradigm, 2013); Angus Burgin, *The Great Persuasion: Reinventing Free Markets Since the Depression* (Cambridge, MA; Harvard University Press, 2012); Quinn Slobodian, *Globalists: The End of Empire and the Birth of Neoliberalism* (Cambridge, MA: Harvard University Press, 2018); Jamie Peck, *Constructions of Neoliberal Reason* (New York: Oxford University Press, 2013); Kim Phillips-Fein, *Invisible Hands: The Businessmen's Crusade Against the New Deal* (New York: Norton, 2009); Jane Mayer, *Dark Money: The Hidden History of the Billionaires Behind the Rise of the New Right* (New York: Anchor, 2017); Nancy MacLean, *Democracy in Chains: The Deep History of the Radical Right's Stealth Plan for America* (New York: Viking, 2017); Donald T. Crichlow, *The Conservative Ascendancy: How the GOP Right Made Political History* (Cambridge, MA: Harvard University Press, 2007); Daniel Stedman Jones, *Masters of the Universe: Hayek, Friedman, and the Birth of Neoliberal Politics* (Princeton, NJ: Princeton University Press, 2012); and Jennifer Burns, *Goddess of the Market: Ayn Rand and the American Right* (New York: Oxford University Press, 2011).

23. Nancy MacLean, "How Milton Friedman Exploited White Supremacy to Privatize Education" (working paper, Institute for New Economic Thinking, New York, September 2021), https://www.ineteconomics.org/research/research-papers/how-milton-friedman-exploited-white-supremacy-to-privatize-education.

24. Max Weber, "The Meaning of Ethical Neutrality in Sociology and Economics," in *The Methodology of the Social Sciences*, ed. E. A. Shils and H. A. Finch (New York: Free Press, 1949), 9. Another vested interest with long-standing ties to academia is intelligence services, most notably the Central Intelligence Agency, which has a tradition of employing academics. See David N. Gibbs, "Academics and Spies: The Silence That Roars," *Los Angeles Times*, January 28, 2001.

25. Upton Sinclair, *The Goosestep: A Study of American Education* (Whitefish, MT: Kessinger, 2004. For a more recent debunking of the "radical" professor, see also Russell Jacoby, *The Last Intellectuals: American Culture in the Age of Academe* (New York: Basic Books, 2000). The Sinclair study was originally published in 1923.

26. In 1928, a member of Harvard's Board of Overseers wrote to Thomas Lamont, a partner in J. P. Morgan and Company, asking Lamont for input. "The following appointments in the Department of Economics at Harvard will come before the Overseers at the next meeting. . . . I shall be glad to know *if these meet with your approval.*" Several job candidates were listed. Lamont wrote back: "I approve of all these names if you do." Letter from James H. Perkins to Thomas Lamont, June 4, 1928; and letter from Lamont to Perkins, June 5, 1928; emphasis added. Both letters in Thomas W. Lamont Papers, box 264, folder 32, Baker Library, Harvard Business School.

27. Dwight D. Eisenhower, "Farewell Address," January 17, 1961, Eisenhower Presidential Library, https://www.eisenhowerlibrary.gov/sites/default/files/research/online-documents/farewell-address/1961-01-17-press-release.pdf. Note that prior to becoming president, Eisenhower had briefly served as president of Columbia University. On the overall influence of the military, see the classic study by C. Wright Mills, *The Power Elite* (New York: Oxford University Press, 2000), chaps. 8, 9.

28. The influence of the Kochs has extended to my own institution, the University of Arizona, where the Center for the Philosophy of Freedom has become heavily subsidized by a series of wealthy and overtly right-wing figures, including Charles Koch. See Tim Vanderpool, "Freedom from Regulation: The Koch Brothers Pump Money Into a New UA Center," *Tucson Weekly*, May 5, 2011.

29. Jagdish Bhagwati quoted and paraphrased in Liza Featherstone and Doug Henwood, "Clothes Encounters: Activists and Economists Clash Over Sweatshops," *Lingua Franca*, March 2001.

30. Paul Krugman, "The 1 Percent's Solution," *New York Times*, April 25, 2013.

31. Elizabeth Popp Berman, *Thinking Like an Economist: How Efficiency Replaced Equality in Public Policy* (Princeton, NJ: Princeton University Press, 2022).

32. Sabastian Mallaby, *The Man Who Knew: The Life and Times of Alan Greenspan* (New York: Penguin, 2016), 131.

33. Sun Tzu, *The Art of War* (New York: Columbia University Press, 2009); and Carl von Clausewitz, *On War* (Princeton, NJ: Princeton University Press, 1989).

Regarding the influence of military classics on business executives, see Albert Madansky, "Is War a Business Paradigm? A Literature Review," *Journal of Private Equity* 8, no. 3 (2005).

34. The use of crises as strategic opportunities to impose conservative agendas is explored in Naomi Klein, *The Shock Doctrine: The Rise of Disaster Capitalism* (New York: Picador, 2007).

35. On the concept of "class compromise" in the advanced industrialized countries, see Adam Przeworski and Michael Wallerstein, "The Structure of Class Conflict in Democratic Capitalist States," *American Political Science Review* 76, no. 2 (1982).

1. THE RICH ACCEPT A COMPROMISE

The epigraph is from Henry A. Wallace, "The Century of the Common Man," speech at the Commodore Hotel, New York City, May 8, 1942, in American Rhetoric Online Speeches, https://www.americanrhetoric.com/speeches/henry wallacefreeworldassoc.htm.

1. Claudia Goldin and Robert Margo, "The Great Compression: The Wage Structure of the United States at Mid-Century," *Quarterly Journal of Economics* 107, no. 1 (1992).

2. President Franklin Delano Roosevelt, "State of the Union Message to Congress," January 11, 1944, in American Presidency Project, Gerhard Peters and John T. Woolley, eds., University of California, Santa Barbara, https://www .presidency.ucsb.edu/documents/state-the-union-message-congress.

3. John Maynard Keynes, *The General Theory of Employment, Interest, and Money* (New York: Harcourt, Brace, 1936).

4. Perhaps the best characterization of Roosevelt's presidency was "a careerist on the people's side, but working to wrangle some concessions from the powers that be." From Lincoln Steffens, *The Autobiography of Lincoln Steffens* (New York: Harcourt, Brace, 1958), 514. On business support for the New Deal, see Thomas Ferguson, "From Normalcy to New Deal: Industrial Structure, Party Competition, and American Public Policy During the New Deal," *International Organization* 38, no. 1 (1984).

5. Roosevelt, "State of the Union Message to Congress," January 11, 1944.

6. Dewey's views on full employment were noted in Claude Pepper, "Sixty Million Jobs, Pro and Con," *New York Times*, September 9, 1945.

7. On the economic effects of wartime military spending and fears of postwar stagnation, see "Richard M. Bissell, Jr: Oral History Interview, July 9, 1971," sec. 12, Harry S. Truman Presidential Library, https://www.trumanlibrary.gov/library /oral-histories/bissellr. On the unique historical circumstances that made

the New Deal possible, see Jefferson Cowie, *The Great Exception: The New Deal and the Limits of American Politics* (Princeton, NJ: Princeton University Press, 2016).

8. Robert J. Gordon, *The Rise and Fall of American Growth: The U.S. Standard of Living Since the Civil War* (Princeton, NJ: Princeton University Press, 2016), 547.

9. U.S. Congress, *Full Employment Act of 1945: Hearings Before the Committee on Expenditures in the Executive Departments* (Washington, DC: U.S. Government Printing Office, 1945); and Henry A. Wallace, *The Price of Vision: The Diary of Henry A. Wallace, 1942–1946* (Boston: Houghton Mifflin, 1973), 404.

10. See retrospective analysis by Senator Paul H. Douglas, "Evaluating the Employment Act," *Challenge* 12, no. 1 (1963).

11. Gerald Mayer, "Union Membership Trends in the United States" (CRS Report for Congress, Congressional Research Service, Washington, DC, August 31, 2004), 22, https://sgp.fas.org/crs/misc/RL32553.pdf. The number refers to "Percent of Nonagricultural Workers" in Appendix A.

12. Michael Honey, "Operation Dixie: Labor and Civil Rights in the Postwar South," *Mississippi Quarterly* 45, no. 4 (1992); and Ken Fones-Wolf and Elizabeth A. Fones-Wolf, *Struggle for the Soul of the South: White Evangelical Protestants and Operation Dixie* (Urbana: University of Illinois Press, 2015).

13. The long-standing role of racism in impeding class solidarity in the United States forms a theme in the classic W. E. B. Dubois, *Black Reconstruction in America: 1860–1880* (New York: Free Press, 1998).

14. The quoted Populist is Thomas Watson, who later changed his views and acceded to the dominant racism of the era. The career of Watson nicely exemplifies the Janus-faced character of U.S. populism, especially with regard to issues of race. Quote from Watson, "The Negro Question in the South," *The Arena*, October 1892, https://msuweb.montclair.edu/~furrg/spl/tomwatson .html. The first two sentences appear to be Watson quoting from the platform of the People's Party.

15. T. Harry Williams, *Huey Long: A Biography* (New York: Knopf, 1969), 703–106; Carl Grafton and Anne Permaloff, *Big Mules and Branchheads: James E. Folsom and Political Power in Alabama* (Athens: University of Georgia Press, 2008), chap. 6. On multiracial politics in the post–Civil War South, see the classic C. Vann Woodward, *The Strange Career of Jim Crow* (New York: Oxford University Press, 1955).

16. Governor James Folsom, "Christmas Message," December 25, 1949, in *Lend Me your Ears: Great Speeches in History*, ed. William Safire (New York: Norton, 1997), 661–63.

17. Governor Orval Faubus, who famously championed continued segregation of Arkansas's schools in 1957, had grown up in a socialist family. Faubus's father

"detested capitalism and bigotry with equal fervor." Roy Reed, "Orval E. Faubus: Out of Socialism to Realism," *Arkansas Historical Journal* 66, no. 2 (2007): 167. On Faubus's socialist background, see also Roy Reed, "Sister Who Opposed Faubus Died: Bonnie Lou Faubus Salcido Publicly Called Out Her Brother for Blocking the Integration of Central High," *Arkansas Times*, May 23, 2013.

18. See "Operation Dixie: Wooing the Negro," *New York Amsterdam News*, March 8, 1947. The CIO's organizing activities spurred its competitors at the AFL to aim recruitment efforts at Black workers as well.

19. See accounts by the former OPA economist John Kenneth Galbraith, *A Life in Our Times: A Memoir* (Boston: Houghton Mifflin, 1981), chaps. 8–12; and Galbraith, "The Selection and Timing of Inflation Controls," *Review of Economics and Statistics* 23, no. 2 (1941).

20. Testimony by OPA administrator Chester Bowles in U.S. Congress, *Inflation Control Program of OPA* (Washington, DC: U.S. Government Printing Office, 1945), 13. See also Chester Bowles, *Promises to Keep: My Years in Public Life, 1941–1969* (New York: Harper & Row, 1971), pt. I.

21. Former OPA employee Richard Nixon misleadingly stated that World War II showed that "rationing does not work well even in wartime when patriotism inspires sacrifice." From Richard M. Nixon, *RN: The Memoirs of Richard Nixon* (New York: Grosset & Dunlap, 1978), 986. In fact, the OPA worked sufficiently well that it received overwhelming public support.

22. Meg Jacobs, *Pocketbook Politics: Economic Citizenship in Twentieth Century America* (Princeton, NJ: Princeton University Press, 2005), 211–13, 218–20; Nelson Lichtenstein, *State of the Union: A Century of American Labor* (Princeton, NJ: Princeton University Press, 2002), 102.

23. On administered pricing by oligopolies, see the following verbatim transcript: "The Council of Economic Advisors Under Chairman Leon H. Keyserling, 1949–1953: Oral History Interview," in *The President and the Council of Economic Advisers: Interviews with CEA Chairmen*, ed. Erwin C. Hargrove and Samuel A. Morley (Boulder, CO: Westview, 1984), 76–77.

24. Keynes, *General Theory*, chap. 24.

25. Keynes, *General Theory*, 374.

26. Paul Krugman, "The Smith/Klein/Kalecki Theory of Austerity," The Conscience of a Liberal, May 16, 2013, https://archive.nytimes.com/krugman.blogs.nytimes.com/2013/05/16/the-smithkleinkalecki-theory-of-austerity/. Krugman referenced the views of the late economist Michal Kalecki. On the issue of business confidence, see also Mark Blyth, *Austerity: The History of a Dangerous Idea* (New York: Oxford University Press, 2013), 121–22.

27. Quotes are paraphrases of Olof Palme in Hendrik Hertzberg, "Death of a Patriot," *New Republic*, March 31, 1986. On Palme's travels in the United States,

see also "Remembering Olof Palme," *Kenyon College Alumni Bulletin*, Winter 2012; and "Swedish Prime Minister Olof Palme Discusses His Socialist Political Viewpoints with Studs Turkel in Sweden at the House of Parliament," Studs Turkel Radio Archive, November 5, 1973, https://studsterkel.wfmt.com /programs/swedish-prime-minister-olaf-palme-discusses-his-socialist-political -viewpoints-studs?t=NaN%2CNaN&a=%2C.

28. On Keynes's proposals for multinational capital controls, see full-text source material in Elizabeth Johnson and Donald Moggridge, eds., *The Collected Writings of John Maynard Keynes: Volume 25, Activities 1940–1944, Shaping the Post-War World, the Clearing Union* (Cambridge: Cambridge University Press, 1978), chap. 1.

29. Ruth Ellen Wasem, *Tackling Unemployment: The Legislative Dynamics of the Employment Act of 1946* (Kalamazoo, MI: Upjohn Institute for Employment Research, 2013), 58–68, 101; Gary Mucciaroni, *The Political Failure of Employment Policy, 1945–1982* (Pittsburgh: University of Pittsburgh Press, 1990), 218.

30. Senator Robert A. Taft, "Statement on the Full Employment Bill," January 18, 1945, in *The Papers of Robert A. Taft, Volume III, 1945–1948*, ed. Clarence E. Wunderlin, Jr. (Kent, Oh: Kent State University Press, 2003), 9–12.

31. Jacobs, *Pocketbook Politics*, 221–31.

32. See letter from Robert Taft to Herbert Hoover, March 23, 1945, in *The Papers of Robert A. Taft, Volume III*, 47–48.

33. Barbara S. Griffith, *The Crisis of American Labor: Operation Dixie and the Defeat of the CIO* (Philadelphia: Temple University Press, 1988), chaps. 5–7.

34. Full text of the Employment Act of 1946, Public Law 304, 79th Congress, FRED Economic Data, Federal Reserve Bank of St. Louis, https://fraser.stlouisfed.org /files/docs/historical/trumanlibrary/srf_014_002_0002.pdf.

35. On the politics of the OPA during this period, see Wallace's account in *The Price of Vision*, 582–83.

36. President Harry S. Truman, "Executive Order 10161—Delegating Certain Functions of the President Under the Defense Production Act of 1950," September 9, 1950, in American Presidency Project, https://www.presidency.ucsb.edu /documents/executive-order-10161-delegating-certain-functions-the-president -under-the-defense.

37. Griffith, *Crisis of American Labor*, 42–43.

38. Samuel Huntington, "United States," in *The Crisis of Democracy: Report on the Governability of Democracies to the Trilateral Commission*, ed. Michel J. Crozier, Samuel P. Huntington, and Joji Watanuki (New York: New York University Press, 1975), 98. On Truman's business ties, see also Nomi Prins, *All the Presidents' Bankers: The Hidden Alliances That Drive American Power* (New York: Nation Books, 2014), 182; and Philip H. Burch, Jr., *Elites*

in American History: The New Deal to the Carter Administration (New York: Holmes & Meier, 1980), chap. 3.

39. Keyserling in "The Council of Economic Advisors Under Chairman Leon H. Keyserling," in Hargrove and Morley, eds., *The President and the Council of Economic Advisers*, 81. Note that during his service in Truman's cabinet, George Marshall was a retired general.

40. President Harry S. Truman, "The President's News Conference," December 7, 1945, in Truman Library, https://www.trumanlibrary.gov/library/public-papers /208/presidents-news-conference.

41. Harry S. Truman, *Memoirs: Years of Trial and Hope* (Garden City, NY: Double-day, 1956), 24–29.

42. Regarding the massive scale of the 1946 strike wave, see Melvyn Dubufsky, "Labor Unrest in the United States, 1906–90," *Review* (Fernand Braudel Center) 18, no. 1 (1995): 131.

43. For full text of Taft-Hartley, see Section 1. [§ 141.] (a) of the National Labor Relations Act, U.S. National Labor Relations Board, https://www.nlrb.gov/guidance /key-reference-materials/national-labor-relations-act. Technically, Taft-Hartley is an amendment to the 1935 National Labor Relations Act. For analysis, see Sumner H. Slichter, "The Taft-Hartley Act," *Quarterly Journal of Economics* 63, no. 1 (1949).

44. For an ideological defense of Taft-Hartley by one of its authors, see Senator Robert Taft, "Speech Before Inland Daily Press Association," February 10, 1948, in Wunderlin, Jr., ed., *The Papers of Robert A. Taft, Volume III*, 385–91.

45. On the racist motives that contributed to Taft-Hartley, see Richard D. Kahlen-berg and Moshe Z. Marvit, "The Ugly Racial History of 'Right to Work,'" *Dissent*, December 20, 2012.

46. Mancur Olson, *The Logic of Collective Action: Public Goods and the Theory of Groups* (Cambridge, MA: Harvard University Press, 1965), chap. 3.

47. National Right to Work Committee, "Right to Work States: Timeline," 2016, https://nrtwc.org/facts-issues/state-right-to-work-timeline-2016/. Note that several states had already adopted some form of right-to-work legislation even before the Taft-Harley Act. However, the act placed such legislation on a much stronger legal footing.

48. Lawrence Richards, *Union-Free America: Workers and Anti-Union Culture* (Urbana: University of Illinois Press, 2008), 5.

49. Strom Thurmond, "Houston Acceptance Speech of August 11, 1948," in Strom Thurmond Papers, Clemson University, https://tigerprints.clemson.edu/strom /597/; and "Speech by Henry A. Wallace [on U.S. relations with the Soviet Union], September 20, 1948," W. E. B. Dubois Papers, University of Massachusetts, online resources, https://credo.library.umass.edu/view/full/mums312-b121-i323.

50. "Democratic Party Platform," July 12, 1948, https://www.presidency.ucsb.edu /documents/1948-democratic-party-platform; and Harry S. Truman, "Address in Philadelphia Upon Accepting the Nomination of the Democratic National Convention," July 15, 1948, https://www.presidency.ucsb.edu/documents/address -philadelphia-upon-accepting-the-nomination-the-democratic-national-convention. Both documents are in American Presidency Project.

51. Harry S. Truman, "Labor Day Address in Cadillac Square, Detroit," September 6, 1948, https://www.presidency.ucsb.edu/documents/labor-day-address-cadillac -square-detroit; see also Truman, "Address at the State Capitol in Denver," September 20, 1948, https://www.presidency.ucsb.edu/documents/address-the -state-capitol-denver. Both speeches in American Presidency Project.

52. Regarding the economic motives for the surge in military spending, see U.S. Department of State, "Memorandum Prepared for the Department of State: Legislation for Foreign Aid Programs," undated [probably November 16, 1950], document 135 in *Foreign Relations of the United States 1950, Volume I, National Security Affairs, Foreign Economic Policy*, ed. Neal H. Petersen et al. (Washington, DC: U.S. Government Printing Office, 1977), 409.

53. The full text of NSC-68 is in U.S National Security Council, "NSC-68: United States Objectives and Programs for National Security," April 14, 1950, from Federation of American Scientists, https://irp.fas.org/offdocs/nsc-hst/nsc-68 .htm. Note that the document's recommendations were secretly approved in April 1950, though the massive increase in military spending occurred after the Communist invasion of South Korea in June. The April approval of NCS-68 was revealed in Dean Acheson's memoir, *Present at the Creation: My Years in the State Department* (New York: Norton, 1969), 374.

54. Benjamin O. Fordham, *Building the Cold War Consensus: The Political Economy of U.S. National Security Policy, 1949–1951* (Ann Arbor: University of Michigan Press, 1998), especially chaps. 6, 7. Fordham does not cite any explicit agreement between Truman and congressional Republicans, but he argues persuasively that such an agreement is strongly indicated by the chain of events.

55. "Longhand Note of President Harry S. Truman," May 12, 1945, Truman Presidential Library, https://www.trumanlibrary.gov/library/truman-papers/longhand -notes-presidential-file-1944-1953/may-12-1945?documentid=NA&pagenumber=2. See also the exposé "The Truth About J. Edgar Hoover," *Time*, December 22, 1975.

56. Truman, *Memoirs*, 171–72.

57. According to one source, "The Council Against Communist Aggression . . . was organized largely by liberals and trade unionists during the Korean War. The driving force behind this organization . . . was Arthur G. McDowell, an official of the Upholsterers' Union." Letter from Abraham H. Kalish, Executive Secretary,

Accuracy in Media, to Wesley McCune, September 20, 1971, in Group Research Inc. Papers, box 2, folder "Accuracy in Media," Columbia University.

58. "Text of the AFL-CIO Merger Agreement," *Monthly Labor Review* 78, no. 4 (1955).

59. On labor union ties to the CIA, see Ted Morgan, *A Covert Life, Jay Lovestone: Communist, Anti-Communist, and Spymaster* (New York: Random House, 1999); Tim Shorrock, "Labor's Cold War: Freshly Unearthed Documents May Force AFL-CIO to Face Up to Past Betrayals," *The Nation*, May 19, 2003; Thomas W. Braden, "I'm Glad the CIA Is Immoral," *Saturday Evening Post*, May 20, 1967; and Harry Bernstein, "CIA Linked to AFL-CIO Foreign Unit," *Detroit News*, May 23, 1966.

60. On the enthusiasm felt by the AFL-CIO leadership for the Cold War as a basic *raison d'être*, see "Lane Kirkland, Aristocratic American Labor Leader, Died on August 14th, Aged 77," *Economist*, August 28, 1999.

61. Michal Kalecki, "Political Aspects of Full Employment," *Political Quarterly* 14, no. 4 (1943): 323. Specifically, Kalecki advocated a national tax on capital as a means of reducing the budget deficit, though it would also have had the effect of restraining inflation.

62. The official announcement appeared as "Treasury-Federal Reserve Accord," March 1–2, 1951, in *Thirty Eighth Annual Report of the Federal Reserve System, Covering Operations for the Year 1951*, 98–102, Federal Reserve historical website, https://www.federalreserve.gov/monetarypolicy/files/fomcropa19510302 .pdf. See also Allan H. Meltzer, *A History of the Federal Reserve, Vol. I, 1913–1951* (Chicago: University of Chicago Press, 2003), 707–24.

63. The anti-inflation character of the accord is emphasized in Robert L. Hetzel and Ralph F. Leach, "The Treasury-Fed Accord: A New Narrative Account," *Federal Reserve Bank of Richmond Economic Quarterly* 87, no. 1 (2001): 34, 52, 53; and Christina D. Romer and David H. Romer, "The Rehabilitation of Monetary Policy in the 1950s," *American Economic Review* 92, no. 2 (2002): 121. The latter authors emphasize the "abhorrence of inflation by virtually all members of the [Fed's] Open Market Committee."

64. Lyn Turgeon, *Bastard Keynesianism: The Evolution of Economic Thinking and Policy Making Since World War II* (Westport, CT: Praeger, 1996), 11. The abiding influence of finance during this period is a central theme of Prins, *All the Presidents' Bankers*, 173–95.

65. On the Phillips curve, see A. W. Phillips, "The Relation Between Unemployment and the Rate of Change of Money Wage Rates in the United Kingdom, 1861–1957," *Economica* 25, no. 100 (1958); and Paul A. Samuelson and Robert M. Solow, "Analytical Aspects of Anti-Inflation Policy," *American Economic Review* 50, no. 2 (1960). Though the Phillips curve itself was not formalized

until the late 1950s, the anti-inflation ideas associated with it were established well before.

66. Samuelson, quoted in William Breit and John H. Huston, "Reputation Versus Influence: The Evidence from Textbook References," *Eastern Economic Journal* 23, no. 4 (1997): 451.

67. The 4 percent "full employment" rate was advocated in a 1947 report by the Committee for Economic Development. Robert Skidelsky, *John Maynard Keynes, Fighting for Freedom, 1937–1946* (New York: Penguin, 2000), 504. See also Richard B. DuBoff, "Full Employment: History of a Receding Target," *Politics & Society* 7, no. 1 (1977).

68. Turgeon, *Bastard Keynesianism*, especially 15, 25, 26. Turgeon's book provides an especially useful discussion of the Phillips curve as a fundamentally "bastard Keynesian" innovation.

69. On the Red Scare and its effects on the teaching of economics, see extended interviews with Paul Samuelson, Lorie Tarshis, and Paul Sweezy in David C. Colander and Harry Landreth, eds., *The Coming of Keynesianism to America: Conversations with the Founders of Keynesian Economics* (Northampton, MA: Edward Elgar, 1996), chaps. 3, 4, 8.

70. By the late 1970s, economic theory had moved beyond the Phillips curve as a means of fighting inflation, toward the much more draconian idea of monetarism associated with Milton Friedman. See discussion in chapter 6.

71. David Kotz, *The Rise and Fall of Neoliberal Capitalism* (Cambridge, MA: Harvard University Press, 2015), 90, 99. Note that the figures on GDP growth are calculated in "chained 2005 U.S. dollars."

72. Claudia Goldin and Robert A. Margo, paraphrased in Wasem, *Tackling Unemployment*, 160. On rising economic equality during this period, see also Thomas Piketty, *Capital in the Twenty-First Century* (Cambridge, MA: Belknap Press of Harvard University Press, 2014), 292; and Robert M. Collins, *More: The Politics of Economic Growth in Postwar America* (New York: Oxford University Press, 2000), chap. 2.

73. Servicemen's Readjustment Act, Public Law 346, June 22, 1944, full text from U.S. National Archives, https://www.archives.gov/milestone-documents/servicemens-readjustment-act#transcript.

74. Glenn C. Altschuler and Stuart M. Blumin, *The GI Bill: A New Deal for Veterans* (New York: Oxford University Press, 2009); Suzanne Mettler, *From Soldiers to Citizens: The GI Bill and the Making of the Greatest Generation* (New York: Oxford University Press, 2007). For a retrospective analysis, see Michael Schaller, "GI Bill: The Law that Changed America," *Arizona Daily Star*, October 18, 2020. From the right, Senator Robert Taft objected that the housing provisions of the GI Bill were administered to "prevent someone making the usual industry profit."

See Taft, "Speech to Republican State Convention," September 11, 1946, in Wunderlin, Jr., ed., *The Papers of Robert A. Taft, Volume III*, 171–85.

75. Daniel Mitchell, "Historical Lessons of Lower Tax Rates" (report, Heritage Foundation, Washington, DC, April 13, 2003), https://www.heritage.org/taxes /report/the-historical-lessons-lower-tax-rates.

76. Gordon, *Rise and Fall of American Growth*, 617. Gordon paraphrases the views of Frank Levy and Peter Temin.

77. From NSC 68, "United States Objectives and Programs for National Security," Section I, https://history.state.gov/milestones/1945-1952/NSC68.

78. Robert Pollin, *Back to Full Employment* (Cambridge, MA: MIT Press, 2012), 102–3. See also Seymour Melman, *The Demilitarized Society: Disarmament and Conversion* (Montreal, QC: Harvest House, 1988); and Robert Pollin and Heidi Garrett-Peltier, "The U.S. Employment Effects of Military and Domestic spending Priorities: 2011 Update" (Political Economy Research Institute, University of Massachusetts, Amherst, December 2011).

79. Eisenhower did reluctantly acknowledge using federal highway funds as a means of Keynesian stimulus during the 1958 recession. See letter from Eisenhower to William Fife Knowland and Joseph William Martin, Jr., March 8, 1958, in Louis Galambos and Daun Van Ee, eds., *The Papers of Dwight D. Eisenhower: The Presidency, Keeping the Peace*, vol. 19 (Baltimore: Johns Hopkins University Press, 2001), 760–65. On the military impetus for the highway system, see Lee Lacy, "Dwight D. Eisenhower and the Birth of the Interstate Highway System," February 20, 2018, U.S. Army website, https://www.army.mil/article/198095 /dwight_d_eisenhower_and_the_birth_of_the_interstate_highway_system.

80. Public Law 85-864—September 2, 1958, National Defense Education Act, Discover U.S. Government Information, https://www.govinfo.gov/content/pkg/STATUTE -72/pdf/STATUTE-72-Pg1580.pdf.

81. "America's Interstate Highways: America's Splurge," *Economist*, February 16, 2008; and Thomas F. Keane, "The Economic Importance of the National Highway System," *Public Roads* 59, no. 4 (1996).

82. Gordon, *Rise and Fall of American Growth*, 542. See also Lane Windham, *Knocking on Labor's Door: Union Organizing in the 1970s and the Roots of a New Economic Divide* (Chapel Hill: University of North Carolina Press, 2017), 20; and Richard B. Freeman, *What Do Unions Do?* (New York: Basic Books, 1985).

83. "The Treaty of Detroit: GM May Have Paid a Billion for Peace, It Got a Bargain," *Fortune*, July 1950; Victor G. Reuther, *The Brothers Reuther and the Story of the UAW: A Memoir by Victor G. Reuther* (Boston: Houghton Mifflin, 1976), chap. 23; and Daniel J. Clark, *Disruption in Detroit: Auto Workers and the Elusive Postwar Boom* (Champaign: University of Illinois Press, 2018), chap. 2.

84. Lichtenstein, *State of the Union*, 123-28

85. Quoted in Dwight D. Eisenhower, *Mandate for Change: The White House Years, 1953–1956* (New York: Doubleday, 1963), 491.

86. Herbert Hill, "Labor Unions and the Negro: The Record of Discrimination," *Commentary*, December 1959. On the Jim Crow system, see the memoir Adolph L. Reed, Jr., *The South: Jim Crow and Its Afterlives* (London: Verso, 2022).

87. Hilary Herbold, "Never a Level Playing Field: Blacks and the GI Bill," *Journal of Blacks in Higher Education*, no. 6 (1994–1995); and Isabel Wilkerson, *The Warmth of Other Suns: The Epic Story of America's Great Migration* (New York: Vintage Books, 2011).

88. On the Pullman Porters, see A. Phillip Randolph, "Report at Brotherhood of Sleeping Car Porters' Convention (1968)," in Andrew E. Kersten and David Lucander, eds, *For Jobs and Freedom: Selected Speeches and Writings of A. Phillip Randolph* (Amherst: University of Massachusetts Press, 2014), 65–73.

89. Harry S. Truman, "Executive Order 9981—Establishing the President's Committee on Equality of Treatment and Opportunity in the Armed Services," July 26, 1948, Truman Presidential Library, https://www.trumanlibrary.gov/library/executive-orders/9981/executive-order-9981. For political context, see also "Oral History Interview with [retired General] Bruce C. Clarke," January 14, 1970, Truman Presidential Library, https://www.trumanlibrary.gov/library/oral-histories/clarkeb.

90. See U.S. Supreme Court decision in *Shelley v. Kraemer*, 334 U.S. 1 (1948), https://supreme.justia.com/cases/federal/us/334/1/#annotation; and *Brown v. Board of Education of Topeka*, 347 U.S. 483 (1954), https://supreme.justia.com/cases/federal/us/347/483/. Both document sets are in the Justia: U.S. Supreme Court website. The 1930s and 1940s also saw advancements for Native Americans associated with the "Indian New Deal." See documentation in David E. Wilkins, ed., *On the Drafting of Tribal Constitutions: Felix S. Cohen* (Norman: University of Oklahoma Press, 2007).

91. Amitabh Chandra, "Labor Market Dropouts and the Racial Wage Gap: 1940–1990," *American Economic Review* 90, no. 2 (2000): 334.

92. Kotz, *Rise and Fall of Neoliberal Capitalism*, 55. Regarding the role of the CED, see Robert M. Collins, *The Business Response to Keynes, 1929–1964* (New York: Columbia University Press, 1981); and Andrew Rich, *Think Tanks, Public Policy, and the Politics of Expertise* (Cambridge: Cambridge University Press, 2004), 44.

93. On Brookings's funding, see memorandum for Secretary Stans, from Peter M. Flanagan, February 16, 1970, in White House Central Files, Staff Member Office Files, Charles Colson Papers, box 32, folder: 14," Nixon Presidential Library.

94. "The New Conservatism: A Bold, New Creed for Modern Capitalism," *Wall Street Journal*, November 21, 1956. The article originally appeared in *Time* magazine.

95. Mayer, *Union Membership Trends in the United States*, 22 (figure for "Percent of Nonagricultural Workers"). Public support for unions also peaked during this period, reaching 75 percent approval by the mid-1950s. See historical data in Justin McCarthy, "U.S. Support of Labor Unions at Highest Point Since 1965," *Gallup News*, August 20, 2022, https://news.gallup.com/poll/398303/approval-labor-unions-highest-point-1965.aspx.

96. Eisenhower, quoted in speech by Senator Hubert H. Humphrey, "What Is Right with American Labor," June 24, 1959, in Hubert H. Humphrey Papers, Minnesota Historical Society, http://www2.mnhs.org/library/findaids/00442/pdfa/00442-00852.pdf.

97. Letter from Dwight D. Eisenhower to Edgar Newton Eisenhower, November 8, 1954, in Louis Galambos and Daun Van Ee, eds., *The Papers of Dwight D. Eisenhower: The Presidency, The Middle Way*, vol. 15 (Baltimore: Johns Hopkins University Press, 1996), 1386–89.

98. G. William Domhoff, *Who Rules America? The Triumph of the Corporate Rich* (New York: McGraw-Hill, 2013); E. Digby Baltzell, *Philadelphia Gentlemen: The Making of a National Upper Class* (Glencoe, Il: Free Press, 1958); Ferdinand Lundburg, *The Rich and the Superrich: A Study in the Power of Money Today* (New York: Lyle Stuart, 1968_; and Burch, *Elites in American History*, vol. 3.

99. E. E. Schattschneider, *The Semisovereign People: A Realist's View of Democracy in America* (Hinsdale, IL: Dryden, 1960), 30, 32. Emphasis in original has been deleted.

100. Burch, *Elites in American History*, vol. 3, chaps. 2–4; Kim Phillips-Fein, *Invisible Hands: The Businessmen's Crusade Against the New Deal* (New York: Norton, 2009), chaps. 3–6; Philip H. Burch, Jr., "The NAM as an Interest Group," *Politics & Society* 4, no. 1 (1973); and Jonathan Soffer, "The National Association of Manufacturers and the Militarization of American Conservatism," *Business History Review* 75, no. 4 (2001).

101. Charles J. V. Murphy, "Texas Business and McCarthy," *Fortune*, May 1954.

102. On the role of the candy magnate Robert Welch in creating the John Birch Society, see Michael Seiler, "Robert Welch, Founder of Birch Society, Dies at 85," *Los Angeles Times*, January 8, 1985. See also the extended study, Edward H. Miller, *A Conspiratorial Life: Robert Welch, the John Birch Society, and the Revolution of American Conservatism* (Chicago: University of Chicago Press, 2021).

103. Elizabeth Fones-Wolf, *Selling Free Enterprise: The Business Assault on Labor and Liberalism, 1945–1960* (Champaign: University of Illinois Press, 1994), chap. 9. The idea of restraining labor power was quietly encouraged by the president; see letter from Eisenhower to Eric Harlow Heckett, October 18, 1958, in Galambos and Van Ee, eds., *The Papers of Dwight D. Eisenhower*, vol. 19, 1153–56.

104. See Kazan's own account regarding the context for *On the Waterfront* in Elia Kazan, *A Life* (New York: Knopf, 1988), 499–500.

105. Public Law 86–257, Landrum-Griffin Act, September 14, 1959, 73 Stat. 519–546, as amended; full text at United Auto Workers, http://uaw.org/landrum-griffin-act.

106. Fones-Wolf, *Selling Free Enterprise*, chap. 7; and Richards, *Union-Free America*, 2–3, 44–45.

107. Dorothy Day, "Hooverville," *Catholic Worker*, March 1940. This and other Day writings are available at The Catholic Worker Movement, https://catholicworker.org/941-html/.

108. Kevin M. Kruse, *One Nation Under God: How Corporate America Invented Christian America* (New York: Basic Books, 2015), 14–20. On Spiritual Mobilization's ties to libertarian politics, see Brian Doherty, *Radicals for Capitalism: A Freewheeling History of the American Libertarian Movement* (New York: Public Affairs, 2007), 272–82; and Irving E. Howard, "Christ and the Libertarians," *Christianity Today*, March 17, 1958.

109. Quoted in James L. MacAllister, "Evangelical Faith and Billy Graham," *Social Action*, March 1953, 23.

110. Grant Wacker, *America's Pastor: Billy Graham and the Shaping of a Nation* (Cambridge, MA: Belknap Press of Harvard University Press, 2014), 154; Jane Wolfe, *The Murchisons: The Rise and Fall of a Texas Dynasty* (New York: St. Martin's, 1989), 233. See also Steven P. Miller, *Billy Graham and the Rise of the Republican South* (Philadelphia: University of Pennsylvania Press, 2009), 169, 175.

111. Kim Phillips-Fein, "Business Conservatives and the Mont Pèlerin Society," in *The Road from Mont Pèlerin: The Making of a Neoliberal Thought Collective.*, ed. Philip Mirowski and Dieter Plehwe (Cambridge, MA: Harvard University Press, 2009), 296; Dieter Plehwe, "Introduction," in *Road from Mont Pèlerin: The Making of a Neoliberal Thought Collective*, ed. Philip Mirowski and Dieter Plehwe (Cambridge, MA: Harvard University Press, 2009), 15; Phillips-Fein, *Invisible Hands*, 42, 51, 55; Angus Burgin, *The Great Persuasion: Reinventing Free Markets Since the Depression* (Cambridge, MA: Harvard University Press, 2012), 171; and Quinn Slobodian, *Globalists: The End of Empire and the Birth of Neoliberalism* (Cambridge, MA: Harvard University Press, 2018), 144. Slobodian notes that after 1945, "neoliberals worked with and alongside the International Chamber of Commerce."

112. Nancy MacLean, "How Milton Friedman Exploited White Supremacy to Privatize Education" (Working Paper no. 161, Institute for New Economic Thinking, New York, September 1, 2021), https://www.ineteconomics.org/uploads/papers/WP_161-MacLean.pdf.

113. One of the MPS's most prominent members was Friedman, whose profile was elevated considerably in 1962 with the publication of the widely read *Capitalism and Freedom*, which was written with support from the Volker Fund. Friedman acknowledged Volker support for a series of conferences that formed the basis of his book. See Milton Friedman, *Capitalism and Freedom* (Chicago: University of Chicago Press, 2002), xv. See also discussion in Milton Friedman and Rose D. Friedman, *Two Lucky People: Memoirs* (Chicago: University of Chicago Press, 1998), 161, 622.

114. Rob Van Horn, "Reinventing Monopoly and the Role of Corporations: The Roots of Chicago Law and Economics," in *Road from Mont Pèlerin: The Making of a Neoliberal Thought Collective*, ed. Philip Mirowski and Dieter Plehwe (Cambridge, MA: Harvard University Press, 2009), 204, 215. The undated quote from Simons is a direct quote; the one from Friedman is a paraphrase by Van Horn. Note that the "Chicago economists" were not yet fully established at the University of Chicago; I use the term "Chicago economists" in a generic sense.

115. Friedman, *Capitalism and Freedom*, chap. 8; and Van Horn, "Reinventing Monopoly and the Role of Corporations." Friedman was especially critical of "closed shop" labor agreements, with mandated union membership.

116. On administered pricing in general, see the interview in "Leon Keyserling, 1949–1953: Oral History Interview," in Hargrove and Morley, eds, *The President and the Council of Economic Advisers*, 76–77. See also the classic Paul A. Baran and Paul M. Sweezy, *Monopoly Capital: An Essay on the American Economic and Social Order* (New York: Monthly Review Press, 1966). On administered pricing by U.S. Steel, see Arthur M. Schlesinger, Jr., *A Thousand Days: John F. Kennedy in the White House* (Boston: Houghton Mifflin, 1965), 636.

117. Yves Steiner, "The Neoliberals Confront the Trade Unions," in *Road from Mont Pèlerin: The Making of a Neoliberal Thought Collective*, ed. Philip Mirowski and Dieter Plehwe (Cambridge, MA: Harvard University Press, 2009), 190. On MPS funding from U.S. Steel and General Electric, see Phillips-Fein, "Business Conservatives and the Mont Pèlerin Society," 292, 296; and Phillips-Fein, *Invisible Hands*, p. 48.

118. Plehwe, "Introduction," 30.

119. Regarding the mainstream skepticism toward Friedman's economics during the 1960s, see Paul Volcker and Christine Harper, *Keeping at It: The Quest for Sound Money and Good Government* (New York: Public Affairs, 2018), 32–33; and David Rockefeller, *Memoirs* (New York: Random House, 2002), 88.

120. MPS meetings often entailed uncritical celebration of free market ideas. One book editor who attended a 1980 meeting of the MPS later reflected, "I was struck by the very political nature of the society's theme. . . . In most instances,

there was no debate whatsoever." Letter from Richard J. Bishirjian, senior edi-
tor, Arlington House Publishers, to Edwin J. Feulner, September 18, 1980, in
Mont Pèlerin Society Papers, box 23, folder 5, Hoover Institution Archives,
Stanford University.

121. See sources noted in Mark S. Mizruchi, *The Fracturing of the American Corporate Elite* (Cambridge, MA: Harvard University Press, 2013), 98.

122. Leo Panitch and Sam Gindin, *The Making of Global Capitalism: The Political
Economy of American Empire* (London: Verso, 2012), 87; "The 1957–1958 Reces-
sion: Recent or Current?," *Monthly Review* [Federal Reserve Bank of St. Louis],
August 1958.

123. Claire Jackson, "History Lessons: The Asian Flu Pandemic," *British Journal of
General Practice* 59, no. 565 (2009).

124. Elizabeth Tandy Shermer, "Sunbelt Boosterism: Industrial Recruitment, Economic Development, and Growth Politics in the Developing South," in Michelle
Nickerson and Darren Dochuk, eds., *Sunbelt Rising: The Politics of Place, Space,
and Region* (Philadelphia: University of Pennsylvania Press, 2011).

125. On the political effects of the 1960 recession, see letter from Adlai Stevenson to
Barbara Jackson, October 8, 1960, in Walter Johnson, ed., *The Papers of Adlai
E. Stevenson: Continuing Education and the Unfinished Business of American
Society, 1957–1961, Vol. VII* (Boston: Little, Brown, 1977), 573.

126. John. F. Kennedy, "Remarks of Senator John F. Kennedy, Allentown, PA,"
October 28, 1960, Kennedy Presidential Library, https://www.jfklibrary.org
/archives/other-resources/john-f-kennedy-speeches/allentown-pa-19601028.

127. On the administration's strategy of military buildup, see "Robert S. McNamara
Oral History Interview," April 4, 1964, Kennedy Presidential Library, 2–5, https://
www.jfklibrary.org/sites/default/files/archives/JFKOH/McNamara%2C%20
Robert%20S/JFKOH-RSM-01/JFKOH-RSM-01-TR.pdf.

128. David N. Gibbs, "Political Parties and International Relations: The United
States and the Decolonization of Sub-Saharan Africa," *International History
Review* 17, no. 2 (1995): 322–26.

129. See comments on military spending by Council of Economic Advisers chairman
Walter Heller in "Oral History Interview with Walter Heller, Kermit Gordon,
James Tobin, Gardner Ackley, Paul Samuelson," August 1, 1964, Kennedy Pres-
idential Library, https://docs.google.com/viewerng/viewer?url=https://www
.jfklibrary.org/sites/default/files/archives/JFKOH/Council+of+Economic+Advisers
/JFKOH-CEA-01/JFKOH-CEA-01-TR.pdf.

130. Schlesinger, *A Thousand Days*, 634–36.

131. See the following memoirs by Kennedy-era officials: Theodore C. Sorensen,
Kennedy (New York: Harper & Row, 1965), 443–69; and Schlesinger, *A Thousand Days*, 634–43.

132. Quoted in Sorensen, *Kennedy*, 449, 452, 461. Sorensen plausibly claimed that Kennedy disparaged steel men but that it was widely misreported in the press as disparaging all businessmen, thus inflaming the situation.

133. "The Wrong War: Washington's Assault on U.S. Steel Will Cost the Nation Dear," *Barron's National Business and Financial Weekly*, April 16, 1962.

134. Stock prices during the 1962 steel crisis were discussed in Robert M. Bleiberg, "Benevolent Uncle? Washington Is Rigging the Market Against Investors," *Barron's National Business and Financial Weekly*, October 16, 1972.

135. "Presidential Approval Ratings—Gallup Historical Statistics and Trends," Gallup Polling, accessed October 12, 2023, https://www.gallup.com/poll/116677 /presidential-approval-ratings-gallup-historical-statistics-trends.aspx.

136. See, for example, Mitchell, "Historical Lessons of Lower Tax Rates." Regarding the politics of the Kennedy/Johnson tax cut, see the verbatim transcript, "Lyndon Johnson and Walter Heller on 14 December 1963," in Presidential Recordings, Miller Center for Public Affairs, https://prde.upress.virginia.edu /conversations/9020195. The tax revision was likely gratifying to the MPS economists. On Friedman's hostility toward redistribution, see his letter to James Buchanan, in Milton Friedman Papers, March 19, 1975, box 22, folder 9, Hoover Institution Archives.

137. President Lyndon Baines Johnson, "Radio and Television Remarks Upon Signing the Tax Bill," February 26, 1964, in American Presidency Project, https:// www.presidency.ucsb.edu/documents/radio-and-television-remarks-upon-signing-the-tax-bill. See analysis of the tax cut by Walter Heller, who served as chairman of the Council of Economic Advisers during the Kennedy and early Johnson administrations, in Milton Friedman and Walter W. Heller, *Fiscal vs. Monetary Policy* (New York: Norton, 1969), 27–36.

138. Johnson, quoted in "Hey! Hey! LBJ," *Economist*, September 28, 2013. Regarding the relatively modest economic accomplishments of the Kennedy administration, see Neil A. Jacoby, "The Fiscal Policy of the Kennedy-Johnson Administration," *Journal of Finance* 19, no. 2 (1964).

139. On Johnson and civil rights, see "Oral History Transcript, A. Phillip Randolph, Interview, 1 (I)," October 29, 1968, Johnson Presidential Library, https://www .discoverlbj.org/item/oh-randolpha-19681029-1-72-15.

140. "Gross Domestic Product," U.S. data from 1947 to present, FRED Economic Data, Federal Reserve Bank of St. Louis, accessed November 3, 2023, https:// fred.stlouisfed.org/series/GDP.

141. See historical statistics on profitability, figure 3, in Chuck Marr, Chye-Ching Huang, and Brendan Duke, "Tax Plans Must Not Lose Revenue and Should Focus on Raising Working Class Incomes" (Center for Budget and

Policy Priorities, Washington, DC, September 8, 2017), https://www.cbpp.org/research/federal-tax/tax-plans-must-not-lose-revenue-and-should-focus-on-raising-working-class.

142. Edwin L. Dale, Jr., "Are Recessions a Thing of the Past?," *New York Times*, June 7, 1964.

143. Robert Brenner, "The Economics of Global Turbulence: A Special Report on the World Economy, 1950–1998," *New Left Review*, no. 229 (1998): 7, figure 3. These statistics reference U.S. net rates of profit for manufacturing.

144. On the economic impact of the Vietnam War, see the memoirs of Treasury official Robert Solomon, *The International Monetary System, 1945–1976: An Insider's View* (New York: Harper & Row, 1977), 100–104.

145. Johnson did reluctantly implement a tax surcharge in 1968, combined with domestic spending restraints. Solomon, *The International Monetary System*, 103; and Alan S. Blinder, *A Monetary and Fiscal History of the United States, 1961–2021* (Princeton, NJ: Princeton University Press, 2022), 21–23.

146. The 1968 tax increase may be viewed as a mild form of austerity, though it produced no recession. See Joseph W. Barr, Arthur M. Okun, and Charles J. Zwick, "Memorandum for the President, Subject: Troika Review of the Economic and Budgetary Outlook," August 5, 1968, FRED Economic Data, Federal Reserve Bank of St. Louis, https://fraser.stlouisfed.org/files/docs/historical/johnson/barmem680805.pdf.

147. Brenner, "Economics of Global Turbulence," 93.

2. THE RICH REVOLT

The chapter epigraph comes from Robert M. Bleiberg, "Benevolent Uncle? Washington Is Rigging the Market Against Investors," *Barron's National Business and Financial Weekly*, October 16, 1972.

1. Philip Mirowski and Dieter Plehwe, eds., *The Road from Mont Pèlerin: The Making of a Neoliberal Thought Collective* (Cambridge, MA: Harvard University Press, 2009).

2. Public Broadcasting System, "Commanding Heights: The Battle for the World Economy," interview with George Shultz, October 2, 2000, https://www.pbs.org/wgbh/commandingheights/shared/minitext/int_georgeshultz.html. Note that the quote is from the unnamed PBS interviewer.

3. "Three of the Men Who Serve as Goldwater's Advisors," *New York Times*, March 31, 1964. Both Friedman and Gottfried Haberler advised the campaign. See also Jason Michael Shahl, "Selling Conservatism: Think Tanks, Conservative Ideology, and the Undermining of Liberalism, 1945–Present" (PhD diss., Department of History, University of Minnesota, 2008), 59–62.

4. Kim Phillips-Fein, "Business Conservatives and the Mont Pèlerin Society," in *The Road from Mont Pèlerin: The Making of a Neoliberal Thought Collective*, ed. Philip Mirowski and Dieter Plehwe (Cambridge, MA: Harvard University Press, 2009), 292, 296. However, business support for the MPS economists was not universal. An economist with the business-oriented Conference Board derided "Friedman's obsession and hatred for the Keynesians." Letter from Juan de Torres to Irving Kristol, June 14, 1974, Irving Kristol Papers, box 11, folder 3, Wisconsin Historical Society.

5. On the MPS economist Gottfried Haberler's ties to AEI, see Bryce N. Harlow and Charles W. Colson, "Memorandum for the President," April 30, 1970, White House Special Files, Staff Member and Office Files, Charles Colson Papers, box 32, folder 12, Nixon Presidential Library. Friedman later joined the staff of the Hoover Institution.

6. Phillip L. Zweig, *Wriston: Walter Wriston, Citibank, and the Rise and Fall of American Financial Supremacy* (New York: Crown, 1995), 448–49, 709.

7. Milton Friedman, "The Adam Smith Address: The Suicidal Impulse of the Business Community (1989)," in *The Best of Business Economics: Highlights from the First Fifty Years*, ed. Robert Thomas Crow (London: Palgrave Macmillan, 2016), 184–85.

8. Avner Offer and Gabriel Söderberg, *The Nobel Factor: The Prize in Economics, Social Democracy, and the Market Turn* (Princeton, NJ: Princeton University Press, 2016).

9. Phillips-Fein, "Business Conservatives and the Mont Pèlerin Society," 296.

10. Milton Friedman, "The Paradox of Doing Good," *Readers Digest*, October 1971; William E. Simon, "Big Government and Our Economic Woes," *Readers Digest*, April 1975; and Walter B. Wriston, "The Trouble with Government Regulation," *Readers Digest*, July 1974. Regarding the magazine's ties to the DeWitt Wallace family, see "About Wallace: A Brief History," Wallace Foundation, n.d., accessed November 20, 2023, https://www.wallacefoundation.org/about-wallace/pages/history.aspx.

11. Quoted from "Republicans: Candidate in Crisis," *Time*, October 31, 1960.

12. Richard Nixon, "Remarks at the Swearing-In of William D. Ruckelshaus as Administrator of the Environmental Protection Agency," December 4, 1970, https://www.presidency.ucsb.edu/documents/remarks-the-swearing-william-d-ruckelshaus-administrator-the-environmental-protection; and "Remarks on Signing the Occupational Safety and Health Act of 1970," December 29, 1970, https://www.presidency.ucsb.edu/documents/remarks-signing-the-occupational-safety-and-health-act-1970. Both speeches in American Presidency Project, Gerhard Peters and John T. Woolley, eds., University of California, Santa Barbara.

13. See Judson MacLaury, "Nixon and Ford Administrations 1969-1977," in *History of the Department of Labor, 1913–1988* (Washington, DC: U.S. Department of Labor, 1988), chap. 7, https://www.dol.gov/general/aboutdol/history/dolchp07.

14. Quoted in "Tips for a Keynesian Convert," Chicago *Tribune*, January 10, 1971.

15. Quote from "Memorandum for the File, Subject: 'Meeting with Messrs. Connally, Haldeman, Rumsfeld, Shultz, and Colson,'" probably November 19, 1971, Colson Papers, box 28, folder 17, Nixon Presidential Library. The administration did have recurring conflicts with labor, notably the AFL-CIO, but these were always kept within certain bounds. On labor, see also "Nixon Strategy Aims at Blocking Efforts to Label Him 'Anti-Union,'" *Politics: A Digest of Trends and Developments*, July/August 1971.

16. Dean J. Kotlowski, "Richard Nixon and the Origins of Affirmative Action," *The Historian* 60, no. 3 (1998); Elizabeth Hinton, *From the War on Poverty to the War on Crime: The Making of Mass Incarceration in America* (Cambridge, MA: Harvard University Press, 2017).

17. James Reichley, "Conservatism May Have a Future After All," *Fortune*, July 1972; Jonathan Riehl and David Frisk, "The Third-Party Trap: What a Failed 1970s Crusade Can Teach a GOP at War with Itself," *Politico*, December 20, 2013. Regarding Rusher's complex views of Nixon, see William A. Rusher, *The Rise of the Right* (New York: National Review Press, 1993), 182–86.

18. Quotes from Milton Friedman and Rose Friedman, *Two Lucky People: Milton and Rose D. Friedman, Memoirs* (Chicago: University of Chicago Press, 1998), 375, 382, 387.

19. William L. Silber, *Volcker: The Triumph of Persistence* (New York: Bloomsbury, 2012), 73. On Friedman's role, see also the memoir by Herbert Stein, *Presidential Economics: The Making of Economic Policy from Roosevelt to Clinton* (Washington, DC: American Enterprise Institute for Public Policy Research, 1994), 138.

20. Stein, *Presidential Economics*, 145. On Friedman's continuing role, see also Chairman of the Council of Economic Advisers, "Meeting with the Council of Economic Advisers and Five Outside Economists, April 27, 1970," Declassified Documents Reference System, Gale-Cengage; and George P. Shultz, *Learning from Experience* (Palo Alto, CA: Hoover Institution Press, 2016), 47.

21. William E. Simon, *A Time for Reflection: An Autobiography* (Washington, DC: Regnery, 2004), 73; John B. Connally and Mickey Herskowitz, *In History's Shadow: An American Odyssey* (New York: Hyperion, 1993), 237; and Friedman and Friedman, *Two Lucky People*, 377.

22. "Remembering Paul McCracken: U-M Economists and Advisor to Many U.S. Presidents," *Michigan News*, August 3, 2012, https://news.umich.edu/remembering -paul-mccracken-u-m-economist-and-adviser-to-many-u-s-presidents/.

23. Quote from Richard McCormack, "Herbert Stein," American Enterprise Institute, November 16, 1999, https://www.aei.org/articles/herbert-stein/.

24. Butz's strongly ideological worldview was frankly stated in letter from Butz to Milton Friedman, October 28, 1975, Milton Friedman Papers, box 22, folder "Butz, Earl L.," Hoover Institution Archives, Stanford University. Friedman praised "the skill of Secretary Earl Butz in promoting free markets" in agriculture. From Milton Friedman, "Henry, Stick to Politics," *Newsweek*, March 31, 1975. On Butz's agribusiness ties, including membership on Ralston-Purina's board, see Julius Duscha, "Up, Up, Up: Butz Makes Hay Down on the Farm," *New York Times*, April 16, 1972.

25. His views on antitrust were later spelled out in Robert H. Bork, *The Antitrust Paradox: A Policy at War with Itself* (New York: Basic Books, 1978). During his time as a professor at Yale Law School, "His students dubbed his class on antitrust law 'pro-trust.'" Quoted from Binyamin Applebaum, *The Economists' Hour: False Prophets, Free Markets, and the Fracture of Society* (Boston: Little, Brown, 2019), 149. Regarding Friedman's view of monopoly, see Milton Friedman, *Capitalism and Freedom* (Chicago: University of Chicago Press, 2002), chap. 8.

26. Haberler's consulting to the presidential transition team is noted in memo from Tilford C. Haines, Transmitting Report on Task Force on U.S. Balance of Payments Policies to the President Elect, December 17, 1968, White House Central Files, Staff Member and Office Files, Hendrick S. Houthakker Papers, box 31, folder, "Haberler Task Force, No. 2," Nixon Presidential Library. On Matchlup's role as consultant to the Treasury Department, see Joanne Gowa, *Closing the Gold Window: Domestic Politics and the End of Bretton Woods* (Ithaca, NY: Cornell University Press, 1983), 193.

27. Arthur Burns in Robert H. Ferrell, ed., *Inside the Nixon Administration: The Secret Diary of Arthur Burns, 1969–1974* (Lawrence: University Press of Kansas, 2010), 73.

28. Letter from Gerald Ford to Milton Friedman, October 14, 1976, in Friedman Papers, box 27, folder: "Ford, Gerald R.," Hoover Institution Archives, Stanford University.

29. This topic is discussed at length in the Colson Papers, box 32; see multiple folders on the "American Enterprise Institute," Nixon Presidential Library.

30. See "An Expanded American Enterprise Institute," attached to White House memorandum to Bryce Harlow, December 30, 1969, in White House Central Files, Staff Member and Office Files, Bryce N. Harlow Papers, box 8, folder 1, Nixon Presidential Library.

31. For general background on AEI, see Nick Thimmesch, "American Enterprise Institute: The Right Kind of Think Tank at the Right Time," *Human Events*,

October 7, 1978. Note that at the time of its founding, the institute was called American Enterprise Association, later changed to American Enterprise Institute.

32. Friedman and Friedman, *Two Lucky People*, 344. On Friedman's praise for AEI's activities, see letter from Milton Friedman to Paul M. McCracken, June 10, 1977, in William J. Baroody Sr. Papers, box 33, folder 5, Library of Congress.

33. In 1970, AEI Trustees included executives from Mobil Oil, Standard Oil of Indiana, Procter & Gamble, Metropolitan Life, Avon Products, and U.S. Steel. See "Minutes of the Annual Meeting of the Board of Trustees, American Enterprise Institute for Public Policy Research, February 19, 1970," in Baroody Papers, box 39, folder 6.

34. Barry M. Goldwater, *With No Apologies: The Personal and Political Memoirs of Barry M. Goldwater* (New York: William Morrow, 1979), 163–64. Goldwater described AEI director Baroody as a key policy adviser in the 1964 presidential election.

35. Memorandum, Charles W. Colson to Dwight Chapin, April 5, 1971, in Colson Papers, box 32, folder "American Enterprise Institute—AEI Fundraising Dinner," Nixon Presidential Library. Emphasis added.

36. Memorandum, Charles Colson to H. R. Haldeman, December 30, 1970, in Colson Papers, box 32, folder 15. It appears likely that presidential staff gave copies of their vast index card files of corporate contacts to the AEI director, William Baroody, facilitating still further the institute's efforts at generating corporate support. A large number of fund-raising files referencing specific individuals appears in Baroody's personal papers. The wording in these files strongly implies that the files originated from the White House. See Baroody Papers, boxes 57 and 58.

37. The lack of political savvy among business executives was noted in "An Expanded American Enterprise Institute," attached to White House Memorandum, December 30, 1969, Harlow Papers, box 8, folder 1, Nixon Presidential Library.

38. That Nixon was personally close to Baroody is strongly implied in Robert H. Bork, *Saving Justice: Watergate, The Saturday Night Massacre, and Other Adventures of a Solicitor General* (New York: Encounter, 2013), 88.

39. Memorandum from Charles W. Colson to Dwight Chapin, April 5, 1971, in Colson Papers, box 32, folder "American Enterprise Institute—AEI Fundraising Dinner," Nixon Presidential Library.

40. Memo for Charles W. Colson from Dwight L. Chapin, "Re: American Enterprise Institute," February 2, 1971, in Colson Papers, box 32, folder "American Enterprise Institute [1 of 2]," Nixon Presidential Library.

41. See the following memoranda: Tom Charles Huston to H. R. Haldeman, July 16, 1970; Tom Huston to George Bell, January 25, 1971; and Charles Colson to John

Dean, May 1, 1972, in *From the President: Richard Nixon's Secret Files*, ed. Bruce Oudes (New York: Harper & Row, 1989), 147–48, 207–8, 435.

42. Memorandum for Secretary Stans from Peter M. Flanagan, February 16, 1970, Colson Papers, box 32, folder "American Enterprise Institute—IV [202]," Nixon Presidential Library. There was a concerted effort to attack institutions of the Eastern Establishment. See memorandum for Secretary Stans from Peter M. Flanagan, February 16, 1970, in Colson Papers, box 32, folder "American Enterprise Institute IV [2 of 2]"; and unsigned White House memorandum, March 24, 1970, Colson Papers, box 32, folder "American Enterprise Institute III [2 of 2]." Both documents from the Nixon Presidential Library. See also comments by Deputy Secretary of Defense David Packard, as described in James J. Kilpatrick, "Why Students Are Hostile to Free Enterprise," *Nation's Business*, July 1975.

43. Presidential transcripts of conversation among Nixon, H. R. Haldeman, and Henry Kissinger, November 13, 1972, in *Abuse of Power: The New Nixon Tapes*, ed. Stanley I. Kutler (New York: Free Press, 1997), 8. Emphasis in the original has been deleted.

44. Presidential transcripts of conversation between Nixon and H. R. Haldeman, November 13, 1972, in Kutler, *Abuse of Power*, 176.

45. Presidential transcripts of conversations with H. R. Haldeman and Ronald Ziegler, July 5, 1971, in Kutler, *Abuse of Power*, 24.

46. Richard M. Nixon, *RN: The Memoirs of Richard Nixon* (New York: Grosset & Dunlap, 1978), 512–13.

47. Agnew quoted verbatim in William J. Baroody, "The Corporate Role in the Decade Ahead," October 20, 1972, 7, in W. Averell Harriman Papers, box 612, folder "Post Govt: Business Council, 1969," Library of Congress. Emphasis in the original document has been deleted.

48. Allen J. Matusow, *Nixon's Economy: Booms, Busts, Dollars, and Votes* (Lawrence: University Press of Kansas, 1998), 215, 252.

49. Nixon, *RN*, 761. In this section of this memoirs, Nixon was referencing an earlier interview he did with the *Washington Star.*

50. Quoted from Dan Rather and Gary Paul Gates, *The Palace Guard* (New York: Harper & Row, 1974), 8; emphasis added. Rather and Gates do not identify the quoted official. Along similar lines, Attorney General John Mitchell stated: "This country is going so far to the right that you won't recognize it." Quote from Hunter S. Thompson, "Fear and Loathing on the Campaign Trail in '72," *Rolling Stone*, July 5, 1972.

51. William J. Baroody Jr., "Memorandum for the President: Letters to Congress," March 6, 1973, White House Special Files, Staff Member and Office Files, Staff Secretary, box 81, folder "Presidential Memos—1973–1974, Baroody," Nixon Presidential Library.

52. Memorandum from Charles W. Colson to John Ehrlichman, April 7, 1971, in Colson Papers, box 82, folder 25, Nixon Presidential Library.

53. Sam Rosenfeld, *The Polarizers: Postwar Architects of Our Partisan Era* (Chicago: University of Chicago Press, 2018), 173–76. On the Southern strategy, see also Kevin P. Phillips, *The Emerging Republican Majority* (New Rochelle, NY: Arlington House, 1969); and Matthew D. Lassiter, *The Silent Majority: Suburban Politics in the Sunbelt South* (Princeton, NJ: Princeton University Press, 2007).

54. Elizabeth Hinton, *America on Fire: The Untold Story of Police Violence and Black Rebellion Since the 1960s* (New York: Norton, 2021), pt. I.

55. See Senator Goldwater's views on Watergate in Goldwater, *With No Apologies*, 252–69.

56. Memo from Bell to Irving Kristol, Nathan Glazer, and James Q. Wilson, "On Watergate," September 10, 1973, from Daniel Bell Papers, box 167, folder 7, Harvard University. Emphasis in original. Note that Bell was widely characterized as a neoconservative (accurately in my view), though Bell himself resisted the label.

57. "After Watergate: Putting Business Ethics in Perspective," *Business Week*, September 15, 1973. For a similar view about Watergate's impact, see Llewellyn King, "Energy: The Crisis in Society," 3, speech before meeting of the Business Council, May 11, 1979, in Harriman Papers, box 987, folder "Post-Government—Business Council, 1978–85".

58. On business anxiety about the prospect of Democratic gains in November 1974, see "Labor's Push for a Veto-Proof Congress: Its Leaders Hope to Elect Enough Friends to Be Able to Override any Presidential Veto," *Nation's Business*, August 1974. Note that *Nation's Business* was the official publication of the U.S. Chamber of Commerce.

59. "Right-Wing Rolls Along as Reagan Clinches Nomination," *Group Research Report*, May 29, 1980.

60. See two documents from Baroody Papers: "American Enterprise Institute, Board of Trustees, April 1975" [attached to letter from Richard M. Lee to J. F. Burditt, May 20, 1975], box 35, folder 10; and American Enterprise Institute, list of "Active Corporation Contributions (Contributions in 1974 or 1975)," box 56, folder 5.

61. Stephen Klaidman, "A Look at Former President Ford's Think Tank Institution," *Washington Post*, February 20, 1977.

62. Thimmesch, "American Enterprise Institute." See also Steven Rattner, "A Think Tank for Conservatives," *New York Times*, March 23, 1975; Karlyn Bowman, "Melvin Laird, RIP," American Enterprise Institute, November 17, 2016, https://www.aei.org/politics-and-public-opinion/melvin-laird-rip; and "Herbert Stein, 1916–1999," American Enterprise Institute, October 1, 1999, https://www.aei.org/articles/herbert-stein-1916-1999/.

63. On Haberler's ties to the Nixon administration, see Arthur Selden, "Obituary: Gottfried Haberler," *Independent*, May 15, 1995; and memo from Tilford C. Gaines, December 17, 1968, transmitting "Task Force on U.S. Balance of Payments Policies to the President Elect," Houthakker Papers, box 31, folder "Haberler Task Force, No. 2," Nixon Presidential Library.

64. David R. Henderson, "A Feel for Economics: Murray Weidenbaum, 1927–2014," *Regulation*, Winter 2014–15. See also Weidenbaum's AEI biography in *Government-Mandated Price Increases: A Neglected Aspect of Inflation*, accessed November 20, 2023, https://www.aei.org/research-products/book/government-mandated-price-increases/; and Thimmesch, "American Enterprise Institute."

65. Thimmesch, "American Enterprise Institute." On public outreach, see also letter from William Baroody to Howard W. Blauvelt, May 31,1974, in Baroody Papers, box 56, folder 5.

66. Max Kampelman, a former aide to Senator Hubert Humphrey, served on the advisory board to AEI's project on government regulation. Noted in Thimmesch, "American Enterprise Institute."

67. Letter from Robert F. Dee to Lacy Hunt, November 6, 1975, in Baroody Papers, box 46, folder 2.

68. Letter from Richard B. Madden to Robert E. Cannon, November 21, 1977, in Baroody Papers, box 38, folder 6. On AEI connections to the American Petroleum Institute, see memo from Gordon Hodgson to William Baroody, "Energy Project," October 5, 1973, in Baroody Papers, box 72, folder 8.

69. Quote from Council on Foreign Relations associate Alton Fry in Peter H. Stone, "Conservative Brain Trust," *New York Times Magazine*, May 10, 1981.

70. Letter from William Baroody to Robert R. Richardson, June 19, 1974; letter from Glenn Campbell to R. R. Richardson, June 25, 1974. Both documents are in Baroody Papers, box 45, folder 3. Note that the official name was Hoover Institution of War, Revolution, and Peace.

71. "Hoover Institution on War, Revolution and Peace, Board of Overseers, November 1971," James Buchanan Papers, box 63, folder "Correspondence, The Heritage Foundation, 1976–1987," series 2 ("Correspondence"), subseries 1 ("Alphabetical Correspondence"), George Mason University.

72. "The Hoover Institution Edges Toward the Middle," *Business Week*, August 23, 1982. See also Stewart McBride, "Hoover Institution: Leaning to the Right," *Christian Science Monitor*, March 27, 1980.

73. Martin Arnold, "Papers Cite Transcripts in Ending Support of Nixon," *New York Times*, May 20, 1974.

74. Robert G. Kaiser, "Money, Family Name Shaped Scaife," *Washington Post*, May 3, 1999.

75. Quote from Karen Rothmyer, "Citizen Scaife," *Columbia Journalism Review*, July/August 1981.

76. David Warner, "Scaife: Financier of the Right," *Pittsburgh Post-Gazette*, April 20, 1981; Kaiser, "Money, Family Name Shaped Scaife"; and John S. Saloma III, *Ominous Politics: The New Conservative Labyrinth* (New York: Hill & Wang, 1984), 14–15. 35.

77. Saloma, *Ominous Politics*, 14–15.

78. Morton Kondracke, "The Heritage Model," *New Republic*, December 20, 1980.

79. Letter from Irving Kristol to Frank Shakespeare, February 13, 1980, in Kristol Papers, box 12, folder 3.

80. See discussion in chapter 3 of this study and Joseph E. Lowndes, *From the New Deal to the New Right: Race and the Southern Origins of Modern Conservatism* (New Haven, CT: Yale University Press, 2009), chaps. 4, 5.

81. Thomas Byrne Edsall, *The New Politics of Inequality* (New York: Norton, 1984), 118, 219–20, 224. For an extended study of the Miami program, see Steven M. Teles, *The Rise of the Conservative Legal Movement: The Battle for Control of the Law* (Princeton, NJ: Princeton University Press, 2008), chap. 4.

82. Letter from Henry G. Manne to William W. Weston, January 31, 1975, in Kristol Papers, box 15, folder 8; Walter Guzzadri Jr., "Judges Discover the World of Economics," *Fortune*, May 21, 1979. Note that the Miami institution was originally named "Center for Studies in Law and Economics."

83. Guzzadri, "Judges Discover the World of Economics."

84. During the 1970s, the CSIS Executive Board included the retired Admiral Arleigh Burke and former chairman of the Joint Chiefs of Staff Thomas Moorer, while its executive director was the former CIA officer Ray S. Cline. See Tim Weiner, "Ray S. Cline: Chief CIA Analyst Is Dead at 77," *New York Times*, March 16, 1996; and James Allen Smith, *Strategic Calling: The Center for Strategic and International Studies, 1962–1992* (Washington, DC: Center for Strategic and International Studies, 1993), 250. On the probable ties between CSIS cofounder Richard Allen and the Grumman Corporation, see Barry Schweid, "Allen: Trouble Keeping His Head Down," Associated Press, November 13, 1981.

85. Letter from James Buchanan to Francis A. O'Connell Jr., June 30, 1978, in Buchanan Papers, series 2 ("Correspondence"), subseries 1 ("Alphabetical Correspondence"), box 74, folder "Grants, Olin Foundation [2 of 2]."

86. Patrick J. Akard, "The Return of the Market: Corporate Mobilization and the Transformation of U.S. Economic Policy, 1974–1984" (PhD thesis, Department of Sociology, University of Kansas, 1989), chap. 2; Russ Bellant, *The Coors Connection: How Coors Family Philanthropy Undermines Democratic Pluralism* (Boston: South Bend Press, 1991); and Nicole Hoplin and Ron Robinson,

Funding Fathers: The Unsung Heroes of the Conservative Movement (Washington, DC: Regnery, 2008), especially chaps. 1, 8.

87. Michael C. Jensen, "Young Millionaires Are Big Contributors to McGovern," *New York Times*, August 23, 1972; "The Money Man for McGovern," *Business Week*, June 3, 1972; and "Institute for Policy Studies (Executive Summary)," Heritage Foundation, April 19, 1977, https://www.heritage.org/conservatism/report/institute-policy-studies.

88. Robert H. Malott, "Self Interest Should Guide Corporate Giving," *FMC Progress*, Spring 1977, in Baroody Papers, box 38, folder 7.

89. William Whyte quoted in "Why the Corporate Lobbyist Is Necessary: More and More Companies Rely on Lobbyists to Cope with Big Government," *Business Week*, March 18, 1972.

90. "Remarks by Bryce N. Harlow before the Annual Meeting of the Business Roundtable," June 17, 1974, 3–4, in Baroody Papers, box 64, folder 3. Harlow stated that the aforementioned views were expressed by Washington politicians in their assessments of business; Harlow made it clear that he agreed with the assessments. For a similar view, see letter from Henry G. Manne to Lemuel Boulware, February 7, 1974, in William Banowsky Papers, box 6, folder "Business Industry Education Seminar, May 9, 1974," Pepperdine University.

91. Friedman, quoted in Malott, "Self Interest Should Guide Corporate Giving." Similar views were expressed by the chairman of the Board of Cyanamid, James G. Affleck, "Remarks Before the NEA/Industry Meeting," November 9, 1976, 2, in Paul M. Weyrich Papers, box 18, folder 10, American Heritage Center, University of Wyoming; and Lee Drutman, *The Business of America Is Lobbying: How Corporations Became Politicized and Politics Became More Corporate* (New York: Oxford University Press, 2015), 9.

92. Quotes from William Baroody, "Public Policy Trends: Implications for the Future," speech before the Annual Meeting of the Mutual Insurance Alliance, New Orleans, May 24, 1976, 15, in Baroody Papers, box 85, folder 5. The embedded quote is from Daniel Bell, who is referenced with approval by Baroody.

93. "You're Still the Answer," editorial, *Nation's Business*, May 1974.

94. Bleiberg, "Benevolent Uncle?" See also letter from Karl R. Bendetsen to D. K. Ludwig, September 26, 1978, in Baroody Papers, box 61, folder 6.

95. D. J. Kirchhoff speech before the Merchants & Manufacturers Association, verbatim in "Corporate Missionary: Those Who Believe in Capitalism Must Fight Back," *Barron's National Business and Financial Weekly*, February 19, 1979.

96. Speech by Elisha Gray II before the Business Council, Hot Springs, Virginia, "The Imperatives for Business for the Next Ten Years," October 20, 1972, 5–6, in Harriman Papers, box 612, folder "Post Govt—Business Council, 1969" Emphasis in the original has been deleted.

97. The idea of defunding liberal or centrist institutions became a staple of discussion in corporate circles. See James J. Kilpatrick, "Why Students Are Hostile to Free Enterprise," *Nation's Business*, July 1975; and Irving Kristol, "On Corporate Philanthropy," *Wall Street Journal*, March 21, 1977.

98. James Grant, "Government in Exile? The Brookings Institution Wields Tremendous Clout," *Barron's National Business and Financial Weekly*, October 27, 1975. On the rightward shift at Brookings, see also statements by Robert Roosa and Herbert Stein, quoted in Leonard Silk and Mark Silk, *The American Establishment* (New York: Basic Books, 1980), 179, 182.

99. Ford Foundation support for AEI is noted in a letter from Don A. Goodall to William Baroody, February 27, 1976, in Baroody Papers, box 12, folder 1; and Jason Michael Shahl, "Selling Conservatism: Think Tanks, Conservative Ideology, and the Undermining of Liberalism, 1945–Present" (PhD diss., Department of History, University of Minnesota, 2008), 72.

100. Letter from William Baroody to David Packard, January 5, 1979, in Baroody Papers, box 24, folder 4.

101. Kim McQuaid, "The Roundtable: Getting Results in Washington," *Harvard Business Review*, May/June 1981. See also the well-documented study, Benjamin C. Waterhouse, *Lobbying America: The Politics of Business from Nixon to NAFTA* (Princeton, NJ: Princeton University Press, 2014). Note that Burns and Connally helped form the "March Group," which soon evolved into the Business Roundtable.

102. Walter Guzzardi Jr., "Business Is Learning How to Win in Washington: With Top Corporate Leaders Now Out in Front, the Business Lobby Is Bigger and More Influential Than Ever," *Fortune*, March 27, 1978.

103. Memorandum from Ray Bowie, "Rough Draft of [Right to Work Legal Defense] Foundation History," October 17, 1979, 9, in John Davenport Papers, box 25, folder 1, Hoover Institution, Stanford University. The attached report stated, "Financial support of the Foundation increased dramatically. . . . [In 1970, the Foundation president] invited over 200 business and community leaders . . . to serve on the Foundation's new National Advisory Council of Business Leaders. . . . In 1969, 10,866 contributors had financially supported the new Foundation; by the end of 1970, the number of contributors had already reached 71,124." Still, in 1971, one executive with Sun Oil believed that right to work remained "a lost cause" and advised against contributing. Letter from Clyde Wheeler [Sun Oil letterhead] to Miriam E. Bisbing, September 23, 1971, in J. Howard Pew Papers, box 107, folder "Political Contributions, 1971," Hagley Center Archive, Wilmington, Delaware. In reality, the "lost cause" of antiunionism would prove increasingly successful despite Pew's judgment.

104. Douglas Martin, "Labor Nemesis: When the Boss Calls in this Expert, the Union May be in Real Trouble—Philadelphia Lawyer Cabot Helped Keep Unions Out, Unseat Those Already In," *Wall Street Journal*, November 19, 1979.

105. "Conservatives Are Working on State Legislatures," *Group Research Report*, March 29, 1978. On Scaife support for ALEC, see the memoir by the conservative activist Alan Crawford, *Thunder on the Right: The "New Right" and the Politics of Resentment* (New York: Pantheon, 1980), 12–14.

106. "1977: Suggested State Legislation, ALEC, American Legislative Exchange Council," in Papers of the Conservative Party of New York, series 7, box 1, folder "American Legislative Exchange Council," State University of New York, Albany.

107. On the U.S. Chamber and the National Association of Manufacturers, see Alyssa Katz, *The Influence Machine: The U.S. Chamber of Commerce and the Corporate Capture of American Life* (New York: Spiegel & Grau, 2015), pt. I; memorandum from William Baroody Jr., "Meeting with the National Association of Manufacturers and the U.S. Chamber of Commerce," September 5, 1974, in White House Central File, Name File, 1974–77, box 2292, folder "National Association of Manufacturers," Ford Presidential Library; Juan Cameron, "What Businessmen Like and Don't Like About Nixon," *Fortune*, July 1972; and Richard I. Kirkland Jr., "Lobbies: Fat Days for the Chamber of Commerce," *Fortune*, September 21, 1981.

108. "Membership in NAM Public Relations Council," attached to letter from Richard L. Cutler to William J. Baroody, November 27, 1970, in Baroody Papers, box 75, folder 10. On earlier perceptions that NAM and the chamber were ineffective, see Philip H. Burch Jr., *Elites in American History: The New Deal to the Carter Administration* (New York: Holmes & Meier, 1980), 234.

109. Adam Bernstein, "Amway Cofounder Jay Van Andel Dies at 80," *Washington Post*, December 8, 2004. On the Marriott connection, see "The Chamber of Commerce of the U.S.," *Group Research Report*, July/August 1979. On Armco Steel, Raytheon, Bristol-Myers, and other corporate interests, see "How to Get Along: There Have Been Many Recriminations Between Business and the Mass Media—Now Efforts Are Increasing to Shift from Confrontation to Cooperation," *Nation's Business*, April 1978.

110. Burch, *Elites in American History*, 281; Bill Black, "The Powell Memorandum's 40th Anniversary: Impunity for Control Fraud," *Business Insider*, April 25, 2011.

111. Lewis F. Powell Jr., "Attack on the Free Enterprise System: Confidential Memorandum for the U.S. Chamber of Commerce," August 23, 1971, 1, 29–30, Lewis Powell Papers, Washington and Lee University, https://scholarlycommons.law.wlu.edu/cgi/viewcontent.cgi?article=1000&context=powellmemo.

112. Jack Anderson, "FBI Missed Blueprint by Powell," *Washington Post*, September 29, 1972.

113. See numerous admiring letters referencing the Powell Memorandum in Powell Papers, "Reaction—Attack on the Free Enterprise System," accessed November 20, 2023, https://scholarlycommons.law.wlu.edu/powellmemo/3/. Note that the Chamber of Commerce formed the "Task Force on the Powell Memorandum," in letter from William S. Lowe to William G. Whyte, "December 15, 1972, Baroody Papers, box 88, folder 6. See also mention of the Powell Memorandum in Connie Marshner, Heritage Foundation, "Essentials and Benefits of the Free Enterprise System: A Course of Study in Public Schools of Texas," 1976, 2, in Weyrich Papers, box 18, folder 10; and letter from Reed Irvine to J. Roderick MacArthur, March 28, 1979, Accuracy in Media Papers, box 31, folder "Reed Irvine Chron File, January 1979," Brigham Young University.

114. "Big Business, Ecologists Clash Nears," *Sacramento Bee*, March 4, 1973.

115. Dana L. Thomas, "On the Right Side: The Pacific Legal Foundation Is Doing Yeoman Work," *Barron's National Business and Financial Weekly*, February 2, 1976.

116. Oliver A. Houck, "Charity for All," *Yale Law Journal* 93, no. 8 (1984); and "New Legal Network Takes Conservative Cases," *Group Research Report*, November 30, 1977.

117. Saloma, *Ominous Politics*, 8–9, 66. The Committee for the Survival of a Free Congress also received contributions from the Pittsburgh-Des Moines Steel Company. See letter from W. R. Jackson Jr., to Joseph Coors, March 31, 1976, Weyrich Papers, box 36, folder 6.

118. "NAM Is Pushing Business PACs," *Group Research Report*, October 26, 1979.

119. Paul H. Weaver, "Corporations Are Defending Themselves with the Wrong Weapon," *Fortune*, June 1977; emphasis added. Note that this article was somewhat critical of the economics education courses and stressed the need for improved course materials.

120. "Industry's Schoolhouse Clout," *Business Week*, October 13, 1980.

121. "Teaching Young People to Understand Business," *Nation's Business*, May 1975.

122. "1977: Suggested State Legislation, ALEC, American Legislative Exchange Council," 48–49, in Papers of the Conservative Party of New York, Series 7, box 1, folder "American Legislative Exchange Council." For a history of ALEC, see Alexander Hertel-Fernandez, *State Capture: How Conservative Activists, Big Business, and Wealthy Donors Reshaped the American States—and the Nation* (New York: Oxford University Press, 2019), 27–38.

123. "Conservatives Are Working on State Legislatures," *Group Research Report*, March 29, 1978.

124. Ann Crittenden, "The Economic Wind's Blowing Toward the Right—for Now," *New York Times*, July 16, 1978.

125. Sheila Harty, *Hucksters in the Classroom: A Review of Industry Propaganda in Schools* (Washington, DC: Center for Responsive Law, 1979), 78.

126. Raymond D'Argenio of Mobil Oil, quoted in Irwin Ross, "Public Relations Isn't Kid Glove Stuff at Mobil," *Fortune*, September 1976. A congressional source stated that "oil companies have spent hundreds of millions of dollars" on political advertising. Letter from Congressman Thomas J. Downey to William Tavoulareas, Mobil Oil, November 11, 1977, in Jack Anderson Papers, box 315, folder 4, George Washington University.

127. Ross, "Public Relations Isn't Kid Glove Stuff at Mobil."

128. Sally Quinn, "Herb Schmertz, Kennedy's Mobil Superflack: From Oil Company Image-Maker to the Teddy Kennedy Campaign," *Washington Post*, November 28, 1979.

129. Robert J. Samuelson, "The Oil Companies and the Press," *Columbia Journalism Review*, January/February 1974. Sun Oil funded efforts to influence the press in a probusiness direction, as indicated by a letter from Charles Hull Wolfe to Robert G. Dunlop of Sun Oil, January 28, 1975, in Kristol Papers, box 15, folder 8. On Atlantic Richfield's media efforts, see letter from William A. Rusher to Philip M. Crane, May 12, 1976, in William A. Rusher Papers, box 21, folder 11, Library of Congress.

130. Letter from Reed Irvine to Mrs. St. John Garwood, March 23, 1977, in Accuracy in Media Papers, box 6, folder "G Misc—General Correspondence."

131. James J. Kilpatrick, "A Short Course in Media Relations," *Nation's Business*, June 1979.

132. "Scaife Buys Into Newspaper Empire," *Group Research Report*, December 28, 1977.

133. Letter from Alexander Haig Jr., to William Rusher, October 30, 1980, in Rusher Papers, box 37, folder 7.

134. Bob Chitester, "How *Free to Choose* Changed the World," *Reason*, October 21, 2020.

135. Peter W. Bernstein, "The Man Who Brought You Milton Friedman," *Fortune*, February 25, 1980. The funds associated with National Presto Industries were provided by the company chairman through a charity that he controlled. On Bechtel funding, see Saloma, *Ominous Politics*, 34.

136. Letter from William Rusher to John Connally, August 28, 1975; memorandum to Bill Buckley and Bill Rusher, October 13, 1975; and "List of Acceptances for the Luncheon in Honor of John B. Connally," October 2, 1975. Documents in Rusher Papers, box 20, folder 10.

137. Regarding funding for AIM and the Media Institute from oil companies, Scaife, and other wealthy interests, see the following: "New Right-Wing Organization Is Taking on the Media," *Group Research Report*, September 25, 1979; "United States Industrial Council Education Foundation," *Group Research Report*, October 22, 1980; and "Memo for Jack—with AIM Memo," November 9, 1975, in

Anderson Papers, box 275, folder 2. Also see the following documents, all from Accuracy in Media Papers: Letter from Reed Irvine to Mrs. St. John Garwood, March 23, 1977, box 6, folder "G Misc—General Correspondence"; letter from Irvine to Shelby Cullom Davis, February 22, 1979, in box 31, folder "Reed Irvine Chron File, 1979"; and letter from Irvine to Richard M. Larry, December 28, 1978, in box 31, folder "Reed Irvine Chron File, 1979."

138. On Roger Ailes's failed TVN venture, see Gabriel Sherman, *The Loudest Voice in the Room: How the Brilliant, Bombastic Roger Ailes Built Fox News—and Divided a Country* (New York: Random House, 2017), 97–107; and Stanhope Gould, "Coors Brews the News," *Columbia Journalism Review*, March/April 1975.

139. Dinesh D'Souza, "Retreat from Radicalism: The Times, It Is a-Changing," *Policy Review*, Fall 1984, 26. On earlier negative perspectives on the *Times*, see "Interview of Secretary Simon," May 30, 1976, 72, in William E. Simon Papers, series V, drawer 43, box 86, folder 39, Lafayette College.

140. Regarding fears that U.S. political culture was turning against private enterprise, see the following: "Who Will the New Advocates of Business Be?," speech by William J. Baroody at the Conference Board, February 8, 1973, Baroody Papers, box 96, folder 4; Llewellyn King, "Energy: The Crisis in Society," speech before the Business Council, May 11, 1979, in Harriman Papers, box 987, folder "Post-Government—Business Council, 1978–85"; "Egalitarianism: Threat to a Free Market," *Business Week*, December 1, 1975; and "The Unconventional Becomes Respectable," *Business Week*, January 9, 1971.

141. Martin Feldstein, Lawrence Summers, and Michael Wachter, "Is the Rate of Profit Falling?," *Brookings Papers on Economic Activity* no. 1 (1977): 221; emphasis in quotes added. The authors speculated optimistically that low profitability was a temporary phenomenon, but this predication was proven wrong, as profits remained low for an extended period. See statistics on profitability in Thomas L. Hungerford, "Corporate Tax Rates and Economic Growth Since 1947," (Issue Brief 364, Economic Policy Institute, Washington, DC, June 4, 2013), https://www.epi.org/publication/ib364-corporate-tax-rates-and-economic-growth/.

142. The long-term decline of U.S. profit rates forms a central theme in Robert Brenner, "The Economics of Global Turbulence: A Special Report on the World Economy, 1950–1998," *New Left Review*, no. 229 (1998).

143. Alicia H. Munnell, "Why Has Productivity Growth Declined? Productivity and Public Investment," *New England Economic Review* [Federal Reserve Bank of Boston], January/February 1990. The economic historian Robert Gordon emphasizes that the rise in productivity in post–Civil War American history was associated with technological advances and improvements in educational attainment that had mostly run their course by the early 1970s. One particularly significant factor cited by Gordon was effective completion of the Interstate

Highway System in 1972, with only limited improvements in highways and other transportation after that date. See Robert J. Gordon, *The Rise and Fall of American Growth: The U.S. Standard of Living Since the Civil War* (Princeton, NJ: Princeton University Press, 2016), pt. II, especially 390–91.

144. The central importance of the energy crisis as a cause of productivity decline is presented in study by William Nordhaus, "Retrospective on the 1970s' Productivity Slowdown" (NBER Working Papers Series, no. 10950, National Bureau of Economic Research, Cambridge, MA, 2004), 29–30, https://www.nber.org/papers/w10950. Note that federal pollution controls were often cited as a major cause of economic stress, but that appears doubtful, a point emphasized by the Council of Economic Advisers during the Nixon presidency. See memorandum for the president, July 20,1971, in White House Central Files, Staff Member and Office Files, Ezra Solomon Papers, box 1, folder "Memos for the President [2of2]," Nixon Presidential Library.

145. Concern about declining profits was noted in Andrew Brimmer, "Why Inflation Hits Some People Less Than Others," *Nation's Business*, February 1977, 39.

146. Joseph J. Minarik, "The Distributional Effects of Inflation and Their Implications," in U.S. Congress, Joint Economic Committee, *Stagflation: The Causes, Effects, and Solutions* (Washington, DC: U.S. Government Printing Office, 1980), 229.

147. Edward N. Wolff, "The Distributional Effects of the 1969–1975 Inflation on Holdings of Household Wealth in the United States," *Review of Income and Wealth* 25, no. 2 (1979): 206–7.

148. See George L. Perry, Martin Neil Bailey, and William Poole, "Slowing the Wage Price Spiral: The Macroeconomic View," *Brookings Papers in Economic Activity*, no. 2 (1978).

149. Minarik, "The Distributional Effects of Inflation and Their Implications," 229.

150. Stein, *Presidential Economics*, 219. Stein noted that inflation caused macroeconomic dysfunctions due to increased uncertainty and risk, which discouraged investment. However, the standard solution to inflation—austerity through increased unemployment—causes even greater dysfunctions.

151. See U.S. data on income inequality, 1900–2010, table S8.2, in "Technical Appendix to *Capital in the 21st Century*" (Cambridge, MA: Belknap Press of Harvard University, 2014), http://piketty.pse.ens.fr/files/capital21c/en/pdf/supp/TS8.2.pdf.

152. Richard M. Nixon, "Address to the Nation Outlining a New Economic Policy: 'The Challenge of Peace,'" August 15, 1971, in American Presidency Project, https://www.presidency.ucsb.edu/documents/address-the-nation-outlining-new-economic-policy-the-challenge-peace. In his speech, Nixon also emphasized inflation's negative impact on the elderly.

153. Jimmy Carter, "Atlanta Georgia, Remarks Accepting the Martin Luther King, Jr. Nonviolent Peace Prize," January 14, 1979, in American Presidency Project, https://www.presidency.ucsb.edu/documents/atlanta-georgia-remarks-accepting -the-martin-luther-king-jr-nonviolent-peace-prize.

154. Milton Friedman, "Inflation and Unemployment," December 13, 1976, Nobel Memorial Lecture, https://www.nobelprize.org/uploads/2018/06/friedman-lecture -1.pdf.

155. During 1984–85, Israel reached a point "bordering on hyperinflation." The Israeli inflation constituted an unusual case, since it was associated with excessively high levels of military spending and an almost continuous state of warfare since independence. The economy became particularly stressed during the "lost decade" that followed the 1973 war, which Israel nearly lost. See Rafi Melnick and Yosef Mealem, "Israel Studies, an Anthology: Israel's Economy, 1986–2008," September 2009, *Jewish Virtual Encyclopedia*, https://www.jewish virtuallibrary.org/israel-studies-an-anthology-israel-s-economy.

156. James M. Buchanan and Richard E. Wagner, *Democracy in Deficit: The Political Legacy of Lord Keynes* (New York: Academic, 1977), 65.

157. Friedman, *Capitalism and Freedom*, xiv.

158. Inflation was also used as a pretext for implementing a free market policy turn in Great Britain under Margaret Thatcher. See comments by former adviser to the UK Treasury Alan Budd, quoted in Robert Wade, "How High Inequality Plus Neoliberal Governance Weakens Democracy," *Challenge* 56, no. 6 (2013): 7.

159. Quotes from William Simon, "Talking Points for the Business Council," December 12, 1974, William Simon Papers, series V, drawer 38, folder 91. The document is a draft speech. Emphasis in original.

160. On standing ovations, see the following documents, both from Willam Simon Papers: letter from John P. Roche, President of the American Iron and Steel Institute, May 29, 1975, series V, drawer 39, folder 12; and letter from Carl E. Bagge, president of the National Coal Association, June 20, 1975, series V, drawer 39, folder 28.

161. For first-hand accounts, see Gerald R. Ford, *A Time to Heal: The Autobiography of Gerald R. Ford* (New York: Harper & Row, 1979), 315–19; David Gergen, *Eyewitness to Power: The Essence of Leadership, Nixon to Clinton* (New York: Simon & Schuster, 2000), 115; James Cannon, *Gerald R. Ford: An Honorable Man* (Ann Arbor: University of Michigan Press, 2013), 359–64; Robert T. Hartmann, *Palace Politics: An Inside Account of the Ford Years* (New York: McGraw-Hill, 1980), 355–59; Alan Greenspan, Oral History Interview, December 17, 2008, Ford Presidential Library, https://geraldrfordfoundation.org/centennial-docs /oralhistory/wp-content/uploads/2013/05/Alan-Greenspan.pdf; and Donald Rumsfeld, Oral History Interview, March 31, 2009, Ford Presidential Library,

https://geraldrfordfoundation.org/centennial-docs/oralhistory/wp-content /uploads/2013/05/Donald-Rumsfeld.pdf.

162. Simon, *Time for Reflection*, 150–51. Regarding the role of David Rockefeller and George Ball in advocating for leniency toward New York, see "Interview of Honorable William E. Simon, Secretary of the Treasury," pt. II, 310, n.d. (probably 1976), William Simon Papers, series V, drawer 43, box 86, folder 44. On the business community's reluctance to accept a full default, see "Bailing Out New York," *Business Week*, October 20, 1975.

163. "Fiscal Cuts or Racial Cuts?," *New York Amsterdam News*, February 28, 1976.

164. On the role of inflation in influencing President Ford's decision to limit the federal bailout of New York, see Gerald R. Ford, "Remarks at a Republican Party Rally in Milwaukee," October 30, 1975, in American Presidency Project, https:// www.presidency.ucsb.edu/documents/remarks-republican-party-rally -milwaukee.

165. Letter from Ford to Earl C. Johnson, September 26, 1974, in White House Central Files, Name File, 1974–77, box 555, folder "Chamber of Commerce, 8/74– 3/75," Ford Presidential Library.

166. Simon, *Time for Reflection*, 151. In his memoirs, Simon quoted directly from his congressional testimony.

167. Patrick J. Buchanan, "New York," New York *Daily News*, April 11, 1978. On the enthusiasm of conservative activists for a "scorched earth" policy vis-à-vis New York, see "Kingston Minutes," October 31, 1975, Paul Weyrich Papers, box 32, folder 19.

168. Letter from Jude Wanniski to Donald Rumsfeld and Richard Cheney, October 8, 1975, in Jude Wanniski Papers, box 18, folder 5, Hoover Institution Archives, Stanford University.

169. Nicholas Freudenberg, Marianne Fahs, Sandro Galea, and Andrew Greenberg, "The Impact of New York City's 1975 Fiscal Crisis on the Tuberculosis, HIV, and Homicide Syndemic," *American Journal of Public Health* 96, no. 3 (2006): 424. On the long-term effects of the New York fiscal crisis, see Kim Phillips-Fein, *Fear City: New York City's Fiscal Crisis and the Rise of Austerity Politics* (New York: Metropolitan, 2017), pt. III.

170. On the increasingly unified character of U.S. business during this period, see Dan Clawson, Alan Neustadtl, and James Bearden, "The Logic of Business Unity; Corporate Contributions to the 1980 Elections," *American Sociological Review* 51, no. 6 (1986); J. Craig Jenkins and Craig M. Eckert, "The Right Turn in Economic Policy: Business Elites and the New Conservative Economics," *Sociological Forum* 15, no. 2 (2000); Tie-Ting Su, Alan Neustadtl, and Dan Clawson, "Business and the Conservative Shift: Corporate PAC Contributions, 1976–1986," *Social Science Quarterly* 76, no. 1 (1995); Dan Clawson and Alan

Neustadtl, "Interlocks, PACs, and Corporate Conservatism," *American Journal of Sociology* 94, no. 4 (1989); and Patrick J. Akard, "Corporate Mobilization and Political Power: The Transformation of U.S. Economic Policy in the 1970s," *American Sociological Review* 57, no 5 (1992).

3. BUILDING A MASS BASE

The chapter epigraph is from Jefferson Davis, quoted in "Peace Prospects South," *New York Times*, August 18, 1864.

1. See data in Gerald Mayer, "Union Membership Trends in the United States" (CRS Report for Congress, Congressional Research Service, Washington, DC, August 31, 2004), 22, https://sgp.fas.org/crs/misc/RL32553.pdf. I note union membership as the "Percent of wage and salary workers."

2. Thomas Ferguson and Joel Rogers, "The Myth of America's Turn to the Right," *The Atlantic*, May 1986.

3. The pivotal role of Weyrich in the New Right is emphasized in "Confidential Memorandum" from Jeffrey St. John to Richard DeVos, October 24, 1978, in Paul M. Weyrich Papers, box 17, folder 32, American Heritage Center, University of Wyoming.

4. See sources in chapter 2, notes 76 and 77.

5. Weyrich had long lamented the Republican weakness in the area of mass organizing, noting, "For reasons known only to itself, the Republican party does very little with the organizational aspect of politics. This is in fact the area where organized labor scores its greatest gains. . . . This is why conservative candidates must meet organized labor on its own ground." Memo from Weyrich to Jerry Guth, "Various CSFC Activities," August 31, 1978, Weyrich Papers, box 36, folder 6.

6. Paul Weyrich, interviewed in Adam Curtis, dir., "The Power of Nightmares, Part 1: Baby, It's Cold Outside," BBC 2004, available from YouTube video, https://www.youtube.com/watch?v=7O90svFKdjQ.

7. The phrase "silent majority" was originally used in reference to supporters of Nixon's Vietnam policy, though it later assumed much broader cultural connotations as well. See Richard Nixon, "Address to the Nation on the War in Vietnam," November 3, 1969, Nixon Presidential Library, https://www.nixonlibrary.gov/sites/default/files/2018-08/silentmajority_transcript.pdf.

8. Letter from L. Brent Bozell, director of the Society for Christian Commonwealth, to William F. Buckley, July 11, 1973, William F. Buckley Papers, box 101, folder 354, Yale University.

9. Weyrich liked to present himself as a populist set apart from the business establishment, but this self-perception had little basis in fact in light of his corporate

ties. Regarding Weyrich's populist identity, see memo from Paul Weyrich "To the Committee," October 18, 1976, Weyrich Papers, box 36, folder 6.

10. Nixon, quoted and paraphrased in Josh Mound, "What Democrats Must Do," *Jacobin*, September 30, 2017, https://jacobin.com/2017/09/democratic-party -2016-election-working-class.

11. Richard M. Nixon, *RN: The Memoirs of Richard M. Nixon* (New York: Grosset & Dunlap, 1978), 491.

12. On the "Southern strategy," see Kevin P. Phillips, *The Emerging Republican Majority* (New Rochelle, NY: Arlington House, 1969), sec. III. See also John Ehrlichman, *Witness to Power: The Nixon Years* (New York: Simon & Schuster, 1982), 213–14; Edward H. Miller, *Nut Country: Right-Wing Dallas and the Birth of the Southern Strategy* (Chicago: University of Chicago Press, 2015); "Interview: Lee Atwater's Infamous 1981 Interview on the Southern Strategy," The Nation, available from YouTube video, https://www.youtube.com/watch?v=X _8E3ENrKrQ; and Joseph E. Lowndes, *From the New Deal to the New Right: Race and the Southern Origins of Modern Conservatism* (New Haven, CT: Yale University Press, 2008), chap. 5.

13. John Ehrlichman, quoted in Dan Baum, "Legalize It All: How to Win the War on Drugs," *Harper's*, April 2016. However, the issue of "law and order" resonated to some degree with African Americans given concerns about rising crime. See Michael Javen Fortner, *Black Silent Majority: The Rockefeller Drug Laws and the Politics of Punishment* (Cambridge, MA: Harvard University Press, 2015).

14. Agnew, quoted in "Agnew Describes Strategy for '72," *New York Times*, October 6, 1971.

15. Quoted in Deborah Huntington and Ruth Kaplan, "Corporate Ties to the Evangelical Christian Groups: A Report to the World Student Christian Federation," August 28, 1980, 13. Unpublished report in Group Research Inc. Papers, box 125, folder 8, Columbia University.

16. Quoted in Huntington and Kaplan, "Corporate Ties to the Evangelical Christian Groups," 13. Note that the "emotional" issues that Weyrich alluded to included "gun control, abortion, taxes, and crime."

17. On the historical legacy of fusionism, see Reihan Salem, "The Origins of the Trump Revolution—Nixon Lives Again," *Wall Street Journal*, November 12, 2016; and Daniel Parker, "CPAC: The Origins and Role of the Conference in the Expansion and Consolidation of the Conservative Movement, 1974–1980" (PhD thesis, Department of Political Science, University of Pennsylvania, 2015), 55–57.

18. Hal Lindsay, *The Late Great Planet Earth* (Grand Rapids, MI: Zondervan, 1970). On the book's influence, see Erin A. Smith, "The *Late Great Planet Earth* Made the Apocalypse a Popular Concern," *Humanities*, Winter 2017.

19. Daniel K. Williams, *God's Own Party: The Making of the Christian Right* (New York: Oxford University Press, 2010), 160; David Frum, *How We Got Here: The 70s—The Decade That Brought You Modern Life—For Better or Worse* (New York: Basic Books, 2000), 148–55; and Jerome L. Himmelstein, *To the Right: The Transformation of American Conservatism* (Berkeley: University of California Press, 1990), 115. And in 1979, Christian conservatives managed to take over the Southern Baptist Convention, much to the chagrin of President Carter, who was himself a Southern Baptist. See Jimmy Carter, *White House Diary* (New York: Picador, 2010), 455.

20. See his memoirs and Patrick J. Buchanan, *Nixon's White House Wars: The Battles That Made and Broke a President and Divided America Forever* (New York: Crown Forum, 2017). See also Mark Galli, "Inside the Nixon Years: Chuck Colson Tells the Inside Story of the Most Controversial Relationship in Billy Graham's Life," *Christianity Today*, April 1, 2018.

21. Nixon, *RN*, 491.

22. Billy Graham, "Inaugural Prayer," January 20, 1969, from Billy Graham Evangelical Association, https://billygraham.org/story/inauguration-prayers-billy-graham-franklin-graham/.

23. Anthea Butler, *White Evangelical Racism: The Politics of Morality in America* (Chapel Hill: University of North Carolina Press, 2021, chaps. 2 and 3; and Randall Balmer, *Bad Faith: Race and the Rise of the Religious Right* (Grand Rapids, MI: Eerdmans, 2021). On the role of Billy Graham, see "Graham, Ministers Say South Will Be First to Solve Race Problem," *New York Amsterdam News*, January 26, 1963; and "Graham Crusade Can Disturb the Blacks," *New York Amsterdam News*, April 18, 1970.

24. Grant Wacker, *America's Pastor: Billy Graham and the Shaping of a Nation* (Cambridge, MA: Belknap Press of Harvard University Press, 2014), 154. On Graham's business connections, see Jane Wolfe, *The Murchisons: The Rise and Fall of a Texas Dynasty* (New York: St. Martin's, 1989), 233; Steven P. Miller, *Billy Graham and the Rise of the Republican South* (Philadelphia: University of Pennsylvania Press, 2009), 169, 175; and Kevin M. Kruse, *In God We Trust: How Corporate America Created Christian America* (New York: Basic Books, 2015), 50–54.

25. Letter from Lemuel Bell to Frank P. Stelling, December 18, 1971, Lemuel Bell Collection, box 41, folder 19, Billy Graham Center, Wheaton College.

26. Quoted in Dominic Sandbrook, *Mad as Hell: The Crisis of the 1970s and the Rise of the Populist Right* (New York: Knopf, 2011), 177. On Nixon's relationship with evangelicals, see also Kristin Kobes du Mez, *Jesus and John Wayne: How White Evangelicals Corrupted a Faith and Fractured a Nation* (New York: Liveright, 2020), 44–48.

27. "An Evening at the White House with Merle Haggard," Richard Nixon Foundation, March 17, 1973, available from YouTube video, https://www.youtube.com/watch?v=EylEuU5x6TU.

28. Nixon's use of country music was quite cynical. The presidential aide H. R. Haldeman privately wrote in his diary that while listeners appreciated Haggard's political lyrics, "the audience obviously had no appreciation for country-western music and there wasn't much rapport." From "H. R. Haldeman Diaries Collection, January 18, 1969–April 30, 1973," entry for March 17, 1973, Nixon Presidential Library, https://www.nixonlibrary.gov/sites/default/files/virtuallibrary/documents/haldeman-diaries/37-hrhd-audiocassette-ac31b32a-19730317-pa.pdf.

29. Kevin Phillips, *American Theocracy: The Peril and Politics of Radical Religion, Oil, and Borrowed Money in the 21st Century* (New York: Viking, 2006), 184.

30. See Collin Hansen, "What I Would Have Done Differently: Billy Graham's Regrets, in His Own Words," *Christianity Today*, April 1, 2018. Despite his personal secularism, President Nixon enjoyed a friendly correspondence with Graham, which extended even after the president's resignation from office. See the research collection "Post Presidential Correspondence with Rev. Billy Graham (1974–1990)," Nixon Presidential Library.

31. On Phillips's pivotal role in rallying Nixon loyalists for a post-Nixon conservatism, see "Memo for Rabbi Korff," from Howard Phillips, December 30, 1974, Howard Phillips Papers, RG-04, CC4:2, box 14, Conservative Caucus Materials, part 6, folder 4W, Liberty University.

32. "Yoking Politics and Proclamation—Can It Be Done? An Interview with Bill Bright," *Christianity Today*, September 24, 1976.

33. Robert C. Liebman, "Mobilizing the Moral Majority," in *The New Christian Right: Mobilization and Legitimation*, ed. Robert C. Liebman and Robert Wuthnow (New York: Aldine, 1983), 50–53; and Marjorie Hyer, "Christian Embassy Is Opened: Group Seeks to Evangelize U.S. Officials," *Washington Post*, February 27, 1976.

34. Allan J. Lichtman, *White Protestant Nation: The Rise of the American Conservative Movement* (New York: Atlantic Monthly Press, 2008), 342.

35. Darren Dochuk, *From Bible Belt to Sun Belt: Plain Folks Religion, Grassroots Politics, and the Rise of Evangelical Conservatism* (New York: Norton, 2011), 386. The *Los Angeles Times* characterized Shakarian himself as a "businessman" as well as a Christian leader. See Russell Chandler, "Gospel Fellowship Draws Charismatics," *Los Angeles Times*, July 5, 1975. On the distinctive role of Orange County, California, in America's conservative transformation, see Lisa McGirr, *Suburban Warriors: The Origins of the New American Right* (Princeton, NJ: Princeton University Press, 2015).

36. Darren Elliott Grem, "The Blessings of Business: Corporate America and Conservative Evangelicalism in the Sunbelt Age, 1945–2000" (PhD thesis, Department of History, University of Georgia, 2010), 199.

37. Robison's 1980 statements from the BBC documentary, "The Power of Nightmares." See also "A Fiery Baptist Evangelist Adopts Some New Doctrines," *Christianity Today*, June 15, 1984.

38. Quoted in "Results of the 1978 Campaign," *Clean Up America Newsletter*, April 1979, in Papers of the Old Time Gospel Hour, FM 3–3, series 1, box 2, folder 1, Liberty University.

39. Jerry Falwell, *Listen America!* (New York: Doubleday, 1980), 13. On the politicization of Falwell's religious activities: "What Is a Right-Winger? Americans 'Who Care,'" *Moral Majority Report*, May 26, 1980, in Moral Majority Papers, Jerry Falwell Library Liberty University, https://cdm17184.contentdm.oclc.org /digital/collection/p17184coll1/id/1702/rec/6.

40. Frances FitzGerald, quoted in Michael Lienesch, *Redeeming America: Piety and Politics in the New Christian Right* (Chapel Hill: University of North Carolina Press, 1993), 11. See also Jerry Falwell, *Falwell: An Autobiography* (Lynchburg, VA: Liberty House, 1997), chap. 14. In his sermons, Falwell openly boasted about his connections to the wealthy. "Chapel Sermon, 01/30/80," Falwell Family Papers, Jerry Falwell Library, Liberty University, https://cdm17184.contentdm .oclc.org/digital/collection/p17184coll4/id/4230/rec/2.

41. See Jerome L. Himmelstein, "The New Right," in *The New Christian Right: Mobilization and Legitimation*, ed. Robert C. Liebman and Robert Wuthnow (New York: Aldine, 1983), 26; Dirk Smillie, *Falwell Inc: Inside a Religious, Political, Educational, and Business Empire* (New York: St. Martin's, 2008), 105; and Steven V. Roberts, "Evangelicals Press Political Activities: Fundamentalists in Sun Belt Ally with Conservative Groups—Expected to Aid Reagan," *New York Times*, September 29, 1980.

42. Grem, "Blessings of Business," 199. On the Hunt dynasty, see "Nelson Hunt Loses a Bundle But Raises a Billion," *Christianity Today*, May 2, 1980.

43. Grem, "Blessings of Business, 159, 161, 187, 191, 203, 210–11. Additional information on business funding can be found in Huntington and Kaplan, "Corporate Ties to the Evangelical Christian Groups," Columbia University.

44. On the corresponding globalization of religion in tandem with conservative economics, see Sabine Dreher, *Religions in International Political Economy* (Cham, Switzerland: Palgrave Macmillan, 2020), especially chap. 3.

45. Bethany Moreton, *To Serve God and Walmart: The Making of Christian Free Enterprise* (Cambridge, MA: Harvard University Press, 2009), chap. 6.

46. *Charleston Gazette* as quoted in Ben A. Franklin, "Textbook Dispute Has Many Causes," *New York Times*, October 14, 1974.

47. "Klan Holds Rally in Textbook Fight," *New York Times*, February 1, 1975. A consultant for the former Alabama governor George Wallace also supported the demonstrators. Memo from Wesley McCune, March 18, 1975, Group Research Inc. Papers box 48, folder "Busing," Columbia University.

48. See statements by the Heritage staffer Connie Marshner in Trey Kay, Deborah George, and Stan Bumgardner, "The Great Textbook War," American Public Media radio program, n.d., http://americanradioworks.publicradio.org/features /textbooks/transcript.html; and Lichtman, *White Protestant Nation*, 314.

49. See Anita Bryant, *The Anita Bryant Story: The Survival of our Nation's Families and the Threat of Militant Homosexuality* (Grand Rapids, MI: Revell, 1977). See also "Interview with Phyllis Schlafly on the Equal Rights Amendment, November 1978," in *Jerry Falwell and the Rise of the Religious Right: A Brief History with Documents*, ed. Matthew Avery Sutton (New York: Bedford/St. Martin's, 2012).

50. At the time that Schlafly was employed with AEI, it was called the American Enterprise Association. See Karlyn Bowman, "The First Lady of Conservatism: Phyllis Schlafly, RIP," American Enterprise Institute, September 6, 2016, https://www.aei.org/society-and-culture/phyllis-schlafly-rip/. The standard study from a conservative standpoint is Donald T. Crichlow, *Phyllis Schlafly and Grassroots Conservatism: A Woman's Crusade* (Princeton, NJ: Princeton University Press, 2005).

51. On Schlafly's ties to Coors, see Russ Bellant, *The Coors Connection: How Coors Family Philanthropy Undermines Democratic Pluralism* (Boston: South End, 1991), 56. With regard to her likely ties to Amway, one of the founders of Amway recommended Schlafly to the Reagan administration for a possible cabinet appointment. See Randall Balmer, "Phyllis Schlafly: The Antifeminist Who Wanted a Job in the Reagan Administration," *Los Angeles Times*, September 8, 2016.

52. On Schlafly's ties to ALEC, see "American Legislative Exchange Council, A Brief Review," n.d. (probably 1980), 3, from Papers of the New York Conservative Party, series 7, box 13, folder "American Legislative Exchange Council, Programs for State Senators," State University of New York, Albany.

53. On Marshner's affiliation with Heritage and also with the Committee for the Survival of a Free Congress, see Eileen White, "Heritage's Influence Is Rooted in Broad Network," *Education Week*, October 5, 1981.

54. Letter from Donald E. Santarelli to Hartford Gunn, June 26, 1974, William J. Baroody Sr. Papers, box 67, folder 14, Library of Congress; and Robert O. Self, *All in the Family: The Realignment of American Democracy Since the 1960s* (New York: Hill & Wang, 2012), 381.

55. The National Pro-Life PAC was backed by the Conservative Caucus, American Conservative Union, Committee for the Survival of a Free Congress, and

ALEC. Regarding corporate support for these latter groups, see chapter 2. On the Pro-Life PAC, see "A Catholic Leader Questions Some Ties with New Right," *Group Research Report*, October 22, 1980.

56. On outreach to Catholics, see Fr. Robert E. Burns, "Catholic 'Thrilled with Success of Moral Majority,' " *Moral Majority Report*, November 13, 1980, in Moral Majority Papers, Jerry Falwell Library, https://cdm17184.contentdm.oclc.org/digital/collection/p17184coll1/id/1685/rec/12.

57. Religious News Service, "Graham's Friendship Toward Jews Applauded by Rabbi Tanenbaum," June 4, 1970, in Grady Baxter Wilson Papers, collection 544, box 29, folder 1, Billy Graham Research Center, Charlotte, North Carolina. On evidence that Graham and other evangelical leaders privately expressed anti-Semitic views, see David Neff, "Billy Graham and the Jews," *Christianity Today*, April 2018; and Patrick Allitt, *Religion in America Since 1945: A History* (New York: Columbia University Press, 2003), 153.

58. Regarding working-class association with evangelical Christianity, see Sara Diamond, *Roads to Dominion: Right-Wing Movements and Political Power in the United States* (New York: Guilford, 1995), 163. Diamond notes research from the early 1980s that showed that viewers of religious television programs tended to be "lower than average in education and income." Regarding evidence that the less educated tended to be conservative on social issues, see letter from Seymour Martin Lipset, April 10, 1978, in Baroody Papers, box 79, folder 2.

59. On working-class economic stresses during this period, see letter from Podhoretz to Morris B. Abrams, April 19, 1971, in Normon Podhoretz Papers, box 1, folder "General Correspondence, 1969–1977," Library of Congress.

60. Robert D. Putnam, *Bowling Alone: The Collapse and Revival of American Community* (New York: Simon & Schuster, 2000), 161; emphasis in original. On Rev. Jerry Falwell's organization, see Harry Covert, "The Sacred Duty for Moral Americans: Vote," *Moral Majority Report*, November 13, 1980, in Moral Majority Papers, Jerry Falwell Library, https://cdm17184.contentdm.oclc.org/digital/collection/p17184coll1/id/1677/rec/12.

61. "Group of Libertarians Pushes Pure Free Enterprise," *Group Research Report*, December 28, 1979.

62. All quotes from Brian Doherty, *Radicals for Capitalism: A Freewheeling History of the Modern American Libertarian Movement* (New York: Public Affairs, 2007), 409–10. On libertarianism, see also Jennifer Burns, *Goddess of the Market: Ayn Rand and the American Right* (New York: Oxford University Press, 2011). Regarding Ayn Rand's long-standing popularity in corporate America, see Michael Hiltzik, "Has Ayn Rand's Day as a Business Guru Finally Passed?," *Los Angeles Times*, February 5, 2015.

63. Doherty, *Radicals for Capitalism*, 409.

64. Charles G. Koch, "Anti-Capitalism and Business," Institute for Humane Studies, 1974. Document provided to me by Samantha Parsons of the organization Un-Koch My Campus, originally obtained from the University of Virginia Special Collections.

65. Jane Mayer, *Dark Money: The Hidden History of the Billionaires Behind the Rise of the Radical Right* (New York: Doubleday, 2016), 56, 87–88, 149–50; emphasis added. For additional information regarding corporate funding for the IHS, see "Institute for Humane Studies," *Group Research Report*, December 22, 1980. Koch also chaired the Council for a Competitive Economy, with a laissez-faire bent and ties to the Conservative Caucus. See "Group of Libertarians Pushes Pure Free Enterprise."

66. On tensions between libertarians and YAF, see Doherty, *Radicals for Capitalism*, 353–59. On YAF's historical connection with *National Review*, see M. Stanton Evans, "Sharon Statement," *National Review*, September 24, 1960. See also "Listen YAF," originally published in *Libertarian Forum*, August 15, 1969, https://www.libertarianism.org/articles/listen-yaf.

67. "Famed Economist Speaks to Truckers," *Overdrive: Magazine of the American Trucker*, March 1973. On the MPS effort to build blue-collar support, see letter from James Buchanan to Milton Friedman, April 2, 1969, in Friedman Papers, box 22, folder 9, Hoover Institution Archives, Stanford University.

68. Steve Viscelli, *The Big Rig: Trucking and the Decline of the American Dream* (Berkeley: University of California Press, 2016). See also Shane Hamilton, "The Populist Appeal of Deregulation: Independent Truckers and the Politics of Free Enterprise, 1935–1980," *Enterprise & Society* 10, no. 1 (2009); Hamilton, *Trucking Country: The Road to America's Walmart Economy* (Princeton, NJ: Princeton University Press, 2014); and Michael H. Belzer, *Sweatshops on Wheels: Winners and Losers in Trucking Deregulation* (New York: Oxford University Press, 2000).

69. Friedman letter, quoted in Nancy MacLean, *Democracy in Chains: The Deep History of the Radical Right's Stealth Plan for America* (New York: Viking, 2017), 68.

70. Milton Friedman, *Capitalism and Freedom* (Chicago: University of Chicago Press, 2002), chap. 6.

71. Memo from R. R. Richardson, "Notes on Conversation with Professor Milton Friedman," November 12, 1973, Irving Kristol Papers, box 14, folder 42, Wisconsin Historical Society.

72. Diane Ravitch, *Reign of Error: The Hoax of the Privatization Movement and the Danger to America's Public Schools* (New York: Knopf, 2014), chap. 19.

73. On the growing conservatism of U.S. business, see Anthony Harrigan, U.S. Industrial Council, "Sensing the News," press release, November 28, 1974, in

Phillips Papers, RG-04, CC4:2, box 14, Conservative Caucus Materials, part 6, folder 4W.

74. Kemp actively promoted the libertarian brand, though he stopped short of calling himself a libertarian. See Alessandra Stanley, "Campaign Portrait, Jack Kemp: Quarterback of Supply Side," *Time*, April 13, 1987.

75. Letter from Irving Kristol to Jack Kemp, April 3, 1978, Kristol Papers, box 12, folder 28.

76. Letter from Irving Kristol to Jack Kemp, May 30, 1978, Kristol Papers, box 12, folder 28.

77. Marjorie J. Spruill, *Divided We Stand: The Battle Over Women's Rights and Family Values That Polarized American Politics* (New York: Bloomsbury, 2017), 92.

78. Ronald Reagan, "The New Republican Party," speech before the Conservative Political Action Committee, February 6, 1977, Ronald Reagan Institute, https://www.reaganfoundation.org/media/358057/reagan-cpac-speech.pdf.

79. Taylor E. Dark, *The Unions and the Democrats: An Enduring Alliance* (Ithaca, NY: Cornell University Press, 1999), 85–86.

80. "Last Angry Man? Douglas Fraser, Head of the UAW, Talks Tough," *Barron's Business and Financial Weekly*, June 9, 1980; and Jefferson Cowie, *Stayin' Alive: The 1970s and the Last Days of the Working Class* (New York: New Press, 2010), chap. 1.

81. "U.S. Needs '30,000 New Jobs a Week Just to Break Even': Interview with George Meany, President, AFL-CIO," *U.S. News & World Report*, February 21, 1972; emphasis added.

82. The role of women in labor organizing is emphasized in Lane Windham, *Knocking on Labor's Door: Union Organizing in the 1970s and the Roots of a New Economic Divide* (Chapel Hill: University of North Carolina Press, 2017). These unionization efforts elicited some anxiety on the right. See "Unionization of the Textile Industry: A Case Study of J. P. Stevens," Heritage Foundation, August 3, 1977, https://www.heritage.org/jobs-and-labor/report/unionization-the-textile-industry-case-study-j-p-stevens.

83. On the AFL-CIO's concerns about international trade and offshoring, see comments by the union officials Andrew Biemiller and Nat Goldfinger in U.S. Senate, *Multinational Corporations: Hearings Before the Subcommittee on International Trade of the Committee on Finance, United States Senate, Ninety-Third Congress, First Session* (Washington, DC: U.S. Government Printing Office, 1973), 299–332.

84. Sterling G. Slappey, "Will Unions Win International Bargaining?" *Nation's Business*, June 1975.

85. See verbatim transcript of statements by Bernard Norwood, former official with the U.S. Office of the Special Trade Representative at the Kennedy Round

of trade negotiations during the mid-1960s, in Alfred E. Eckes Jr., ed., *Revisiting U.S. Trade Policy: Decisions in Perspective* (Athens: Ohio University Press, 2000), xviii, 73.

86. On the AFL-CIO's heavy focus on foreign policy, see Memo from I. Irving Davidson to Rose Mary Woods, "Subject: Accidental Meeting with George Meany, EAL Flight 190 (Washington to Miami) Tuesday, January 18, 1972," White House Special Files, Staff Member and Office Files, Charles Colson Papers box 28, folder: "AFL-CIO Convention (Meany, 11/14/71 [3 of 8]," Nixon Presidential Library. Meany was paraphrased in the document as stating that the AFL-CIO possessed "a little State Department of their own."

87. A laudatory biography of Kirkland later underscored his foreign policy achievements. The book was written by an associate of Freedom House, which is part of the U.S. foreign policy establishment. The Amazon listing for the book presents endorsements from Zbigniew Brzezinski, Lech Wałęsa, George Shultz, and Helmut Schmidt but no comment from anyone with a background in U.S. labor organizing. See Arch Puddington, *Lane Kirkland: Champion of American Labor* (New York: Wiley, 2008). On Puddington's long-standing affiliation with Freedom House, see the biography in "A Life Devoted to the Cause of Freedom," October 20, 2020, https://freedomhouse.org/article/life-devoted-cause-global -freedom. Meany's heavy interest in foreign policy is evident in the AFL-CIO Papers, now at the University of Maryland.

88. George Meany, "No Appeasement: Meany Backs Johnson's Policy in Vietnam, Santo Domingo," *AFL-CIO News*, May 8, 1965. The tendency of Meany to use red-baiting tactics against critics of the Vietnam War was also noted in letter from Charles Colson to Jay Lovestone, October 25, 1972, in Colson Papers, box 73, folder 3, Nixon Presidential Library. Colson stated, "It is terribly important that McGovern be portrayed as the apologist for the Communists that he is. Only Meany has been able to make the charge and make it stick. We can't; we would be accused of red baiting if we did, but Meany can get away with it brilliantly."

89. The AFL-CIO was listed as a contributor to the Committee on the Present Danger in "Contributors $5000 and Over, Calendar Year 1980," in Papers of the Committee on the Present Danger, box 464, folder "Contributors—Lists," Hoover Institution Archives, Stanford University. The AFL-CIO staffer Lane Kirkland served as a "founding member and cochairman of the Committee." A. H. Raskin, "Land Kirkland: New Style," *New York Times*, October 28, 1979.

90. Regarding organized labor's estrangement from the McGovern campaign, see analysis by Joshua Muravchik, National Chairman, Social Democrats USA, n.d. (probably summer 1972), from Carl Gershman Papers, box 14, folder 4, Hoover Institution Archives, Stanford University.

91. Self, *All in the Family*, 250.

92. Seymour Martin Lipset letter to William Baroody, November 26, 1973, Baroody Papers, box 79, folder 2. Lipset referenced activism at Harvard, but clearly his statements applied much more broadly.

93. On Black, Chicano, and Native American political activism from this period, see Margo V. Perkins, *Autobiography as Activism: Three Black Women of the Sixties* (Oxford: University Press of Mississippi, 2000); Juan Gómez-Quiñones and Irene Vásquez, *Making Aztlán: Ideology and Culture of the Chicana and Chicano Movement, 1966–1977* (Albuquerque: University of New Mexico Press, 2014); and David E. Wilkins, *Red Prophet: The Punishing Intellectualism of Vine Deloria Jr.* (Golden, CO: Fulcrum, 2018).

94. "Combahee River Collective Statement," April 1977, in *Home Girls: A Black Feminist Anthology*, ed. Barbara Smith (New Brunswick, NJ: Rutgers University Press, 2000), 264–74. Full text is also available through Yale University's Department of American Studies, https://americanstudies.yale.edu/sites/default /files/files/Keyword%20Coalition_Readings.pdf. See also analysis in Madeleine Janover, "Wading Toward Common Ground," *Off Our Backs: A Women's New Journal*, August 1975.

95. David R. Swartz, "Identity Politics and the Fragmenting of the 1970s Left," *Religion and American Culture: A Journal of Interpretation* 21, no. 1 (2011). Note also that the American Enterprise Institute was working to undermine left-leaning efforts to build support in religious communities. See letter from Irving Kristol to Edward Littlejohn, October 24, 1977, Kristol Papers, box 12, folder 42; and Ernest W. Lefever to Kristol, October 13, 1977, Kristol Papers, box 12, folder 42.

96. Ruth Rosen, *The World Split Open: How the Modern Women's Movement Changed America* (New York: Penguin, 2006), 138–40.

97. On strategic action: the Institute for Policy Studies (IPS), founded in 1963, widely known as the "think tank of the left." During the 1970s, it did offer some intellectual guidance to left-wing activism, especially with regard to foreign policy and international economics. However, IPS lacked any strategic allies among like-minded think tanks that could provide political and intellectual support of the type enjoyed by the numerous think tanks on the right. In the late 1970s, IPS was subjected to a series of McCarthy-style attacks, which further limited its influence. See "Institute for Policy Studies," Heritage Foundation, May 1977, https://www.heritage.org /conservatism/report/institute-policy-studies. On successful strategic action by the left, see Thomas E. Ricks, *Waging a Good War: A Military History of the Civil Rights Movement, 1954–1968* (New York: Farrar, Straus and Giroux, 2022).

98. Morton Kondracke, "The Heritage Model," *New Republic*, December 20, 1980; emphasis added.

99. Michael Drosnin, "After 'Bloody Friday,' New Yorkers Wonder if Wall Street is Becoming a Battleground," *Wall Street Journal*, May 11, 1970; and David Paul Kuhn, *Hardhat Riot: Nixon, New York City, and the Dawn of White Working-Class Revolution* (New York: Oxford University Press, 2020).

100. Letter from Seymour Martin Lipset, April 10, 1978, Baroody Papers, box 79, folder 2.

101. Dialogue from *Joe*, 1970, directed by John G. Avildsen.

102. J. Hoberman, "Off the Hippies: 'Joe' and the Chaotic Summer of '70," *New York Times*, July 30, 2000.

103. "'All in the Family': THR's 1971 Review," *Hollywood Reporter*, October 1, 2014.

104. The public discussion of growth and its negative consequences was influenced by the following: E. F. Schumacher, *Small Is Beautiful: A Study of Economics as If People Mattered* (London: Blond & Briggs, 1973); and Donella H. Meadows, Dennis L. Meadows, Jorgen Randers, and William W. Behrens III, *The Limits to Growth: A Report to the Club of Rome's Project on the Predicament of Mankind* (New York: Universe Books, 1974). Corporate interests appear to have been alarmed by these antigrowth tendencies, as noted in "Remarks of J. K. Jamieson [CEO, Exxon Corporation]," *Exxon News*, June 1975.

105. Despite some contemporary recognition about the need for sustainable growth, there also has been a renewed emphasis on "de-growth," aiming to terminate economic growth altogether. See "Meet the De-Growers," *Economist*, May 20, 2023.

106. On the failed 1971 effort to achieve universal childcare services, see Joan Beck, "A Major Issue for the '70s: The Fight for Daycare," *Chicago Tribune*, January 5, 1971; and Richard M. Nixon, "Veto Message—Economic Opportunity Amendments of 1971," December 9, 1971, in Gerhard Peters and John T. Woolley, eds., American Presidency Project, University of California, Santa Barbara, https://www.presidency.ucsb.edu/documents/veto-the-economic-opportunity-amendments-1971.

107. I surveyed *Ms.* magazine from July 1973 through June 1980. Regarding the upscale tone, note especially the following articles: Irma Kurtz, "I Have Contempt for Money and the Feeling Is Mutual," *Ms.*, August 1973; and "Why Does this Woman Work? Jacqueline Onassis and Gloria Steinem, a Conversation," *Ms.*, March 1979 (cover story).

108. See survey findings in Kristin Luker, *Abortion and the Politics of Motherhood* (Berkeley: University of California Press, 1984), chap. 8 and appendix 1. This study includes surveys conducted by the author with 212 persons engaged in abortion politics, beginning in 1977.

109. The role of Vietnam veterans in the peace movement is a major theme in Jerry Lembcke, *The Spitting Image: Myth, Memory, and the Legacy of Vietnam* (New

York: NYU Press, 2000). It seems highly likely that—in the era of the military draft—many antiwar veterans were working class. See also Penny Lewis, *Hard-hats, Hippies, and Hawks: The Vietnam Antiwar Movement in Myth and Memory* (Ithaca, NY: Cornell University Press, 2013). The role of Vietnam veterans in the far right is emphasized in Kathleen Belew, *Bring the War Home: The White Power Movement and Paramilitary America* (Cambridge, MA: Harvard University Press, 2018).

110. On the elitist style that inevitably flowed from the focus on celebrities, see Shirley MacLaine, *You Can Get There from Here* (New York: Norton, 1975), 72. MacLaine openly acknowledged the problem, based on her own experiences in political organizing. See also John C. Boland, "Anti-Capitalist Roadshow: Jane Fonda, Tom Hayden, Head a Cast of Thousands," *Barron's Business and Financial Weekly*, October 29, 1979.

111. Herbert Marcuse, *One-Dimensional Man: Studies in the Ideology of Advanced Industrial Society* (Boston: Beacon, 1964), 30, 256–57; and Charles A. Reich, *The Greening of America* (New York: Bantam, 1970), chap. II. Both books were widely influential among political activists in the 1970s.

112. Jack Newfield, "A Populist Manifesto: The Making of a New Majority," *New York Magazine*, July 19, 1971. See also Jim Squires, "Fred Harris: Populism, 'Cornpone': Presidential Campaign Is Geared to Activist Left," *Chicago Tribune*, February 4, 1976.

113. On alleged elitism of this period and the right's use of this issue, see Steve Fraser, *The Limousine Liberal: How an Incendiary Image United the Right and Fractured America* (New York: Basic Books, 2016); and Lily Geismer, *Don't Blame Us: Suburban Liberals and the Transformation of the Democratic Party* (Princeton, NJ: Princeton University Press, 2015).

114. Quoted in "Spiro Agnew: The King's Taster," *Time*, November 14, 1969.

115. The populist style of the New Right is emphasized in this insider account: Alan Crawford, *Thunder on the Right: The "New Right" and the Politics of Resentment* (New York: Pantheon, 1981).

116. "Civil Rights Commission Finds Segregation in Boston," *Boston Globe*, January 19, 1965.

117. Milton J. Valencia, "Massachusetts Is Segregated: Here's Why," *Boston Globe*, May 7, 2022; and "The Controversial Mortgage/Redlining Debate," *New York Amsterdam News*, December 9, 1978. For the larger context, see Keeanga-Yamahtta Taylor, *Race for Profit: How Banks and the Real Estate Industry Undermined Black Homeownership* (Chapel Hill: University of North Carolina Press, 2019); and Richard Rothstein, *The Color of Law: A Forgotten History of How our Government Segregated America* (New York: Liveright, 2018).

118. Louise Day Hicks, quoted in Sandbrook, *Mad as Hell*, 109.

119. Ronald P. Formisano, *Boston Against Busing: Race, Class, and Ethnicity in the 1960s and 1970s* (Chapel Hill: University of North Carolina Press, 1991), 174. Note that Hicks carefully sought to distance herself from Wallace, at least publicly. Elizabeth Gillespie McRae, *Mothers of Massive Resistance: White Women and the Politics of White Supremacy* (New York: Oxford University Press, 2018), 227. See also Earl Smith, "Racism and the Boston Schools Crisis," *Black Scholar* 6, no. 6 (1975).

120. King, paraphrased in Maria Karagianis, "Racism, Not Busing, the Real Issue, Mrs. King Says on Eve of Hub Rally," *Boston Globe*, November 30, 1974.

121. Formisano, *Boston Against Busing*, 16, 66. In the quote concerning connection between unemployment and antibusing activism, Formisano is paraphrasing "several writers"; however, he acknowledges that the writers' conclusions were mostly correct. See additional account of the Boston busing crisis in Senator Edward M. Kennedy, *True Compass: A Memoir* (New York: Twelve Books, 2009), 346–52.

122. The opposition to busing was supported by a young senator from Delaware, Joseph Biden, who worked closely with prominent Southern Senators with a long history of opposition to integration. See letter from Biden to Senator James O. Eastland, June 30, 1977, available through CNN, http://cdn.cnn.com/cnn/2019/images/04/11/biden.eastland.letter.2.pdf.

123. Thomas Ascik, "The Anti-Busing Constitutional Amendment," Heritage Foundation, July 18, 1979, https://www.heritage.org/report/the-anti-busing-constitutional-amendment.

124. "1977: Suggested State Legislation, ALEC, American Legislative Exchange Council," 60, Papers of the Conservative Party of New York, Series 7, box 1, folder "American Legislative Exchange Council," State University of New York, Albany.

125. An early concept of the Humphrey-Hawkins bill was described in "Remarks by Senator Hubert H. Humphrey at Congressional Breakfast for Full Employment," January 15, 1975," Minnesota Historical Society, http://www2.mnhs.org/library/findaids/00442/pdfa/00442-03756.pdf.

126. Humphrey-Hawkins emerged from a series of conferences in 1974. See "A Call for Action from the Black Economic Summit," advertisement in the *Washington Post*, September 27, 1974. See also the following account from a former advocate for the bill: Helen Ginsburg, "Historical Amnesia: The Humphrey-Hawkins Act, Full Employment, and Employment as a Right," *Review of Black Political Economy* 39, no. 1 (2012).

127. Rep. Augustus Hawkins, "Joblessness Leads to an Empty Belly," *New York Amsterdam News*, September 24, 1977. Note that the Hawkins personal archival collection at the University of California, Los Angeles, contains significant information on Humphrey-Hawkins.

128. On reparations, see Robert S. Browne, "Black Economic Autonomy," *Black Scholar* 3, no. 2 (1971): 30; "'No Reparations,' Says LI Episcopal," *New York Amsterdam News*, September 20, 1969; and James Farmer, "The Core of It: Reparations," *New York Amsterdam News*, September 18, 1965.

129. Jackson, paraphrased in Barbara Bowman, "Martin Luther King's Birth Commemorated," *Washington Post*, January 16, 1975.

130. See chapter 1 for discussion.

131. For example, William K. Stevens, "Shutdown of Steelworks Stuns Youngstown," *New York Times*, September 21, 1977.

132. See, for example, Lacy H. Hunt, "The High Price of Full Employment Legislation," *Nation's Business*, November 1976; and James Grant, "Left Turn? Hubert Humphrey Has Never Gotten Over the New Deal," *Barron's National Business and Financial Weekly*, April 19, 1976.

133. Supporters of Humphrey-Hawkins insisted that sustained economic growth was inherently noninflationary. See Hubert Humphrey, "Full Employment Interview," July 15, 1976, Minnesota Historical Society, http://www2.mnhs.org/library /findaids/00442/pdfa/00442-04022.pdf. See also quotes from Senator Humphrey in Grant, "Left Turn?"

134. Michal Kalecki, "Political Aspects of Full Employment," *Political Quarterly* 14, no. 4 (1943): 323; and Humphrey, "Full Employment Interview," 6.

135. Weir, *Politics and Jobs*, 136; and Walter Guzzardi Jr., "Business Is Learning How to Win in Washington," *Fortune*, March 27, 1978.

136. The National Organization for Women nominally endorsed the bill but made no serious effort to build broad support for it. See also Leslie Smith and Toni White, "'Our Story/Her Story': The Washington DC Feminist Community from 1969 to 1979," *Off Our Backs*, February 1980.

137. On the AFL-CIO position, see Weir, *Politics and Jobs*, 136. Note that some of the leading figures in the Black Caucus—notably John Conyers—opposed military spending. See Vernon Jarrett, "Conyers Jostles Democrats' Boat," *Chicago Tribune*, July 16, 1976; Edward Walsh and Mary Russell, "Humphrey-Hawkins Provokes Confrontation," *Washington Post*, September 27, 1978.

138. Regarding endorsements for the bill, see Augustus Hawkins, "Testimony on Full Employment," *Congressional Record*, May 13, 1975, 14141–142.

139. Helen Ginsburg, *Full Employment and Public Policy: The United States and Sweden* (Lanham, MD: Lexington Books, 1983), 78.

140. On the overwhelming hostility toward the bill in the Carter administration, see Charlie Schultze, "Memorandum for the Economic Policy Group," March 14, 1977, in Carter Presidential Papers, Staff Offices, Council of Economic Advisers, box 530, folder "Humphrey-Hawkins Bill [3]," Carter Presidential Library.

141. Text of the Full Employment and Balanced Growth Act ("Humphrey-Hawkins Act"), Public Law 95–323, October 27, 1978, FRED Economic Data, Federal Reserve of St. Louis, https://fraser.stlouisfed.org/title/full-employment -balanced-growth-act-humphrey-hawkins-act-1034.

142. "Employment Measure Attracts Growing List of Symbolic Gestures," *Wall Street Journal*, March 10, 1978.

143. "Humphrey-Hawkins," *Hartford Courant*, November 18, 1977.

144. Herbert Stein, *Presidential Economics: The Making of Economic Policy from Roosevelt to Clinton* (Washington, DC: American Enterprise Institute for Public Policy Research, 1994), 218. Stein had recently served as chairman of the Council of Economic Advisers.

145. Douglas Foster, "Jesse Jackson: He Thinks He Can Win," *Mother Jones*, October 1, 1987. For further background on the Jackson campaign, see Mfanya D. Tryman, "Was Jesse Jackson a Third-Party Candidate in 1988?" *Black Scholar* 20, no. 1 (1989); and Adolph L. Reed Jr., *The Jesse Jackson Phenomenon: The Crisis of Purpose in Afro-American Politics* (New Haven, CT: Yale University Press, 1986).

4. SELLING A NEW COLD WAR

The chapter epigraph comes from Sir Rodric Braithwaite, "The British Public Will Decide in the End If Prime Minister Oversold His Wares on Iraq Risk," letter to the editor, *Financial Times*, July 10, 2003.

1. On My Lai, see account by the journalist who originally broke the story: Seymour M. Hersh, *Reporter: A Memoir* (New York: Knopf, 2018), chaps. 9, 10. Regarding the Nixon administration's private reaction to My Lai, see "Telecon, Secretary Laird, 11/21/69, 3:50pm," from National Security Archive, George Washington University, "The Kissinger Telcons" file, https://nsarchive2.gwu.edu /NSAEBB/NSAEBB123/doc%201%20%2011-21-1969.pdf.

2. Daniel Ellsberg, *Papers on the War* (New York: Simon & Schuster, 2009); Ellsberg, *Secrets: A Memoir of Vietnam and the Pentagon Papers* (New York: Penguin, 2003), pt. III.

3. Daniel Ellsberg, quoted in the 1974 documentary film *Hearts and Minds*, 1974, dir. Peter Davis, available from YouTube video, January 15, 2018, 1:52:06, https:// youtube.com/watch?v=WzxNRoGoSKU.

4. See comments on official lying by Senator J. William Fulbright, interviewed in *Hearts and Minds*.

5. The full contents of these Senate investigations are now available online. See U.S. Senate, *Senate Select Committee to Study Governmental Operations with Respect to Intelligence Activities, 1975–76 (Church Committee)*, https://www .intelligence.senate.gov/resources/intelligence-related-commissions.

6. Robert Buzzanco, "Whatever Happened to the New Left? Toward a Radical Reading of American Foreign Relations," *Diplomatic History* 23, no. 4 (1999).

7. From *The Godfather, Part II*," 1974, dir. Francis Ford Coppola; emphasis added.

8. George H. Gallup, *The Gallup Poll: Public Opinion, 1935–1971* (New York: Random House, 1972), vol. III, 2135, 2153, 2164, 2199.

9. Gallup, *The Gallup Poll*, 2210.

10. Henry Kissinger, *The White House Years* (Boston: Little, Brown, 1979), 195, 199. Dissatisfaction with the Vietnam War extended to some elements of American business. In 1970, representatives from several corporations sponsored an anti-war business organization. See "Business Executives Move for Vietnam Peace," June 9, 1970, in W. Averell Harriman Papers, box 612, folder "Post Government—Business Executives Move for Vietnam Peace," Library of Congress.

11. Richard M. Nixon, "Informal Remarks in Guam with Newsmen," July 25, 1969, in Gerhard Peters and John T. Woolley, eds, American Presidency Project, University of California, Santa Barbara, https://www.presidency.ucsb.edu/documents/informal-remarks-guam-with-newsmen; and Nixon, *RN: The Memoirs of Richard Nixon* (New York: Grosset & Dunlap, 1978), 394–95.

12. The Nixon administration furnished support to South Africa through semi-covert means, as set forth in National Security Study Memorandum 39. It is reproduced in Mohamed A. Elkhawas and Barry Cohen, eds, *The Kissinger Study of Southern Africa* (Westport, CT: Lawrence Hill, 1976).

13. As Nixon was being inaugurated in 1969, there was widespread concern about the security of the Persian Gulf region owing to a British decision to withdraw its forces; Iran was used as a substitute for British power. George W. Ball, *The Past Has Another Pattern: Memoirs* (New York: Norton, 1982), 453–55; National Security Decision Memorandum 92, "U.S. Policy Toward the Persian Gulf," November 7, 1970, Federation of American Scientists, Intelligence Resource Program, https://fas.org/irp/offdocs/nsdm-nixon/nsdm-92.pdf.

14. "U.S. Foreign Aid to Israel: Total Aid (1949–Present)," Jewish Virtual Library, accessed November 21, 2023, http://www.jewishvirtuallibrary.org/total-u-s-foreign-aid-to-israel-1949-present.

15. Jussi M. Hanhimäki, *The Rise and Fall of Détente: American Foreign Policy and the Transformation of the Cold War* (Sterling, VA: Potomac, 2012); Jeremi Suri, *Power and Protest: Global Revolution and the Rise of Détente* (Cambridge, MA: Harvard University Press, 2005).

16. "Interim Agreement Between the United States of America and the Union of Soviet Socialist Republics on Certain Measures with Respect to the Limitation of Strategic Offensive Arms," signed May 26, 1972, Federation of American Scientists, https://fas.org/nuke/control/salt1/text/salt1.htm; and "Treaty Between the United States of America and the Union of Soviet Socialist Republics on

the Limitation of Anti-Ballistic Missile Systems," signed May 26, 1972, State Department website, https://2009-2017.state.gov/t/avc/trty/101888.htm.

17. On the diplomacy leading to the famous table tennis matches, see memorandum from Henry Kissinger to the president, "My Talks with Chou En-Lai," July 14, 1971, https://nsarchive2.gwu.edu/NSAEBB/NSAEBB66/ch-40.pdf; and Intelligence Brief from Ray S. Cline, April 14, 1971, https://nsarchive2.gwu.edu /NSAEBB/NSAEBB66/ch-13.pdf. Both documents from National Security Archive, George Washington University.

18. In courting the PRC government, Nixon accepted its framing of the Taiwan issue, which was now viewed as a "part of China." See "U.S.-PRC Joint Communique (Shanghai Communique)," February 27, 1972, in Congressional Research Service, "China/Taiwan: Evolution of the 'One China' Policy—Key Statements from Washington, Beijing, and Taipei," January 5, 2015, https://www.everycrsreport .com/reports/RL30341.html, 34.

19. Quoted in Colin Dueck, *Hard Line: The Republican Party and U.S. Foreign Policy Since World War II* (Princeton, NJ: Princeton University Press, 2010), 163. The verbatim Nixon-Mao conversation is available in William Burr, ed., *The Kissinger Transcripts: The Top-Secret Talks with Beijing and Moscow* (New York: New Press, 1998), 61.

20. "Press Release by Burson-Marsteller, 'Leaders Organize the American Committee on U.S.-Soviet Relations to Assure Détente Continuation,'" July 10, 1974, Henry M. Jackson Papers, accession #3560-005, box 117, folder 15, University of Washington. See also information on Chase Manhattan's loans to the Soviets in letter from Jay Lovestone to George Meany, March 23, 1973, Jay Lovestone Papers, box 380, folder 1, Hoover Institution Archives, Stanford University.

21. Letter from William J. Casey to Thomas Corcoran, July 15, 1974, Thomas G. Corcoran Papers, box 53, folder "General Correspondence, Cline, Ray," Library of Congress.

22. Regarding reduced business enthusiasm for military interventionism during the early 1970s, see Bruce M. Russett and Betty C. Hanson, "How Corporate Executives See America's Role in the World," *Fortune*, May 1974. Even the very conservative Treasury secretary William Simon was a supporter of détente. See his comments in "Department of the Treasury: Interview with Secretary Simon," July 9, 1976, in William E. Simon Papers, series V, drawer 43, box 86, folder 42, 32, Lafayette College.

23. Kissinger, quoted in Daniel Shorr, "Telling It Like It Is: Kissinger and the Kurds," *Christian Science Monitor*, October 18, 1996.

24. For U.S. combat deaths in Vietnam during the Nixon presidency, see U.S. National Archives, "Vietnam War, U.S. Military Fatal Casualty Statistics:

Electronic Records Reference Report," January 2018, https://www.archives.gov
/research/military/vietnam-war/casualty-statistics.

25. Paul W. McCracken, "The Double Economic Transition," attached to "Memorandum for Arthur J. Sohmer," August 3, 1970, White House Central Files, Staff Member and Office Files, Paul W. McCracken Papers, box 44, folder "Agnew, Spiro [1 of 2]," Nixon Presidential Library.

26. Charles J. V. Murphy, "The Pentagon Enters Its Era of Austerity," *Fortune*, December 1972. Nixon aide Charles Colson expressed satisfaction with the administration's "successful transition from a wartime to a peacetime economy." Charles Colson, "Closing Days of the Presidential Campaign," October 28, 1972, Earl Butz Papers, box L, folder "White House Correspondence," Purdue University.

27. Bruce Cumings, "Still the American Century," *Review of International Studies* 25, no. 5 (1999): 283.

28. David Shribman, "Henry M. Jackson, Dead at 71," *New York Times*, September 3, 1983.

29. Robert G. Kaufman, *Senator Henry M. Jackson: A Life in Politics* (Seattle: University of Washington Press, 2000), 22.

30. On labor support for Jackson, see letter from Benjamin Rubenstein to Richard Perle, October 13, 1971, Jackson Papers, accession #3560-004, box 261, folder 3.

31. Philip S. Foner, *U.S. Labor and the Viet-Nam War* (New York: International Publishers, 1989).

32. Henry Kissinger, *Years of Upheaval* (Boston: Little, Brown, 1982), 985.

33. Kissinger is quoted by Averell Harriman in "Specially Private: Memorandum of Conversation," June 26, 1974, Harriman Papers, box 1072, folder 6.

34. Andrew Feickert and Stephen Daggett, "A Historical Perspective on 'Hollow Forces,'" U.S. Congressional Research Service, January 31, 2012, 2–3, https://fas
.org/sgp/crs/natsec/R42334.pdf.

35. François LeRoy, "Mirages Over the Andes: Peru, France, and the United States and Military Jet Procurement During the 1960s," *Pacific Historical Review* 71, no. 2 (2002).

36. Stockholm International Peace Research Institute, *SIPRI Yearbook* (Stockholm: Almqvist & Wiksell, 1973), 308–9. On competition for arms sales, see Captain Eric W. Stewart, "The Political Economy of United States Arms Transfers to Latin America During the Cold War" (MA thesis, Department of Latin American Studies, University of Arizona, 1999).

37. On the ASC's ties to the military-industrial complex, see list of military supporters in letter from John M. Fisher, American Security Council, July 29, 1971, Group Research Inc. Papers, box 355, folder 1, Columbia University.

The ASC was termed "the soul" of the military-industrial complex. Harold C. Relyea, "The American Security Council," *The Nation*, January 24, 1972. Later in the decade, aggrieved former CIA and FBI operatives also began working closely with the military-industrial complex, as noted by Wesley McCune, "Another Defense Fund Is Organized for U.S. Intelligence Agents," *Group Research Report*, January 31, 1978.

38. Quoted in Jerry W. Sanders, *Peddlers of Crisis: The Committee on the Present Danger and the Politics of Containment* (Boston: South End, 1983), 223.

39. Thomas Ferguson and Joel Rogers, "The Reagan Victory: Corporate Coalitions and the 1980 Campaign," in *The Hidden Election: Politics and Economics in the 1980 Presidential Campaign*, ed. Thomas Ferguson and Joel Rogers (New York: Pantheon, 1981), 17, 59.

40. According to Group Research, Georgetown's CSIS was established in 1962 by the American Enterprise Institute, which "used a subsidiary . . . as a conduit to set up the Center." See "American Enterprise Institute for Public Policy Research, Some Background and Information," May 6, 1971, William J. Baroody Sr. Papers, box 64, folder 2, Library of Congress. CSIS is also discussed in chapter 2 of this study.

41. See the following document, which implicitly disparaged the ASC: letter from Lloyd H. Smith to Charls E. Walker, August 21, 1976, Charls E. Walker Papers, box 30, folder 9, Hoover Institution Archives, Stanford University.

42. Regarding the role of U.S. covert operations in protecting investors, see Arindrajit Dube, Ethan Kaplan, and Suresh Naidu, "Coups, Corporations, and Classified Information," *Quarterly Journal of Economics* 126, no. 3 (2011).

43. The reduced effectiveness of the CIA is strongly implied in a letter from Barry Goldwater to Frank Church, July 16, 1975, Barry M. Goldwater Papers, box 4, folder 12, Arizona State University.

44. Regarding the growth of U.S. foreign direct investment, see Joseph LaPalombara and Stephen Blank, *Multinational Corporations and Developing Countries* (New York: Conference Board, 1979), 7.

45. Barbara Stallings, *Banker to the Third World: U.S. Portfolio Investment in Latin America, 1900–1986* (Berkeley: University of California Press, 1987).

46. Bill Warren, "Imperialism and Capitalist Industrialization," *New Left Review*, I/81 (1973).

47. John McCloy, "Notes on Meeting on January 7, 1971, with Under-Secretary Johnson," from series 20, box "Oil 2," folder 4; and "Memorandum on Private Investment," undated document submitted by a group of multinational corporations to the State Department, attached to cover letter, January 11, 1971, box "Oil 2," folder 5. Both documents from John J. McCloy Papers, Amherst College.

48. Dan Haendel, *Corporate Strategic Planning: The Political Dimension*) Washington, DC: Center for Strategic and International Studies, 1981), 14–15. See also Robert M. Bleiberg, "Worth Its SALT? The U.S. Is in Danger of Becoming a Second-Rate Power," editorial, *Barron's National Business and Financial Weekly*, December 8, 1975.

49. "The Decline of U.S. Power: The New Debate Over Guns and Butter," *Business Week*, March 12, 1979. Criticisms of détente also emanated from the Trilateral Commission. Letter from Zbigniew Brzezinski on commission letterhead to Senator Henry Jackson, February 25, 1974, Jackson Papers, accession #3560-005, box 117, folder 15.

50. The issue of resource scarcity would become a new justification for military intervention. See "An Interview with General Maxwell D. Taylor in Washington DC, 12 June 1974," 25–26, Maxwell D. Taylor Papers, box 76, folder C, National Defense University Archives, Washington D.C.

51. The United States briefly considered leading a military takeover of Persian Gulf oil fields in Abu Dhabi and possibly Saudi Arabia, though that was never undertaken. Memorandum of conversation, Henry Kissinger, James R. Schlesinger, and Brent Scowcroft, August 2, 1974, in National Security Adviser, Memoranda of Conversations, 1973–1977, Ford Presidential Library, https://www. fordlibrarymuseum.gov/library/document/0314/1552738.pdf. See also Glenn Frankel, "U.S. Mulled Seizing Oil Fields in '73," *Washington Post*, January 1, 2004; and "Editorial Note," document 244, in *Foreign Relations of the United States, 1969–1976: Volume XXXVI, Energy Crisis, 1969–1974*, ed. Linda Qaimmaqami (Washington, DC: U.S. Government Printing Office, 2011).

52. Robert Novick, *The Holocaust in American Life* (Boston: Houghton Mifflin, 1999), 149.

53. Andrew Cockburn, "Secretary of Nothing: John Kerry and the Myth of Foreign Policy," *Harper's*, December 2013. Note that U.S. support for Israel elicited considerable opposition from major oil companies, as well as other interests connected with Saudi Arabia and other Gulf States. See "Memorandum for the President," from J. K. Jamieson, Rawleigh Warner Jr., M. F. Granville, and Otto N. Miller, October 12, 1973, in Jack Anderson Papers, attached to letter from Alexander Haig, October 12, 1973, box 319, folder 7, George Washington University.

54. "Task Force, World of the 70s: Revised Report," American Jewish Committee, February 24, 1972, from AJC Archives, FAD-D, box 30, folder 2, New York.

55. John Rosenberg, "The Quest Against Détente: Eugene Rostow, the October War, and the Origins of the Anti-Détente Movement, 1969–1976," *Diplomatic History* 39, no. 4 (2015).

56. Senator Jackson's pro-Israel stance created tensions with the largest oil companies, which were dependent on the Arab states of the Persian Gulf region.

However, Jackson enjoyed support from independent oil companies in Texas and Oklahoma, which counterbalanced the oil majors. See letter from John Kyle, vice president, Oklahoma Oil Marketers Association, to Jackson, March 1, 1978; and letter from W. P. Wright Jr., president of Texas Oil Marketers Association, to Jackson, February 28, 1978. Both documents from Jackson Papers, accession #3560-005, box 172, folder 20. Jackson's public criticisms for the major oil companies were noted by William Simon. See "Interview with Secretary Simon," May 30, 1974, 52, in Simon Papers, series V, drawer 43, box 86, folder 39. On Jackson's longstanding support for Israel, see Hadas Binyami, "Senator 'Scoop' Jackson and the Jewish Cold Warriors," *Jewish Currents*, May 24, 2022.

57. The Jackson-Vanik Amendment was part of the 1974 Trade Act. See discussion in Gerald R. Ford, *A Time to Heal: The Autobiography of Gerald R. Ford* (New York: Harper & Row, 1979), 138–39, 200. Treasury Secretary William Simon was evidently eager to continue and expand U.S.-Soviet trade. See U.S. Department of the Treasury, memorandum of conversation, "Subject: U.S.-Soviet Bilateral Economic Relations," February 19, 1975, in Correspondence of the Secretary [W. E. Simon], entry number UD-UP-777, box 2, folder "Memo of Conversation C (1975)," collection RG 56, National Archives.

58. George Perkovich, "U.S. Can Aid Soviet Jews by Lifting a Dubious Law," *Los Angeles Times*, March 20, 1988.

59. Daniel K. Williams, *God's Own Party: The Making of the Christian Right* (New York: Oxford University Press, 2010), 160. Williams cites a 1976 poll noting that a third of U.S. adults claimed they had been "born again."

60. Rev. Harold Fickett, paraphrased in memorandum to Rabbi Marc Tanenbaum and Neil Sandberg, August 8, 1973, in AJC Archives, FAD-IM, box 25, folder 11. On Zionist evangelicals, see also Barry Covert, "Falwell Says America Must Support Israel," *Moral Majority Report*, March 14, 1980, in Moral Majority Papers, Jerry Falwell Library, Liberty University, https://cdm17184.contentdm .oclc.org/digital/collection/p17184coll1/id/1851/rec/3.

61. Regarding the Jewish response to the emerging Christian Zionists, see letter from Rabbi Marc H. Tanenbaum to Hertzel Fishman, January 3, 1978, AJC Archives, FAD-IM, box 31, folder 8.

62. The need for a Jewish political alliance with evangelicals is strongly implied in "For AJC," memorandum from Irving Kristol, 1981, Irving Kristol Papers, box 9, folder 28, Wisconsin Historical Society.

63. Quoted in Fred Halliday, *The Making of the Second Cold War* (London: Verso, 1983), 116. In one sermon, Rev. Falwell blithely declared, "I believe one day this entire universe will be destroyed by nuclear blast." From Jerry Falwell, "Nuclear War & the Second Coming of Christ," n.d. (probably 1983), 5 in Papers of the Old Time Gospel Hour, FM 3:4, box 9, series 12, folder 4, Liberty University.

64. On the strongly pro-Israel position of Lieutenant General Daniel O. Graham, who was closely affiliated with the neoconservative intellectuals, see letter from Graham to Frank R. Barnett, November 26, 1974, in Daniel O. Graham Papers, box 2, folder 5, University of Miami, Florida.

65. Justin Vaïsse, *Neoconservatism: The Biography of a Movement* (Cambridge, MA: Belknap Press of Harvard University Press, 2010), 93.

66. For a harshly critical view of the neoconservatives, see three-part BBC documentary, *The Power of Nightmares*, 2004, dir. Adam Curtis. Part 1: https://www.youtube.com/watch?v=7O9osvFKdjQ; Part 2: https://www.youtube.com/watch?v=EjKZmlA1zDU; Part 3: https://www.youtube.com/watch?v=IZqieiYzJqE. All links accessed on November 20, 2023. Despite the critical tone, this series presented the neocons as a band of ideologues who acted on the basis of political principle.

67. Letter from Paul Nitze to Ruben F. Mettler, March 11, 1980; and letter from Nitze to Charles F. Adams, March 12, 1980. Both documents from Paul H. Nitze Papers, box 35, folder 22, Library of Congress.

68. Seymour M. Hersh, "Lunch with the Chairman: Why Was Richard Perle Meeting with Adnan Khashoggi?," *New Yorker*, March 17, 2003.

69. Center for Media and Democracy, "Paul Dundes Wolfowitz," Sourcewatch, Center for Media and Democracy, June 21, 2017, https://www.sourcewatch.org/index.php/Paul_Dundes_Wolfowitz.

70. Letter from Charles Wohlstetter to Irving Kristol, November 23, 1977, in Baroody Papers, box 78, folder 10. Wohlstetter's letter was written on Continental Telephone stationary.

71. On Kristol's extensive business connections and consulting activities, see correspondence in Kristol Papers, especially boxes 11–15 and 24. On his central role in neoconservatism, see "Godfather of Neoconservatism Dies," BBC, September 19, 2009, http://news.bbc.co.uk/2/hi/americas/8264260.stm.

72. On the neoconservatives' self-image as "outsiders" see Richard Pipes, *Vixi: Memoirs of a Non-Belonger* (New Haven, CT: Yale University Press, 2003).

73. Quoted in Barbara J. Keys, *Reclaiming American Virtue: The Human Rights Movement of the 1970s* (Cambridge, MA: Harvard University Press, 2014), 220.

74. "Statement by J. W. Fulbright, *Pacem in Terris* Convocation, October 8, 1973, Sheraton Park Hotel, Washington DC," 6, Clark M. Clifford Papers, box 24, folder "Fulbright, J. William," Library of Congress.

75. This was famously argued in Jean J. Kirkpatrick, "Dictatorships and Double Standards," *Commentary*, November 1979.

76. The questioning was conducted by the late University of Texas professor James A. Bill, and the verbatim interview appeared in Bill, *The Eagle and the Lion: The Tragedy of American-Iranian Relations* (New Haven, CT: Yale University

Press, 1988), 186–87. See also film footage of the shah in which he came close to admitting systematic torture in the BBC documentary, *Decadence and Downfall: The Shah of Iran's Ultimate Party*, dir. Hassan Amini, BBC, 2016, available from YouTube video, September 7, 2022, 1:16:11, https://www.youtube .com/watch?v=I2JXYHZKZE8. On U.S. complicity, see J. J. Langguth, "Torture's Teachers," *New York Times*, June 11, 1979.

77. Even at this early phase, however, some figures in the neocon camp advocated for a human rights justification for their political stance. See, for example, "For Peace in Vietnam," unpublished paper by David Jessup, Mike Grimes, and Carl Gershman, October 28, 1971, Carl Gershman Papers, box 14, folder 1, Hoover Institution, Stanford University.

78. Daniel Patrick Moynihan, "The Politics of Human Rights," *Commentary*, August 1977.

79. Keys, *Reclaiming American Virtue*, 226.

80. In reality, Solzhenitsyn was not the angelic figure his supporters often claimed him to be. See Jeri Laber, "The Selling of Solzhenitsyn: The Stereotype of the Russian Author Does Not Entirely Fit the Facts," *Columbia Journalism Review*, May 1974; and Hedrick Smith, *The Russians* (New York: Quadrangle/New York Times, 1976), chap. XVII.

81. Moynihan, quoted and paraphrased in Daniel J. Sargent, *A Superpower Transformed: The Remaking of American Foreign Relations in the 1970s* (New York: Oxford University Press, 2015), 200.

82. Norman Podhoretz, *Why We Were in Vietnam* (New York: Simon & Schuster, 1982).

83. The complete multivolume set of the Pentagon Papers can be found at *The Pentagon Papers* (Washington, DC: U.S. National Archives), https://www.archives .gov/research/pentagon-papers. See the very readable shortened version by *New York Times* reporters: Neil Sheehan, Hedrick Smith, E. W. Kenworthy, and Fox Butterfield, *The Pentagon Papers* (New York: Bantam, 1971). The official title of the classified Pentagon report was "Report of the Office of the Secretary of Defense, Vietnam Task Force."

84. William Shawcross, *Sideshow: Kissinger, Nixon, and the Destruction of Cambodia* (New York: Harper-Collins, 1979).

85. See Noam Chomsky, "East Timor Retrospective," *Le Monde Diplomatique*, October 1999. On the U.S. role in East Timor, see the memoirs of former UN ambassador Daniel Patrick Moynihan, *A Dangerous Place* (Boston: Little, Brown, 1978), 245–46.

86. "Report on Trip to the People's Republic of China, 1977," Nitze Papers, box 68, folder 6.

87. Richard Pipes, "Resisting the Elephant," *Commentary*, May 1988. Also see sources in David N. Gibbs, "Forgotten Coverage of Afghan 'Freedom Fighters':

The Villains of Today's News Were Heroes in the '80s," *Extra*, January/February 2002.

88. Letter from Max Kampelman to Joan Baez, December 2, 1980, Max M. Kampelman Papers, 151.C.5.1B, box 4, folder "Madrid Conference on Security and Cooperation in Europe," Minnesota Historical Society; and Rick Perlstein, *Reaganland: America's Right Turn, 1976–1980* (New York: Simon & Schuster, 2020), 839.

89. George C. Wilson, "Former Government Officials Warn About Soviet Expansionism," *Washington Post*, November 9, 1976.

90. Nicholas Thompson, *The Hawk and the Dove: Paul Nitze, George Kennan, and the History of the Cold War* (New York: Picador/Henry Holt, 2009), 263.

91. For a complete CPD membership list, see Sanders, *Peddlers of Crisis*, 154–60.

92. Quoted from memorandum from Terry O'Donnell, "Dinner Meeting with the Business Council," December 11, 1974, in Ford Presidential Library, White House Central Files, Name File, box 2411, folder "Packard, David."

93. Bart Barnes, "Charls E. Walker: Tax Lobbyist for GOP and Big Business, Dies at 91," *Washington Post*, June 25, 2015.

94. Letter from Charls E. Walker to Herbert Allen, August 11, 1976, Walker Papers, box 30, folder 9.

95. See "Contributions $5000 and Over—Calendar Year 1980," in Papers of the Committee on the Present Danger, box 464, folder "Contributor Lists," Hoover Institution Archives, Stanford University.

96. Sanders, *Peddlers of Crisis*, 217–18. Note that Schlafly was connected with the hawkish Coalition for Peace Through Strength (CPS). See "Soviet SALT Deception," CPS press release, December 13, 1979, Liberty University, https://liberty .contentdm.oclc.org/digital/collection/p17184coll12/id/11255/rec/1. On the close connections between the CPS and the Committee on the Present Danger, see Center for Media and Democracy, "Committee on the Present Danger," Sourcewatch, Center for Media and Democracy, June 21, 2017, https://www.sourcewatch .org/index.php?title=Committee_on_the_Present_Danger.

97. Letter to Colgate W. Darden Jr., March 7, 1977, Papers of the Committee on the Present Danger, box 60, folder 14. While the letter was unsigned, the wording and contents suggest that the author was likely Rostow. Note that substantial quantities of CPD papers can be found in the Foy Kohler Papers, boxes 20 and 80, University of Toledo.

98. Vaïsse, *Neoconservatism*, 164–65.

99. Letter from Donald G. Brennan to Eugene Rostow, March 3, 1977, Papers of the Committee on the Present Danger, box 60, folder 14.

100. Admiral Elmo R. Zumwalt Jr., *On Watch: A Memoir* (New York: Quadrangle/ New York Times, 1976), 427–30, 506. Note that at the time of his CPD membership, Zumwalt was a retired officer.

101. Letter from Max Kampelman to Hubert Humphrey, January 28, 1976, Kampelman Papers, 151.C.6.6F, box 25, folder "Memoranda for Humbert H. Humphrey, 1971–1976."

102. Letter from Frank Barnett to Eugene Rostow, July 12, 1976, Nitze Papers, box 68, folder 8. This statement and the previous one from Kampelman were made during the time that the committee was in the process of being formed.

103. The politically astute Edward Teller sought out the TRW Corporation to assist in publicizing *First Strike*. See memorandum from Edward Teller to John S. Foster Jr., of TRW, n.d.; and "KRON TV Proudly Presents 'First Strike,'" 1979. From Edward Teller R. Papers, box 28, folder 7, Hoover Institution Archives, Stanford University. For the film, itself, see *First Strike: Part 1*, available from YouTube video, accessed November 21, 2023, https://www.youtube.com/watch?v=jlPEBROvR9w.

104. Letter from CPD member Jay Lovestone to James R. Schlesinger, December 15, 1978, Lovestone Papers, box 707, folder 36. Regarding perceived dire threats to U.S. security, see letter from Frank R. Barnett to Clare Boothe Luce, December 4, 1979, in Clare Boothe Luce Papers, box 711, folder 10, Library of Congress; and Norman Podhoretz, "The Present Danger," *Commentary*, March 1980.

105. Letter from Clare Boothe Luce to Frank R. Barnett, August 12, 1980, in Luce Papers, box 711, folder 10.

106. Vaïsse, *Neoconservatism*, 153.

107. Eugene Rostow, quoted and paraphrased in Anne Hessing Cahn, *Killing Détente: The Right Attacks the CIA* (University Park: Penn State University Press, 1998), 29–30.

108. Peter C. Stuart, "Anti-SALT Lobbyists Outspend Pros by 15 to 1: Treaty Opponents Build Momentum Before Senate Launches Formal Action," *Christian Science Monitor*, March 23, 1979.

109. Quote in letter from Max Kampelman to Myer Feldman, November 21, 1979, Kampelman Papers, 147.J.13.7B, box 36, folder "Kennedy, Edward M. Campaign, 1979–1980." The letter referenced a study by the Harvard political scientist Samuel Huntington.

110. Letter from Eugene Rostow to William Loeb, July 15, 1977, Papers of the Committee on the Present Danger, box 109, folder "CPD, Eugene V. Rostow, 1977." Rostow's letter specifically stated that his wife worked in "psychiatry," though his 2002 obituary referred to his widow as a "psychotherapist."

111. Ford, *A Time to Heal*, chaps. 4, 5.

112. President Gerald Ford, "Remarks Upon Signing Instruments of Ratification of the Geneva Protocol of 1925 and the Biological Weapons Convention," January 22, 1975, in Gerhard Peters and John T. Woolley, eds, American Presidency

Project, https://www.presidency.ucsb.edu/documents/remarks-upon-signing
-instruments-ratification-the-geneva-protocol-1925-and-the-biological.

113. Cahn, *Killing Détente*, 83–84.

114. Pipes, *Vixi*, 132–43; and Paul H. Nitze, *From Hiroshima to Glasnost: At the Center of Decision* (New York: Grove-Weidenfeld, 1989), 350–55.

115. According to the former CIA analyst Melvin Goodman, Chief of Staff Richard Cheney and Defense Secretary Donald Rumsfeld played key roles in persuading Ford to accept Team B. See Melvin Goodman, *Whistleblower at the CIA: An Insider's Account of the Politics of Intelligence* (San Francisco: City Lights, 2017), 64.

116. Richard Pipes, "Team B: The Reality Behind the Myth," *Commentary*, October 1986. The principal Team B report is Central Intelligence Agency, "Intelligence Community Experiment in Competitive Analysis: Soviet Strategic Objectives, An Alternative View, Report of Team 'B,'" December 1976, National Security Archive, George Washington University, https://nsarchive2.gwu.edu//NSAEBB /NSAEBB139/nitze10.pdf.

117. Regarding Kennan's less confrontational views, see letter from Kennan to James Reston, November 28, 1978, in Carter Presidential Library, National Security Affairs, Brzezinski Material, Name File, box 2, folder "Kennan, Geroge F. 11/78." On Harriman, see "Specially Private: Memorandum of Conversation," June 26, 1974, Harriman Papers, box 1072, folder 6.

118. Raymond L. Garthoff, *Détente and Confrontation: American-Soviet Relations from Nixon to Reagan* (Washington, DC: Brookings Institution, 1985), 551.

119. Pipes, "Team B."

120. Cahn, *Killing Détente*, 176.

121. Raymond Garthoff, *A Journey Through the Cold War: A Memoir of Containment and Coexistence* (Washington, DC: Brookings Institution, 2001), chap. 17; Cahn, *Killing Détente*, 1–2, 67–168, 194; and Pavel Podvig, "The Window of Vulnerability That Wasn't: Soviet Military Buildup in the 1970s," *International Security* 33, no. 1 (2008).

122. White House, Memorandum of Conversation, President Ford, Clare Boothe Luce, Brent Scowcroft, February 25, 1976, Ford Presidential Library, https:// www.fordlibrarymuseum.gov/library/document/0314/1553381.pdf.

123. Ford's disavowal of the word "détente" was noted by the press in the following: "The President's News Conference," April 29, 1976, in American Presidency Project, https://www.presidency.ucsb.edu/documents/the-presidents-news-conference-50.

124. The shift away from détente was also evident at the vice presidential level. See Nelson Rockefeller, "Remarks of the Vice President at the Ceremony Launching of the Dwight D. Eisenhower Nuclear-Powered Aircraft Carrier, Newport News Shipbuilding, Newport News, Virginia," October 11, 1975, Teller Papers, box 3, folder 12.

125. "Editorial: Why Détente Is in Trouble," *Fortune*, April 1976.
126. "Treaty Between the United States of America and the Union of Soviet Socialist Republics on the Limitation of Strategic Offensive Arms (SALT II)," June 18, 1979, State Department website, https://2009-2017.state.gov/t/isn/5195.htm. Note that this treaty was not ratified by the Senate and never went into effect.
127. "Joint Communique on the Establishment of Diplomatic Relations Between the United States of America and the People's Republic of China," January 1, 1979, read by Carter in a public address, in Kristin L. Ahlberg, ed., *Foreign Relations of the United States, 1977–1980, Volume 1: Foundations of Foreign Policy* (Washington, DC: U.S. Government Printing Office, 2014), document 104.
128. Jimmy Carter, *White House Diary* (New York: Picador/Farrar, Straus & Giroux, 2010), 74–75, 36–137.
129. "Carter Aims for the Moon," *Euromoney*, February 1977.
130. Jimmy Carter, "Address at Commencement Exercises at the University of Notre Dame," May 22, 1977, in American Presidency Project, https://www.presidency.ucsb.edu/documents/address-commencement-exercises-the-university-notre-dame.
131. Carter, *White House Diary*, 76, 123; David Skidmore, *Reversing Course: Carter's Foreign Policy, Domestic Politics, and the Failure of Reform* (Nashville, TN: Vanderbilt University Press, 1996), chaps 2–5.
132. Stuart, "Anti-SALT Lobbyists Outspend Pros by 15 to 1."
133. Zbigniew Brzezinski, *Power and Principle: Memoirs of a National Security Advisor, 1977–1981* (New York: Farrar, Straus & Giroux, 1983).
134. George C. Wilson, "Business Booms for Weapons Makers," *Washington Post*, January 21, 1979.
135. Regarding Carter-era interventions, see Halliday, *The Making of the Second Cold War*, chaps. 4, 5.
136. Quoted from C. Robert Zelnick, "Paul Nitze: The Nemesis of SALT II," *Washington Post*, June 24, 1979.
137. *New York Times*/CBS News poll, discussed in Adam Clymer, "Carter Budget Gets Support in Survey," *New York Times*, January 31, 1979.
138. Gallup, *The Gallup Poll*, 176–77.
139. Jimmy Carter, "The State of the Union Address Delivered Before a Joint Session of the Congress," January 23, 1980, in American Presidency Project, https://www.presidency.ucsb.edu/documents/the-state-the-union-address-delivered-before-joint-session-the-congress. On Carter's response to the invasion, see also "Talking Points for Discussions on Afghanistan with Allied Leaders," declassified document previously marked "Secret," n.d. (probably January 1980), Remote Archives Capture (RAC files), box 1, folder 1, NLC 128-1-1-6, Carter Presidential Library.

140. U.S. Joint Chiefs of Staff, "Program of Assistance for the General Area of China," January 16, 1950, 35, Declassified Documents Reference System, Gale-Cengage.

141. On the declassified government documents, see David N. Gibbs, "Does the USSR Have a 'Grand Strategy'? Reinterpreting the Invasion of Afghanistan," *Journal of Peace Research* 24, no. 4 (1987): 367–69.

142. Louis Dupree, "Afghanistan Under the Khalq," *Problems of Communism* 28, no. 4 (1979): 38, 50.

143. Marshall I. Goldman, *Soviet Foreign Aid* (New York: Praeger, 1967), 122–23.

144. Peter R. Kann, "Do the Russians Covet Afghanistan? If So, It's Hard to Figure Why," *Wall Street Journal*, December 27, 1973. And U.S. officials continued to view the country as holding little strategic significance, as indicated in memo from Robert B. Oakley to Brent Scowcroft, "Request for Appointment with You and Afghanistani Deputy Foreign Minister Waheed Abdullah, October 7, 1974," Presidential Country Files for the Middle East and South Asia, box 2, folder "Afghanistan (1)," Ford Presidential Library. This memo stated, "Afghanistan is of no major importance to us."

145. This conclusion is based on a JSTOR search of Brzezinski's writings during the period 1950–1977. The search revealed a single mention of the word "Afghanistan," which appeared only in passing, as part of a list of countries, in terms of how they voted in the United Nations.

146. Fred Halliday, "Revolution in Afghanistan," *New Left* Review, no. 112, 1978.

147. See the authoritative account by Diego Cordovez and Selig S. Harrison, *Out of Afghanistan: The Inside Story of the Soviet Withdrawal* (New York: Oxford University Press, 1995), 25–28. This study cites a 1993 interview conducted with Alexander Morozov, who served as deputy chief of the KGB station in Afghanistan during the 1978 coup.

148. Unnamed Soviet official, quoted in Dupree, "Afghanistan Under the Khalq," 50;emphasis in original.

149. The record of Soviet documentation is presented in David N. Gibbs, "Reassessing Soviet Motives for Invading Afghanistan: A Declassified History," *Critical Asian Studies* 36, no. 2 (2006): 250–52.

150. Soviet Government, "Transcript of CPSU CC Politburo Discussions on Afghanistan," March 17, 1979, English translation, Cold War International History Project, Wilson Center, http://digitalarchive.wilsoncenter.org/document/113260.pdf ?v=9a14e68ffecd3c52f4655b8da4a4a08e.

151. Robert M. Gates, *From the Shadows: The Ultimate Insider's Story of Five Presidents and How They Won the Cold War* (New York: Simon & Schuster, 1996), 146–47. Note that Gates had a long career in the CIA, including during the Carter presidency.

152. USSR Government, "CPSU CC Politburo Decision on Afghanistan, with Report by Gromyko, Andropov, Ustinov, and Zagladin, 7 April 1980," English translation, Cold War International History Project, Woodrow Wilson, http://digitalarchive.wilsoncenter.org/document/111590. Though the views in this document were expressed shortly after the invasion occurred, it appears likely that these attitudes contributed to the invasion decision. See also Soviet security fears expressed in A. Petrov, "On Events in Afghanistan," *Pravda*, December 31, 1979, English translation, in *Current Digest of the Soviet Press*, January 23, 1980.

153. Fred Halliday, "War and Revolution in Afghanistan," *New Left Review*, no. 119 (1980): 35–36.

154. The Carter Doctrine was first presented in "Address by President Carter on the State of the Union Before a Joint Session of Congress," January 23, 1980, in Ahlberg, *Foreign Relations of the United States: 1977–1980, Volume I, Foundations of Foreign Policy*, document 138.

155. Jimmy Carter, *Keeping Faith: Memoirs of a President* (New York: Bantam, 1982), 472–78. On the 1980 Olympics, see "Letter by President Jimmy Carter to the President of the United States Olympic Committee, Robert Kane," January 20, 1980, Cold War International History Project, Wilson Center, https://digitalarchive.wilsoncenter.org/document/letter-president-jimmy-carter-president-united-states-olympic-committee-robert-kane.

156. George C. Wilson, quoted in Hobart Rowan, "Fiscal '81 Budget a Victim of New Cold War," *Washington Post*, January 20, 1980.

157. Department of Defense, Memorandum for the President from Harold Brown, "Subject: Strategic Review of our Unified Command Structure," April 6, 1980, Declassified Documents Reference System, Gale-Cengage. For background on the Rapid Deployment Joint Task Force, see memorandum from General William E. Odom to Zbigniew Brzezinski, "Strategy for the Persian Gulf in 1980," November 28, 1979, William E. Odom Papers, box 36, folder 5, Library of Congress.

158. Daniel Southerland, "Washington Toughens Stance with 'Realistic View' of Soviet Aims," *Christian Science Monitor*, January 7, 1980.

159. Quoted in Jonathan Haslam, *Russia's Cold War: From the October Revolution to the Fall of the Wall* (New Haven, CT: Yale University Press, 2011), 326. Brzezinski's comment was made to Lieutenant General William Odom, who communicated it to Haslam in a later conversation. For further information on Brzezinski's role, corroborating the account in Haslam, see *"Les Révélations d'un Ancien Conseilleur de Carter: 'Oui, la CIA est Entré en Afghanistan avant les Russes . . .'" Le Nouvel Observateur* (Paris), January 15–21, 1998. An English translation appears in David N. Gibbs, "Afghanistan: The Soviet Invasion in Retrospect," *International Politics* 37, no. 2 (2000), 241–42. For further evidence on

Brzezinski's role in provoking the invasion, see Jonathan Haslam, "Response to H-Diplo Article Review 966 (2020): There Really Was an 'Afghan Trap,'" H-Diplo, May 13, 2022, https://networks.h-net.org/node/28443/discussions/10247063 /response-h-diplo-article-review-966-2020-there-really-was-afghan.

160. Brzezinski perfunctorily expressed regret at the invasion, but he also expressed pleasure that the invasion had vindicated his hardline views of the Soviets and that the invasion enabled President Carter to project an image of toughness. See Brzezinski, *Power and Principle*, 429.

161. George C. Wilson, quoted in Hobart Rowan, "Fiscal '81 Budget a Victim of New Cold War," *Washington Post*, January 20, 1980.

162. John L. Frisbee, "Afghanistan: A Watershed," *Air Force Magazine*, February 1980. The article did express some pro forma regret about the invasion.

5. THE RICH GO GLOBAL

The chapter epigraph comes from Charles Murray, "The Shape of Things to Come," *National Review*, July 8, 1991.

1. For the popularized image of globalization as an inevitable process, see Thomas L. Friedman, *The Lexus and the Olive Tree* (New York: Farrar, Straus & Giroux, 1999), 88–89.

2. Some academics have mistakenly predicted that the decline of U.S. manufacturing would lead to a loss of its great power status, on the model of British decline during the first half of the twentieth century. Missed in this interpretation was America's ability to draw in foreign funds, which compensated for weak industrial exports, enabling the United States to continue its great power status long after it emerged as a net debtor state. On U.S. "decline," see the classic by Paul Kennedy, *The Rise and Fall of the Great Powers: Economic Change and Military Conflict from 1500 to 2000* (New York: Random House, 1987).

3. The records of the 1944 Bretton Woods meetings are now available. See Kurt Schuler and Andrew Rosenberg, eds., *The Bretton Woods Transcripts* (New York: Center for Financial Stability, 2012). See also the online document collection at http://www.centerforfinancialstability.org/brettonwoods_docs.php.

4. See "Articles of Agreement of the International Monetary Fund," July 22, 1944, article IV, section 3, Avalon Project, Yale Law School, http://avalon.law.yale .edu/20th_century/decad047.asp.

5. Elizabeth Borgwardt, *A New Deal for the World: America's Vision for Human Rights* (Cambridge, MA: Belknap Press of Harvard University Press, 2007), chaps. 3, 4; Eric Rauchway, *The Money Makers: How Roosevelt and Keynes Ended the Depression, Defeated Fascism, and Secured a Prosperous Peace* (New York: Basic Books, 2015), chaps. 11, 12. On how the legacy of the Depression

influenced postwar economic policy, see Charles P. Kindleberger, *The World in Depression, 1929–1939* (Berkeley: University of California Press, 1973); and Perry Mehrling, *Money and Empire: Charles P. Kindleberger and the Dollar System* (Cambridge: Cambridge University Press, 2022).

6. I. de Vegh, "Why International Lending Is Planned: Mechanism Sought to Replace Now Unworkable Gold Standard," *Barron's National Business and Financial Weekly*, January 1, 1945.

7. Gerald Epstein and Thomas Ferguson, "Monetary Policy, Loan Liquidation, and Industrial Conflict: The Federal Reserve and the Open Market Operations of 1932," *Journal of Economic History* 44, no. 4 (1984).

8. "Banking Act of 1933 (Glass-Steagall Act)," June 16, 1933, FRED Economic Data, Federal Reserve Bank of St. Louis, https://fraser.stlouisfed.org/title/banking -act-1933-glass-steagall-act-991.

9. Board of Governors of the Federal Reserve System, 12 CFR part 217, "Capital Adequacy of Bank Holding Companies, Savings and Loan Holding Companies, and State Member Banks (Regulation Q)," August 29, 1933, Legal Information Institute, Cornell Law School, https://www.law.cornell.edu/cfr/text/12 /part-217.

10. Paul A. Baran and Paul M. Sweezy, *Monopoly Capital: An Essay on the American Economic and Social Order* (New York: Monthly Review, 1966), 16. There was, however, a gradual rise in consumer loans after World War II; see Louis Hyman, *Debtor Nation: The History of America in Red Ink* (Princeton, NJ: Princeton University Press, 2011), chap. 5.

11. MacroTrends, LLC, "Dow Jones, DJIA, 100 Year Historical Chart," 1915–2020, by month. Accessed on November 20, 2023, https://www.macrotrends .net/1319/dow-jones-100-year-historical-chart. The stock market's pre-Depression value peaked in real terms on August 1, 1929; this level was not reached again until May 1, 1959.

12. Mark Blyth, *Austerity: History of a Dangerous Idea* (New York: Oxford University Press, 2013), 24.

13. This overseas migration of U.S. banking was connected with the liberalization of European finance and the lifting of most capital controls during the late 1950s. See Atish R. Ghosh and Mahvash S. Qureshi, "What's in a Name? That Which We Call Capital Controls" (Working Paper 16/25, International Monetary Fund, Washington, DC, February 2016), 18, https://www.imf.org/external /pubs/ft/wp/2016/wp1625.pdf.

14. Barry Bluestone and Bennett Harrison, *The Deindustrialization of America: Plant Closings, Community Abandonment, and the Dismantling of Basic Industry* (New York: Basic Books, 1982), 113; William D. Cohan, *Money and Power: How Goldman Sachs Came to Rule the World* (New York: Doubleday, 2011), 210; and

Eric Helleiner, *States and the Reemergence of International Finance: From Bretton Woods to the 1990s* (Ithaca, NY: Cornell University Press, 1994), 83–84.

15. On U.S. export of inflation during this period, see Paul Volcker and Toyoo Gyohten, *Changing Fortunes: The World's Money and the Threat to American Leadership* (New York: Times Books, 1992), 66. On Vietnam and international finance, see John J. Deutsch, "Inflation, 1950–1975: A Social and Political Perspective, a Paper for the Bilderberg Conference," April 1975, 9, in William F. Buckley Papers, pt. II, series 1, box 89, folder 212, Yale University.

16. Michael Moffitt, *The World's Money: International Banking from Bretton Woods to the Brink of Insolvency* (New York: Simon & Schuster, 1983), 146.

17. On the gradual loss of international confidence in the dollar, see Barry Eichengreen, *Exorbitant Privilege: The Rise and Fall of the Dollar and the Future of the International Monetary System* (New York: Oxford University Press, 2011), 49–54. In September 1970, U.S. officials expressed concern about the possibility of "renewed speculation in gold." From "Volcker Working Paper," September 10, 1970, document 148 in *Foreign Relations of the United States, 1969–1976, Volume III: Foreign Economic Policy, International Monetary Policy, 1969–1972*, ed. Bruce F. Duncombe (Washington, DC: U.S. Government Printing Office, 2001), https://history.state.gov/historicaldocuments/frus1969-76v03/d148.

18. See IET full text at Public Law 88-563—September 2, 1964, "Interest Equalization Tax," Discover U.S. Government Information, https://www.govinfo.gov/content/pkg/STATUTE-78/pdf/STATUTE-78-Pg809.pdf#page=36.

19. For the FDIP, see U.S. Department of Treasury, "Memorandum from Secretary of the Treasury Fowler to President Johnson, Subject: Balance of Payments Program for 1969—Early Announcement of the Foreign Direct Investment Program," November 12, 1968, document 204 in *Foreign Relations of the United States, 1964–1968, Volume VIII, International Monetary and Trade Policy*, ed. Evan Duncan, David S. Patterson, and Carolyn Yee (Washington, DC: U.S. Government Printing Office, 1998).

20. Helleiner, *States and the Reemergence of International Finance*, 84–91; John A. C. Conybeare, *United States Foreign Economic Policy and International Capital Markets: The Case of Capital Export Countries, 1963–1974* (New York: Garland, 1988), 6–7.

21. Paul E. Erdman, *The Crash of '79* (New York: Simon & Schuster, 1976).

22. At Bretton Woods, Keynes had in fact advocated for much tighter international controls on private finance, but this was blocked by the American delegation. On Keynes's original proposal for multinational financial controls, see Eric Helleiner, "Controlling Capital Flows 'at Both Ends': A Neglected (but Newly Relevant) Keynesian Innovation from Bretton Woods," *Challenge* 58, no. 5 (2015). Original documentation can be found in Elizabeth Johnson and Donald

Moggridge, eds., *The Collected Writings of John Maynard Keynes: Volume 25, Activities 1940–1944, Shaping the Post-War World, the Clearing Union* (Cambridge: Cambridge University Press, 1978). See also John Maynard Keynes, "Proposals for an International Currency (or Clearing) Union," February 11, 1942; and "Proposals for an International Clearing Union," April 1943, both in *The International Monetary Fund, 1945–1965: Twenty Years of International Monetary Cooperation, Vol. 3, Documents,* ed. J. K. Horsefield (Washington, DC: International Monetary Fund, 1969).

23. Wriston's views are noted in Milton Friedman, "The Adam Smith Address: The Suicidal Approach of the Business Community (1989)," in *The Best of Business Economics: Highlights from the First Fifty Years,* ed. Robert Crow (London: Palgrave Macmillan, 2016), 184–85.

24. Patricia Sullivan, "Walter B. Wriston, 85: Chairman of Citicorp," *Washington Post,* January 21, 2005; Nicholas Lemann, "The Man Who Freed the Banks," *New York Times,* May 12, 1996.

25. Herbert Stein, *Presidential Economics: The Making of Economic Policy from Roosevelt to Clinton* (Washington, DC: American Enterprise Institute for Public Policy Research, 1994), 165.

26. Helleiner, *States and the Reemergence of Global Finance,* 99–100. The rise in multinational investment was closely connected with the declining profit rates during the late 1960s. See Ronald W. Cox, *Corporate Power, Class Conflict, and the Crisis of the New Globalization* (Lanham, MD: Lexington, 2019).

27. See "Testimony by Joseph W. Leimert, Vice President CPC International Inc for the National Association of Manufacturers on International Monetary Reform Before the House Subcommittee on International Trade, Investment, and Monetary Policy, June 1976," 2, attached to U.S. Department of the Treasury, memorandum, "Department of the Treasury to the International Monetary Group (Info Distribution)," June 2, 1976, Office of the Assistant Secretary for International Affairs, Subject Files of the Secretariat, 1974–1976, collection RG 56, entry number A1-862, box 1, folder "Vastine Chron II," U.S. National Archives. Note that during this period, NAM was gaining increasing interest in multinational enterprise and finance. Jennifer A. Delton, *The Industrialists: How the National Association of Manufacturers Shaped American Capitalism* (Princeton, NJ: Princeton University Press, 2020), 258.

28. Milton Friedman, "The Case for Flexible Exchange Rates," in Friedman, *Essays in Positive Economics* (Chicago: University of Chicago Press, 1953). See also Paul Volcker and Christine Harper, *Keeping at It: The Quest for Sound Money and Good Government* (New York: Public Affairs, 2018), 62–63.

29. Carol M. Connell, *Reforming the World Monetary System: Fritz Machlup and the Bellagio Group* (London: Pickering & Chatto, 2013), 99.

30. For a detailed analysis of the MPS support for globalization, see Quinn Slobo-dian, *Globalists: The End of Empire and the Birth of Neoliberalism* (Cambridge, MA: Harvard University Press, 2018), especially chap. 4. See also Jessica Whyte, *The Morals of the Market: Human Rights and the Rise of Neoliberalism* (London: Verso, 2019).

31. The Wriston-Friedman collaboration is noted in Friedman, "The Adam Smith Address," 184–85.

32. Milton Friedman and Rose Friedman, *Two Lucky People: Milton and Rose D. Friedman, Memoirs* (Chicago: University of Chicago Press, 1998), 376.

33. Memo from Tilford C. Haines, transmitting report on Task Force on U.S. Balance of Payments Policies to the President Elect, December 17, 1968, in White House Central Files, 1969–71, Hendrick S. Houthakker Papers, box 31, folder "Haberler Task Force, No. 2," Nixon Presidential Library. This document was presented as a draft, although it appears to have been very close to final completion.

34. On Nixon's lack of interest in international economics, see H. S. Houthakker, "The Breakdown of Bretton Woods" (Discussion Paper no. 543, Harvard Institute of Economic Research, April 1977), in Carter Presidential Papers, Staff Offices, Council of Economic Advisers, George C. Eads File, subject files, box 230, folder "Houthakker, Hendrik (Harvard University)," Carter Presidential Library.

35. Nixon's obsession with reelection was a major concern for Arthur Burns, who chaired the Federal Reserve. These concerns were repeatedly noted in his diary, Robert H. Ferrell, ed., *Inside the Nixon Administration: The Secret Diary of Arthur Burns, 1969–1974* (Lawrence: University Press of Kansas, 2010), 53, 63. At one point, Burns noted, "The president's preoccupation with the [1972] election frightens me."

36. Allen J. Matusow, *Nixon's Economy: Booms, Busts, Dollars, and Votes* (Lawrence: University Press of Kansas, 1998), chaps. 5, 6.

37. Benn Steil, *The Battle of Bretton Woods: John Maynard Keynes, Harry Dexter White, and the Making of a New World Order* (Princeton, NJ: Princeton University Press, 2013), 338. See also Burton A. Abrams, "How Richard Nixon Pressured Arthur Burns: Evidence from the Nixon Tapes," *Journal of Economic Perspectives* 20, no. 4 (2006).

The policy of reduced interest rates and monetary growth elicited complaint from Milton Friedman. Letter from Milton Friedman to Arthur Burns, December 13, 1971, in White House Central Files, Staff Members and Office Files, Arthur Burns Papers, box K12, folder "Friedman, Milton (2)," Ford Presidential Library.

38. Richard M. Nixon, *RN: The Memoirs of Richard Nixon* (New York: Grosset & Dunlap, 1978), 518; Robert Solomon, *The International Monetary System: 1945–1976: An Insider's View* (New York: Harper & Row, 1977), 182.

39. Paul W. McCracken, memorandum for the president, August 9, 1971, White House Central Files, Subject Files, FO, Foreign Affairs, box 44, folder "Ex FO 4-1, 1/1/71-12/31/71 [2 of 3]," Nixon Presidential Library.

40. World Bank, "Current Account Balance (Percent of GDP)—United States," 1970–2020, accessed November 1, 2023, https://data.worldbank.org/indicator /BN.CAB.XOKA.GD.ZS?end=2017&locations=US&start=1970&view=chart.

41. Robert Solomon, "The Spector of an International Monetary Crisis," March 12, 1971, in Burns Papers, box C15, folder "Solomon, Robert (9) Mar-Apr 10, 1971," Ford Presidential Library. On the dollar crisis of this period, see the memoirs of the former official of the New York Federal Reserve, Charles A. Coombs, *The Arena of International Finance* (New York: Wiley, 1976), chap. 12.

42. On Nixon's close relationship with Connally, see the accounts by the former presidential aide John Ehrlichman, *Witness to Power: The Nixon Years* (New York: Simon & Schuster, 1982), 259–60; and by former Justice Department official Robert H. Bork, *Saving Justice: Watergate, the Saturday Night Massacre, and Other Adventures of a Solicitor General* (New York: Encounter, 2013), 76.

43. John B. Connally and Mickey Herskowitz, *In History's Shadow: An American Odyssey* (New York: Hyperion, 1993), 237. Connally noted that his views were influenced by MPS member George Shultz. Regarding Friedman's efforts to influence Connally, see Friedman and Friedman, *Two Lucky People*, 377.

44. Richard M. Nixon, "Address to the Nation Outlining a New Economic Policy: 'The Challenge of Peace,'" August 15, 1971, American Presidency Project, University of California, Santa Barbara, https://www.presidency.ucsb.edu /documents/address-the-nation-outlining-new-economic-policy-the-challenge -peace. On the politics leading to the Nixon Shock, see Solomon, *The International Monetary System*, chap. XI.

45. Nixon, *RN*, 519.

46. Robert B. Semple Jr., "Import Surtax Ended by Nixon," *New York Times*, December 21, 1971.

47. Letter from Gottfried Haberler to David Rockefeller, February 2, 1970, in Gottfried Haberler Papers, box 28, folder "GH-David Rockefeller," Hoover Institution Archives, Stanford University. Haberler cited discussions with White House personnel as the basis for his claims.

48. Speech by Robert Bleiberg, "Farewell to Wage and Price Controls," *Imprimis* 3, no. 7 (July 1974), https://imprimis.hillsdale.edu/farewell-to-wage-and-price -controls-july-1974/. Bleiberg was the publisher of *Barron's* financial weekly. See also Benjamin C. Waterhouse, *Lobbying America: The Politics of Business from Nixon to NAFTA* (Princeton, NJ: Princeton University Press, 2014), chap. 4.

49. See Nixon, "Address to the Nation."

50. Ezra Solomon, "The International Monetary System: Opportunities and Options," August 22, 1971, in White House Central Files, Staff Member and Office Files, Paul W. McCracken Papers, box 109, folder "International [1 of 2]," Nixon Presidential Library.

51. Quoted in Phillip L. Zweig, *Wriston: Walter Wriston, Citibank and the Rise and Fall of American Financial Supremacy* (New York: Crown, 1995), 350.

52. Connally and Herskowitz, *In History's Shadow*, 237.

53. Juan Cameron, "What Businessmen Like and Don't Like About Nixon," *Fortune*, July 1972.

54. White House Memorandum, "Conversation with David Rockefeller," April 7, 1972, Foreign Affairs, box 43, folder "Ex For 4, Financial Relations, 1/1/71-12/31/72," Nixon Presidential Library.

55. Letter from Milton Friedman to John Connally, December 3, 1971, in Burns Papers, box K12, folder "Friedman, Milton (2)," Ford Presidential Library. Friedman did, however, criticize the administration's import surcharge and also worried about a possible shift toward a renewed fixed exchange rate regime in future.

56. Nomi Prins, *All the Presidents' Bankers: The Hidden Alliances That Drive American Power* (New York: Nation, 2014), 286.

57. William L. Silber, *Volcker: The Triumph of Persistence* (New York: Bloomsbury, 2012), 58, 75–76.

58. George P. Shultz, *Learning from Experience* (Palo Alto, CA: Hoover Institution, 2016), 47. Shultz adds that Friedman advocated floating rates, while maintaining "the appearance of par values," to achieve some cosmetic continuity with the older Bretton Woods system.

59. Silber, *Volcker*, 113. Note that there was significant currency floating even before the March 1973 decision. See "Some Essentials of International Monetary Reform: Remarks of Arthur F. Burns, Chairman, Board of Governors of the Federal Reserve System Before the 1972 International Banking Conference, Montreal Canada, May 12, 1972," 1, in Burns Papers, box B75, folder "International Monetary Reforms, Issues, Papers Misc (3)" Ford Presidential Library.

60. For the diplomatic record, see documents 1–37, "The End of Fixed Exchange Rates, January-March 1973," in *Foreign Relations of the United States, 1969–1976, Volume XXXI: Foreign Economic Policy, 1973–1976*, ed. Kathleen B. Rasmussen (Washington, DC: U.S. Government Printing Office, 2009), https://history.state.gov/historicaldocuments/frus1969-76v31/ch1.

61. William Glenn Gray, "Floating the System: Germany, the United States, and the Breakdown of Bretton Woods, 1969–1973," *Diplomatic History* 31, no. 2 (2007): 321. Despite deregulation, states still retained some role through "managed" or "dirty" floats, whereby central bankers and finance ministries would

manipulate the values of their currencies to achieve political objectives. On dirty floats, see "Some Essentials of International Monetary Reform: Remarks of Arthur F. Burns," 1, Ford Presidential Library.

62. The quote is a paraphrase from Treasury Secretary Shultz in "U.S. Ends 3 Bars on Capital Flows Overseas: Steps Were Expected to Come Later," *Wall Street Journal*, January 30, 1974. On the ideological motive for removal of capital controls, see Robert M. Bleiberg, "Government and Business: Federal Regulation Has Reached a Dead End," *Barron's National Business and Financial Weekly*, April 18, 1975.

63. U.S. Department of the Treasury, memorandum from Gerald Parsky, assistant secretary for International Affairs, "Subject: The Major Lines of Treasury International Economic Policy, and Actions to Implement Them in Coming Months," November 25, 1976, in Correspondence of the Secretary [W. E. Simon], entry number UD-UP-777, box 1, collection RG 56, folder "Memo to Secy, Nov-Dec, C, 1976," National Archives.

64. Gordon Mitchell, "Beyond Bretton Woods? Floating Currencies Says BankAmerica Works Fine," *Barron's National Business and Financial Weekly*, November 11, 1974.

65. David Rockefeller was somewhat critical of Friedman, noting that his views "have now come to symbolize a Chicago School that is strongly doctrinaire." David Rockefeller, *Memoirs* (New York: Random House, 2002), 88.

66. David Rockefeller, "Living in an Energy Scarce World," February 9, 1974, 16, in Joseph and Stewart Alsop Papers, box 152, folder 5, Library of Congress. Emphasis in original.

67. Daniel S. Sargent, *A Superpower Transformed: The Remaking of American Foreign Relations in the 1970s* (New York: Oxford University Press, 2015), 108. A similar conclusion is reached by the following well-researched study: Christoffer J. P. Zoeller, "Closing the Gold Window: The End of Bretton Woods as a Contingency Plan," *Politics & Society* 47, no. 1 (2019).

68. Quote from Muammer Wali and Meher Manzur, "Exchange Rate Volatility Before and After the Float," *World Economy* 36, no. 8 (2013): 1091. For similar views, see also Selahattin Dibooğlu, "International Monetary Regimes and the Incidence and Transmission of Macroeconomic Shocks: Evidence from the Bretton Woods and Modern Floating Periods," *Southern Economic Journal* 66, no. 3 (2000): 605; Fred Block and Margaret R. Somers, *The Power of Market Fundamentalism: Karl Polanyi's Critique* (Cambridge, MA: Harvard University Press, 2014), 17–18; and Paul Krugman, *Exchange Rate Instability* (Cambridge, MA: MIT Press, 1989), 2, 100–101.

69. Jacob Dreyer, Gottfried Haberler, and Thomas Willett, "Conference on International Monetary System Under Stress, February 28–29, 1980, American

Enterprise Institute, Washington, DC," in Arthur Burns Papers, box E47, folder "AEI Conference on the IMF Under Stress—Introductory Remarks, 2/28/1980," Ford Presidential Library.

70. The idea that floating rates would have a stabilizing effect (exchange rates "would smoothly adjust") had long been advocated by Milton Friedman, as described in "Interview with Paul A. Volcker," December 29, 2009, 258, Federal Reserve Board Oral History Project, https://www.federalreserve.gov /aboutthefed/files/paul-a-volcker-interview-20080225.pdf.

71. Joseph W. Barr, "The Last Days of Franklin National Bank," *Administrative Law Review* 27, no. 4 (1975); Edward P. Foldessy, "Fed's Lending to Franklin National Bank Is About $1.1 Billion, a High for Such Aid," *Wall Street Journal*, May 23, 1974.

72. Letter from Milton Friedman to William Proxmire, May 26, 1971, in Milton Friedman Papers, box 171, folder "Proxmire, William, 1967–1987," Hoover Institution Archives, Stanford University. This specific letter notes Friedman's objections to the federal loan guarantee for the Lockheed Corporation; Friedman's objections to this bailout would apply with equal force to the bailout of Franklin National and other failed banks.

73. Moffitt, *The World's Money*, 136. For a similar view by the former chairman of the Federal Reserve, see Arthur F. Burns, "Maintaining the Soundness of Our Banking System," speech before the American Bankers Convention, October 21, 1974, in Arthur Burns, *Reflections of an Economic Policy Maker: Speeches and Congressional Statements: 1969–1978* (Washington, DC American Enterprise Institute for Public Policy Research, 1978), 358–59.

74. Bank for International Settlements, Basel, "International Liquidity and International Bank Lending, 1974–1978," April 27, 1979, 8, from A.BISA.1.3.a.3.B.vol 2, "International Liquidity and International Bank Lending 1974–1978, 27/04/1979," Bank for International Settlements Archives.

75. FRED Economic Data, Federal Reserve Bank of St. Louis, "Nonfarm Business Sector: Labor Productivity (Output per Hour) for All Workers," U.S. data from 1947 to present, FRED Economic Data, Federal Reserve Bank of St. Louis, accessed November 3, 2023, https://fred.stlouisfed.org/series/OPHNFB. Note especially data from 1973–1980.

76. A representative of the Business Council openly expressed concern about the possibility of a severe recession or depression. Memo from Kenneth B. Williams to Chairman Burns, Subject: "Meeting of Technical Consultants to the Business Council, October 1, Part II," October 7, 1974, 6, in Burns Papers, box B12, folder "Business Council, Technical Consultants to," Ford Presidential Library.

77. In 1973, OPEC comprised the following twelve countries: Algeria, Ecuador, Indonesia, Iran, Iraq, Kuwait, Libya, Nigeria, Qatar, Saudi Arabia, United Arab Emirates, and Venezuela. During the early phase of the energy crisis, another

significant player was the Organization of Arab Petroleum Exporting Countries, OAPEC.

78. On profiteering by the oil companies as a motive for OPEC: "One of the Arab diplomats is reported to have said . . . 'you screwed us, and condescended to us too, for three hundred years and we are going to enjoy screwing you too.'" From "Memorandum to the Files: Thoughts on Our Energy Problem," March 19, 1974, in Trilateral Commission Papers, box 98, folder 1104, Rockefeller Archive Center.

79. Stein, *Presidential Economics*, 191–92.

80. This is strongly implied in John M. Fisher, president, ASC to William D. Desilva Jr., April 1, 1974, in Group Research Inc. Papers, box 355, folder "American Security Council, 1974," Columbia University.

81. See President Richard M. Nixon, "Annual Message to Congress on the State of the Union," January 30, 1974, American Presidency Project, https://www.presidency .ucsb.edu/documents/annual-message-the-congress-the-state-the-union.

82. Treasury Secretary William Simon, quoted in Memorandum of Conversation, President Nixon, William Simon, and Brent Scowcroft, July 9, 1974, in National Security Adviser, Memoranda of Conversations, 1973–1977, Ford Presidential Library, https://www.fordlibrarymuseum.gov/library/document/0314/1552732 .pdf. Simon also emphasized the importance of Venezuela in raising oil prices.

83. Andrew Scott Cooper, *The Oil Kings: How the U.S., Iran, and Saudi Arabia Changed the Balance of Power in the Middle East* (New York: Simon & Schuster, 2011), 42.

84. Andrew Cooper, "Showdown at Doha: The Secret Oil Deal That Helped Sink the Shah of Iran," *Middle East Journal* 62, no. 4 (2008): especially 578–91. However, there was a gradual move away from the shah on oil pricing toward the end of the Ford presidency.

85. Memorandum of Conversation, July 9, 1974, Ford Presidential Library; emphasis added. Simon was a consistent advocate of lowering world oil prices as a basic priority. See U.S. Department of Treasury, Memorandum of Conversation, "Subject: IMF Interim Committee Work Program," November 29, 1974, 4, in Correspondence of the Secretary [W. E. Simon], collection RG 56, entry number UD-UP-777, box 2, folder "Memo of Conversation C (1975)."

86. William E. Simon, undated document, "Memorandum for the President," in Jack Anderson Papers, box 329, folder 2, George Washington University. The wording of the document suggests it was probably written during either the late Nixon presidency or the Ford presidency.

87. White House, Memorandum of Conversation: President Nixon, William Simon, Kenneth Rush, Brent Scowcroft, July 30, 1974, from Declassified Documents Reference System, Gale-Cengage.

88. Jack Anderson, "Nixon Let Shah Drive Up Oil Prices," *Washington Post*, June 1, 1979. For further evidence of Saudi willingness to restrain prices, see the following two documents from the William E. Simon Papers at Lafayette College: "Department of Treasury: Interviews of Secretary Simon," n.d. (probably 1976), 2, series V, drawer 43, box 86, folder 36; and "Department of Treasury: Interview of Secretary Simon," May 1, 1976, 3–4, series V, drawer 43, box 86, folder 38.

89. Letter from Ahmed Zaki Yamani to William Simon, September 3, 1975, in Anderson Papers, box 329, folder 2. Yamani added—unconvincingly—that he did not believe that the U.S. government was encouraging the oil price increases. The Saudis' willingness to use their influence to restrain price rises was also noted in "NSSM 238: U.S. Policy Toward the Persian Gulf," undated report, 8, attached to National Security Council memorandum, "NSSM 238—U.S. Policy Toward the Persian Gulf," November 19, 1976, in Correspondence of the Secretary [W. E. Simon], collection RG 56, entry number UD-UP-777, box 3, folder "White House 1976."

90. V. H. Oppenheim, "Why Oil Prices Go Up: The Past—We Pushed Them," *Foreign Policy*, no. 25 (1976–1977): 24. See also Amin Mirzadegan, "Nixon's Folly: The White House and the 1970s Oil Price Crisis," *Yale Historical Review* 5, no. 2 (Spring 2016); and Debra K. Piot, "Kissinger Accused of OPEC Prod," *Christian Science Monitor*, May 5, 1980.

91. Jonathan Kwitny, *Endless Enemies: The Making of an Unfriendly World* (New York: Penguin, 1984), 187–89. On fawning press coverage of the shah, see James A. Bill, *The Eagle and the Lion: The Tragedy of American-Iranian Relations* (New Haven, CT: Yale University Press, 1988), 369–70.

92. John Kifner, "Documents Show Shah Sought U.S. Lobby," *New York Times*, May 30, 1979; Jacob K. Javits and Rafael Steinberg, *Javits: The Autobiography of a Public Man* (New York: Houghton Mifflin, 1981), 486.

93. Walter Pincus and Dan Morgan, "Arming the Shah: U.S. Interests Confused by Push for Profits," *Washington Post*, January 20, 1980.

94. On oil company profits during mid-decade, see Robert Sherrill, "The Case Against the Oil Companies," *New York Times*, October 14, 1979; John M. Blair, *The Control of Oil* (New York: Vintage, 1978), 280.

95. Letter from Richard Helms, December 11, 1974, in Barry M. Goldwater Papers, box 4, folder 12, Arizona State University.

96. Regarding extensive private-sector support for the shah, notably from the Rockefeller family, see telegram from U.S. Embassy, Tehran, November 22, 1978, from WikiLeaks Public Library of U.S. Diplomacy, https://search.wikileaks.org/plusd/cables/1978TEHRAN11498_d.html#efmAp-Auj.

97. With regard to the devastating effects of the energy crisis on less developed countries, especially in sub-Saharan Africa, see Fantu Cheru, *The Silent Revolution in Africa: Debt, Development, and Democracy* (London: Zed, 1989).

98. Peter Gowan, *The Global Gamble: Washington's Faustian Bid for World Dominance* (London: Verso, 1999), 49–50. On debt, see also Barbara Stallings, *Banker to the Third World: U.S. Portfolio Investment in Latin America, 1900–1986* (Berkeley: University of California Press, 1987).

99. On official corruption and misuse of oil revenues, see the excellent BBC documentary, dir. Hassan Amini, "Decadence and Downfall: The Shah of Iran's Ultimate Party," February 14, 2016, available from YouTube video, September 7, 2022, 1:16:11, https://www.youtube.com/watch?v=dWxwtILhfvE.

100. The trade deficit would briefly disappear during the mid-1970s due to lowered imports associated with the severe recession, but that was clearly understood to be a transitory phenomenon. On U.S. current account deficits over time, see World Bank, "Current Account Balance (Percent of GDP)—United States."

101. On the early history of ARAMCO, see "Memorandum by Mr. James A. Moffett for President Roosevelt," April 16, 1941, in *Foreign Relations of the United States, Diplomatic Papers, 1941, the British Commonwealth, the Near East, and Africa, Volume III*, ed. N. O. Sappington, Francis C. Prescott, and Kieran J. Carroll (Washington, DC: U.S. Government Printing Office, 1959), document 645; and Irvine H. Anderson Jr., *ARAMCO, the United States, and Saudi Arabia: A Study in the Dynamics of Foreign Oil Policy, 1933–1950* (Princeton, NJ: Princeton University Press, 1981). The name ARAMCO was not used until 1944.

102. See the fiercely adversarial negotiations between Saudi petroleum minister Yamani and representatives of the top Western oil companies. "Report of Meeting Held in Geneva at Intercontinental Hotel 4pm, 21 January 1972," in John J. McCloy Papers, series 20, box OIL2, folder 5, Amherst College. There was an ever-present danger that Persian Gulf states might destroy their oil installations in response to any external effort to seize the oil fields by force—a possibility that Saudi officials would pointedly bring up from time to time. See quotes from Ahmed Zaki Yamani in "Transcript of Talk Given by Ambassador James E. Akins on December 12, 1979," in Elbridge Durbrow Papers, box 4, folder "Iran-Afghanistan, April 1980–September 1980," Hoover Institution, Stanford University.

103. This paragraph paraphrases Andrea Wong, "The Untold Story Behind Saudi Arabia's 41-Year U.S. Trade Secret: How a Legendary Bond Trader from Salomon Brothers Brokered a Do-or-Die Deal That Reshaped U.S.-Saudi Relations for Generations," *Bloomberg News*, May 30, 2016.

104. Shultz, quoted in William E. Simon, *A Time for Reflection: An Autobiography* (Washington, DC: Regnery, 2004), 73.

105. Simon's intentions before the meeting with the Saudis were discussed in Memorandum of Conversation, President Nixon, William Simon, and Brent Scowcroft, July 9, 1974, Declassified Documents Reference System.

106. On the Jeddah agreement see Wong, "The Untold Story Behind Saudi Arabia's 41-Year U.S. Trade Secret." See also Duccio Basosi, "Oil, Dollars, and U.S. Power in the 1970s: Reviewing the Connections," *Journal of Energy History*, no. 3 (2019); and David E. Spiro, *The Hidden Hand of American Hegemony: Petrodollar Recycling and International Markets* (Ithaca, NY: Cornell University Press, 1999), 42–44, 106–9. The need to recycle petrodollars was widely recognized at the time. See "Remarks by David Rockefeller at the Business Council Meeting: Redistribution of International Capital," May 11, 1974, in Melvin Laird Papers, box A131, folder "Business Council Meeting, May 1974," Ford Presidential Library.

107. A joint commission was established to funnel U.S. development expertise and investment into Saudi Arabia. See U.S. Department of the Treasury, "Fact Sheet: U.S./Saudi Arabian Joint Commission on Economic Cooperation," attachment 3 with Memo to Secretary Simon from Gerald L. Parsky, "Briefing Material for Your Meeting with U.S. Ambassador to Saudi Arabia William Porter," January 9, 1976, in Correspondence of the Secretary [W. E. Simon], collection RG 56, entry number UD-UP-777, box 1, folder "Briefing Memos, C, Jan-May 1976 C."

108. Some officials expressed anxiety about the Arab League boycott of Israel and how it affected the emerging U.S.-Saudi alliance, though the problems were viewed as manageable. See U.S. Department of Treasury, "Recent Developments in the Arab Boycott and Related Practices," attached to Memo to Secretary Simon from Gerald L. Parsky, "Briefing Material for Your Meeting with the New Saudi Arabian Ambassador to the U.S.: Ali Abdullah Alireza," January 23, 1976, Tab A attached, in Correspondence of the Secretary [W. E. Simon], collection RG 56, entry number UD-UP-777, box 1, folder "Briefing Memos, C, Jan-May 1976 C."

109. On the Saudi Arabian Monetary Authority (SAMA), a 1975 Treasury document refers casually to "the direct SAMA/Treasury connection." U.S. Department of Treasury, Memorandum from Gerald L. Parsky to Secretary Simon and Undersecretary Yeo, "Subject: Briefing Material for Your Meeting with Abd Al-Aziz al-Quraishi, Governor of the Saudi Arabian Monetary Agency," August 29, 1975, 3, in Correspondence of the Secretary [W. E. Simon], collection RG 56, entry number UD-UP-777, box 2, folder "Briefing Memos, June, C, 1975."

110. Kuwait also invested in U.S.-based assets, effectively propping up the dollar. U.S. Department of Treasury, Memorandum of Conversation, "Subject: Meeting for Abdulrahman S. Al-Ateeqi, Kuwait Minister of Finance, with US Business Leaders," August 29, 1975, in Correspondence of the Secretary [W. E. Simon], collection RG 56, entry number UD-UP-777, box 2, folder "Memo of Conversation C (1975)."

111. U.S. Treasury Department, "Implications of Capital Flows for Medium Term Current Account Outlook," May 19, 1978, 5, in Subject Files of Anthony M.

Solomon, collection RG 56, entry number A1-858, box 1, folder "Ad Hoc (Inter-agency Bal of Payments, GRP)," National Archives. Some 20 percent of OPEC surpluses were invested directly in the United States; nearly 80 percent were in dollar-denominated assets.

112. Roosa's comments appear verbatim in *Conference on Inflation: Held at the Request of President Gerald R. Ford and the Congress of the United States* (Washington, DC: U.S. Government Printing Office, 1974), 33. Roosa was a former Treasury official who later joined the Brown Brothers, Harriman investment bank.

113. For recent data on foreign holdings of U.S. Treasuries, see Marc Labonte and Ben Leubsdorf, "Foreign Holdings of Federal Debt," Congressional Research Service, June 9, 2023, https://sgp.fas.org/crs/misc/RS22331.pdf.

114. "Iranian Revolution (1979-)," DNSA Collection, Iran-Contra Affair, n.d., Digital National Security Archive, George Washington University.

115. Cooper, "Showdown at Doha," 579–80; Rachel Bronson, *Thicker Than Oil: America's Uneasy Partnership with Saudi Arabia* (New York: Oxford University Press, 2006), chaps. 5–7.

116. Steven Emerson, *The American House of Saud: The Secret Petrodollar Connection* (New York: Franklin Watts, 1985). It appears that affiliates of the American Enterprise Institute discreetly counseled Saudi officials on how to conduct their public relations efforts. See letter from Robert J. Pranger, director of Foreign Policy and Defense Policy Studies, AEI to Prince Bander Al-Sultan, May 11, 1978, in William J. Baroody Sr. Papers, box 4, folder 2, Library of Congress.

117. The lack of concern about Saudi violations of human rights was apparent even during the administration of Jimmy Carter, which sought to "strengthen the close ties" with the Saudis. Letter from Treasury Secretary G. William Miller to R. Bayly Winder, September 12, 1980, in G. William Miller Papers, box 31, folder "Saudi Arabia," Carter Presidential Library.

118. Charles Mohr, "Sale to Saudis Just Got By, But It Didn't Just Happen," *New York Times*, November 1, 1981.

119. Shultz's affiliation with Bechtel was noted in Alan Abelson, "Up and Down on Wall Street," *Barron's National Business and Financial Weekly*, November 14, 1983. Shultz later became president of Bechtel. See also Hussam Al May-man, "Bechtel: Partners in Transformation," *Saudi Gazette*, April 26, 2018; and Bechtel Newsroom, "George Shultz, Former President of Bechtel, Passes at 100," February 8, 2021, https://www.bechtel.com/newsroom/releases/2021/02/george-schultz-former-bechtel-president-passes/.

120. Tad Szulc, "Recycling Petrodollars: The $100 Billion Understanding," *New York Times*, September 20, 1981.

121. The Saudi deal may have postponed the need for austerity as a means of cor-recting the trade deficit, which was always another option. For an early mention

of austerity, see memorandum by Gaylord Freeman, chairman, First National Bank of Chicago, "Observations on the Dollar," April 21, 1971, in McCracken Papers, box 51, folder "Peterson, Peter [1 of 2]," Nixon Presidential Library.

122. Deutsch, "Inflation, 1950–1975," 9; emphasis added.

123. Richard Clark and Lindsay R. Dolan, "Pleasing the Principal: U.S. Influence in World Bank Policymaking," *American Journal of Political Science* 66, no. 1 (2021). On the strategic importance of U.S. economic power, see Department of Defense, "Army Special Operations Force: Unconventional Warfare," September 2008, appendix E, "The Financial Instrument of National Power," in WikiLeaks Public Library of U.S. Diplomacy, https://file.wikileaks.org/file/us-fm3-05-130.pdf.

124. "Defense is a major drain on our balance of payments," according to one White House document. Quoted from "Coordinating Group—Planning the Negotiations for the New Economic Policy Abroad," September 20, 1971, in McCracken Papers, box 51, folder "Peterson, Peter [2of 2]," Nixon Presidential Library. For a similar view, see also verbatim statements by Senator Alan Cranston in *Conference on Inflation*, 70.

125. Ronald I. McKinnon, *The Unloved Dollar Standard: From Bretton Woods to the Rise of China* (New York: Oxford University Press, 2013), 91–92.

126. This quote is a paraphrase of Casey's views. From Leo Panitch and Sam Gindin, *The Making of Global Capitalism: The Political Economy of American Empire* (London: Verso, 2012), 148. This was a period when a wide range of innovative proposals were at least briefly contemplated. Even so conservative a figure as George Shultz advocated changes to the international financial system that would have penalized surplus countries; and, by implication, such measures would have subsidized deficit countries—which now included the United States. See letter to George Shultz, October 4, 1972, in White House Central Files, Staff Members and Office Files, Herbert Stein Papers, box 21, folder "Haberler, Gottfried," Nixon Presidential Library.

127. Marina Whitman, "Reflections on the International Monetary System," August 27, 1971, in McCracken Papers, box 109, folder "International [1 of 2]," Nixon Presidential Library.

128. David Rockefeller's views were paraphrased in "Outline of Proposals for Interim Monetary Arrangements," September 10, 1971, Foreign Affairs, box 44, folder "Ex FO 4-1, 1/1/71-12/31/71 [2 of 3]," Nixon Presidential Library.

129. Solomon, "The International Monetary System," 183–84, 242. The idea of using special drawing rights (SDRs) as a replacement for dollars seems to have been widely favored, at least for a time. At a 1973 meeting of the Trilateral Commission, "Most participants had favored the substitution of SDRs for national currencies or gold as reserve assets," according to a Japanese business

representative who participated in the meeting, as paraphrased in a British Foreign Office report. From British Embassy, Commercial Department, "Monte Carlo Talks," June 7, 1973, FCO 82/277, in Archives Direct: Sources from the National Archives, UK.

130. Comments made in 1973 by William Casey, as quoted in Panitch and Gindin, *The Making of Global Capitalism*, 148.

131. James K. Jackson, "Financing the U.S. Trade Deficit," Congressional Research Service, October 7, 2016, https://sgp.fas.org/crs/misc/RL33274.pdf.

132. Robert Wade and Frank Veneroso, "The Asian Crisis: The High Debt Model Versus the Wall Street-Treasury-IMF Complex," *New Left Review*, no. I/228 (1998), 18–19.

133. Quoted in Jeffrey Fleishman, "Here's Why Bruce Springsteen's Blue-Collar Heroes Have Made Donald Trump Their Rock Star," *Los Angeles Times*, October 27, 2016.

134. On the perception that financial deregulation began in 1980, see Kevin R. Brine and Mark Poovey, *Finance in America: An Unfinished Story* (Chicago: University of Chicago Press, 2017), chap. 10.4a, "Deregulation and the Growth of Finance in America After 1980."

135. Jonathan Kirshner, *American Power After the Financial Crisis* (Ithaca, NY: Cornell University Press, 2014), 51. After having succeeded in deregulating the international economy, Walter Wriston began turning his attention to domestic deregulation, notably the abolition of Regulation Q. See letter to Congressman Edward Koch, September 10, 1974, in Walter B. Wriston Papers, series 5, box 033, folder "Political Correspondence, 1973–1978, 1 of 2," Tufts University.

136. Robin Greenwood and David Scharfstein, "The Growth of Finance, "*Journal of Economic Perspectives* 27, no. 2 (2013): 3. They calculate that "the financial sector's share of GDP increased at a faster rate since 1980 . . . than it did in the prior 30 years." The link between deregulation and the growth of financialization has been widely noted. See, for example, David M. Kotz, *The Rise of Neoliberal Capitalism* (Cambridge, MA: Harvard University Press, 2015), 33; and Greta R. Krippner, *Capitalizing on Crisis: The Political Origins of the Rise of Finance* (Cambridge, MA: Harvard University Press, 2011), 82–85.

137. Panitch and Gindin, *The Making of Global Capitalism*, 187.

138. Kevin Phillips, *American Theocracy: The Peril and Politics of Radical Religion, Oil, and Borrowed Money in the 21st Century* (New York: Viking, 2006), 28.

139. Jeff Madrick, *Age of Greed: The Triumph of Finance and the Decline of America, 1970 to the Present* (New York: Knopf, 2011), chap.4; James Crotty, "The Neoliberal Paradox: The Impact of Destructive Product Market Competition and 'Modern' Financial Markets on Nonfinancial Corporation Performance in the Neoliberal Era," in *Financialization and the World Economy*, ed. Gerald A.

Epstein (Cheltenham, UK: Edward Elgar, 2005), 88; Krippner, *Capitalizing on Crisis*, 142–43; and Bluestone and Harrison, *The Deindustrialization of America*, 6. On shareholder value, see Neil Fligstein and Taekjin Shin, "Shareholder Value and the Transformation of the U.S. Economy, 1984–2000," *Sociological Forum* 22, no. 4 (2007).

140. Mike Collins, "Wall Street and the Financialization of the Economy," *Forbes*, February 4, 2015.

141. Charles de Gaulle, verbatim transcript of 1940 radio speech, *"Commémoration Annuelle de l'Appel du 18 Juin, 1940 (70e Anniversaire),"* Alliance Française, London, https://www.alliancefrancaise.london/L'appel-du-18-juin-70e-Alliance -Francaise-de-Londres.php. Translated from the French.

142. At one point in 1985, U.S. officials did seek to lower the value of the dollar; but over the long term, the policy tended toward maintaining a strong dollar. Art Pine, "To Avert a Trade War, U.S. Joins with Major Allies to Lower Dollar," *Wall Street Journal*, September 23, 1985.

143. McKinnon, *The Unloved Dollar Standard*, 91–92. McKinnon discusses "foreign borrowing" as the problem, which includes the foreign purchase of Treasury bonds.

144. Jane D'Arista, "The Role of the International Monetary System in Financialization," in *Financialization and the World Economy*, ed. Gerald A. Epstein (Cheltenham, UK: Edward Elgar, 2005), 222.

145. Avraham Ebenstein, Ann Harrison, and Margaret McMillan, "Why Are American Workers Getting Poorer? China, Trade, and Offshoring," in *The Factory-Free Economy: Outsourcing, Servitization, and the Future of Industry*, ed. Lionel Fontagné and Ann E. Harrison (New York: Oxford University Press, 2017). Part of the problem was the secular decline in profit rates, which contributed to the "growth of multinational manufacturing, as corporations seek areas of lowest material and labor costs." From speech before the Business Council by Irwin Miller, "The Corporate Role in the Decade Ahead," October 20, 1972, 3, in W. Averell Harriman Papers, box 612, folder "Post Gov't—Business Council, 1969," Library of Congress.

146. Robert Johnson, quoted in William Greider, *One World, Ready or Not: The Manic Logic of Global Capitalism* (New York: Simon & Schuster, 1997), 24.

147. Nelson Lichtenstein, *State of the Union: A Century of American Labor* (Princeton, NJ: Princeton University Press, 2002), 223.

148. The globalization of laissez-faire economics is a major theme in Naomi Klein, *The Shock Doctrine: The Rise of Disaster Capitalism* (New York: Picador, 2007); and Slobodian, *Globalists*.

149. Letter from Juan Carlos Simons to Edwin J. Feulner Jr., September 24, 1980, in Mont Pèlerin Society Papers, box 23, folder 5, Hoover Institution Archives, Stanford University.

150. One MPS document noted, "The Chileans now enjoy a degree of economic freedom not only unknown but unimaginable in Europe. This is the merit of the 'Chicago Boys' . . . who drafted the reforms and the generals who implemented them." Letter from Max Thurn, MPS Secretary, to Edwin Feulner, May 9, 1980, in Mont Pèlerin Society Papers, box 23, folder 2.

151. See Andrew James Tesseyman, "The New Right Think Tanks and Policy Change in the UK" (DPhil thesis, Department of Politics, University of York, 1999). The Adam Smith Institute, with branches in the UK and United States, formed a nexus that was influential in the Thatcher government. Letter from Peter Young, Director Adam Smith Institute, Washington, DC, July 3, 1985, in Mont Pèlerin Society Papers, box 4, folder 2.

152. See William Echikson, "Poland Launches Sweeping Reforms: Plan Is Bolder Than Changes Seen So Far in Soviet Union," *Christian Science Monitor*, October 9, 1987; Dan Morgan and Bradley Graham, "Money Is Often Bottom Line in East-West Ties," *Washington Post*, May 11, 1982; Robert C. Toth, "Hungarian Asks U.S. Help for Reform Program," *Los Angeles Times*, July 27, 1988; and John Tagliabue, "East's 'Garbage Can Economies' Get a Whiff of Capitalism," *New York Times*, October 4, 1987. On Yugoslavia, see Susan L. Woodward, *Balkan Tragedy: Chaos and Dissolution After the Cold War* (Washington, DC: Brookings Institution, 1995), chap. 3.

153. Jagdish Bhagwati, "The Capital Myth: The Difference Between Trade in Widgets and Dollars," *Foreign Affairs*, 77, no. 3 (May-June 1998): 10–12.

154. On the considerable U.S. influence over the IMF, see testimony by James Ortega of Saenz Hofmann Financial in U.S. Congress, *Quota Increase of the International Monetary Fund* (Washington, DC: U.S. Government Printing Office, 1991), 31.

155. Andrei Shleifer, "The Age of Milton Friedman," *Journal of Economic Literature* 47, no. 1 (2009).

156. For data on U.S. growth rates over time, see "Real Gross Domestic Product," United States, 1947–2020, FRED Economic Data, Federal Reserve Bank of St. Louis, accessed November 3, 2023, https://fred.stlouisfed.org/series/A191RL1Q225SBEA.

157. Neil Irwin, "America Is Driving the Global Economy: When Does That Become a Problem?," *New York Times*, June 8, 2021. On how the unregulated Euromarket constrained the ability of individual countries to control inflation, see letter from Harvey Williams, president of the International Chamber of Commerce, to Sol Linowitz, July 16, 1974, in Sol M. Linowitz Papers, box 408, folder 11, Library of Congress.

158. W. Carl Biven, *Jimmy Carter's Economy: Policy in an Age of Limits* (Chapel Hill: University of North Carolina Press, 2002), chaps. 8–11. The MIT economist Charles Kindleberger took the view that the move to flexible exchange rates

and increased capital flows meant that "independent monetary policies are compromised." Quoted in Mehrling, *Money and Empire*, 181.

159. Susan Strange, *Casino Capitalism* (Manchester, UK: Manchester University Press, 1997), 50. On offshore havens, see also Ronen Palan, *The Offshore World: Sovereign Markets, Virtual Places, and Nomad Millionaires* (Ithaca, NY: Cornell University Press, 2006).

6. THE TRIUMPH OF LAISSEZ-FAIRE

The chapter epigraphs come from Senate testimony by Paul Volcker, October 17, 1979, reprinted verbatim in "Volcker: 'Standard of Living Has to Decline,'" *Wall Street Journal*, October 29, 1979; and from Tom Redburn, "Volcker Goes from Villain to Hero, But Will He Stay?," *Los Angeles Times*, April 5, 1987.

1. Carter was not above periodic appeals to the segregationist vote, a technique he used in his 1970 campaign for governor of Georgia and in his 1976 campaign for president. In the latter case, candidate Carter defended the right of whites to protect the "ethnic purity" of their neighborhoods; he later apologized. See Ron Nesson, "Ethnic Purity," April 13, 1976, Ron Nessen Papers, box 119, folder "Ethnic Purity," Gerald R. Ford Presidential Library, https://www.fordlibrarymuseum .gov/library/document/0204/1512889.pdf.

2. On Carter's complicated relationship with the civil rights movement, see Robert A. Strong, "Politics and Principle: Jimmy Carter in the Civil Rights Era," *Irish Association for American Studies: IJAS Online*, no. 3 (2014).

3. Carter later acknowledged that Kirbo was "my closest friend and adviser" during his period as governor of Georgia. From Jimmy Carter, *A Full Life: Reflections at Ninety* (New York: Simon & Schuster, 2015), 108.

4. Philip H. Burch Jr., *Elites in American History: The New Deal to the Carter Administration* (New York: Holmes & Meier, 1980), 313–14.

5. Peter G. Bourne, *Jimmy Carter: A Comprehensive Biography from Plains to Post-Presidency* (New York: Scribner, 1997), 201. Bourne served as an adviser to Governor Carter on health policy and drug issues.

6. "Dixie Whistles a Different Tune: Georgia Governor Jimmy Carter," *Time*, May 31, 1971.

7. W. Carl Biven, *Jimmy Carter's Economy: Policy in an Age of Limits* (Chapel Hill: University of North Carolina Press, 2002), 16.

8. Bourne, *Jimmy Carter*, 240.

9. Paraphrases of Carter's views, quoted from "The Summary of Proceedings of Meetings of the Trilateral Commission of North America, Monday Evening, October 15, 1973," 5, in Papers of the Trilateral Commission, box 1, folder 14, Rockefeller Archive Center.

10. A widespread belief in the Carter White House was that traditional ideological and partisan categories were becoming less relevant, even obsolete; this view was echoed in the memoirs of Carter's chief of staff, Hamilton Jordan, *Crisis: The Last Year of the Carter Presidency* (New York: Putnam, 1982), 329.

11. "Carter Presidency Project: Final Edited Transcript (Redacted Version): Interview with Stuart Eizenstat," January 29–30, 1982, 100, Miller Center of Public Affairs, University of Virginia, https://s3.amazonaws.com/web.poh.transcripts/ohp_1982_0129_eizenstat.pdf.

12. "Carter Presidency Project, Final Edited Transcript: Interview with Robert Bergland, November 21, 1986," 14, Miller Center of Public Affairs, University of Virginia, https://s3.amazonaws.com/web.poh.transcripts/ohp_1986_1121_bergland.pdf.

13. On the deregulatory role of Agriculture Secretary Earl Butz, see James Risser and George Anthan, "Why They Love Earl Butz," *New York Times*, June 13, 1976; and Earl Butz, "An Emerging Market-Oriented Food and Agricultural Policy," *Public Administration Review* 36, no. 2 (1976).

14. "Interview with Stuart Eizenstat, January 29–30, 1982," 22.

15. Quote from David Rubinstein in "Final Edited Transcript, Interview with Bertram Carp and David M. Rubenstein with Alice Rogoff," March 6, 1982, 36, Miller Center of Public Affairs, University of Virginia, https://s3.amazonaws.com/web.poh.transcripts/ohp_1982_0306_carp.pdf.

16. Jimmy Carter, diary entry, January 19, 1978, reprinted in *Keeping Faith: Memoirs of a President* (New York: Bantam, 1982), 102.

17. Burch, *Elites in American History*, chap. 7; Thomas R. Dye, *Who's Running America? The Carter Years* (Englewood Cliffs, NJ: Prentice-Hall, 1979), 58–62.

18. "In the Age of Ron, Celebrity Lobbies Are Losing the Limelight," *Fortune*, September 21, 1981.

19. Martin Tolchin, "Carter's Corporate Brain Trust: Talks on More than Business and the Economy," *New York Times*, July 24, 1978. During the 1976 presidential campaign, the conservative activist Paul Weyrich complained about corporate willingness to contribute to Democrats, quoted in *Right Report*, October 18, 1976, in Paul M. Weyrich Papers, box 36, folder 7, American Heritage Center, University of Wyoming.

20. Kai Bird, *The Outlier: The Unfinished Presidency of Jimmy Carter* (New York: Crown, 2021), 204.

21. Louis M. Kohlmeier, "The Big Businessmen Who Have Jimmy Carter's Ear," *New York Times*, February 5, 1978.

22. The initially warm relations between the Carter administration and elite business interests were emphasized in Steve Selig, memorandum for the president, "Reactions to Last Night's Speech," February 3, 1977, in Carter Presidential

Papers, Staff Offices, Chief of Staff (Jordan), Selig Files, Office of Public Liaison File, box 162, folder "Business Correspondence, 1/11/77–1/23/77," Carter Presidential Library.

23. Surface Mining Control and Reclamation Act, PL 95–87, enacted August 3, 1977, full text at U.S. Department of Interior website, https://www.osmre.gov /sites/default/files/inline-files/SMCRA_0.pdf.

24. Jimmy Carter, "Report to the American People: Remarks from the White House Library," February 2, 1977, in Gerhard Peters and John T. Woolley, eds., American Presidency Project, University of California, Santa Barbara, https://www .presidency.ucsb.edu/documents/report-the-american-people-remarks-from -the-white-house-library.

25. Charles R. Babcock, "Carter Names Record Number of Minorities to Federal Bench," *Washington Post*, May 25, 1980.

26. Vince Guerrieri, "On the 40th Anniversary of Youngstown's 'Black Monday': An Oral History," *Belt Magazine*, September 19, 2017.

27. Austin Scott, "Carter Signs $20.1 Billion Jobs, Stimulus Measure," *Washington Post*, May 14, 1977.

28. On the politics of Humphrey-Hawkins, see discussion in chapter 3.

29. See verbatim interview in "The Council of Economic Advisors Under Chairman Alan Greenspan, 1974–1977," in *The President and the Council of Economic Advisers: Interviews with CEA Chairmen*, ed. Erwin C. Hargrove and Samuel A. Morley (Boulder, CO: Westview, 1984), 453. Greenspan also implied that he was pleasantly surprised by Carter's fiscal restraint and the mildness of his stimulus package.

30. Walter Dean Burnham, "The 1980 Earthquake: Realignment, Reaction, or What?," in *The Hidden Election: Politics and Economics in the 1980 Presidential Campaign*, ed. Thomas Ferguson and Joel Rogers (New York: Random House, 1981), 108.

31. Herbert Stein, *Presidential Economics: The Making of Economic Policy from Roosevelt to Clinton* (Washington, DC: American Enterprise Institute for Public Policy Research, 1994), 219.

32. Barry Ritholtz, "The Death of Equities: How Inflation Is Destroying the Stock Market," *Business Week*, August 13, 1979.

33. Edward N. Wolff, "The Distributional Effects of the 1969–1975 Inflation on Holdings of Household Wealth in the United States," *Review of Income and Wealth* 25, no. 2 (1979): 206–7.

34. Joseph J. Minarik, "The Distributional Effects of Inflation and Their Implications," in *Stagflation: The Causes, Effects, and Solutions*, prepared for U.S. Congress, Joint Economic Committee (Washington, DC: U.S. Government Printing Office, 1980), 225–40.

35. In 1978, the Federal Reserve began moving toward a harder line regarding the perceived inflation threat. See "Trade, Capital Flows, and Currencies: Remarks by Henry C. Wallich, Member of the Board of Governors of the Federal Reserve System at the 8th International Management Symposium," St. Gallen, Switzerland, May 8, 1978, 9, in White House Central Files, Staff Members and Office Files, Arthur Burns Papers, box B62, folder "International Economic Developments, Briefing Book, 6/6/78 (3)," Ford Presidential Library.

36. Jimmy Carter, "January 19, 1978: State of the Union Address," audio file, 46:25, Miller Center of Public Affairs, University of Virginia, https://millercenter.org /the-presidency/presidential-speeches/january-19-1978-state-union-address.

37. Art Pine, "'Lean and Tight,' Carter Budget Seeks $500.2 Billion," *Washington Post*, January 24, 1978.

38. James P. Gannon, "Carter Budget Proposes Restrained Spending, Lacks Bold New Plans," *Wall Street Journal*, January 24, 1978.

39. The politics of military spending are discussed in chapter 4.

40. Jimmy Carter, "Memphis, Tennessee Remarks at the Opening Session of the 1978 National Democratic Party Conference," December 8, 1978, in American Presidency Project, https://www.presidency.ucsb.edu/documents/memphis -tennessee-remarks-the-opening-session-the-1978-national-democratic-party.

41. This follows from a 1943 proposal for taxation on capital as a means of reducing federal budget deficits. See Michal Kalecki, "Political Aspects of Full Employment," *Political Quarterly* 14, no. 4 (1943): 323.

42. Quote from Alfred Kahn in "Carter Presidency Project: Final Edited Transcript: Interview with Alfred E. Kahn," December 10–11, 1981, 59, Miller Center of Public Affairs, University of Virginia, https://s3.amazonaws.com/web.poh .transcripts/ohp_1981_1210_kahn.pdf.

43. Regarding Carter's reluctance in signing the October 1978 tax package, see Stuart E. Eizenstat, *President Carter: The White House Years* (New York: Thomas Dunne, 2018), 316–20. See also M. S. Forbes Jr., "Good Can Come from the New Recession," *Forbes*, June 11, 1979. The increase in the Social Security tax was legislated several months before the corporate tax cut. On the former, see U.S. Department of the Treasury, *The President's 1978 Tax Program: Detailed Descriptions and Supporting Analyses of the Proposals*, January 30, 1978, 3, https://home.treasury.gov/system/files/131/Report-Presidents-1978-Part1.pdf.

44. Steven S. Andreder, "No More 'Soak the Rich': The Revenue Act of 1978 Looms as a Fiscal Landmark," *Barron's National Business and Financial Weekly*, October 16, 1978. See also Robert G. Kaiser and Mary Russell, "Compromise Reached on Key Tax Cuts: A Middle-Class Congress, Haves Over Have Nots," *Washington Post*, October 15, 1978; and Patrick J. Akard, "The Return of the Market: Corporate Mobilization and the Transformation of U.S. Economic

Policy, 1974–1984" (PhD thesis, Department of Sociology, University of Kansas, 1989), 281–84.

45. During the 1976 campaign, Carter advocated a "comprehensive national health care program," which "guarantees to every person as much care as he or she needs." Jimmy Carter, "Response to Questions for 'Nation's Business,'" September 1, 1976, in American Presidency Project, https://www.presidency.ucsb.edu /documents/response-questions-for-nations-business. On the complex politics of health care during this period, see Mary E. Gwin, "National Health Insurance in an Age of Limits: Jimmy Carter's Abandoned Agenda" (PhD thesis, Department of History, Vanderbilt University, 2018).

46. "How Business Won a Major Washington Victory," *Nation's Business*, March 1978; Benjamin C. Waterhouse, *Lobbying America: The Politics of Business Nixon to NAFTA* (Princeton, NJ: Princeton University Press, 2014), 151–73. With regard to Carter's lack of interest in a proposed consumer protection agency, in his unpublished presidential diary, the only mention of a consumer protection agency comes in a single meeting that the president attended for exactly twenty minutes. From "The Daily Diary of President Jimmy Carter," June 1, 1977, Carter Presidential Library, https://www.jimmycarterlibrary.gov /assets/documents/diary/1977/d060177t.pdf.

47. During 1977, prolabor members of Congress proposed "common situs picketing" legislation that aimed to facilitate union efforts to organize strikes, but the president openly acknowledged making no effort to lobby for the legislation, which was defeated in Congress. See Jimmy Carter, "Interview with the President: Remarks and a Question and Answer Session with a Group of Publishers, Editors, and Broadcasters," March 25, 1977, in American Presidency Project, https://www.presidency.ucsb.edu/documents/interview-with-the-president-remarks-and-question-and-answer-session-with-group-1. See also "Labor and Congress: New Day A-Dawning?," *Charls E. Walker's Washington Economic Report*, March 29, 1977, in Paul Nitze Papers, box 68, folder 9, Library of Congress; and memo from Jeffrey St. John to Richard DeVos, October 24, 1978, in Weyrich Papers, box 17, folder 22.

48. "Seething Impotence in the Labor Camp," *Fortune*, July 31, 1978. Similarly, in 1979, environmentalists received only weak support from the administration. See Philip Shabecoff, "Environmentalists See End to a Golden Era," *New York Times*, August 6, 1979.

49. Nelson Lichtenstein, *State of the Union: A Century of American Labor* (Princeton, NJ: Princeton University Press, 2002), 234.

50. "Interview with Alfred E. Kahn," December 10–11, 1981, 38.

51. On background on the CAB, see Elizabeth E. Bailey, David R. Graham, and Daniel P. Kaplan, *Deregulating the Airlines: An Economic Analysis* (Washington,

DC: Civil Aeronautics Board, 1983), chaps. 1–3. On Kahn and deregulation, see also Naomi Oreskes and Erik M. Conway, *The Big Myth: How American Business Taught Us to Loathe Government and Love the Free Market* (New York: Bloomsbury, 2023), chap. 12.

52. I do not deny that many of the regulatory regimes were often dysfunctional; and regulation was one of the weakest features of the New Deal. My point is that in the political context of the 1970s, the main motive behind deregulation was to attack unions and working-class living standards; this was also the main effect of deregulation, once it was implemented.

53. Alfred Kahn, notes for a planned talk before the National Council of State Legislatures, Panel on Reg Reform, July 10, 1980, in Alfred Kahn Papers, box 55, folder 26, Cornell University.

54. Alfred Kahn, "The Stock Market Attitude Toward Airlines," February 2, 1978, 9, in Kahn Papers, box 34, folder 16.

55. Letter from Kahn to R. C. Clarke, September 1, 1978, in Kahn Papers, box 28, folder 18.

56. Letter from Kahn to John C. Whitney, June 26, 1978, in Kahn Papers, box 28, folder 18.

57. On monopoly, see Milton Friedman, *Capitalism and Freedom* (Chicago: University of Chicago Press, 2002), chaps. 8, 9.

58. The long-serving director of the AEI, William Baroody Sr., delivered speeches endorsing the idea of deregulation in the months leading up to the Carter administration's application of this idea to airlines. See William Baroody, "Government Regulation: Who's Responsible to Whom?," speech to Public Relations Society of America, November 14, 1977, 4–5, in William J. Baroody Sr. Papers, box 97, folder 8, Library of Congress. See also letter from William J. Baroody Jr. to Randolph Richardson of the Smith Richardson Foundation, January 17, 1979, in Irving Kristol Papers, box 24, folder 6, Wisconsin Historical Society. Note that Baroody Jr., succeeded his father as president of AEI.

59. On opposition to deregulation emanating from Delta and Eastern, see Waterhouse, *Lobbying America*, 185. On support from NAM, see Con Hitchcock, "Review of *Deregulating the Airlines*. Elizabeth E. Bailey, David R. Graham, and Daniel P. Kaplan. Cambridge, MA: MIT Press, 1985," *Cato Journal*, fall 1985; and National Association of Manufacturers, "News from NAM: For Release Friday, October 20, 1978," in Carter Presidential Papers, Staff Offices, DPS—Gov't Reform (Neustadt), box 46, folder "NAM [1978]," Carter Presidential Library.

60. Although generally a political liberal, Ralph Nader and his organization held somewhat negative views of organized labor; it was considered just one more vested interest. See Mark J. Green, James Fallows, and David R. Zwick, *Who*

Runs Congress? The President, Big Business, or You? (New York: Bantam, 1972), 36–37, 44. The book was presented on the cover as coming from the "Ralph Nader Congress Project."

61. Airline Deregulation Act, Public Law 95–504, October 24, 1978, Discover U.S. Government Information, https://www.govinfo.gov/content/pkg/STATUTE-92 /pdf/STATUTE-92-Pg1705.pdf#page=1.

62. On monopoly/oligopoly, see Matt Stoller, *Goliath: The 100-Year War Between Monopoly Power and Democracy* (New York: Simon & Schuster, 2019), chaps. 13–16; Eizenstat, *President Carter,* 371; Larry Kramer, "Carter Withholds Support from Antitrust Plans," *Washington Post,* March 8, 1979; and Marcy Gordon, "Airline Industry Consolidation Is Direct Result of Deregulation," *Buffalo News,* August 13, 1989. In his coauthored memoirs, Carter's attorney general barely mentions antitrust. See Griffin B. Bell and Ronald J. Ostrow, *Taking Care of the Law* (New York: William Morrow, 1982).

63. Robert J. Gordon, *The Rise and Fall of American Growth: The U.S. Standard of Living Since the Civil War* (Princeton, NJ: Princeton University Press, 2016), 404; emphasis added.

64. James Peoples, "Deregulation and the Labor Market," *Journal of Economic Perspectives* 12, no. 3 (1998): 128. The study concludes, "Labor earnings premiums fell sharply in trucking, somewhat in airlines, slightly in telecommunications, and barely in railroads."

65. The American Conservative Union also advocated deregulation of airlines. See memorandum from Jim Roberts, ACU executive director, Re: "Airline Deregulation Project," August 16, 1977, in Papers of the Conservative Party of New York, series 7, box 1, folder "American Legislative Exchange Council, Programs for State Senators," State University of New York, Albany.

66. Susan E. Dudley, "Alfred Kahn, 1917–2010: Remembering the Father of Airline Deregulation," *Regulation* [Cato Institute publication], Spring 2011, https://www .cato.org/regulation/spring-2011/alfred-kahn-1917-2010; and Andrea O'Sullivan, "Twelve Economists of Christmas: Alfred E. Kahn," December 23, 2019, Mercatus Center, George Mason University, https://www.mercatus.org/bridge/commentary /12-economists-christmas-alfred-e-kahn.

67. Jimmy Carter, "Motor Carrier Act of 1980: Remarks on Signing S.2245 into Law," July 1, 1980, https://www.presidency.ucsb.edu/documents/motor-carrier-act -1980-statement-signing-s-2245-into-law; and "Staggers Rail Act of 1980: Remarks on Signing S.1946 into Law," October 14, 1980, https://www.presidency.ucsb .edu/documents/staggers-rail-act-1980-statement-signing-s-1946-into-law. Both documents from American Presidency Project. The administration also made some strides in deregulating communications and pharmaceuticals. See

memorandum from Julie Clark to Alfred E. Kahn, "Briefing for Business Council," December 12, 1979, in Special Advisor, Inflation—Kahn, box 8, folder "Business Council, 12/79–1/80," Carter Presidential Library.

68. "Oil Price Decontrol and Beyond," *FRBNY Quarterly* [Federal Reserve Bank of New York], Winter 1980–81, 38.

69. Michael H. Belzer, *Sweatshops on Wheels: Winners and Losers in Trucking Deregulation* (New York: Oxford University Press, 2000). See also Lynda Gorov, "For Workers, Deregulation Has Meant a Rude Awakening: Layoffs, Wage Concessions Spread as Companies Face New Competition," *Boston Globe*, March 9, 1986.

70. The full title of the act was Financial Institutions Deregulation and Monetary Control Act of 1980. See full text at FRED Economic Data, Federal Reserve Bank of St. Louis, https://fraser.stlouisfed.org/title/depository-institutions-deregulation-monetary-control-act-1980-1032.

71. CitiBank CEO Walter Wriston had lobbied for years in favor of repealing Regulation Q. See letter from Wriston to Edward I. Koch, September 10, 1974, in Walter Wriston Papers, series, 5, box 033, folder "Political Correspondence, 1973–1978, 1 of 2," Tufts University. According to Alan Blinder, the 1980 act "defanged" Regulation Q, but the regulation was not fully repealed until the Dodd-Frank Act of 2010. Blinder, *A Monetary and Fiscal History of the United States* (Princeton, NJ: Princeton University Press, 2022), 23.

72. Nomi Prins, *All the Presidents' Bankers: The Hidden Alliances That Drive American Power*. New York: Nation Books, 2014, p. 314; and William Greider, *Secrets of the Temple: How the Federal Reserve Runs the Country*. New York: Simon & Schuster, 1987, pp. 162–166.

73. Prins, *All the Presidents' Bankers*, p. 314.

74. On the politics of student debt that grew out of this period, see Melinda Cooper, *Family Values: Between Neoliberalism and the New Social Conservatism*. (New York: Zone, 2017), chap. 6.

75. Carter's Treasury Secretary Michael Blumenthal reaffirmed the U.S. commitment to the deregulated system of floating exchange rates. "Memorandum from Secretary of the Treasury Blumenthal to President Carter," August 9, 1977, in *Foreign Relations of the United States, 1977–1980: Volume III, Foreign Economic Policy*, ed. Kathleen B. Rasmussen (Washington, DC: U.S. Government Printing Office, 2013), document 50.

76. Regarding the relationship between financialization and deindustrialization, see discussion in chapter 5.

77. See Jerry Brown, interviewed on William F. Buckley's *Firing Line* television program in 1975, available from YouTube video, 5:39, https://www.youtube.com/watch?v=CaDjjJKv7fw.

78. Quoted from Jesse Walker, "Five Faces of Jerry Brown," *American Conservative*, November 1, 2009.

79. Daniel A. Smith, "Howard Jarvis, Populist Entrepreneur: Reevaluating the Causes of Proposition 13," *Social Science History* 23, no. 2 (1999): 175–76, 191–92, 199. See also Irving Thomsen, president, Apartment Association of Los Angeles County, "President's Message," n.d., in Judith Stanley Papers [Proposition 13], box 1, folder 3, University of California, Irvine.

80. "Jarvis and the Tax Rebellion," *Libertarian Review*, editorial, May 1, 1978. On Koch funding for *Libertarian Review*, see Brian Doherty, *Radicals for Capitalism: A Freewheeling History of the Libertarian Movement* (New York: Public Affairs, 2007), 409–10.

81. Regarding Friedman's antitax viewpoint, see letter from James Buchanan to Harrison Fox, research director for Senator Bill Brock, November 20, 1972, in James Buchanan Papers, series 2 (Correspondence), subseries 1 (Alphabetical Correspondence), box 58, folder "Correspondence—Bill Brock, 1972," George Mason University; letter from Friedman to Ronald Reagan, December 9, 1976, Milton Friedman Papers, box 174, folder "Reagan, Ronald, 1976–1991," Hoover Institution Archives, Stanford University; and letter from Friedman to Ronald Reagan, December 9, 1976, in Friedman Papers, box 174, folder "Reagan, Ronald, 1976–1991."

82. "A Special Report on Propositions 8 and 13," *Bank American* [newsletter of Bank of America], April 1978, in Stanley Papers [Proposition 13], box 1, folder 7.

83. Friedman comments in "Top Economist Endorses Jarvis Plan: Chance to Control Government Spending," *Los Angeles Herald Examiner*, March 31, 1978, in Stanley Papers [Proposition 13], box 2, folder 15.

84. Tom Wicker, "A Test in California," *New York Times*, June 11, 1978.

85. See enthusiastic letters regarding the outcome of Proposition 13 and plans for future tax cuts from numerous conservative figures in Paul Gann Papers, box 1416, folder "People's Advocate, Correspondence from Senators and Congressmen, Re Deficit Spending, People's Advocate, 1979–1979," California State Library.

86. Robert M. Bleiberg, "Forgotten Man? The Climate May Be Turning More Hospitable to Investors," *Barron's National Business and Financial Weekly*, June 12, 1978.

87. On the National Tax Limitation Committee, see letter from William F. Rickenbacker to William Niskanen, 1977 [full date not specified], William A. Niskanen Papers, box 49, Hoover Institution, Stanford University; and Isaac William Martin, *Rich People's Movements: Grassroots Campaigns to Untax the One Percent* (New York: Oxford University Press, 2013), 161–69. On the politics of Proposition 13, see also Solon Simmons, *The Eclipse of Equality: Arguing*

America on Meet the Press (Palo Alto, CA: Stanford University Press, 2013), 55–56.

88. Letter from John T. Hay to D. L. Bower, August 1, 1979, in Gann Papers, box 1413, folder "People's Advocate Correspondence, Outgoing, 1979." . See also " 'Spirit of 13': HQ Opened for Initiative Drive," *Los Angeles Times*, January 14, 1979.

89. On Kemp's connections to business interests and the AEI, see the following sources: letter from Irving Kristol to Jack Kemp, April 3, 1978; and letter from Kristol to Kemp, May 30, 1978. Both letters in Kristol Papers, box 12, folder 28.

90. Quote is from "The Old Political Shell Game," *Forbes*, August 21, 1978.

91. Memorandum from Congressman Phillip Crane, subject "Re Tax Limitation," May 22, 1978, Papers of the Conservative Party of New York, series 7, box 1, "American Conservative Union," folder 1."

92. The survey research from this period is summarized in Thomas Ferguson and Joel Rogers, *Right Turn: The Decline of the Democrats and the Future of American Politics* (New York: Hill & Wang, 1986), 12–24.

93. A unique factor that led to Proposition 13 was a rapid rise of real estate prices in California, which simultaneously escalated property taxes. Thomas Piketty, *Capital and Ideology* (Cambridge, MA: Belknap Press of Harvard University Press, 2020), 836–37.

94. The quote is from Marc F. Plattner, "Liberty and the State: [Review of] *A Time for Truth* by William E. Simon," *Commentary*, February 1979.

95. William E. Simon, *A Time for Truth* (New York: Reader's Digest Press, 1978), 85.

96. Memorandum from Marvin Liebman, "Re: A Time for Truth/GOP Distribution," June 5, 1978, Marvin Liebman Papers, box 143, folder "Simon, William E," Hoover Institution Archives, Stanford University.

97. Letter from John M. Olin to Marvin Liebman, September 7, 1978, Liebman Papers, box 143, folder "Simon, William E." Olin was listed as honorary chairman of the board of the Olin Corporation.

98. Memorandum from Marvin Liebman "Re: A Time for Truth/GOP Distribution Final Report," August 28, 1978, Liebman Papers, box 143, folder "Simon, William E." Frank Shakespeare's affiliation with RKO General was noted in Ronald Reagan, "Nomination of Frank Shakespeare To Be United States Ambassador to Portugal," July 24, 1985, in American Presidency Project, https://www.presidency.ucsb.edu/documents/nomination-frank-shakespeare -be-united-states-ambassador-portugal.

99. In December 1978, former Fed chair Arthur Burns noted "a mood of unease and anxiety," which continued to "haunt the state of business opinion." Arthur F. Burns, "The Condition of the American Economy," speech at the American Enterprise Institute, December 14, 1978, 3, in Clark M. Clifford Papers, box 20, folder "Burns, Arthur F.," Library of Congress.

100. "Carter's Campaign to Regain Momentum," *Business Week*, August 21, 1978; "Twisting Jimmy's Arm," *Forbes*, July 24, 1978. The latter article emphasized Carter's inability to persuade Congress to lower federal spending.

101. See, for example, "Economic Education," *Wall Street Journal*, October 3, 1979.

102. Thomas Byrne Edsall, *The New Politics of Inequality* (New York: Norton, 1984), 77. On the role of the U.S. Chamber of Commerce in the 1978 elections, see Vernon Louviere, "Pro-Business Congress May Come to Washington," *Barron's National Business and Financial Weekly*, September 1980.

103. On congressional enthusiasm for cutting social programs after the 1978 elections, see "First 1981 Budget Resolution: Slim Surplus," subsection "First Balanced Budget," *CQ Almanac*, 1980.

104. "Selling Pressure Pushes the Dollar to Six-Month Low: Dumping That Was Begun Last Month Continues, Gold Hits Another High," *Wall Street Journal*, July 18, 1979; and Charles Schultze and Lyle Gramley, "The Dollar (or 'The June Swoon')," June 26, 1979, in Carter Presidential Library, Staff Offices, Council of Economic Advisors, box 364, folder "Dollar (Value)."

105. Michael Moffitt, *The World's Money: International Banking from Bretton Woods to the Brink of Insolvency* (New York: Simon & Schuster, 1983), 146; "Dollar Plunges as Anti-Inflation Plan Draws Fire: But Treasury Secretary Says Fundamentals Favorable to U.S. Currency," *Wall Street Journal*, October 26, 1978.

106. C. Fred Bergsten, memorandum of conversation between Saudi and U.S. officials, subject: "Secretary Blumenthal's Meeting with [Saudi] Minister of Commerce Soliman Solaim," November 19, 1978, 2, in Office of the Undersecretary for Monetary Affairs, Records of the Assistant Secretary of International Affairs, C. Fred Bergsten, 1977–1979, entry A1-755, box 2, folder "Meetings," record group 56, U.S. National Archives.

107. On the possibility of ending the dollar's international reserve status from the Nixon presidency, see Marina Whitman, "Reflections on the International Monetary System," August 27, 1971, White House Central Files, Staff Member and Office Files, Paul W. McCracken Papers, box 109, folder "International [1 of 2]," Nixon Presidential Library; and "Outline of Proposals for Interim Monetary Arrangements," September 10, 1971, White House Central Files, Subject Files, FO, Foreign Affairs, box 44, folder "Ex FO 4-1, 1/1/71-12/31/71 [2 of 3]," Nixon Presidential Library.

108. "Carter Aims for the Moon," *Euromoney*, February 1977.

109. For a recent iteration of this point of view, see Paul Krugman, "The Greenback Rules: So What?," *New York Times*, May 28, 2021.

110. "Talking Points for G-5 Discussion of World Outlook," attached to U.S. Department of Treasury, memorandum from Tom Leddy to Mr. Solomon,

September 13, 1979, record group 56, Subject Files of Anthony M. Solomon, entry A1-858, box 2, folder "G-5," National Archives. Emphasis added.

111. Quote from David Rockefeller, *Memoirs* (New York: Random House, 2002), 369.

112. On Volcker's close ties to David Rockefeller, see "Federal Reserve Board Oral History Project: Interview with Paul A. Volcker," January 28, 2008, U.S. Federal Reserve Board, 44, https://www.federalreserve.gov/aboutthefed/files/paul-a-volcker-interview-20080225.pdf.

113. Volcker's connection to Rockefeller did elicit some criticism during confirmation hearings before Congress. See U.S. Senate, Committee on Banking, Housing, and Urban Affairs, *The Nomination of Paul A. Volcker To Be Chairman of the Board of Governors of the Federal Reserve System, July 30, 1979* (Washington, DC: U.S. Government Printing Office, 1979), 65, 67.

114. On Volcker as a "nominal Democrat," see Hobart Rowan, "Paul Volcker: In or Out?," *Washington Post*, March 17, 1983. See also Paul Volcker and Christine Harper, *Keeping at It: The Quest for Sound Money and Good Government* (New York: Public Affairs, 2018), 102–4.

115. At times, Carter would directly criticize the Fed. See Kenneth H. Bacon and Timothy D. Schellhardt, "Carter Assails Fed for Policies Boosting Interest Rates," *Wall Street Journal*, October 3, 1980.

116. Stuart E. Eizenstat, "Jimmy Carter's Lesson for Donald Trump: Hands Off the Fed," *Financial Times*, October 16, 2018.

117. Quote from Gerald Friedman, in Craig Phelen, ed., "*Labor History* Symposium: Judith Stein's *Pivotal Decade*," *Labor History* 52, no. 3 (2011)326; emphasis in original.

118. "Bond Yields and Interest Rates: 1900 to 2002," U.S. Census Bureau, accessed November 22, 1923, https://www2.census.gov/library/publications/2004/compendia/statab/123ed/hist/hs-39.pdf.

119. Helmut Schmidt, quoted in Leonard Silk, "The Interest Rate Issue," *New York Times*, July 21, 1981.

120. National Bureau of Economic Research, "Unemployment Rates and Recessions Since 1948," accessed November 4, 2023, https://www.nber.org/research/business-cycle-dating.

121. Long-term changes in the distribution of resources following the recession will be discussed in the concluding chapter of this book.

122. "Paul Volcker Dies: First 'Celebrity' Chairman of the Federal Reserve," *Mercury News* (San Jose), December 9, 2019.

123. "U.S. National Unemployment Rate," MacroTrends, accessed November 4, 2023, https://www.macrotrends.net/1316/us-national-unemployment-rate.

124. "[U.S.] Black Unemployment Rate," MacroTrends, accessed November 4, 2023, https://www.macrotrends.net/2621/black-unemployment-rate.

125. Underemployment is a standard problem during recessions, well recognized in policy circles. See Daniela Dean Avila and Kurt G. Lundsford, "Underemployment Following the Great Recession and the COVID-19 Recession," Federal Reserve Bank of Cleveland, February 3, 2022, https://www.clevelandfed.org /publications/economic-commentary/2022/ec-202201-underemployment -following-the-great-recession-and-the-covid-19-recession. See especially figure 1.

126. Bruce Springsteen, "The River," 1980, live performance in Tempe, Arizona, available from YouTube, 7:43, https://www.youtube.com/watch?v=lc6F47Z6PI4.

127. Blinder, *A Monetary and Fiscal History of the United States*, 106.

128. On the economics of the farm crisis, see the following sources: Dave Kennedy and Thomas Saylor, *Minnesota in the 70s* (St. Paul: Minnesota Historical Society Press, 2013), chap. 6; Neil E. Harl, *The Farm Debt Crisis of the 1980s* (Ames: Iowa State University Press, 1990); Kathryn Marie Dudley, *Debt and Dispossession: Farm Loss in America's Heartland* (Chicago: University of Chicago Press, 2000), chap. 2; and U.S. Federal Deposit Insurance Corporation, *History of the Eighties: Lessons for the Future* (Washington, DC: FDIC, 1997), vol. 1, chap. 8, https://www.fdic.gov/bank/historical/history/259_290.pdf.

129. See Eileen Ogintz, "Emotional Crisis Grips Rural America," *Chicago Tribune*, April 12, 1985; and interviews in the PBS documentary, "Farm Crisis Results in Suicide and Murder," Iowa Public Broadcasting Service, July 1, 2013, https://www.iowapbs.org/shows/farmcrisis/clip/5266/farm-crisis-results -suicide-and-murder.

130. "Hate Group Expert Daniel Levitas Discusses Posse Comitatus, Christian Identity Movement, and More," *Intelligence Report, Southern Poverty Law Center*, June 15, 1998, https://www.splcenter.org/fighting-hate/intelligence -report/1998/hate-group-expert-daniel-levitas-discusses-posse-comitatus -christian-identity-movement-and; and Ellen Isler and Rabbi A. James Rudin, "Anti-Semitism, Extremism, and the Farm Crisis: A Background Memorandum," American Jewish Committee, 1985, from AJC Archives, search at http:// ajcarchives.org/ajcarchive/DigitalArchive.aspx.

131. See verbatim statement by Milton Friedman in *Conference on Inflation: Held at the Request of President Gerald R. Ford and the Congress of the United States* (Washington, DC: U.S. Government Printing Office, 1974), 257. Friedman acknowledged that his recommended course of action would entail "a temporary period of low growth and relatively high unemployment."

132. Lindsey H. Clark Jr., "The Fed's Saturday Surprise," *Wall Street Journal*, October 9, 1979. This article did not directly reference Friedman or use the word "monetarism," but the implication of Volcker's announcement was widely understood as a turn toward monetarism. On the background, see David E. Lindsey,

Athanasios Orphanides, and Robert H. Rasche, "The Reform of October 1979: How It Happened and Why" (Finance and Economics Discussion Series working paper no. 2005-02, Federal Reserve Board, Washington, DC, December 2004), https://www.federalreserve.gov/pubs/feds/2005/200502//200502pap.pdf.

133. Frank Morris, November 17, 1981, statement, as quoted in Alexandre Reichart and Abdelkader Slifi, "The Influence of Monetarism on Federal Reserve Policy During the 1980s," *Cahiers d'Economie Politique*, no. 70 (2016): 140. The Morris comment was made in 1981, the first year of the Reagan presidency, but it was made in reference to the policies of Volcker, not Reagan.

134. Federal Reserve Board Oral History Project, "Interview with Nancy H. Teeters, Former Member, Board of Governors of the Federal Reserve System," October 25, 2008, 32, https://www.federalreserve.gov/aboutthefed/files/nancy-h-teeters-interview-20081025.pdf.

135. Quotes from verbatim interview in "The Council of Economic Advisors Under Chairman Charles Schultze, 1977–1981," in *The President and the Council of Economic Advisers*, ed. Erwin C. Hargrove and Samuel A. Morley (Boulder, CO: Westview, 1984), 486.

136. Volcker acknowledged that at least some members of the Fed Board of Governors believed that monetarism was just "public relations" and a way of deflecting responsibility, though Volcker insisted that he did not hold that view. "An Interview with Paul A. Volcker," in *Inside the Economist's Mind: Conversations with Eminent Economists*, ed. Paul A. Samuelson and William A. Barnett (Malden, MA: Blackwell, 2007), 178.

137. Jimmy Carter, "Philadelphia, Pennsylvania Interview with Correspondents of WCAU-TV," October 2, 1980, in American Presidency Project, https://www.presidency.ucsb.edu/documents/philadelphia-pennsylvania-interview-with-correspondents-wcau-tv.

138. Friedman himself complained that the Fed was not following monetarist doctrine with sufficient strictness. In response, Volcker conceded a lack of doctrinal strictness, stating that his policy was "practical monetarism." On Friedman's complaints: "'Oh Milton,' Volcker's Riposte to Friedman's Talk," *Wall Street Journal*, June 3, 1980; and Milton Friedman and Donald W. Paden, "A Monetarist View," *Journal of Economic Education* 14, no. 4 (1983): 53–54. On Volcker's "practical monetarism," see Federal Reserve Board Oral History Project, "Interview with Paul A. Volcker," January 28, 2008, 67, https://www.federalreserve.gov/aboutthefed/files/paul-a-volcker-interview-20080225.pdf. An academic study concludes that Volcker's policy was "quasi-monetarist"; David R. Hakes and David C. Rose, "The 1979–1982 Monetary Policy Experiment: Monetarist, Anti-Monetarist, or Quasi-Monetarist?," *Journal of Post-Keynesian Economics* 15, no. 2 (1992–93): 287.

139. Jimmy Carter, "Address to the Nation on Energy and National Goals: 'The Malaise Speech,'" July 15, 1979, in American Presidency Project, https://www .presidency.ucsb.edu/documents/address-the-nation-energy-and-national -goals-the-malaise-speech.

140. Memorandum Al From to Alfred Kahn, March 7, 1980, in Kahn Papers, box 15, folder 15.

141. Zbigniew Brzezinski, *Power and Principle: Memoirs of a National Security Advisor, 1977–1981* (New York: Farrar, Straus & Giroux, 1983), 429. He also casually claimed that the invasion constituted a "political blow" to Carter, but in reality, Carter's popularity increased after the invasion (see following source).

142. "Approval Ratings for POTUS," rating for January 25, 1980, in American Presidency Project, accessed November 4, 2023, https://docs.google.com /spreadsheets/d/1iEl565M1mICTubTtoxXMdxzaHzAcPTnb3kpRndsrfyY/edit #gid=566304079.

143. "Taking Charge: 'An Assault Will Be Repelled by Any Means Necessary,'" *Time*, February 4, 1980.

144. For an after-action review of Eagle Claw, see U.S. Joint Chiefs of Staff, "Final Report of the Special Operations Review Group," July 1980, in National Security Archive, George Washington University, https://nsarchive.gwu.edu/document /19709-national-security-archive-doc-10-final-report.

145. Jews and Blacks in the Democratic Party were on somewhat adversarial terms in 1979 due to a controversy surrounding the resignation of UN Ambassador Andrew Young, who was African American. The departure of Young from the administration was advocated by several Jewish groups while strenuously opposed by Blacks. At least some Jewish leaders privately defended Young and complained about how he had been treated. World Jewish Congress President Philip Klutznick stated, "Andrew Young was never an enemy—he was always a friend. You do not destroy friends when they make mistakes." Letter from Klutznick to Moshe Kol, September 12, 1979, Phillip M. Klutznick Papers, box 32, folder 1, University of Chicago. See also "Blacks and Jews," *New York Amsterdam News*, September 8, 1979.

146. On the gradual estrangement of the evangelical movement from President Carter and the Democratic Party more generally, see J. Brooks Flippen, *Jimmy Carter, the Politics of Family, and the Rise of the Religious Right* (Athens: University of Georgia Press, 2011), chaps. 4, 5, 6.

147. One of the triggers to Carter's rupture with evangelicals was a decision by the Internal Revenue Service to deprive religious schools that practiced racial exclusion of their tax exemption. See Vernon E. Jordan Jr., "To Be Equal," *New York Amsterdam News*, January 27, 1979; and "The IRS Pins 'Badge of Doubt' on Tax-Exempt Private Schools," *Christianity Today*, January 5, 1979.

148. Megan Rosenfeld, "The New Moral America and the War of the Religicos," *Washington Post*, August 24, 1980. On the overtly political character of Falwell's organization, see "Dr. Falwell's Notes for Speaking with Ronald Reagan," December 29, 1980, in Falwell Family Papers, Liberty University, https://cdm17184.contentdm.oclc.org/digital/collection/p17184coll4/id/4609 /rec/252.

149. Dirk Smillie, *Falwell Inc: Inside a Religious, Political, Education, and Business Empire* (New York: St. Martin's, 2008), 105. Note that the specific time frame for these contributions is not specified.

150. Russ Bellant, *Coors Connection: How Coors Family Philanthropy Undermines Democratic Pluralism* (Boston: South End, 1991), 50. On the American Security Council, John Fisher, president of the ASC, was "one of the political members of [Religious] Roundtable's Council of 56," according to John Saloma III, *Ominous Politics: The New Conservative Labyrinth* (New York: Hill & Wang, 1984), 61. For more information on Fisher and the Roundtable, see "A Third Religious Force Is Organized by the Right Wing," *Group Research Report*, November 28, 1979. Regarding the close ties between the Religious Roundtable and the Moral Majority, see Robert Wuthnow, *The Restructuring of American Religion: Society and Faith Since World War II* (Princeton, NJ: Princeton University Press, 1988), 205.

151. Jerry Falwell, *Listen America!* (New York: Doubleday, 1980), 13. While the Moral Majority was overwhelmingly white, small numbers of Black Christians were also active in the organization. See Clyde Wilcox, "Blacks and the New Christian Right: Support for the Moral Majority and Pat Robertson Among Washington, D.C. Blacks," *Review of Religious Research* 32, no. 1 (1990).

152. Quoted in Tom Drury, "Kennedy Slams Carter Policies," *Daily Iowan*, November 14, 1979. Kennedy's liberalism had its limits; he had been a strong supporter of Carter's deregulation program. See "Interview with Stephen Breyer," June 17, 2008, 3–13, in Edward M. Kennedy Oral History Project, http://web1 .millercenter.org/poh/transcripts/ohp_2008_0617_breyer.pdf. Kennedy also had close ties to neoconservative circles whose members were quietly lobbying him to drop his antimilitarist stance. It appears that Kennedy resisted these efforts. See multiple documents in Max M. Kampelman Papers, 147.J.13.7B, box 36, folder "Kennedy, Edward M. Campaign, 1979–1980," Minnesota Historical Society.

153. "Kennedy Hits Carter Budget," *Washington Post*, February 12, 1980.

154. On the Kennedy candidacy, see Timothy Randolph Stanley, " 'Sailing Against the Wind': A Reappraisal of Edward Kennedy's Campaign for the 1980 Democratic Party Presidential Nomination," *Journal of American Studies* 43, no. 2 (2009); Jon Ward, *Camelot's End: Kennedy vs. Carter, and the Fight That Broke the Democratic Party* (New York: Twelve Books, 2019); and Joshua Zeitz, "The

Bobby Kennedy Myth: Many on the Left Have Learned the Wrong Lessons from His Ill-Fated Presidential Bid," *Politico*, June 5, 2018.

155. On Kennedy's disastrous November 4, 1979, interview, see "The Interview That Blindsided the Ted Kennedy Presidential Campaign," *Boston Globe*, video, 5:12, available from YouTube, https://www.youtube.com/watch?v=e5TkhNWPspM.

156. Quoted in Robert G. Kaiser and Bill Peterson, "GOP to Spend $4.3 Million More on Nationwide TV Ads," *Washington Post*, August 27, 1980.

157. Reagan placed special emphasis on threats in the Persian Gulf, often based on sensationalized and inaccurate claims about the Soviet role in Afghanistan. "Afghanistan," from Reagan, Ronald 1980 Campaign Papers, series XVII, Briefing Material File, box 513, folder "Briefing Material File [Reagan-Bush International Briefing Book, James T. Lynn personal copy [1/3], October 13, 1980, section Afghanistan," Reagan Presidential Library.

158. On August 3, 1980, Reagan delivered a speech in Nashoba County, Mississippi, that extoled the importance of "states' rights." The speech took place several miles from the location of a notorious killing of civil rights workers that had taken place sixteen years before. A written transcript of the speech is available through the website of the *Neshoba Democrat*, https://neshobademocrat.com /stories/ronald-reagans-1980-neshoba-county-fair-speech,49123.

159. Eizenstat, *President Carter*, 877.

160. "Carter-Reagan Presidential Debate," October 28, 1980, Commission on Presidential Debates, https://www.debates.org/voter-education/debate-transcripts /october-28-1980-debate-transcript/.

161. New information has emerged suggesting that figures close to the Reagan presidential campaign may have intentionally prolonged the Iranian hostage crisis by encouraging the Islamic Republic to continue holding the hostages until after the election. These claims of a covert Republican deal with Iran are plausible, and it may well have contributed somewhat to the Republicans' 1980 victory. However, it seems doubtful that the hostage crisis alone was the decisive factor, given the huge scale of Reagan's election victory. Peter Baker, "A Four Decade Secret: One Man's Story of Sabotaging Carter's Reelection," *New York Times*, March 18, 2023. Similarly, the third-party candidate John B. Anderson could not have affected the 1980 election outcome, since the number of votes Anderson received was well below Reagan's margin of victory.

162. There have been efforts in recent years to rehabilitate Carter's legacy, notably Jonathan Alter, *His Very Best: Jimmy Carter, A Life* (New York: Simon & Schuster, 2020); Kevin Mattson, *What the Heck Are You Up To, Mr. President? Jimmy Carter, America's Malaise, and the Speech that Should Have Changed America* (London: Bloomsbury, 2009); and Bird, *The Outlier*. See also the documentary "Jimmy Carter: Rock and Roll President," 2020, dir. Mary Wharton. A notably

superficial analysis of the Carter presidency appears in Gary Gerstle, *The Rise and Fall of the Neoliberal Order: America and the World in the Free Market Era* (New York: Oxford University Press, 2022), 64–69.

163. Zaid Jilani, "Barack Obama Is Using His Presidency to Cash in, But Harry Truman and Jimmy Carter Refused," *The Intercept,* May 1, 2017.

164. Jonathan Kwitny, *Endless Enemies: The Making of an Unfriendly World* (New York: Congdon & Weed, 1984), 177–78. Emphasis added.

165. Quoted in Zaid Jilani, "Jimmy Carter and Bernie Sanders Explain How Inequality Breeds Authoritarianism," *The Intercept,* May 9, 2017.

166. I thank an anonymous reviewer for suggesting this phrase.

CONCLUSION

The chapter epigraph comes from Warren Buffett, quoted in Ben Stein, "In Class Warfare, Guess Which Class Is Winning," *New York Times,* November 26, 2006.

1. Bob Dylan, "Gotta Serve Somebody," 1979, https://www.bobdylan.com/songs /gotta-serve-somebody/.

2. As discussed in chapter 3, Humphrey-Hawkins was officially signed into law in 1978, but only after its guarantee of full employment was removed. At the point of passage, it was purely symbolic—and irrelevant.

3. Regarding business influence on Reagan's conversion to conservatism, see Thomas Evans, *The Education of Ronald Reagan: The General Electric Years and the Untold Story of his Conversion to Conservatism* (New York: Columbia University Press, 2006).

4. I have searched all of Reagan's speeches, interviews, and press conferences during 1981–1987 from the American Presidency Project and have found no criticism of Volcker.

5. See table 6.1 in of this study.

6. On Reagan's relationship with Volcker, see Paul Volcker and Christine Harper, *Keeping at It: The Quest for Sound Money and Good Government* (New York: Public Affairs, 2018), 112–13. On Volcker's relationship with Carter, see chapter 6.

7. Art Pine, "Carter Unveils Plan to 'Fight Inflation,'" *Washington Post,* March 9, 1980; Robert Benenson, "Social Welfare Under Reagan," *CQ Researcher,* March 9, 1984, https://library.cqpress.com/cqresearcher/document.php?id =cqresrre1984030900.

8. Economic Recovery Tax Act of 1981 (PL 97-34), August 13, 1981, Discover U.S. Government Information, https://www.govinfo.gov/content/pkg/STATUTE-95 /pdf/STATUTE-95-Pg172.pdf.

9. U.S. Treasury Department, *Report to Congress on the Capital Gains Tax Reductions of 1978* (Washington, DC: U.S. Government Printing Office, 1985).

10. Joseph A. McCartin, *Collision Course: Ronald Reagan, the Air Traffic Controllers, and the Strike That Changed America* (New York: Oxford University Press, 2011).

11. Gerald Mayer, "Union Membership Trends in the United States," (CRS Report for Congress, Congressional Research Service, Washington, DC, August 31, 2004), 22.

12. Paul Volcker, quoted in Binyamin Applebaum, *The Economists' Hour: False Prophets, Free Markets, and the Fracture of Society* (Boston: Little, Brown, 2019), 83. See also Volcker and Harper, *Keeping at It*, 113.

13. Inflation-adjusted military spending from table 7.2, "National Defense," in U.S. Department of Defense, Office of the Undersecretary (Comptroller), *National Defense Budget Estimates for FY 2020* (Washington, DC: Office of the Undersecretary [Comptroller], May 2019), 251–52, https://comptroller.defense.gov /Portals/45/Documents/defbudget/fy2020/FY20_Green_Book.pdf. The GDP figure for 1986 is from MacroTrends, "U.S. Military Spending/Defense Budget," 1960–present, accessed November 5, 2023, https://www.macrotrends.net/countries /USA/united-states/military-spending-defense-budget.

14. William E. Odom, "The Cold War Origins of the U.S. Central Command," *Journal of Cold War Studies* 8, no. 2 (2006).

15. Charles J. Elia, "Prospect of Military Outlay Boost Spurs Rush to Add Defense Stocks to Investors' Arsenals," *Wall Street Journal*, January 8, 1980.

16. President Ronald Reagan, "Remarks in an Interview with Managing Editors on Domestic Issues," December 3, 1981, in Reagan Presidential Library, https:// www.reaganlibrary.gov/archives/speech/remarks-interview-managing-editors -domestic-issues. See also Carly Hayden Foster, "The Welfare Queen: Race, Gender, Class, and Public Opinion," *Race, Gender, & Class* 15, no. 3/4 (2008).

17. "A Talk with James Watt," *High Country News*, October 1, 1982; Robyn Morrison, "What About Watt?," *High Country News*, June 15, 2010.

18. David Bielo, "Where Did the Carter White House Solar Panels Go?" *Scientific American*, August 6, 2010.

19. Herbert Stein, *Presidential Economics: The Making of Economic Policy from Roosevelt to Clinton* (Washington, DC: American Enterprise Institute for Public Policy Research, 1994), 19.

20. On the macroeconomics of this period, see Alan S. Blinder, *A Monetary and Fiscal History of the United States* (Princeton, NJ: Princeton University Press, 2022), chaps. 8–9.

21. "Inflation, Consumer Prices for the United States," 1960–present, FRED Economic Data, Federal Reserve Bank of St. Louis, accessed November 5, 2023, https://fred.stlouisfed.org/series/FPCPITOTLZGUSA.

22. "Federal Funds Effective Rate," July 1954 to present, FRED Economic Data, Federal Reserve Bank of St. Louis, accessed November 5, 2023, https://fred.stlouisfed .org/series/FEDFUNDS.

23. "Presidential Ad: 'It's Morning Again in America,'" 1984, https://www.youtube.com/watch?v=pUMqic2IcWA. Note that the "It's Morning" phrase was not the official slogan of Reagan's 1980 campaign, but this is the phrase that has been most remembered in retrospect.

24. "Presidential Approval Ratings—Gallup Historical Statistics and Trends," list for average approval ratings for presidents Harry Truman to Donald Trump, accessed November 5, 2023, https://news.gallup.com/poll/116677/presidential-approval-ratings-gallup-historical-statistics-trends.aspx.

25. On public opinion data, see Thomas Ferguson and Joel Rogers, *Right Turn: The Decline of the Democrats and the Future of American Politics* (New York: Hill & Wang, 1986), 12–24; and Benjamin I. Page and Lawrence R. Jacobs, *Class War? What Americans Really Think About Economic Inequality* (Chicago: University of Chicago Press, 2009).

26. See discussion in chapter 2.

27. Jason DeSena Trennert, "Remembering the Reagan Bull Market," *Wall Street Journal*, August 13, 2009. I am, of course, aware of the 1987 crash on the New York Stock Exchange, but that crash proved only a temporary setback in the upward trend of stock values over the longer term. Regarding the negative effects of inflation on investors, see discussion in chapter 2.

28. MacroTrends, "Dow Jones—DJIA—100 Year Historical Chart," 1915 to present, accessed November 5, 2023, https://www.macrotrends.net/1319/dow-jones-100-year-historical-chart.

29. Thomas Piketty, *Capital in the Twenty-First Century* (Cambridge, MA: Belknap Press of Harvard University Press, 2014), 330–35.

30. Matt Stoller, *Goliath: The 100-Year War Between Monopoly Power and Democracy* (New York: Simon & Schuster, 2019), 376–82.

31. See figures in the "data" section of "The Productivity Pay Gap," Economic Policy Institute, updated October 2022, https://www.epi.org/productivity-pay-gap/.

32. From table A4 in Kayla Fontenat, Jessica Semega, and Melissa Kollar, *Income and Poverty in the United States, 2017* (Current Population Reports, U.S. Census Bureau, Washington, DC, September 12, 2018), https://www.census.gov/library/publications/2018/demo/p60-263.html. See also data in Lawrence Mishel, Josh Bivens, Elise Gould, and Heidi Shierholz, *The State of Working America*, 12th ed. (Ithaca, NY: ILR/Cornell University Press, 2012), 29, table 1.2. To the extent that families enjoyed higher average incomes after 2001, it resulted from increasing employment of women, whose participation in the workforce has accelerated considerably. Philip L. Rones, Randy E. Ilg, and Jennifer M. Gardner, "Trends in Hours of Work Since the Mid-1970s," *Monthly Labor Review*, April 1997, 12, https://stats.bls.gov/opub/mlr/1997/04/art1full.pdf.

33. Anne Case and Angus Deaton, *Deaths of Despair and the Future of Capitalism* (Princeton, NJ: Princeton University Press, 2020). For the latest data on low U.S. life expectancy, see Steven H. Woolf, "Falling Behind: The Growing Gap in Life Expectancy Between the United States and Other Countries, 1933–2021," *American Journal of Public Heath* 113 (2023), https://ajph.aphapublications.org/doi/abs/10.2105/AJPH.2023.307310. On the role of economics and health, see Justin R. Pierce and Peter K. Schott, "Trade Liberalization and Mortality: Evidence from U.S. Counties," *American Economic Review Insights* 2, no. 1 (2020).

34. Amitabh Chandra, "Labor Market Dropouts and the Racial Wage Gap, 1940–1990," *American Economic Review* 90, no. 2 (2000): 334; emphasis added. For a powerful class-based analysis of African American deprivation, see Adolph Reed, Jr., "Socialism and the Argument Against Race Reductionism," *New Labor Forum* 29, no. 2 (2020).

35. See table 1 in Valerie Wilson and William M. Rodgers III, *Black-White Wage Gaps Expand with Rising Wage Inequality* (report, Economic Policy Institute, Washington, DC, September 20, 2016), https://www.epi.org/publication/black-white-wage-gaps-expand-with-rising-wage-inequality/. See also Molly Redden and Jana Kasperkevic, "Wage Gap Between White and Black Americans Is Worse Today Than in 1979," *The Guardian*, September 20, 2016. Note that there was a brief reduction in the racial wage gap during the late 1990s, but this trend proved transitory.

36. President Bill Clinton, "Remarks on Signing the Personal Responsibility and Work Opportunity Reconciliation Act of 1996 and an Exchange with Reporters," August 22, 1996, Discover US Government Information, https://www.govinfo.gov/content/pkg/PPP-1996-book2/pdf/PPP-1996-book2-doc-pg1325.pdf.

37. President Bill Clinton, "Remarks on Signing the Gramm-Leach-Bliley Act," November 12, 1999, in Gerhard Peters and John T. Woolley, eds., American Presidency Project, University of California, Santa Barbara, https://www.presidency.ucsb.edu/documents/remarks-signing-the-gramm-leach-bliley-act. Technically, this did not repeal the 1933 Glass-Steagall Act, but it did end Glass-Steagall's separation of investment and commercial banking, the legislation's main feature.

38. Bill Clinton, "Address Before a Joint Session of the Congress on the State of the Union," January 23, 1996, in American Presidency Project, https://www.presidency.ucsb.edu/documents/address-before-joint-session-the-congress-the-state-the-union-10. There were significant gains in labor productivity during the Clinton administration. However, this achievement was mostly the result of long-term trends in the use of information technology in the workplace rather than any specific policy being adopted by the administration. Stephen D. Oliner and Daniel E. Sichel, "The Resurgence of Growth in the Late

1990s: Is Information Technology the Story?," *Journal of Economic Perspectives* 14, no. 4 (2000).

39. Lawrence Summers, "The Great Liberator," *New York Times*, November 19, 2006.

40. Quoted in Thomas Frank, *Listen Liberal: What Ever Happened to the Party of the People?* (New York: Picador, 2016), 173.

41. Ian Swanson, "Obama Says He'd Be Considered as Moderate Republican in 1980s," *The Hill*, December 14, 2012.

42. Joseph E. Stiglitz, "Of the 1 Percent, by the 1 Percent, for the 1 Percent," *Vanity Fair*, May 2011.

43. Quoted in Jim Geraghty, "Chuck Schumer: Democrats Will Lose Blue-Collar Whites, But Will Gain in the Suburbs," *National Review*, July 28, 2016. See also Amory Gethin, Clara Martínez-Toledano, and Thomas Piketty, "Brahmin Left Versus Merchant Right: Changing Political Cleavages in 21 Western Democracies, 1948–2020," *Quarterly Journal of Economics* 137, no. 1 (2022).

44. For a detailed analysis of elite control of U.S. politics, focusing on the top 10 percent of earners, see Martin Gilens, *Affluence and Influence: Economic Inequality and Political Power in America* (Princeton, NJ: Princeton University Press, 2012).

45. Larry M. Bartels, *Unequal Democracy: The Political Economy of the Gilded Age* (Princeton, NJ: Princeton University Press, 2008), chap. 2.

46. Regarding inaccessible vocabulary, see Gareth Sparks, "The Complexity of 'Intersectionality' Is Explored at March Socialist Salon," *Washington Socialist*, April 2017, https://washingtonsocialist.mdcdsa.org/ws-articles/17-04 -intersectionality-salon.

47. Stephen Hawkins, Daniel Yudkin, Miriam Juan-Torres, and Tim Dixon, *Hidden Tribes: A Study of America's Polarized Landscape* (report, More in Common Foundation, New York, 2018), 6, 142, 143, https://hiddentribes.us/media /qfpekz4g/hidden_tribes_report.pdf. The study identifies "progressive activists" with the political left. Similar results were reached in a Pew study, which found that supporters of the "progressive left" tended to be highly educated. See "11. Progressive Left," in *Beyond Red vs. Blue: The Political Typology* (report, Pew Research Center, Washington, DC, November 9, 2021), https://www .pewresearch.org/politics/2021/11/09/progressive-left/. On the left's drift toward the highly educated, see this useful study: Catherine Liu, *Virtue Hoarders: The Case Against the Professional Managerial Class* (Minneapolis: University of Minnesota Press, 2021).

48. Quote from Thomas Piketty, *Capital and Ideology* (Cambridge, MA: Belknap Press of Harvard University Press, 2020), 813; emphasis added. On the class structure of the 2016 vote, see Ruth Igielnik and Rakesh Kochhar, "GOP Gained

Ground in Middle Class Communities in 2016," Pew Research Center, December 8, 2016, https://www.pewresearch.org/fact-tank/2016/12/08/gop -gained-ground-in-middle-class-communities-in-2016/.

49. On the 2016 and 2020 elections, the most serious studies are the following: Thomas Ferguson, Paul Jorgensen, and Jie Chen, "The Knife Edge Election: Between Washington, Kabul, and Weimar" (working paper, Institute for New Economic Thinking, New York, December 2021), https://www.ineteconomics .org/research/research-papers/the-knife-edge-election-of-2020-american-politics -between-washington-kabul-and-weimar; and Ferguson, Jorgensen, and Chen, "Industrial Structure and Political Outcomes: The Case of the 2016 U.S. Presidential Election," in *Palgrave Handbook of Political Economy*, ed. Ivano Cardinale and Roberto Scazzieri (London: Palgrave Macmillan, 2018). See also Ruy Teixeira, "The Power of the Working-Class Vote," *Liberal Patriot*, October 14, 2021, https://theliberalpatriot.substack.com/p/the-power-of-the -working-class-vote.

50. Union membership has fallen continuously up to the present. See U.S. Bureau of Labor Statistics, "Union Membership Fell by 0.2 Percent to 10.1 Percent in 2022," TED: The Economics Daily, January 24, 2023, https://www.bls.gov /opub/ted/2023/union-membership-rate-fell-by-0-2-percentage-point-to-10-1 -percent-in-2022.htm.

51. On the enduring salience of racial tensions, see the following recent studies: Corey Robin, *The Enigma of Clarence Thomas* (New York: Metropolitan, 2019); and Arlie Russell Hochschild, *Strangers in Their Own Land: Anger and Mourning on the American Right* (New York: New Press, 2018).

ACKNOWLEDGMENTS

1. Doug Bandow, "Book Review: *First Do No Harm: Humanitarian Intervention and the Destruction of Yugoslavia*," Cato Institute, July 28, 2009, https://www .cato.org/commentary/book-review-first-do-no-harm-humanitarian-intervention -destruction-yugoslavia.

Bibliography

MANUSCRIPT COLLECTIONS

Accuracy in Media, Brigham Young University
AFL-CIO, George Meany Memorial Archives, National Labor College, now relocated to University of Maryland
AJC Archives [American Jewish Committee], New York
Richard V. Allen, Hoover Institution, Stanford University
Joseph and Stewart Alsop, Library of Congress
American Conservative Union, Brigham Young University
Jack Anderson, George Washington University
Atlantic Council, Hoover Institution, Stanford University
George W. Ball, Princeton University
Bank for International Settlements Archives, Basel, Switzerland
William Banowsky, Pepperdine University
William J. Baroody Sr., Library of Congress
Lemuel Bell, Billy Graham Center, Wheaton College
Daniel Bell, Pusey Library, Harvard University
James Buchanan, George Mason University
William F. Buckley, Yale University
James Burnham, Hoover Institution, Stanford University
Earl L. Butz, Purdue University

William J. Casey, Hoover Institution, Stanford University
Chamber of Commerce of the United States, Hagley Museum and Library, Wilmington, DE
Clark M. Clifford, Library of Congress
Ray S. Cline, Library of Congress
Committee on the Present Danger, Hoover Institution, Stanford University
Conservative Party of New York, State University of New York, Albany
Thomas G. Corcoran, Library of Congress
Brian Crozier, Hoover Institution, Stanford University
John Davenport, Hoover Institution, Stanford University
Deaver & Hannaford Inc., Hoover Institution, Stanford University
Elbridge Durbrow, Hoover Institution, Stanford University
Freedom House, Princeton University
Milton Friedman, Hoover Institution, Stanford University
Paul Gann, California State Library, Sacramento
Carl Gershman, Hoover Institution, Stanford University
Barry M. Goldwater, Arizona State University
Daniel O. Graham, University of Miami, Florida
Group Research Inc., Columbia University
Gottfried Haberler, Hoover Institution, Stanford University
Alexander M. Haig, Library of Congress
Peter Hannaford, Hoover Institution, Stanford University
W. Averell Harriman, Library of Congress
Augustus Hawkins, University of California, Los Angeles
James D. Hodgson, University of California, Los Angeles
Henry M. Jackson, University of Washington
Alfred Kahn, Cornell University
Max M. Kampelman, Minnesota Historical Society, St. Paul
Jack Kemp, Library of Congress
George F. Kennan, Princeton University
Philip M. Klutznick, University of Chicago
Foy Kohler, University of Toledo
Irving Kristol, Wisconsin Historical Society, Madison
Thomas W. Lamont, Baker Library, Harvard Business School
Marvin Liebman, Hoover Institution, Stanford University
Sol M. Linowitz, Library of Congress
Jay Lovestone, Hoover Institution, Stanford University
Clare Boothe Luce, Library of Congress
John J. McCloy, Amherst College

Mont Pèlerin Society, Hoover Institution, Stanford University
William A. Niskanen, Hoover Institution, Stanford University
Paul H. Nitze, Library of Congress
William E. Odom, Library of Congress
Old Time Gospel Hour, Liberty University.
J. Howard Pew, Hagley Museum and Library, Wilmington, DE
Howard Phillips, Liberty University
Normon Podhoretz, Library of Congress
A. Philip Randolph, Library of Congress
Henry Regnery, Hoover Institution, Stanford University
Elliot Richardson, Library of Congress
Nelson A. Rockefeller, Rockefeller Archive Center, Sleepy Hollow, NY
William A. Rusher, Library of Congress
Bayard Rustin, Library of Congress
Daniel Shorr, Library of Congress
William E. Simon, Lafayette College
Judith Stanley [Proposition 13], University of California, Irvine
Maxwell D. Taylor, National Defense University, Washington, DC
Edward R. Teller, Hoover Institution, Stanford University
Trilateral Commission, Rockefeller Archive Center, Sleepy Hollow, NY
Friedrich A. von Hayek, Hoover Institution, Stanford University
Charls E. Walker, Hoover Institution, Stanford University
Jude Wanniski, Hoover Institution, Stanford University
James G. Watt, American Heritage Center, University of Wyoming
Paul M. Weyrich, American Heritage Center, University of Wyoming
Edward Bennett Williams, Library of Congress
Grady Baxter Wilson, Billy Graham Research Center, Charlotte, NC
Walter B. Wriston, Tufts University

PRESIDENTIAL LIBRARIES

Jimmy Carter Presidential Library
Gerald R. Ford Presidential Library
Richard M. Nixon Presidential Library
Ronald Reagan Presidential Library

U.S. NATIONAL ARCHIVES

Department of Treasury, RG 56

ORAL HISTORY COLLECTIONS

Jimmy Carter Presidential Oral History, Miller Center, University of Virginia, https://millercenter.org/the-presidency/presidential-oral-histories/jimmy-carter

Edward M. Kennedy Oral History Project, Edward M. Kennedy Institute, https://millercenter.org/the-presidency/presidential-oral-histories/edward-kennedy

U.S. Federal Reserve System, Board of Governors Oral History Project, https://www.federalreserve.gov/aboutthefed/centennial/federal-reserve-oral-history-interviews.htm

ONLINE ARCHIVES AND DOCUMENTARY MATERIALS

American Enterprise Institute for Public Policy Research, https://aei.org

American Rhetoric, Online Speeches, https://americanrhetoric.com

American Presidency Project, ed. Gerhard Peters and John T. Woolley, University of California, Santa Barbara, https://presidency.ucsb.edu

Center for Budget and Policy Priorities, https://www.cbpp.org/research

Center for Financial Stability, https://centerforfinancialstability.org/

Cold War International History Project, Woodrow Wilson Center, https://wilsoncenter.org/program/cold-war-international-history-project

Cornell Law School, Legal Information Institute, https://law.cornell.edu/supremecourt/

W. E. B. Dubois Papers, 1803–1999, University of Massachusetts, Amherst, https://credo.library.umass.edu/view/collection/mums312

Economic Policy Institute, https://epi.org

Dwight D. Eisenhower Presidential Library, https://eisenhowerlibrary.gov

Falwell Family Papers, Liberty University, https://cdm17184.contentdm.oclc.org/digital/collection/p17184coll4

Federation of American Scientists, Intelligence Resource Program, https://irp.fas.org/.

Gallup Polling, https://gallup.com

GovInfo, Discover U.S. Government Information, https://govinfo.gov

Billy Graham Evangelical Association, https://billygraham.org/

Heritage Foundation, https://heritage.org

Jewish Virtual Library, https://jewishvirtuallibrary.org

Lyndon Baines Johnson Presidential Library, https://lbjlibrary.org/

Justia: U.S. Supreme Court, https://supreme.justia.com

John F. Kennedy Presidential Library, https://jfklibrary.org/archives

MacroTrends, LLC, https://macrotrends.net/

National Bureau of Economic Research, https://nber.org/

National Right to Work Committee, https://nrtwc.org/

National Security Archive, George Washington University, https://nsarchive.gwu.edu/
Nobel Prize in Economic Sciences, Lectures, https://nobelprize.org/prizes/economic
-sciences/.
Pew Research Center, https://pewresearch.org
Lewis Powell Archive, Washington & Lee University, https://law.wlu.edu/powell
-archives/digital-materials
Presidential Recordings, Digital Edition, Miller Center for Public Affairs, University
of Virginia, https://prde.upress.virginia.edu/
Ronald Reagan Institute, https://reaganfoundation.org/.
Thomas Piketty, "Technical Appendix of the Book, *Capital in the 21st Century*"
(Cambridge, MA: Belknap Press of Harvard University Press, 2014). piketty.pse
.ens.fr/files/capital21c/en/Piketty2014FiguresTablesSuppLinks.pdf.
Strom Thurmond Papers, Clemson University, https://tigerprints.clemson.edu/strom
Harry S. Truman Presidential Library, https://trumanlibrary.gov/library/truman-papers
United Auto Workers, https://uaw.org
U.S. Bureau of Labor Statistics, https://bls.gov
U.S. Census Bureau, https://census.gov
U.S. Department of State, https://state.gov
U.S. Federal Reserve System, online documents, https://federalreserve.gov/
U.S. Federal Reserve of St. Louis, https://fraser.stlouisfed.org/
U.S. National Labor Relations Board, https://nlrb.gov/guidance/key-reference-materials
Wallace Foundation, https://wallacefoundation.org/
WGBH, Boston, https://www.wgbh.org//
WikiLeaks Public Library of U.S. Diplomacy, http://wikileaks.org
World Bank, http://data.worldbank.org
Yale Law School, Avalon Project, https://avalon.law.yale.edu/

PUBLISHED TRANSCRIPTS, DOCUMENT COLLECTIONS, AND STATISTICAL COMPENDIA

Archives Direct: Sources from the National Archives, UK (proprietary database).
Burns, Arthur. *Reflections of an Economic Policy Maker: Speeches and Congressional Statements: 1969–1978*. Washington, DC: American Enterprise Institute for Public Policy Research, 1978.
Burr, William, ed. *The Kissinger Transcripts: The Top-Secret Talks with Beijing and Moscow*. New York: New Press, 1998.
Colander, David C., and Harry Landreth Brookfield, eds. *The Coming of Keynesianism to America: Conversations with the Founders of Keynesian Economics*. Northampton, MA: Edward Elgar, 1996.

Declassified Documents Reference System, Gale-Cengage (proprietary database).

Eckes, Alfred E., Jr., ed. *Revisiting U.S. Trade Policy: Decisions in Perspective.* Athens: Ohio University Press, 2000.

Friedman, Milton, and Walter W. Heller. *Fiscal vs. Monetary Policy.* New York: Norton, 1969.

Galambos, Louis, and Daun Van Ee, eds. *The Papers of Dwight D. Eisenhower: The Presidency, The Middle Way,* vol. 15. Baltimore, MD: Johns Hopkins University Press, 1996.

———. *The Papers of Dwight D. Eisenhower: The Presidency, Keeping the Peace,* vol. 19. Baltimore, MD: Johns Hopkins University Press, 2001.

George H. Gallup. *The Gallup Poll: Public Opinion, 1935–1971.* New York: Random House, 1972.

———. *The Gallup Poll: Public Opinion, 1979.* Wilmington, DE: Scholarly Resources, 1980.

Hargrove, Erwin C., and Samuel A. Morley, eds. *The President and the Council of Economic Advisers: Interviews with CEA Chairmen.* Boulder, CO: Westview, 1984.

Horsefield, J. K., ed. *The International Monetary Fund, 1945–1965: Twenty Years of International Monetary Cooperation.* Vol. 3, *Documents.* Washington DC: International Monetary Fund, 1969.

Johnson, Elizabeth, and Donald Moggridge, eds. *The Collected Writings of John Maynard Keynes: Volume 25, Activities 1940–1944, Shaping the Post-War World, the Clearing Union.* Cambridge: Cambridge University Press, 1978.

Johnson, Walter, ed. *The Papers of Adlai E. Stevenson: Continuing Education and the Unfinished Business of American Society, 1957–1961, Vol. VII.* Boston: Little, Brown, 1977.

Kersten, Andrew Edmund, and David Lucander, eds. *For Jobs and Freedom: Selected Speeches and Writings of A. Phillip Randolph.* Amherst: University of Massachusetts Press, 2014.

Kutler, Stanley I., ed. *Abuse of Power: The New Nixon Tapes.* New York: Free Press, 1997.

Oudes, Bruce, ed. *From the President: Richard Nixon's Secret Files.* New York: Harper & Row, 1989.

Safire, William, ed. *Lend Me Your Ears: Great Speeches in History.* New York: Norton, 1997.

Samuelson, Paul A., and William A. Barnett, eds. *Inside the Economist's Mind: Conversations with Eminent Economists.* Malden, MA: Blackwell, 2007.

Schuler, Kurt, and Andrew Rosenberg, eds. *The Bretton Woods Transcripts.* New York: Center for Financial Stability, 2012.

Stockholm International Peace Research Institute, *SIPRI Yearbook.* Stockholm: Almquist & Wiksell, 1973.

——. *SIPRI Yearbook, 1979*. London: Taylor & Francis, 1979.

Sutton, Matthew Avery, ed. *Jerry Falwell and the Rise of the Religious Right: A Brief History with Documents*. New York: Bedford/St. Martin's, 2012.

U.S. Department of State, Office of the Historian. *Foreign Relations of the United States* series, multiple volumes. https://history.state.gov/historicaldocuments.

Wilkins, David E., ed. *On the Drafting of Tribal Constitutions: Felix S. Cohen*. Norman: University of Oklahoma Press, 2007.

Wunderlin, Clarence E., Jr., ed. *The Papers of Robert A. Taft, Volume III, 1945–1948*. Kent, OH: Kent State University Press, 2003.

DOCUMENTARY FILMS

Amini, Hassan, dir. *Decadence and Downfall: The Shah of Iran's Ultimate Party*. BBC, February 14, 2016. Available from YouTube video, September 7, 2022, 1:16:11. https://www.youtube.com/watch?v=I2JXYHZKZE8.

Curtis, Adam, dir. *The Power of Nightmares*. BBC, 2004. Part 1: https://www.youtube.com/watch?v=7O9osvFKdjQ; Part 2: https://www.youtube.com/watch?v=EjKZmlA1zDU; Part 3: https://www.youtube.com/watch?v=IZqieiYzJqE.

Davis, Peter, dir. *Hearts and Minds*. 1974. Available from YouTube video, January 15, 2018, 1:52:06. https://youtube.com/watch?v=WzxNRoGoSKU.

"Farm Crisis Results in Suicide and Murder." Iowa Public Broadcasting Service, July 1, 2013. https://www.iowapbs.org/shows/farmcrisis/clip/5266/farm-crisis-results-suicide-and-murder.

Wharton, Mary, dir. *Jimmy Carter: Rock & Roll President*. 2020.

MEMOIRS AND FIRST-HAND ACCOUNTS

Acheson, Dean. *Present at the Creation: My Years in the State Department*. New York: Norton, 1969.

Ball, George W. *The Past Has Another Pattern: Memoirs*. New York: Norton, 1982.

Bell, Griffin B., and Ronald J. Ostrow. *Taking Care of the Law*. New York: William Morrow, 1982.

Bork, Robert H. *Saving Justice: Watergate, the Saturday Night Massacre, and Other Adventures of a Solicitor General*. New York: Encounter, 2013.

Bourne, Peter G. *Jimmy Carter: A Comprehensive Biography from Plains to Post-Presidency*. New York: Scribner, 1997.

Bowles, Chester. *Promises to Keep: My Years in Public Life, 1941–1969*. New York: Harper & Row, 1971.

Bryant, Anita. *The Anita Bryant Story: The Survival of Our Nation's Families and the Threat of Militant Homosexuality*. Old Tappan, NJ: Revell, 1977.

Brzezinski, Zbigniew. *Power and Principle: Memoirs of a National Security Advisor, 1977–1981.* New York: Farrar, Straus & Giroux, 1983.

Buchanan, Patrick J. *Nixon's White House Wars: The Battles That Made and Broke a President and Divided America Forever.* New York: Crown Forum, 2017.

Burns, Arthur. *Inside the Nixon Administration: The Secret Diary of Arthur Burns, 1969–1974.* Ed. Robert H. Ferrell. Lawrence: University Press of Kansas, 2010.

Cahn, Anne Hessing. *Killing Détente: The Right Attacks the CIA.* University Park: Penn State University Press, 1998.

Cannon, James. *Gerald R. Ford: An Honorable Man.* Ann Arbor: University of Michigan Press, 2013.

Carter, Jimmy. *A Full Life: Reflections at Ninety.* New York: Simon & Schuster, 2015.

——. *Keeping Faith: Memoirs of a President.* New York: Bantam, 1982.

——. *White House Diary.* New York: Picador/Farrar, Straus & Giroux, 2010.

Connally, John B., and Mickey Herskowitz. *In History's Shadow: An American Odyssey.* New York: Hyperion, 1993.

Coombs, Charles A. *The Arena of International Finance.* New York: Wiley, 1976.

Crawford, Alan. *Thunder on the Right: The "New Right" and the Politics of Resentment.* New York: Pantheon, 1980.

Doherty, Brian. *Radicals for Capitalism: A Freewheeling History of the Modern American Libertarian Movement.* New York: Public Affairs, 2007.

Douglas, Senator Paul H. "Challenge Interview: Evaluating the Employment Act." *Challenge* 12, no. 1 (1963).

Ehrlichman, John. *Witness to Power: The Nixon Years.* New York: Simon & Schuster, 1982.

Eisenhower, Dwight D. *Mandate for Change: The White House Years, 1953–1956.* New York: Doubleday, 1963.

Eizenstat, Stuart E. "Jimmy Carter's Lesson for Donald Trump: Hands Off the Fed." *Financial Times,* October 16, 2018.

——. *President Carter: The White House Years.* New York: Thomas Dunne, 2018.

Ellsberg, Daniel. *Secrets: A Memoir of Vietnam and the Pentagon Papers.* New York: Penguin, 2003.

Falwell, Jerry. *Falwell: An Autobiography.* Lynchburg, VA: Liberty House, 1997.

——. *Listen America!* New York: Doubleday, 1980.

Ford, Gerald R. *A Time to Heal: The Autobiography of Gerald R. Ford.* New York: Harper & Row, 1979.

Friedman, Milton. "The Adam Smith Address: The Suicidal Impulse of the Business Community (1989)." In *The Best of Business Economics: Highlights from the First Fifty Years,* ed. Robert Thomas Crow. London: Palgrave Macmillan, 2016.

Friedman, Milton, and Rose D. Friedman, *Two Lucky People: Memoirs.* Chicago: University of Chicago Press, 1998.

Galbraith, John Kenneth. *A Life in Our Times: Memoirs*. Boston: Houghton Mifflin, 1981.

Garthoff, Raymond. *A Journey Through the Cold War: A Memoir of Containment and Coexistence*. Washington, DC: Brookings Institution, 2001.

Gates, Robert M. *From the Shadows: The Ultimate Insider's Story of Five Presidents and How They Won the Cold War*. New York: Simon & Schuster, 1996.

Gergen, David. *Eyewitness to Power: The Essence of Leadership, Nixon to Clinton*. New York: Simon & Schuster, 2000.

Goldwater, Barry M. *With No Apologies: The Personal and Political Memoirs of Barry M. Goldwater*. New York: William Morrow, 1979.

Goodman, Melvin A. *Whistleblower at the CIA: An Insider's Account of the Politics of Intelligence*. San Francisco: City Lights, 2017.

Hartmann, Robert T. *Palace Politics: An Inside Account of the Ford Years*. New York: McGraw-Hill, 1980.

Hersh, Seymour M. *Reporter: A Memoir*. New York: Knopf, 2018.

Javits, Jacob K. *Javits: The Autobiography of a Public Man*. New York: Houghton Mifflin, 1981.

Jordan, Hamilton. *Crisis: The Last Year of the Carter Presidency*. New York: Putnam, 1982.

Kazan, Elia. *A Life*. New York: Knopf, 1988.

Kennedy, Edward M. *True Compass: A Memoir*. New York: Twelve, 2009.

Kissinger, Henry. *The White House Years*. Boston: Little, Brown, 1979.

——. *Years of Upheaval*. Boston: Little, Brown, 1982.

MacLaine, Shirley. *You Can Get There from Here*. New York: Norton, 1975.

Moynihan, Daniel Patrick. *A Dangerous Place*. Boston: Little, Brown, 1978.

Nitze, Paul H. *From Hiroshima to Glasnost: At the Center of Decision*. New York: Grove-Weidenfeld, 1989.

Nixon, Richard M. *RN: The Memoirs of Richard Nixon*. New York: Grosset & Dunlap, 1978.

Pipes, Richard. "Team B: The Reality Behind the Myth." *Commentary*, October 1, 1986.

——. *Vixi: Memoirs of a Non-Belonger*. New Haven, CT: Yale University Press, 2003.

Reed, Adolph L., Jr. *The South: Jim Crow and Its Afterlives*. London: Verso, 2022.

Reuther, Victor G. *The Brothers Reuther and the Story of the UAW: A Memoir by Victor G. Reuther*. Boston: Houghton Mifflin, 1976.

Rockefeller, David. *Memoirs*. New York: Random House, 2002.

Rusher, William A. *The Rise of the Right*. New York: National Review Press, 1993.

Schlesinger, Arthur M., Jr. *A Thousand Days: John F. Kennedy in the White House*. Boston: Houghton Mifflin, 1965.

Shultz, George P. *Learning from Experience*. Palo Alto, CA: Hoover Institution Press, 2016.

Simon, William E. *A Time for Reflection: An Autobiography*. Washington, DC: Regnery, 2004.

———. *A Time for Truth*. New York: Reader's Digest Press, 1978.

Solomon, Robert. *The International Monetary System, 1945–1967: An Insider's View*. New York: Harper & Row, 1977.

Sorensen, Theodore C. *Kennedy*. New York: Harper & Row, 1965.

Steffens, Lincoln. *The Autobiography of Lincoln Steffens*. New York: Harcourt, Brace, 1958.

Stein, Herbert. *Presidential Economics: The Making of Economic Policy from Roosevelt to Clinton*. Washington, DC: American Enterprise Institute for Public Policy Research, 1994.

Truman, Harry S. *Memoirs: Years of Trial and Hope*. Garden City, NY: Doubleday, 1956.

Volcker, Paul, and Toyoo Gyohten. *Changing Fortunes: The World's Money and the Threat to American Leadership*. New York: Times Books, 1992.

Volcker, Paul, and Christine Harper. *Keeping at It: The Quest for Sound Money and Good Government*. New York: Public Affairs, 2018.

Wallace, Henry A. *The Price of Vision: The Diary of Henry A. Wallace, 1942–1946*. Ed. John Morton Blum. Boston: Houghton-Mifflin, 1973.

Zumwalt, Elmo R., Jr. *On Watch: A Memoir*. New York: Quadrangle/New York Times Books, 1976.

GOVERNMENTAL REPORTS

Avila, Daniela Dean, and Kurt G. Lundsford. "Underemployment Following the Great Recession and the COVID-19 Recession." Federal Reserve Bank of Cleveland, February 3, 2022. https://www.clevelandfed.org/publications/economic-commentary/2022/ec-202201-underemployment-following-the-great-recession-and-the-covid-19-recession.

Bailey, Elizabeth E., David R. Graham, and Daniel P. Kaplan. *Deregulating the Airlines: An Economic Analysis*. Washington, DC: Civil Aeronautics Board, 1983.

Conference on Inflation: Held at the Request of President Gerald R. Ford and the Congress of the United States. Washington, DC: U.S. Government Printing Office, 1974.

Congressional Research Service. "China/Taiwan: Evolution of the 'One China' Policy—Key Statements from Washington, Beijing, and Taipei." January 5, 2015. https://www.everycrsreport.com/reports/RL30341.html.

Feickert, Andrew, and Stephen Daggett. "A Historical Perspective on 'Hollow Forces.'" Congressional Research Service, January 31, 2012. https://sgp.fas.org/crs/natsec/R42334.pdf.

Jackson, James K. "Financing the U.S. Trade Deficit." Congressional Research Service, October 7, 2016. https://sgp.fas.org/crs/misc/RL33274.pdf.

Labonte, Marc, and Ben Leubsdorf. "Foreign Holdings of Federal Debt." Congressional Research Service, June 9, 2023. https://sgp.fas.org/crs/misc/RS22331.pdf.

MacLaury, Judson. *History of the Department of Labor, 1913–1988.* Washington, DC: U.S. Department of Labor, 1988. https://www.dol.gov/general/aboutdol/history /dolchp07.

Mayer, Gerald. "Union Membership Trends in the United States." CRS Report for Congress. Washington, DC: Congressional Research Service, August 31, 2004. https://sgp.fas.org/crs/misc/RL32553.pdf.

Minarik, Joseph J. "The Distributional Effects of Inflation and Their Implications." In *Stagflation: The Causes Effects, and Solutions.* Prepared for U.S. Congress, Joint Economic Committee. Washington, DC: U.S. Government Printing Office, 1980.

U.S. Congress. *Full Employment Act of 1945: Hearings before the Committee on Expenditures in the Executive Departments.* Washington, DC: U.S. Government Printing Office, 1945.

——. *Inflation Control Program of OPA.* Washington, DC: U.S. Government Printing Office, 1945.

——. *Quota Increase of the International Monetary Fund.* Washington, DC: U.S. Government Printing Office, 1991.

U.S. Department of Defense. *The Pentagon Papers.* Full text of declassified study of the Vietnam War, 1968. Washington, DC: U.S. National Archives. https://www .archives.gov/research/pentagon-papers.

U.S. Department of Defense, Office of the Undersecretary (Comptroller). *National Defense Budget Estimates for FY 2020.* Washington, DC: Office of the Undersecretary (Comptroller), May 2019.

U.S. Federal Deposit Insurance Corporation. *History of the Eighties: Lessons for the Future.* Washington, DC: FDIC, December 1997, last updated June 12, 2023. https://www.fdic.gov/resources/publications/history-eighties/index.html.

U.S. Senate. *Multinational Corporations: Hearings Before the Subcommittee on International Trade of the Committee on Finance, United States Senate, Ninety-Third Congress, First Session.* Washington, DC: U.S. Government Printing Office, 1973.

——. *Senate Select Committee to Study Governmental Operations with Respect to Intelligence Activities, 1975–76 (Church Committee).* Full text of multiple reports on the CIA from U.S. Senate website, https://www.intelligence.senate.gov/resources /intelligence-related-commissions.

U.S. Senate, Committee on Banking, Housing, and Urban Affairs. *The Nomination of Paul A. Volcker To Be Chairman of the Board of Governors of the Federal Reserve System, July 30, 1979.* Washington, DC: U.S. Government Printing Office, 1979.

U.S. Department of the Treasury, *The President's 1978 Tax Program: Detailed Descriptions and Supporting Analyses of the Proposals*, January 30, 1978, https://home.treasury.gov/system/files/131/Report-Presidents-1978-Part1.pdf.

———. *Report to Congress on the Capital Gains Tax Reductions of 1978*. Washington, DC: U.S. Government Printing Office, 1985.

SECONDARY SOURCES

Abrams, Burton A. "How Richard Nixon Pressured Arthur Burns: Evidence from the Nixon Tapes." *Journal of Economic Perspectives* 20, no. 4 (2006).

Ahlberg, Kristin L., ed. *Foreign Relations of the United States, 1977–1980, Volume 1: Foundations of Foreign Policy*. Washington DC: U.S. Government Printing Office, 2014.

Akard, Patrick J. "Corporate Mobilization and Political Power: The Transformation of U.S. Economic Policy in the 1970s." *American Sociological Review* 57, no 5 (1992).

———. "The Return of the Market: Corporate Mobilization and the Transformation of U.S. Economic Policy, 1974–1984." PhD thesis, Department of Sociology, University of Kansas, 1989.

Albo, Gregory. "Neoliberalism from Reagan to Clinton." *Monthly Review* 52, no. 11 (2001).

Allitt, Patrick. *Religion in America Since 1945: A History*. New York: Columbia University Press, 2003.

Alter, Jonathan. *His Very Best: Jimmy Carter, A Life*. New York: Simon & Schuster, 2020.

Altschuler, Glenn C., and Stuart M. Blumin. *The GI Bill: A New Deal for Veterans*. New York: Oxford University Press, 2009.

Anderson, Irvine H., Jr. *ARAMCO, the United States, and Saudi Arabia: A Study in the Dynamics of Foreign Oil Policy, 1933–1950*. Princeton, NJ: Princeton University Press, 1981.

Applebaum, Binyamin. *The Economists' Hour: False Prophets, Free Markets, and the Fracture of Society*. Boston: Little, Brown, 2019.

Balmer, Randall. *Bad Faith: Race and the Rise of the Religious Right*. Grand Rapids, MI: Eerdmans, 2021.

Baltzell, E. Digby. *Philadelphia Gentlemen: The Making of a National Upper Class*. Glencoe, IL: Free Press, 1958.

Baran, Paul A., and Paul M. Sweezy. *Monopoly Capital: An Essay on the American Economic and Social Order*. New York: Monthly Review, 1966.

Barr, Joseph W. "The Last Days of Franklin National Bank." *Administrative Law Review* 27, no. 4 (1975).

Bartels, Larry M. *Unequal Democracy: The Political Economy of the Gilded Age*. Princeton, NJ: Princeton University Press, 2008.

Bartlett, Randall. *Economic Foundations of Political Power*. New York: Free Press, 1973.

Basosi, Duccio. "Oil, Dollars, and U.S. Power in the 1970s: Reviewing the Connections." *Journal of Energy History*, no. 3 (2019).

Belew, Kathleen. *Bring the War Home: The White Power Movement and Paramilitary America*. Cambridge, MA: Harvard University Press, 2018.

Bellant, Russ. *The Coors Connection: How Coors Family Philanthropy Undermines Democratic Pluralism*. Boston: South End, 1991.

Belzer, Michael H. *Sweatshops on Wheels: Winners and Losers in Trucking Deregulation*. New York: Oxford University Press, 2000.

Berkowitz, Edward D. *Something Happened: A Political and Cultural Overview of the Seventies*. New York: Columbia University Press, 2017.

Berman, Elizabeth Popp. *Thinking Like an Economist: How Efficiency Replaced Equality in Public Policy*. Princeton, NJ: Princeton University Press, 2022.

Bhagwati, Jagdish. "The Capital Myth: The Difference Between Trade in Widgets and Dollars." *Foreign Affairs* 77, no. 3 (May–June 1998).

Bill, James A. *The Eagle and the Lion: The Tragedy of American-Iranian Relations*. New Haven, CT: Yale University Press, 1988.

Bird, Kai. *The Outlier: The Unfinished Presidency of Jimmy Carter*. New York: Crown, 2021.

Biven, W. Carl. *Jimmy Carter's Economy: Policy in an Age of Limits*. Chapel Hill: University of North Carolina Press, 2002.

Blair, John M. *The Control of Oil*. New York: Vintage, 1978.

Bleiberg, Robert. "Farewell to Wage and Price Controls." *Imprimis* 3, no. 7 (July 1974). https://imprimis.hillsdale.edu/farewell-to-wage-and-price-controls-july-1974/.

Blinder, Alan S. *A Monetary and Fiscal History of the United States, 1961–2021*. Princeton, NJ: Princeton University Press, 2022.

Block, Fred, and Margaret R. Somers. *The Power of Market Fundamentalism: Karl Polanyi's Critique*. Cambridge, MA: Harvard University Press, 2014.

Bluestone, Barry, and Bennett Harrison. *The Deindustrialization of America: Plant Closings, Community Abandonment, and the Dismantling of Basic Industry*. New York: Basic Books, 1982.

Blyth, Mark. *Austerity: The History of a Dangerous Idea*. New York: Oxford University Press, 2013.

Borgwardt, Elizabeth. *A New Deal for the World: America's Vision for Human Rights*. Cambridge, MA: Belknap Press of Harvard University Press, 2007.

Bork, Robert H. *The Antitrust Paradox: A Policy at War with Itself*. New York: Basic Books, 1978.

Borstelmann, Timothy. *The 1970s: A New Global History from Civil Rights to Economic Inequality*. Princeton, NJ: Princeton University Press, 2012.

Breit, William, and John H. Huston. "Reputation Versus Influence: The Evidence from Textbook References." *Eastern Economic Journal* 23, no. 4 (1997).

Brenner, Robert. "The Economics of Global Turbulence: A Special Report on the World Economy, 1950–1998." *New Left Review*, no. 229 (1998).

Brine, Kevin R., and Mark Poovey, *Finance in America: An Unfinished Story.* Chicago: University of Chicago Press, 2017.

Bronson, Rachel. *Thicker Than Oil: America's Uneasy Partnership with Saudi Arabia.* New York: Oxford University Press, 2006.

Browne, Robert S. "Black Economic Autonomy." *Black Scholar* 3, no. 2 (1971).

Buchanan, James M., and Richard E. Wagner. *Democracy in Deficit: The Political Legacy of Lord Keynes.* New York: Academic, 1977.

Burch, Philip H., Jr. *Elites in American History: The New Deal to the Carter Administration.* Vol. 3. New York: Holmes & Meier, 1980.

——. "The NAM as an Interest Group." *Politics & Society* 4, no. 1 (1973).

Burgin, Angus. *The Great Persuasion: Reinventing Free Markets Since the Depression.* Cambridge, MA: Harvard University Press, 2012.

Burnham, Walter Dean. "The 1980 Earthquake: Realignment, Reaction, or What?" In *The Hidden Election: Politics and Economics in the 1980 Presidential Campaign,* ed. Thomas Ferguson and Joel Rogers. New York: Random House, 1981.

Burns, Jennifer. *Goddess of the Market: Ayn Rand and the American Right.* New York: Oxford University Press, 2011.

Butler, Anthea. *White Evangelical Racism: The Politics of Morality in America.* Chapel Hill: University of North Carolina Press, 2021.

Butz, Earl. "An Emerging Market-Oriented Food and Agricultural Policy." *Public Administration Review* 36, no. 2 (1976).

Buzzanco, Robert. "Whatever Happened to the New Left? Toward a Radical Reading of American Foreign Relations." *Diplomatic History* 23, no. 4 (1999).

Carroll, Peter N. *It Seemed Like Nothing Happened: America in the 1970s.* New Brunswick, NJ: Rutgers University Press, 1990.

Case, Anne, and Angus Deaton. *Deaths of Despair and the Future of Capitalism.* Princeton, NJ: Princeton University Press, 2020.

Chandra, Amitabh. "Labor Market Dropouts and the Racial Wage Gap: 1940–1990." *American Economic Review* 90, no. 2 (2000).

Cheru, Fantu. *The Silent Revolution in Africa: Debt, Development, and Democracy.* London: Zed, 1990.

Clark, Daniel J. *Disruption in Detroit: Auto Workers and the Elusive Postwar Boom.* Champaign: University of Illinois Press, 2018.

Clark, Richard, and Lindsay R. Dolan. "Pleasing the Principal: U.S. Influence in World Bank Policymaking." *American Journal of Political Science* 66, no. 1 (2021).

Clausewitz, Carl von. *On War.* Princeton, NJ: Princeton University Press, 1989.

Clawson, Dan, and Alan Neustadtl, "Interlocks, PACs, and Corporate Conservatism." *American Journal of Sociology* 94, no. 4 (1989).

Clawson, Dan, Alan Neustadtl, and James Bearden. "The Logic of Business Unity: Corporate Contributions to the 1980 Elections." *American Sociological Review* 51, no. 6 (1986).

Cohan, William D. *Money and Power: How Goldman Sachs Came to Rule the World.* New York: Doubleday, 2011.

Collins, Robert M. *The Business Response to Keynes, 1929–1964.* New York: Columbia University Press, 1981.

——. *More: The Politics of Economic Growth in Postwar America.* New York: Oxford University Press, 2000.

Connell, Carol M. *Reforming the World Monetary System: Fritz Machlup and the Bellagio Group.* London: Pickering & Chatto, 2013.

Conybeare, John A. C. *United States Foreign Economic Policy and International Capital Markets: The Case of Capital Export Countries, 1963–1974.* New York: Garland, 1988.

Cooper, Andrew Scott. *The Oil Kings: How the U.S., Iran, and Saudi Arabia Changed the Balance of Power in the Middle East.* New York: Simon & Schuster, 2011.

——. "Showdown at Doha: The Secret Oil Deal That Helped Sink the Shah of Iran." *Middle East Journal* 62, no. 4 (2008).

Cooper, Melinda. *Family Values: Between Neoliberalism and the New Social Conservatism.* New York: Zone, 2017.

Cordovez, Diego, and Selig S. Harrison, *Out of Afghanistan: The Inside Story of the Soviet Withdrawal.* New York: Oxford University Press, 1995.

Cowie, Jefferson R. *The Great Exception: The New Deal and the Limits of American Politics.* Princeton, NJ: Princeton University Press, 2016.

——. *Stayin' Alive: The 1970s and the Last Days of the Working Class.* New York: New Press, 2012.

Cox, Ronald W. *Corporate Power, Class Conflict, and the Crisis of the New Globalization.* Lanham, MD: Lexington, 2019.

Crichlow, Donald T. *The Conservative Ascendancy: How the GOP Right Made Political History.* Cambridge, MA: Harvard University Press, 2007.

——. *Phyllis Schlafly and Grassroots Conservatism: A Woman's Crusade.* Princeton, NJ: Princeton University Press, 2005.

Crotty, James. "The Neoliberal Paradox: The Impact of Destructive Product Market Competition and 'Modern' Financial Markets on Nonfinancial Corporation Performance in the Neoliberal Era." In *Financialization and the World Economy,* ed. Gerald A. Epstein. Cheltenham, UK: Edward Elgar, 2005.

Crozier, Michel J., Samuel P. Huntington, and Joji Watanuki. *The Crisis of Democracy: Report on the Governability of Democracies to the Trilateral Commission.* New York: NYU Press, 1975.

Cumings, Bruce. "Still the American Century." *Review of International Studies* 25, no. 5 (1999).

D'Arista, Jane. "The Role of the International Monetary System in Financialization." In *Financialization and the World Economy*, ed. Gerald A. Epstein. Cheltenham, UK: Edward Elgar, 2005.

Dark, Taylor E. *The Unions and the Democrats: An Enduring Alliance*. Ithaca, NY: Cornell University Press, 1999.

Delton, Jennifer A. *The Industrialists: How the National Association of Manufacturers Shaped American Capitalism*. Princeton, NJ: Princeton University Press, 2020.

Diamond, Sara. *Roads to Dominion: Right-Wing Movements and Political Power in the United States*. New York: Guilford, 1995.

Dibooğlu, Selahattin. "International Monetary Regimes and Transmission of Macroeconomic Shocks: Evidence from the Bretton Woods and Modern Floating Periods." *Southern Economic Journal* 66, no. 3 (2000).

Dochuk, Darren. *From Bible Belt to Sun Belt: Plain Folks Religion, Grassroots Politics, and the Rise of Evangelical Conservatism*. New York: Norton, 2011.

Domhoff, G. William. *The Myth of Liberal Ascendancy: Corporate Dominance from the Great Depression to the Great Recession*. Boulder, CO: Paradigm, 2013.

——. *Who Rules America? The Triumph of the Corporate Rich*. New York: McGraw-Hill, 2013.

Dreher, Sabine. *Religions in International Political Economy*. Cham, Switzerland: Palgrave Macmillan, 2020.

Drutman, Lee. *The Business of America Is Lobbying: How Corporations Became Politicized and Politics Became More Corporate*. New York: Oxford University Press, 2015.

Dube, Arindrajit, Ethan Kaplan, and Suresh Naidu. "Coups, Corporations, and Classified Information." *Quarterly Journal of Economics* 126, no. 3 (2011).

DuBoff, Richard B. "Full Employment: History of a Receding Target." *Politics & Society* 7, no. 1 (1977).

Dubufsky, Melvyn. "Labor Unrest in the United States, 1906–90." *Review* (Fernand Braudel Center) 18, no. 1 (1995).

Dubois, W. E. B. *Black Reconstruction in America: 1860–1880*. New York: Free Press, 1998.

Dudley, Kathryn Marie. *Debt and Dispossession: Farm Loss in America's Heartland*. Chicago: University of Chicago Press, 2000.

Dueck, Colin. *Hard Line: The Republican Party and U.S. Foreign Policy Since World War II*. Princeton, NJ: Princeton University Press, 2010.

Dupree, Louis. "Afghanistan Under the Khalq." *Problems of Communism* 28, no. 4 (1979).

Dye, Thomas R. *Who's Running America? The Carter Years*. Englewood Cliffs, NJ: Prentice-Hall, 1979.

Ebenstein, Avraham, Ann Harrison, and Margaret Mcmillan. "Why Are American Workers Getting Poorer? China, Trade, and Offshoring." In *The Factory-Free Economy: Outsourcing, Servitization, and the Future of Industry*. Ed. Lionel Fontagné and Ann E. Harrison. New York: Oxford University Press, 2017.

Edsall, Thomas Byrne. *The New Politics of Inequality*. New York: Norton, 1984.

Eichengreen, Barry. *Exorbitant Privilege: The Rise and Fall of the Dollar and the Future of the International Monetary* System. New York: Oxford University Press, 2011.

Elkhawas, Mohamed A., and Barry Cohen, eds. *The Kissinger Study of Southern Africa*. Westport, CT: Lawrence Hill, 1976.

Ellsberg, Daniel. *Papers on the War*. New York: Simon & Schuster, 2009.

Emerson, Steven. *The American House of Saud: The Secret Petrodollar Connection*. New York: Franklin Watts, 1985.

Epstein, Gerald A., ed., *Financialization and the World Economy*. Cheltenham, UK: Edward Elgar, 2005.

Epstein, Gerald A., and Thomas Ferguson. "Monetary Policy, Loan Liquidation, and Industrial Conflict: The Federal Reserve and the Open Market Operations of 1932." *Journal of Economic History* 44, no. 4 (1984).

Erdman, Paul E. *The Crash of 79*. New York: Simon & Schuster, 1976.

Evans, Thomas. *The Education of Ronald Reagan: The General Electric Years and the Untold Story of His Conversion to Conservatism*. New York: Columbia University Press, 2006.

Feldstein, Martin, Lawrence Summers, and Michael Wachter. "Is the Rate of Profit Falling?" *Brookings Papers on Economic Activity* no. 1 (1977).

Ferguson, Thomas. "From Normalcy to New Deal: Industrial Structure, Party Competition, and American Public Policy During the New Deal." *International Organization* 38, no. 1 (1984).

——. *The Investment Theory of Party Competition and the Logic of Money-Driven Political Systems*. Chicago: University of Chicago Press, 1995.

Ferguson, Thomas, and Joel Rogers, "The Reagan Victory: Corporate Coalitions and the 1980 Campaign." In *The Hidden Election: Politics and Economics in the 1980 Presidential Campaign*, ed. Thomas Ferguson and Joel Rogers. New York: Pantheon, 1981.

——. *Right Turn: The Decline of the Democrats and the Future of American Politics*. New York: Hill & Wang, 1986.

Ferguson, Thomas, Paul Jorgensen, and Jie Chen. "Industrial Structure and Political Outcomes: The Case of the 2016 U.S. Presidential Election." In *Palgrave Handbook of Political Economy*. Ed. Ivano Cardinale and Roberto Scazzieri. London: Palgrave Macmillan, 2018.

———. "The Knife Edge Election: Between Washington, Kabul, and Weimar." Working paper. New York: Institute for New Economic Thinking, December 2021. https:// www.ineteconomics.org/research/research-papers/the-knife-edge-election-of -2020-american-politics-between-washington-kabul-and-weimar.

Fligstein, Neil, and Taekjin Shin. "Shareholder Value and the Transformation of the U.S. Economy, 1984–2000." *Sociological Forum* 22, no. 4 (2007).

Flippen, J. Brooks. *Jimmy Carter, the Politics of Family, and the Rise of the Religious Right.* Athens: University of Georgia Press, 2011.

Folsom, James. "Christmas Message," December 25, 1949. In *Lend Me Your Ears: Great Speeches in History,* ed. William Safire. New York: Norton, 1997.

Foner, Philip S. *U.S. Labor and the Viet-Nam War.* New York: International Publishers, 1989.

Fones-Wolf, Elizabeth. *Selling Free Enterprise: The Business Assault on Labor and Liberalism, 1945–1960.* Champaign: University of Illinois Press, 1994.

Fones-Wolf, Ken, and Elizabeth A. Fones-Wolf. *Struggle for the Soul of the South: White Evangelical Protestants and Operation Dixie.* Urbana: University of Illinois Press, 2015.

Fontagné, Lionel, and Ann E. Harrison, eds. *The Factory-Free Economy: Outsourcing, Servitization, and the Future of Industry.* New York: Oxford University Press, 2017.

Fordham, Benjamin O. *Building the Cold War Consensus: The Political Economy of U.S. National Security Policy, 1949–1951.* Ann Arbor: University of Michigan Press, 1998.

Formisano, Ronald P. *Boston Against Busing: Race, Class, and Ethnicity in the 1960s and 1970s.* Chapel Hill: University of North Carolina Press, 1991.

Fortner, Michael Javen. *Black Silent Majority: The Rockefeller Drug Laws and the Politics of Punishment.* Cambridge, MA: Harvard University Press, 2015.

Frank, Thomas. *Listen Liberal: What Ever Happened to the Party of the People?* New York: Picador, 2016.

Fraser, Steve. *The Limousine Liberal: How an Incendiary Image United the Right and Fractured America.* New York: Basic Books, 2016.

Freeman, Richard B. *What Do Unions Do?* New York: Basic Books, 1985.

Friedman, Gerald. "Born in the USA?" In *"Labor History Symposium*: Judith Stein's *Pivotal Decade*," ed. Craig Phelen. *Labor History* 52, no. 3 (2011).

Friedman, Milton. *Capitalism and Freedom.* Chicago: University of Chicago Press, 2002.

———. "The Case for Flexible Exchange Rates." In *Essays in Positive Economics,* ed. Milton Friedman. Chicago: University of Chicago Press, 1953.

Friedman, Milton, and Anna Jacobson Schwartz. *A Monetary History of the United States: 1867–1960.* Princeton, NJ: Princeton University Press, 1963.

Friedman, Milton, and Donald W. Paden. "A Monetarist View." *Journal of Economic Education* 14, no. 4 (1983).

Friedman, Thomas L. *The Lexus and the Olive Tree*. New York: Farrar, Straus & Giroux, 1999.

Freudenberg, Nicholas, Marianne Fahs, Sandro Galea, and Andrew Greenberg. "The Impact of New York City's 1975 Fiscal Crisis on the Tuberculosis, HIV, and Homicide Syndemic." *Journal of Public Health* 96, no. 3 (2006).

Frum, David. *How We Got Here: The 70s—The Decade That Brought You Modern Life, for Better or Worse*. New York: Basic Books, 2000.

Galbraith, John Kenneth. "The Selection and Timing of Inflation Controls." *Review of Economics and Statistics* 23, no. 2 (1941).

Garthoff, Raymond L. *Détente and Confrontation: American-Soviet Relations from Nixon to Reagan*. Washington, DC: Brookings Institution, 1985.

Geismer, Lily. *Don't Blame Us: Suburban Liberals and the Transformation of the Democratic Party*. Princeton, NJ: Princeton University Press, 2015.

Gerstle, Gary. *The Rise and Fall of the Neoliberal Order: America and the World in the Free Market Era*. New York: Oxford University Press, 2022.

Gethin, Amory, Clara Martínez-Toledano, and Thomas Piketty. "Brahmin Left Versus Merchant Right: Changing Political Cleavages in 21 Western Democracies, 1948–2020." *Quarterly Journal of Economics* 137, no. 1 (2022).

Ghosh, Atish R., and Mahvash S. Qureshi. "What's in a Name? That Which We Call Capital Controls." IMF Working Paper 16/25. Washington, DC: International Monetary Fund, February 2016. https://www.imf.org/external/pubs/ft/wp/2016/wp1625.pdf.

Gibbs, David N. "Afghanistan: The Soviet Invasion in Retrospect." *International Politics* 37, no. 2 (2000).

——. "Does the USSR Have a 'Grand Strategy'? Reinterpreting the Invasion of Afghanistan." *Journal of Peace Research* 24, no. 4 (1987).

——. "Political Parties and International Relations: The United States and the Decolonization of Sub-Saharan Africa." *International History Review* 17, no. 2 (1995).

——. "Reassessing Soviet Motives for Invading Afghanistan: A Declassified History." *Critical Asian Studies* 38, no. 2 (2006).

Gilens, Martin. *Affluence and Influence: Economic Inequality and Political Power in America*. Princeton, NJ: Princeton University Press, 2012.

Ginsburg, Helen. *Full Employment and Public Policy: The United States and Sweden*. Lanham, MD: Lexington, 1983.

——. "Historical Amnesia: The Humphrey-Hawkins Act, Full Employment, and Employment as a Right." *Review of Black Political Economy* 39, no. 1 (2012).

Goldin, Claudia, and Robert Margo. "The Great Compression: The Wage Structure of the United States at Mid-Century." *Quarterly Journal of Economics* 107, no. 1 (1992).

Goldman, Marshall I. *Soviet Foreign Aid.* New York: Praeger, 1967.

Gómez-Quiñones, Juan, and Irene Vásquez. *Making Aztlán: Ideology and Culture of the Chicana and Chicano Movement, 1966–1977.* Albuquerque: University of New Mexico Press, 2014.

Gordon, Robert J. *The Rise and Fall of American Growth: The U.S. Standard of Living Since the Civil War.* Princeton, NJ: Princeton University Press, 2016.

Gowa, Joanne. *Closing the Gold Window: Domestic Politics and the End of Bretton Woods.* Ithaca, NY: Cornell University Press, 1983.

Gowan, Peter. *The Global Gamble: Washington's Faustian Bid for World Dominance.* London: Verso, 1999.

Grafton, Carl, and Anne Permaloff. *Big Mules and Branchheads: James E. Folsom and Political Power in Alabama.* Athens: University of Georgia Press, 2008.

Green, Mark J., James Fallows, and David R. Zwick. *Who Runs Congress? The President, Big Business, or You?* New York: Bantam, 1972.

Greenwood, Robin, and David Scharfstein. "The Growth of Finance." *Journal of Economic Perspectives* 27, no. 2 (2013).

Greider, William. *One World, Ready or Not: The Manic Logic of Global Capitalism.* New York: Simon & Schuster, 1997.

——. *Secrets of the Temple: How the Federal Reserve Runs the Country.* New York: Simon & Schuster, 1987.

——. *Who Will Tell the People: The Betrayal of American Democracy.* New York: Simon & Schuster, 2010.

Grem, Darren Elliott. "The Blessings of Business: Corporate America and Conservative Evangelicalism in the Sunbelt Age, 1945–2000." PhD thesis, Department of History, University of Georgia, 2010.

Griffith, Barbara S. *The Crisis of American Labor: Operation Dixie and the Defeat of the CIO.* Philadelphia: Temple University Press, 1988.

Gwin, Mary E. "National Health Insurance in an Age of Limits: Jimmy Carter's Abandoned Agenda." PhD thesis, Department of History, Vanderbilt University, 2018.

Haendel, Dan. *Corporate Strategic Planning: The Political Dimension.* Washington, DC: Center for Strategic and International Studies, 1981.

Hakes, David R., and David C. Rose. "The 1979–1982 Monetary Policy Experiment: Monetarist, Anti-Monetarist, or Quasi-Monetarist?" *Journal of Post-Keynesian Economics* 15, no. 2 (1992–93).

Halliday, Fred. *The Making of the Second Cold War.* London: Verso, 1983.

——. "Revolution in Afghanistan." *New Left* Review, no. 112 (1978).

——. "War and Revolution in Afghanistan." *New Left Review,* no. 119 (1980).

Hamilton, Shane. "The Populist Appeal of Deregulation: Independent Truckers and the Politics of Free Enterprise, 1935–1980." *Enterprise & Society* 10, no. 1 (2009).

——. *Trucking Country: The Road to America's Walmart Economy.* Princeton, NJ: Princeton University Press, 2014.

Hanhimäki, Jussi M. *The Rise and Fall of Détente: American Foreign Policy and the Transformation of the Cold War.* Sterling, VA: Potomac, 2012.

Harl, Neil E. *The Farm Debt Crisis of the 1980s.* Ames: Iowa State University Press, 1990.

Harty, Sheila. *Hucksters in the Classroom: A Review of Industry Propaganda in Schools.* Washington, DC: Center for Responsive Law, 1979.

Haslam, Jonathan. "Response to *H-Diplo* Article Review 966 (2020): There Really Was an 'Afghan Trap.'" *H-Net,* May 13, 2022. https://networks.h-net.org/node /28443/discussions/10247063/response-h-diplo-article-review-966-2020-there -really-was-afghan.

——. *Russia's Cold War: From the October Revolution to the Fall of the Wall.* New Haven, CT: Yale University Press, 2011.

Hawkins, Stephen, Daniel Yudkin, Miriam Juan-Torres, and Tim Dixon. *Hidden Tribes: A Study of America's Polarized Landscape.* New York: More in Common Foundation, 2018. https://hiddentribes.us/media/qfpekz4g/hidden_tribes_report .pdf.

Hayden Foster, Carly."The Welfare Queen: Race, Gender, Class, and Public Opinion." *Race, Gender, & Class* 15, no. 3/4 (2008).

Helleiner, Eric. "Controlling Capital Flows 'at Both Ends': A Neglected (but Newly Relevant) Keynesian Innovation from Bretton Woods." *Challenge* 58, no. 5 (2015).

——. *States and the Reemergence of International Finance: From Bretton Woods to the 1990s.* Ithaca, NY: Cornell University Press, 1994.

Herbold, Hilary. "Never a Level Playing Field: Blacks and the GI Bill." *Journal of Blacks in Higher Education,* no. 6 (1994–1995).

Hertel-Fernandez, Alexander. *State Capture: How Conservative Activists, Big Businesses, and Wealthy Donors Reshaped the American States—and the Nation.* New York: Oxford University Press, 2019.

Hetzel, Robert L., and Ralph F. Leach. "The Treasury-Fed Accord: A New Narrative Account." *Federal Reserve Bank of Richmond Economic Quarterly* 87, no. 1 (2001).

Himmelstein, Jerome L. "The New Right." In *The New Christian Right: Mobilization and Legitimation.* Ed. Robert C. Liebman and Robert Wuthnow. New York: Aldine, 1983.

——. *To the Right: The Transformation of American Conservatism.* Berkeley: University of California Press, 1990.

Hinton, Elizabeth. *America on Fire: The Untold Story of Police Violence and Black Rebellion Since the 1960s.* New York: Norton, 2021.

——. *From the War on Poverty to the War on Crime: The Making of Mass Incarceration in America.* Cambridge, MA: Harvard University Press, 2016.

Hochschild, Arlie Russell. *Strangers in Their Own Land: Anger and Mourning on the American Right*. New York: New Press, 2108.

Honey, Michael. "Operation Dixie: Labor and Civil Rights in the Postwar South." *Mississippi Quarterly* 45, no. 4 (1992).

Hoplin, Nicole, and Ron Robinson. *Funding Fathers: The Unsung Heroes of the Conservative Movement*. Washington, DC: Regnery Press, 2008.

Houck, Oliver A. "Charity for All." *Yale Law Journal* 93, no. 8 (1984).

Hungerford, Thomas L. "Corporate Tax Rates and Economic Growth Since 1947" (Issue Brief 364, Economic Policy Institute, Washington, DC, June 4, 2013), https://www.epi.org/publication/ib364-corporate-tax-rates-and-economic-growth/.

Hyman, Louis. *Debtor Nation: The History of America in Red Ink*. Princeton, NJ: Princeton University Press, 2011.

"Interview with Phyllis Schlafly on the Equal Rights Amendment, November 1978." In *Jerry Falwell and the Rise of the Religious Right: A Brief History with Documents* .Ed. Matthew Avery Sutton. New York: Bedford/St. Martin's, 2012.

Jackson, Claire. "History Lessons: The Asian Flu Pandemic." *British Journal of General Practice* 59, no. 565 (2009).

Jacobs, Meg. *Panic at the Pump: The Energy Crisis and the Transformation of American Politics in the 1970s*. New York: Hill & Wang, 2016.

——. *Pocketbook Politics: Economic Citizenship in Twentieth Century America*. Princeton, NJ: Princeton University Press, 2005.

Jacoby, Neil A. "The Fiscal Policy of the Kennedy-Johnson Administration." *Journal of Finance* 19, no. 2 (1964).

Jenkins, J. Craig, and Craig M. Eckert. "The Right Turn in Economic Policy: Business Elites and the New Conservative Economics." *Sociological Forum* 15, no. 2 (2000).

Jenkins, Philip. *Decade of Nightmares: The End of the Sixties and the Making of Eighties America*. New York: Oxford University Press, 2006.

Jones, Daniel Stedman. *Masters of the Universe: Hayek, Friedman, and the Birth of Neoliberal Politics*. Princeton, NJ: Princeton University Press, 2012.

Kahlenberg, Richard D., and Moshe Z. Marvit. "The Ugly Racial History of 'Right to Work.'" *Dissent*, December 20, 2012.

Kalecki, Michal. "Political Aspects of Full Employment." *Political Quarterly* 14, no. 4 (1943).

Kalman, Laura. *Right Star Rising: A New Politics, 1974–1980*. New York: Norton: 2010.

Katz, Alyssa. *The Influence Machine: The U.S. Chamber of Commerce and the Corporate Capture of American Life*. New York: Spiegel & Grau, 2015.

Kaufman, Robert G. *Senator Henry M. Jackson: A Life in Politics*. Seattle: University of Washington Press, 2000.

Keane, Thomas F. "The Economic Importance of the National Highway System." *Public Roads* 59, no. 4 (1996).

Kennedy, Dave, and Thomas Saylor, *Minnesota in the 70s*. St. Paul: Minnesota Historical Society Press, 2013.

Kennedy, Paul. *The Rise and Fall of the Great Powers: Economic Change and Military Conflict from 1500 to 2000*. New York: Random House, 1987.

Keys, Barbara J. *Reclaiming American Virtue: The Human Rights Movement of the 1970s*. Cambridge, MA: Harvard University Press, 2014.

Keynes, John Maynard. *The General Theory of Employment, Interest, and Money*. New York: Harcourt, Brace, 1936.

Kindleberger, Charles P. *The World in Depression, 1929–1939*. Berkeley: University of California Press, 1973.

Kirshner, Jonathan. *American Power After the Financial Crisis*. Ithaca, NY: Cornell University Press, 2014.

Klein, Naomi. *The Shock Doctrine: The Rise of Disaster Capitalism*. New York: Picador, 2007.

Kobes du Mez, Kristin. *Jesus and John Wayne: How White Evangelicals Corrupted a Faith and Fractured a Nation*. New York: Liveright, 2020.

Kotlowski, Dean J. "Richard Nixon and the Origins of Affirmative Action." *Historian* 60, no. 3, 1998.

Kotz, David. *The Rise and Fall of Neoliberal Capitalism*. Cambridge, MA: Harvard University Press, 2015.

Krippner, Greta R. *Capitalizing on Crisis: The Political Origins of the Rise of Finance*. Cambridge, MA: Harvard University Press, 2011.

Krugman, Paul. *Exchange Rate Instability*. Cambridge, MA: MIT Press, 1989.

Kruse, Kevin M. *One Nation Under God: How Corporate America Invented Christian America*. New York: Basic Books, 2015.

Kuhn, David Paul. *Hardhat Riot: Nixon, New York City, and the Dawn of White Working-Class Revolution*. New York: Oxford University Press, 2020.

Kwitny, Jonathan. *Endless Enemies: The Making of an Unfriendly World*. New York: Congdon & Weed, 1984.

LaPalombara, Joseph, and Stephen Blank. *Multinational Corporations and Developing Countries*. New York: Conference Board, 1979.

Lassiter, Matthew D. *The Silent Majority: Suburban Politics in the Sunbelt South*. Princeton, NJ: Princeton University Press, 2007.

Lembcke, Jerry. *The Spitting Image: Myth, Memory, and the Legacy of Vietnam*. New York: NYU Press, 2000.

Le Roy, François. "Mirages Over the Andes: Peru, France, and the United States and Military Jet Procurement During the 1960s." *Pacific Historical Review* 71, no. 2 (2002).

Lewis, Penny. *Hardhats, Hippies, and Hawks: The Vietnam Antiwar Movement in Myth and Memory*. Ithaca, NY: Cornell University Press, 2013.

Lichtenstein, Nelson. *State of the Union: A Century of American Labor*. Princeton, NJ: Princeton University Press, 2002.

Lichtman, Allan J. *White Protestant Nation: The Rise of the American Conservative Movement*. New York: Atlantic Monthly Press, 2008.

Liebman, Robert C. "Mobilizing the Moral Majority." In *The New Christian Right: Mobilization and Legitimation*. Ed. Robert C. Liebman and Robert Wuthnow. New York: Aldine, 1983.

Lienesch, Michael. *Redeeming America: Piety and Politics in the New Christian Right*. Chapel Hill: University of North Carolina Press, 1993.

Lindsay, Hal. *The Late Great Planet Earth*. Grand Rapids, MI: Zondervan, 1970.

Lindsey, David E., Athanasios Orphanides, and Robert H. Rasche, "The Reform of October 1979: How It Happened and Why." Working paper no. 2005-02. Finance and Economics Discussion Series. Washington, DC: Federal Reserve Board, December 2004. https://www.federalreserve.gov/pubs/feds/2005/200502/200502pap.pdf.

Liu, Catherine. *Virtue Hoarders: The Case Against the Professional Managerial Class*. Minneapolis: University of Minnesota Press, 2021.

Lopez, Ian Haney. *Dog Whistle Politics: How Coded Racial Appeals Have Reinvented Racism and Wrecked the Middle Class*. New York: Oxford University Press, 2015.

Lowndes, Joseph E. *From the New Deal to the New Right: Race and the Southern Origins of Modern Conservatism*. New Haven, CT: Yale University Press, 2009.

Luker, Kristin. *Abortion and the Politics of Motherhood*. Berkeley: University of California Press, 1984.

Lundburg, Ferdinand. *The Rich and the Superrich: A Study in the Power of Money Today*. New York: Lyle Stuart, 1968.

MacLean, Nancy. *Democracy in Chains: The Deep History of the Radical Right's Stealth Plan for America*. New York: Viking, 2017.

——. "How Milton Friedman Exploited White Supremacy to Privatize Education." Working paper no. 161. New York: Institute for New Economic Thinking, September 1, 2021. https://www.ineteconomics.org/uploads/papers/WP_161-MacLean .pdf.

Madansky, Albert. "Is War a Business Paradigm? A Literature Review." *Journal of Private Equity* 8, no. 3 (2005).

Madrick, Jeff. *Age of Greed: The Triumph of Finance and the Decline of America, 1970 to the Present*. New York: Knopf, 2011.

Mallaby, Sabastian. *The Man Who Knew: The Life and Times of Alan Greenspan*. New York: Penguin, 2016.

Marcuse, Herbert. *One-Dimensional Man: Studies in the Ideology of Advanced Industrial Society*. Boston: Beacon, 1964.

Martin, Isaac William. *Rich People's Movements: Grassroots Campaigns to Untax the One Percent*. New York: Oxford University Press, 2013.

Martin, William C. *With God on Our Side: The Rise of the Religious Right in America.* New York: Broadway, 1996.

Mattson, Kevin. *What the Heck Are You Up To, Mr. President? Jimmy Carter, America's Malaise, and the Speech that Should Have Changed America.* London: Bloomsbury, 2009.

Matusow, Allen J. *Nixon's Economy: Booms, Busts, Dollars, and Votes.* Lawrence: University Press of Kansas, 1998.

Mayer, Jane. *Dark Money: The Hidden History of the Billionaires Behind the Rise of the New Right.* New York: Anchor, 2017.

McCartin, Joseph A. *Collision Course: Ronald Reagan, the Air Traffic Controllers, and the Strike That Changed America.* New York: Oxford University Press, 2011.

McGirr, Lisa. *Suburban Warriors: The Origins of the New American Right.* Princeton, NJ: Princeton University Press, 2015.

McKinnon, Ronald I. *The Unloved Dollar Standard: From Bretton Woods to the Rise of China.* New York: Oxford University Press, 2013.

McQuaid, Kim. "The Roundtable: Getting Results in Washington." *Harvard Business Review*, May/June 1981.

McRae, Elizabeth Gillespie. *Mothers of Massive Resistance: White Women and the Politics of White Supremacy.* New York: Oxford University Press, 2018.

Meadows, Donella H., Dennis L. Meadows, Jorgen Randers, and William W. Behrens III. *The Limits to Growth: A Report to the Club of Rome's Project on the Predicament of Mankind.* New York: Universe, 1974.

Mehrling, Perry. *Money and Empire: Charles P. Kindleberger and the Dollar System.* New York: Cambridge University Press, 2022.

Melman, Seymour. *The Demilitarized Society: Disarmament and Conversion.* Montreal, QC: Harvest House, 1988.

Mettler, Suzanne. *From Soldiers to Citizens: The GI Bill and the Making of the Greatest Generation.* New York: Oxford University Press, 2007.

Meltzer, Allan H. *A History of the Federal Reserve, Vol. I, 1913–1951.* Chicago: University of Chicago Press, 2010.

Miller, Edward H. *A Conspiratorial Life: Robert Welch, the John Birch Society, and the Revolution of American Conservatism.* Chicago: University of Chicago Press, 2021.

——. *Nut Country: Right-Wing Dallas and the Origins of the Southern Strategy.* Chicago: University of Chicago Press, 2015.

Miller, Steven P. *Billy Graham and the Rise of the Republican South.* Philadelphia: University of Pennsylvania Press, 2009.

Mills, C. Wright. *The Power Elite.* New York: Oxford University Press, 2000.

Minarik, Joseph J. "The Size Distribution of Income During Inflation." *Review of Income and Wealth* 25, no. 4 (1979).

Mirowski, Philip, and Dieter Plehwe, eds. *The Road from Mont Pèlerin: The Making of a Neoliberal Thought Collective*. Cambridge, MA: Harvard University Press, 2009.

Mirzadegan, Amin. "Nixon's Folly: The White House and the 1970s Oil Price Crisis." *Yale Historical Review* 5, no. 2 (Spring 2016).

Mishel, Lawrence, Josh Bivens, Elise Gould, and Heidi Shierholz. *The State of Working America, 12 ed.* Ithaca, NY: ILR/Cornell University Press, 2012.

Mizruchi, Mark S. *The Fracturing of the American Corporate Elite*. Cambridge, MA: Harvard University Press, 2013.

Moffitt, Michael. *The World's Money: International Banking from Bretton Woods to the Brink of Insolvency*. New York: Simon & Schuster, 1983.

Moreton, Bethany. *To Serve God and Walmart: The Making of Christian Free Enterprise*. Cambridge, MA: Harvard University Press, 2009.

Morgan, Ted. *A Covert Life, Jay Lovestone: Communist, Anti-Communist, and Spymaster*. New York: Random House, 1999.

Mucciaroni, Gary. *The Political Failure of Employment Policy, 1945–1982*. Pittsburgh, PA: University of Pittsburgh Press, 1990.

Munnell, Alicia H. "Why Has Productivity Growth Declined? Productivity and Public Investment." *New England Economic Review* [Federal Reserve Bank of Boston], January/February 1990.

Nordhaus, William. "Retrospective on the 1970s' Productivity Slowdown." NBER Working Papers Series, no. 10950. Cambridge, MA: National Bureau of Economic Research, 2004. https://www.nber.org/papers/w10950.

Novick, Robert. *The Holocaust in American Life*. Boston: Houghton Mifflin, 1999.

Odom, William E. "The Cold War Origins of the U.S. Central Command." *Journal of Cold War Studies* 8, no. 2 (2006).

Offer, Avner, and Gabriel Söderberg, *The Nobel Factor: The Prize in Economics, Social Democracy, and the Market Turn*. Princeton, NJ: Princeton University Press, 2016.

Oliner, Stephen D., and Daniel E. Sichel. "The Resurgence of Growth in the Late 1990s: Is Information Technology the Story?" *Journal of Economic Perspectives* 14, no. 4 (2000).

Olson, Mancur. *The Logic of Collective Action: Public Goods and the Theory of Groups*. Cambridge, MA: Harvard University Press, 1965.

Oppenheim, V. H. "Why Oil Prices Go Up: The Past—We Pushed Them." *Foreign Policy*, no. 25 (1976–1977).

Oreskes, Naomi, and Erik M. Conway. *The Big Myth: How American Business Taught Us to Loathe Government and Love the Free Market*. New York: Bloomsbury, 2023.

Page, Benjamin I., and Martin Gilens. *Democracy in America: What Went Wrong and What We Can Do About It*. Chicago: University of Chicago Press, 2017.

Page, Benjamin I., and Lawrence R. Jacobs. *Class War? What Americans Really Think About Economic Inequality*. Chicago: University of Chicago Press, 2009.

Page, Benjamin I., Jason Seawright, and Mathew J. Lacombe. *Billionaires and Stealth Politics*. Chicago: University of Chicago Press, 2019.

Palan, Ronen. *The Offshore World: Sovereign Markets, Virtual Places, and Nomad Millionaires*. Ithaca, NY: Cornell University Press, 2006.

Panitch, Leo, and Sam Gindin. *The Making of Global Capitalism: The Political Economy of American Empire*. London: Verso, 2012.

Parker, Daniel. "CPAC: The Origins and Role of the Conference in the Expansion and Consolidation of the Conservative Movement, 1974–1980." PhD thesis, Department of Political Science, University of Pennsylvania, 2015.

Peck, Jamie. *Constructions of Neoliberal Reason*. New York: Oxford University Press, 2013.

Peoples, James. "Deregulation and the Labor Market." *Journal of Economic Perspectives* 12, no. 3 (1998).

Perkins, Margo V. *Autobiography as Activism: Three Black Women of the Sixties*. Oxford: University Press of Mississippi, 2000.

Perlstein, Rick. *Nixonland: The Rise of a President and the Fracturing of America*. New York: Scribner, 2008.

——. *Reaganland: America's Right Turn, 1976–1980*. New York: Simon & Schuster, 2020.

Perry, George L., Martin Neil Bailey, and William Poole. "Slowing the Wage Price Spiral: The Macroeconomic View." *Brookings Papers in Economic Activity*, no. 2 (1978).

Petersen, Neal H. et al., eds. *Foreign Relations of the United States 1950, Volume I, National Security Affairs, Foreign Economic Policy*. Washington, DC: U.S. Government Printing Office, 1977.

Phillips, A. W. "The Relation Between Unemployment and the Rate of Change of Money Wage Rates in the United Kingdom, 1861–1957." *Economica* 25, no. 100 (1958).

Phillips, Kevin. *American Theocracy: The Peril and Politics of Radical Religion, Oil, and Borrowed Money in the 21st Century*. New York: Viking, 2006.

——. *The Emerging Republican Majority*. New Rochelle, NY: Arlington House, 1969.

Phillips-Fein, Kim. "Business Conservatives and the Mont Pèlerin Society." In *Road from Mont Pèlerin: The Making of a Neoliberal Thought Collective*. Ed. Philip Mirowski and Dieter Plehwe. Cambridge, MA: Harvard University Press, 2009.

——. *Fear City: New York's Fiscal Crisis and the Rise of Austerity Politics*. New York: Metropolitan, 2017.

——. *Invisible Hands: The Businessmen's Crusade Against the New Deal*. New York: Norton, 2009.

Plehwe, Dieter. "Introduction." In *Road from Mont Pèlerin: The Making of a Neoliberal Thought Collective*. Ed. Philip Mirowski and Dieter Plehwe. Cambridge, MA: Harvard University Press, 2009.

Pierce, Justin R., and Peter K. Schott. "Trade Liberalization and Mortality: Evidence from U.S. Counties." *American Economic Review Insights* 2, no. 1, 2020.

Piketty, Thomas. *Capital and Ideology.* Cambridge, MA: Belknap Press of Harvard University Press, 2020.

——. *Capital in the Twenty-First Century.* Cambridge, MA: Belknap Press of Harvard University Press, 2014.

Podhoretz, Norman. *Why We Were in Vietnam.* New York: Simon & Schuster, 1982.

Podvig, Pavel. "The Window of Vulnerability That Wasn't: Soviet Military Buildup in the 1970s." *International Security* 33, no. 1 (2008).

Pollin, Robert. *Back to Full Employment.* Cambridge, MA: MIT Press, 2012.

Pollin, Robert, and Heidi Garrett-Peltier. "The U.S. Employment Effects of Military and Domestic spending Priorities: 2011 Update." Amherst: Political Economy Research Institute, University of Massachusetts, December 2011.

Price, Carter C., and Kathryn A. Edwards. *Trends in Income from 1975 to 2018.* Working paper no. WR-A516-1. Santa Monica, CA: Rand, 2020, https://www.rand.org/content/dam/rand/pubs/working_papers/WRA500/WRA516-1/RAND_WRA516-1.pdf.

Prins, Nomi. *All the Presidents' Bankers: The Hidden Alliances That Drive American Power.* New York: Nation, 2014.

Przeworski, Adam, and Michael Wallerstein. "The Structure of Class Conflict in Democratic Capitalist States." *American Political Science Review* 76, no. 2 (1982).

Puddington, Arch. *Lane Kirkland: Champion of American Labor.* New York: Wiley, 2008.

Putnam, Robert D. *Bowling Alone: The Collapse and Revival of American Community.* New York: Simon & Schuster, 2000.

Qaimmaqami, Linda, ed. *Foreign Relations of the United States, 1969–1976: Volume XXXVI, Energy Crisis, 1969–1974.* Washington, DC: U.S. Government Printing Office, 2011.

Rasmussen, Kathleen B., ed. *Foreign Relations of the United States, 1977–1980: Volume III, Foreign Economic Policy.* Washington, DC: U.S. Government Printing Office, 2013.

Rauchway, Eric. *The Money Makers: How Roosevelt and Keynes Ended the Depression, Defeated Fascism, and Secured a Prosperous Peace.* New York: Basic Books, 2015.

Rather, Dan, and Gary Paul Gates. *The Palace Guard.* New York: Harper & Row, 1974.

Ravitch, Diane. *Reign of Error: The Hoax of the Privatization Movement and the Danger to America's Public Schools.* New York: Knopf, 2014.

Reed, Adolph L., Jr. *The Jesse Jackson Phenomenon.* New Haven, CT: Yale University Press, 2009.

——. "Socialism and the Argument Against Race Reductionism." *New Labor Forum* 29, no. 2 (2020).

Reed, Roy. "Orval E. Faubus: Out of Socialism to Realism." *Arkansas Historical Journal* 66, no. 2 (2007).

Reich, Charles A. *The Greening of America.* New York: Bantam, 1970.

Reichart, Alexandre, and Abdelkader Slifi. "The Influence of Monetarism on Federal Reserve Policy During the 1980s." *Cahiers d'Economie Politique,* no. 70 (2016).

Rich, Andrew. *Think Tanks, Public Policy, and the Politics of Expertise.* Cambridge: Cambridge University Press, 2004.

Richards, Lawrence. *Union-Free America: Workers and Anti-Union Culture.* Urbana: University of Illinois Press, 2008.

Ricks, Thomas E. *Waging a Good War: A Military History of the Civil Rights Movement, 1954–1968.* New York: Farrar, Straus and Giroux, 2022.

Robin, Corey. *The Enigma of Clarence Thomas.* New York: Metropolitan, 2019.

Romer, Christina D., and David H. Romer. "The Rehabilitation of Monetary Policy in the 1950s." *American Economic Review* 92, no. 2 (2002).

Rosen, Ruth. *The World Split Open: How the Modern Women's Movement Changed America.* New York: Penguin, 2006.

Rosenberg, John. "The Quest Against Détente: Eugene Rostow, the October War, and the Origins of the Anti-Détente Movement, 1969–1976." *Diplomatic History* 39, no. 4 (2015).

Rosenfeld, Sam. *The Polarizers: Postwar Architects of Our Partisan Era.* Chicago: University of Chicago Press, 2018.

Rostker, Bernard. *I Want You! The Evolution of the All-Volunteer Force.* Santa Monica, CA: Rand, 2006.

Rothbard, Murray. "Frank S. Meyer: The Fusionist as Libertarian Manqué." *Modern Age* (Fall 1981).

Rothstein, Richard. *The Color of Law: A Forgotten History of How Our Government Segregated America.* New York: Liveright, 2018.

Rueschemeyer, Dietrich. "Why and How Ideas Matter." In *Oxford Handbook of Contextual Political Analysis.* Ed. Robert E. Goodin and Charles Tilley. New York: Oxford University Press, 2006.

Saloma, John S., III. *Ominous Politics: The New Conservative Labyrinth.* New York: Hill & Wang, 1984.

Samuelson, Paul A., and Robert M. Solow. "Analytical Aspects of Anti-Inflation Policy." *American Economic Review* 50, no. 2 (1960).

Sandbrook, Dominic. *Mad as Hell: The Crisis of the 1970s and the Rise of the Populist Right.* New York: Knopf, 2011.

Sanders, Jerry W. *Peddlers of Crisis: The Committee on the Present Danger and the Politics of Containment.* Boston: South End Press, 1983.

Sappington, N. O., Francis C. Prescott, and Kieran J. Carroll, eds. *Foreign Relations of the United States, Diplomatic Papers, 1941, the British Commonwealth, the*

Near East, and Africa, Volume III. Washington, DC: U.S. Government Printing Office, 1959.

Sargent, Daniel J. *A Superpower Transformed: The Remaking of American Foreign Relations in the 1970s.* New York: Oxford University Press, 2015.

Schattschneider, E. E. *The Semisovereign People: A Realist's View of Democracy in America.* Hinsdale, IL: Dryden, 1960.

Schulman, Bruce J. *The Seventies: The Great Shift in American Culture, Society, and Politics.* Cambridge, MA: Da Capo, 2001.

Schumacher, E. F. *Small Is Beautiful: A Study of Economics as If People Mattered.* London: Blond & Briggs, 1973.

Self, Robert O. *All in the Family: The Realignment of American Democracy Since the 1960s.* New York: Hill & Wang, 2012.

Shawcross, William. *Sideshow: Kissinger, Nixon, and the Destruction of Cambodia.* New York: Harper-Collins, 1979.

Sheehan, Neil, Hedrick Smith, E. W. Kenworthy, and Fox Butterfield. *The Pentagon Papers.* New York: Bantam, 1971.

Sherman, Gabriel. *The Loudest Voice in the Room: How the Brilliant, Bombastic Roger Ailes Built Fox News—and Divided a Country.* New York: Random House, 2017.

Shermer, Elizabeth Tandy. "Sunbelt Boosterism: Industrial Recruitment, Economic Development, and Growth Politics in the Developing South." In *Sunbelt Rising: The Politics of Place, Space, and Region.* Ed. Michelle Nickerson and Darren Dochuk. Philadelphia: University of Pennsylvania Press, 2011.

Shleifer, Andrei. "The Age of Milton Friedman." *Journal of Economic Literature* 47, no. 1 (2009).

Silber, William L. *Volcker: The Triumph of Persistence.* New York: Bloomsbury, 2012.

Silk, Leonard, and Mark Silk. *The American Establishment.* New York: Basic Books, 1980.

Simmons, Solon. *The Eclipse of Equality: Arguing America on Meet the Press.* Palo Alto, CA: Stanford University Press, 2013.

Sinclair, Upton. *The Goosestep: A Study of American Education.* Whitefish, MT: Kessinger, 2004.

Skidelsky, Robert. *John Maynard Keynes: Fighting for Freedom, 1937–1946.* New York: Penguin, 2000.

Skidmore, David. *Reversing Course: Carter's Foreign Policy, Domestic Politics, and the Failure of Reform.* Nashville, TN: Vanderbilt University Press, 1996.

Slichter, Sumner H. "The Taft-Hartley Act." *Quarterly Journal of Economics* 63, no. 1 (1949).

Slobodian, Quinn. *Globalists: The End of Empire and the Birth of Neoliberalism.* Cambridge, MA: Harvard University Press, 2018.

Smillie, Dirk. *Falwell Inc.: Inside a Religious, Political, Educational, and Business Empire*. New York: St. Martin's, 2008.

Smith, Barbara, ed. *Home Girls: A Black Feminist Anthology*. New Brunswick, NJ: Rutgers University Press, 2000.

Smith, Daniel A. "Howard Jarvis, Populist Entrepreneur: Reevaluating the Causes of Proposition 13." *Social Science History* 23, no. 2 (1999).

Smith, Earl. "Racism and the Boston Schools Crisis." *Black Scholar* 6, no. 6 (1975).

Smith, Hedrick. *The Russians*. New York: Quadrangle/New York Times, 1976.

Smith, James Allen. *Strategic Calling: The Center for Strategic and International Studies, 1962–1992*. Washington, DC: Center for Strategic and International Studies, 1993.

Soffer, Jonathan. "The National Association of Manufacturers and the Militarization of American Conservatism." *Business History Review* 75, no. 4 (2001).

Spiro, David E. *The Hidden Hand of American Hegemony: Petrodollar Recycling and International Markets*. Ithaca, NY: Cornell University Press, 1999.

Sproul, Allan. "The Accord—A Landmark in the First Fifty Years of the Federal Reserve System." *Federal Reserve Bank of New York Monthly Review* 46, no. 11 (1964).

Spruill, Marjorie J. *Divided We Stand: The Battle Over Women's Rights and Family Values That Polarized American Politics*. New York: Bloomsbury, 2017.

Stahl, Jason Michael. "Selling Conservatism: Think Tanks, Conservative Ideology, and the Undermining of Liberalism, 1945–Present." PhD diss., Department of History, University of Minnesota, 2008.

Stallings, Barbara. *Banker to the Third World: U.S. Portfolio Investment in Latin America, 1900–1986*. Berkeley: University of California, 1987.

Stanley, Timothy Randolph. "'Sailing Against the Wind': A Reappraisal of Edward Kennedy's Campaign for the 1980 Democratic Party Presidential Nomination." *Journal of American Studies* 43, no. 2 (2009).

Steil, Benn. *The Battle of Bretton Woods: John Maynard Keynes, Harry Dexter White, and the Making of a New World Order*. Princeton, NJ: Princeton University Press, 2013.

Stein, Judith. *Pivotal Decade: How the United States Traded Factories for Finance in the Seventies*. New Haven, CT: Yale University Press, 2010.

Stewart, Captain Eric W. "The Political Economy of United States Arms Transfers to Latin America During the Cold War." MA thesis, Department of Latin American Studies, University of Arizona, 1999.

Stoller, Matt. *Goliath: The 100-Year War Between Monopoly Power and Democracy*. New York: Simon & Schuster, 2019.

Strange, Susan. *Casino Capitalism*. Manchester, UK: Manchester University Press, 1997.

Strong, Robert A. "Politics and Principle: Jimmy Carter in the Civil Rights Era." *Irish Association for American Studies: IJAS Online*, no. 3 (2014).

Su, Tie-Ting, Alan Neustadtl, and Dan Clawson. "Business and the Conservative Shift: Corporate PAC Contributions, 1976–1986." *Social Science Quarterly* 76, no. 1 (1995).

Sun Tzu. *The Art of War*. New York: Columbia University Press, 2009.

Suri, Jeremi. *Power and Protest: Global Revolution and the Rise of Détente*. Cambridge, MA: Harvard University Press, 2005.

Swartz, David R. "Identity Politics and the Fragmenting of the 1970s Left." *Religion and American Culture: A Journal of Interpretation* 21, no. 1 (2011).

Taft, Robert A. "Statement on the Full Employment Bill," January 18, 1945. In *The Papers of Robert A. Taft, Volume III, 1945–1948*. Ed. Clarence E. Wunderlin, Jr. Kent, OH: Kent State University Press, 2003.

Taylor, Keeanga-Yamahtta. *Race for Profit: How Banks and the Real Estate Industry Undermined Black Homeownership*. Chapel Hill: University of North Carolina Press, 2019.

Teles, Steven M. *The Rise of the Conservative Legal Movement: The Battle for Control of the Law*. Princeton, NJ: Princeton University Press, 2008.

Tesseyman, Andrew James. "The New Right Think Tanks and Policy Change in the UK." DPhil thesis, Department of Politics, University of York, 1999.

"Text of the AFL-CIO Merger Agreement." *Monthly Labor Review* 78, no. 4 (1955).

Thompson, Nicholas. *The Hawk and the Dove: Paul Nitze, George Kennan, and the History of the Cold War*. New York: Picador/Henry Holt, 2009.

Tryman, Mfanya D. "Was Jesse Jackson a Third-Party Candidate in 1988?" *Black Scholar* 20, no. 1 (1989).

Turgeon, Lyn. *Bastard Keynesianism: The Evolution of Economic Thinking and Policy Making Since World War II*. Westport, CT: Praeger, 1996.

Vaïsse, Justin. *Neoconservatism: The Biography of a Movement*. Cambridge, MA: Belknap Press of Harvard University Press, 2010.

Viscelli, Steve. *The Big Rig: Trucking and the Decline of the American Dream*. Berkeley: University of California Press, 2016.

Van Horn, Rob. "Reinventing Monopoly and the Role of Corporations: The Roots of Chicago Law and Economics." In *Road from Mont Pèlerin: The Making of a Neoliberal Thought Collective*. Ed. Philip Mirowski and Dieter Plehwe. Cambridge, MA: Harvard University Press, 2009.

Wacker, Grant. *America's Pastor: Billy Graham and the Shaping of a Nation*. Cambridge, MA: Belknap Press of Harvard University Press, 2014.

Wade, Robert. "How High Inequality Plus Neoliberal Governance Weakens Democracy." *Challenge* 56, no. 6 (2013).

Wade, Robert, and Frank Veneroso. "The Asian Crisis: The High Debt Model Versus the Wall Street-Treasury-IMF Complex." *New Left Review*, no. I/228 (1998).

Wali, Muammer, and Meher Manzur. "Exchange Rate Volatility Before and After the Float." *World Economy* 36, no. 8 (2013).

Ward, Jon. *Camelot's End: Kennedy vs. Carter, and the Fight That Broke the Democratic Party*. New York: Twelve, 2019.

Warren, Bill. "Imperialism and Capitalist Industrialization." *New Left Review*, I/81 (1973).

Wasem, Ruth Ellen. *Tackling Unemployment: The Legislative Dynamics of the Employment Act of 1946*. Kalamazoo, MI: Upjohn Institute for Employment Research, 2013.

Waterhouse, Benjamin C. *Lobbying America: The Politics of Business from Nixon to NAFTA*. Princeton, NJ: Princeton University Press, 2014.

Weaver, Richard M. *Ideas Have Consequences*. Chicago: University of Chicago Press, 2013.

Weber, Max. "The Meaning of Ethical Neutrality in Sociology and Economics." In *The Methodology of the Social Sciences*. Ed. E. A. Shils and H. A. Finch. New York: Free Press, 1949.

Whyte, Jessica. *The Morals of the Market: Human Rights and the Rise of Neoliberalism*. London: Verso, 2019.

Wilcox, Clyde. "Blacks and the New Christian Right: Support for the Moral Majority and Pat Robertson Among Washington, D.C. Blacks." *Review of Religious Research* 32, no. 1 (1990).

Wilkerson, Isabel. *The Warmth of Other Suns: The Epic Story of America's Great Migration*. New York: Vintage, 2011.

Wilkins, David E. *Red Prophet: The Punishing Intellectualism of Vine Deloria Jr.* Golden, CO: Fulcrum, 2018.

Williams, Daniel K. *God's Own Party: The Making of the Christian Right*. New York: Oxford University Press, 2010.

Williams, T. Harry. *Huey Long: A Biography*. New York: Knopf, 1969.

Wilson, Valerie, and William M. Rodgers III. *Black-White Wage Gaps Expand with Rising Wage Inequality*. Report. Washington, DC: Economic Policy Institute, September 20, 2016. https://www.epi.org/publication/black-white-wage-gaps-expand-with-rising-wage-inequality/.

Windham, Lane. *Knocking on Labor's Door: Union Organizing in the 1970s and the Roots of a New Economic Divide*. Chapel Hill: University of North Carolina Press, 2017.

Wolfe, Jane. *The Murchisons: The Rise and Fall of a Texas Dynasty*. New York: St. Martin's, 1989.

Wolff, Edward N. "The Distributional Effects of the 1969–1975 Inflation on Holdings of Household Wealth in the United States." *Review of Income and Wealth* 25, no. 2 (1979).

Woodward, C. Vann. *The Strange Career of Jim Crow*. New York: Oxford University Press, 1955.

Woodward, Susan L. *Balkan Tragedy: Chaos and Dissolution After the Cold War*. Washington, DC: Brookings Institution, 1995.

Woolf, Steven H. "Falling Behind: The Growing Gap in Life Expectancy Between the United States and Other Countries, 1933–2021." *American Journal of Public Heath* 113 (2023). https://ajph.aphapublications.org/doi/abs/10.2105/AJPH.2023.307310.

Wuthnow, Robert. *The Restructuring of American Religion: Society and Faith Since World War II*. Princeton, NJ: Princeton University Press, 1988.

Zoeller, Christoffer J. P. "Closing the Gold Window: The End of Bretton Woods as a Contingency Plan." *Politics & Society* 47, no. 1 (2019).

Zweig, Phillip L. *Wriston: Walter Wriston, Citibank, and the Rise and Fall of American Financial Supremacy*. New York: Crown, 1995.

Index

Page numbers with *t* indicate tables; page numbers with *f* indicate figures.

and Friedman, 9, 52, 190; and IMF,
157; and inflation, 28, 44, 75, 204,
250n150; and Johnson, 45; and
Keynes, 28; and militarist policy,
109; and Nixon, 114; and Phillips
curve, 29–30; policy makers for, 7;
and religion, 80; and Springsteen,
189; and Volcker, 200–202, 205
Austin, J. Paul, 169, 172
automobiles, 32

Baez, Joan, 127
bailouts, 76, 152–53, 178, 181, 201,
252n164, 291n72
Baker, Peter, 317n161
Baldwin, James, 87
banking: and Friedman, 48; and
globalization, 141, 144, 146, 153,
284n13; and Scaife, 60
Bank of America, 113, 183
banks: and deregulation, 146, 152–53,
180; and dollar, 143; and Great
Depression, 143; and interest rates,
180, 188; and segregation, 102; and
Third World governments, 118; and
trade, 113; and Volcker, 188
Baroody, William, J., 52, 53, 60, 63, 198,
239n34, 239n36, 239n38, 242n65,
242n68, 242n70, 244n92, 245n99,
249n140, 263n92
Baroody, William, Jr., 56, 306n58
*Barron's National Business and
Financial Weekly*, 42, 63, 67, 72, 177,
183
Bechtel Foundation, 65, 69, 160,
296n119
Bell, Daniel, 57, 241n56, 244n92
Bell Helicopter, 156
Bendix Corporation, 66
Bergland, Robert, 171
Bernstein, Leonard, 101
Bhagwati, Jagdish, 11, 165
Big Rig, The (study), 91
Bildenberg forum, 161
Bill of Rights, 17
Billy Jack (film), 99
Biological Weapons Convention, 131

bioweapons, 131
Bird, Kai, 6
Black activists, 106
Black Caucus, 103–7, 174, 178, 200,
267n137
Blacks: and antiwar movement,
96; and Carter, 169, 176, 194;
economic condition of, 33; entering
mainstream, 44; and Jackson, 106–7;
and racism, 18, 33, 102–4; and
Reagan, 203; unemployment of, 189;
wages of, 33, 207
Bleiberg, Robert M., 47, 234n134, 235n
Blumenthal, Michael, 186, 308n75
Boeing Corporation, 115
bonuses, 205
Bork, Robert H., 51, 238n25, 239n38,
288n42
born again, 82–83, 169, 274n59
Boston busing controversy, 102, 103
Boston Globe, 68
Braithwaite, Rodric, 108, 268n
Brazil, 111
Bretton Woods agreement, 6, 142–46,
149, 150, 157, 163, 283n3, 285n22,
289n58
Bright, Bill, 85
Bristol-Myers, 66, 246n109
Brookings Institution, 34, 35, 52–54, 64,
70, 72, 132, 176, 229n93, 245n98
Brown, Jerry, 181, 183, 308n77
Brown Brothers Harriman & Co., 113
*Brown v. the Board of Education of
Topeka*, 33
Bryant, Anita, 88
Brzezinski, Zbigniew, 134, 137, 139,
171, 192, 262n87, 281n145, 282n157,
282n159, 283n160
Buchanan, James, 62, 74, 234n136,
260n67, 309n81
Buchanan, Patrick, 77, 83, 252n167
Buckley, William F., 69–70, 182, 253n8,
308n77
Buffett, Warren, 198, 318n
Burnham, Walter Dean, 175
Burns, Arthur F., 64, 148, 245n101,
287n35, 289n59, 291n73, 310n99

collective bargaining, transnational, 95
Colorado, 185
Colson, Charles, 53, 83, 236n5, 239n36,
    262n88, 271n26
Columbia Journalism Review, 60
Columbia University, 10, 137, 165, 208
Combahee River Collective, 97
Commentary (magazine), 120, 126
Committee for Economic Development
    (CED), 29, 34, 52, 63–64, 227n67
Committee for the Survival of a Free
    Congress, 67, 247n117, 258n53,
    258n55
Committee on the Present Danger
    (CPD), 9, 95, 96, 128–30, 133–35,
    199, 262n89, 277n96
common situs picketing legislation,
    305n47
communism, 27, 32, 41, 108, 115, 127,
    134, 199
Communist Party, 136
Communists, 108, 112, 124–25, 127, 137,
    148, 165, 225n53, 262n88
compensation: data for, 215n1; from
    1948-2021, 1, 2*f*
Confederacy, 18, 25, 169
Congo, 112
Congress: and Carter, 185, 195;
    conservatives in, 36; controlling,
    79; and Employment Act of
    1946, 23; and environment, 203;
    and evangelicals, 85; and Full
    Employment Act, 17; and Jackson-
    Vanik Amendment, 120; and
    Johnson, 43; and Kemp, 92; and
    Landrum-Griffin Act, 36; and
    lobbying, 8; and Minarik, 72; and
    Nixon, 56–57, 111; and Powell, 66;
    promilitary lobbies in, 117; and
    Reagan, 204; salaries and bonuses,
    205; and Servicemen's Readjustment
    Act, 30; and Social Security, 177; and
    Truman, 24; and unemployment, 17;
    and Volcker, 191, 312n113
Congressional Human Rights Caucus, 123
Congress of Industrial Organizations
    (CIO), 18, 19, 23, 24, 27, 222n18

Connally, John, 51, 64, 149–50, 245n101,
    288nn42–43
conservatism: and AEI, 59, 129; of
    AFL-CIO, 94; and Brown, 182; and
    Carter, 173, 177; Christian, 36–37,
    193; growing, 260n73; and military
    spending, 31; and New Right, 93;
    and Nixon, 4, 256n31; and Reagan,
    318n3; rise of, 47; and Schlafly, 129;
    social, 4, 81, 129, 193; and Weyrich,
    81
Conservative Caucus, 67, 258n55,
    260n65
Conservative Digest (publication), 69
Conservative Political Action
    Committee, 93
conservatives: and AEI, 59–60, 64; and
    ALEC, 65; and austerity, 78; and
    Brookings Institution, 35–36; and
    Carter, 6, 14, 169, 171, 193, 195; and
    CDM, 122; at Chicago School, 39;
    and Chile, 165; class compromise,
    26–30; defined, 14; economists,
    37, 49; efforts of, 198–99; and
    evangelicals, 36–37; institutions for,
    61; and Keynes, 39; in late 1970s,
    181; and libertarians, 90, 92, 93;
    and MPS, 9, 38, 48; at New York
    University, 38; and Nixon, 4, 49–52,
    55–58, 80, 81, 83–85; and political
    manipulation, 80–85; as popular,
    88; on Proposition 13, 184, 185;
    and Reagan, 203; and religion, 88;
    and unions, 23, 36; at University
    of Chicago, 38; U.S. as, 21; and
    Weyrich, 80, 82
construction workers, 98
consumer protection agency, 177,
    305n46
Continental Can, 70
Continental Teléphone, 122
Cooper, Richard, 187
Coors, Joseph, 61, 65, 80, 85, 193,
    247n117, 258n51
Coors Breweries, 67
Coors family, 88
Copeland, Aaron, 100

liberal establishment, 100
liberal institutions, 70, 245n97
liberal intellectuals, 121
liberalism, 15, 34, 50, 65, 95, 316n152
liberal Protestants, 36
liberals: and AEI, 59; and Agnew, 101;
  in Boston, 102; and Carter, 171, 173;
  defined, 14; and FMC Corporation,
  62; and Ford Foundation, 64;
  journalists as, 70; mass media as, 68;
  and Nader, 306n60; and Nixon, 49;
  and Powell Memorandum, 66; and
  race, 102; and religion, 86; on social
  issues, 181; and trucking, 90; and
  working class, 101
liberal views, 193
libertarian, 14
libertarian ideology, 36, 89, 93
libertarianism, 90–92, 107, 259n62
libertarian movement, 182
Libertarian Party, 89
Libertarian Review, 182
libertarians, 14, 89–93, 181, 260n66,
  261n74
Liberty University, 86
Libya, 291n77
Lichtenstein, Nelson, 178
lifestyle, 81, 89, 103, 115
Lilly Endowment, 53
Lindsay, Hal, 83
Lipset, Seymour Martin, 60, 96, 98,
  259n58, 263n92
living standards: and austerity,
  5; damaging effects on, 168;
  decreasing, 152–53, 157, 165, 172, 176,
  187, 189, 190, 192, 200, 203, 207; and
  deregulation, 306n52; increasing, 18,
  45, 144, 166, 183; and inflation, 73;
  and lobbying, 167; protecting, 101,
  104; reducing, 3, 6, 52, 75, 79, 109,
  142; for truckers, 91; working-class,
  5–6, 75, 168, 306n52
loans, 144, 152, 157, 178, 270n20, 284n10
lobby groups, 8, 15, 36, 45, 58, 65–66,
  117, 122, 130, 197
lobbying: and ASC, 117; and Business
  Roundtable, 78; and Carter, 5,

135, 177; and CIA, 131; corporate,
  64–67; and CPD, 134; deep (*see*
  deep lobbying); defined, 7–8; and
  Employment Act of 1946, 23; and
  Friedman, 63; and Full Employment
  Act, 22; and Jews, 120; and Keynes,
  21; and MPS, 167; renaissance of
  corporate, 64–67; and Saudi Arabia,
  160; and Soviet Union, 130; and
  Walker, 128
Long, Huey, 18
Lorillard Tobacco, 70
Los Angeles Times, 68
Louisiana, 18
Lovestone, Jay, 130, 132, 183, 262n88,
  270n20, 278n104
low-income communities, 103
low-income families, 73, 91
low-income groups, 73, 105, 109, 201,
  216n8
low-income whites, 100
Luce, Clare Boothe, 130, 183, 278n104
Luhnow, Harold, 35
Lutherans, 83

Machinists Union, 106
MacKinnon, Ronald, 164
MacLaine, Shirley, 101, 265n110
Maine, 185
Malamud, Bernard, 87
Malott, Robert H., 62, 244n91
managed floats, 289n61
Manne, Henry G., 62, 244n90
manufacturing: airline, 115; and
  deindustrialization, 142; and
  deregulation, 146; effect of finance
  on, 163; as employment, 144; and
  Euromarket, 145; globalization of,
  164; improvements in, 181
Mao Zedong, 112
Marcuse, Herbert, 101
market-based model, 143
market-based pricing, 19
market-based programs, 165
marks, 145
Marriott, J. W., 84
Marriott Hotels, 66

Marshall, George C., 23, 224n39
Marshner, Connie, 88, 258n48, 258n53
Marty (film), 30
Marxist ideas, 97
Mary Kay Cosmetics, 86
Mash (movie), 110
Massachusetts, 61
mass killings, 99, 126
mass media, 8, 60, 66, 68, 70
Masterpiece Theater (television show), 68
Matchlup, Fritz, 51
Matusow, Allen, 55
Mayer, Jane, 90, 260n65
McCarthy, Joseph, 35, 263n97
McCracken, Paul, 51, 58, 113
McGovern, George, 62, 84, 95, 117, 262n90
McIntyre, Thomas, 185
Meany, George, 33, 94–96, 98, 101, 262nn87–88, 270n20
media: and AEI, 59; conservative, 69, 70; and economic sectors, 69; and education, 55; evangelical, 82; and Humphrey-Hawkins, 105; mass, 8, 60, 66, 68, 70; and New York, 78; and oil, 69–70; watchdogs for, 70
Media Institute, 70, 248n137
Medicaid, 43
Medicare, 43
Mercatus Center, 90, 180
Merchants and Manufacturers Association, 21
Methodists, 83
Metropolitan Life, 58, 239n33
middle class, 73
militarism, 5, 8, 14, 80, 95, 110–11, 117, 126, 128, 135, 140
militarist backlash, 114–19
military, 23, 31, 33, 41, 115–18, 134, 159, 218n20, 219n27, 271n37
military adventures, 157
military budget, 5, 106, 115
military buildup, 5, 7, 119, 139, 194, 200, 204, 233n127
military classics, 11, 220n33
military contractors, 9, 122, 129, 134, 202
military equipment, 41, 202

military expansion, 202
military expenditure, 7, 114*t*
military force, 5, 111, 113, 118
military interventionism, 125, 127, 270n22, 273n50
military Keynesianism, 31, 41, 44
military policy, 6, 108–9, 115, 133
military pressure groups, 117
military production, 24
military services, 109
military spending: and austerity, 176; and class compromise, 26, 31, 41; and Communism, 108; and CPD, 96; cuts in, 113; dissatisfaction with, 111; and Ford, 114; hiding, 129; increasing, 117, 126, 133–35, 139–40, 176, 202; introduction to, 5–6, 9; and Jackson, 115; public opinion on, 123; reducing, 131, 177; table of, 114*t*
Milliken, Roger, 184
Minarik, Joseph, 72, 73, 217n10
Minnesota, 185
Mirage fighter plane, 116
Mobil Oil, 58, 68–69, 85, 239n33
Mondale, Walter, 204
monetarism, 11, 48, 52, 190–91, 227n70, 313n132, 314n136, 314n138
Monetary Control Act of 1980, 180–81
monopolies, 38–39, 91, 101, 205, 307n62
Mont Pèlerin Society (MPS): and AEI, 55; and Connally, 288n43; and CPD, 199; and crisis, 148; defined, 38; on deregulation, 179, 180; doctrine, 180; and dollar, 6; economists of, 9, 48, 51, 55, 62, 74–75, 94, 146–48, 151, 158, 164, 171, 179, 190; ideology, 48; influence of, 69; and Nixon, 4, 51, 147, 197; political influence of, 10; and power, 48–49; and Simon, 158
morality, 80, 87, 123, 209
morality wars, 88
Moral Majority, 193, 316nn150–51
mortgages, 102
Moscow Olympics, 139
Mott, Steward III, 62
Moynihan, Daniel Patrick, 122, 123, 126, 127, 276n81, 276n85

MPS. *See* Mont Pèlerin Society (MPS)
Ms. (magazine), 100, 264n107
Mujahidin, 137–38
multiracialism, 19
Murchison, Clint, 84
Murray, Charles, 141, 283n
My Lai massacre, 109, 268n1

Nader, Ralph, 71, 179, 306n60
National Association of Manufacturers
  (NAM), 8, 22, 35–37, 56, 65, 67, 85,
  105, 146, 171, 179, 306n59
National Bureau of Economic Research
  (NBER), 61, 188
National Conservative Political Action
  Committee (NCPAC), 67
national debt, 28
National Defense Education Act, 31
National Economic Council, 208
National Intelligence Estimates (NIE),
  131
nationalism, 202
National Legal Center for the Public
  Interest, 67, 248n135
National Organization for Women, 97,
  267n136
National Presto Industries, 69
National Pro-Life Political Action
  Committee, 88, 258n55
National Review (Buckley), 69–70
National Review network, 90
National Right-to-Work Committee, 65
National Security Council, 26
National Strategy Information Center
  (NSIC), 117
National Tax Limitation Committee,
  183, 309n87
Nation's Business (magazine), 63, 95
Native Americans, 96, 229n90,
  263n93
NATO alliance, 26
Nazis, 102, 130
NBER. *See* National Bureau of
  Economic Research (NBER)
NCPAC. *See* National Conservative
  Political Action Committee
  (NCPAC)

neoconservatism, 121–23, 133–35,
  275n71
neoconservatives, 9, 122–28, 131–34,
  241n56, 275n64, 275n66, 275n72,
  276n77, 316n152
neoliberal, 14
New Deal: and AEI, 58; and business
  executives, 35, 78; and capitalism,
  48; and class compromise, 14,
  52, 62; and Clinton, 208; and
  deregulation, 178, 179; and
  Eisenhower, 34, 208; and equality,
  7; and Friedman, 9; globalization
  undermining, 141, 143, 144, 146–47,
  162–67; and Great Depression,
  17; and Kennedy, 43; laissez-faire,
  168, 169, 171, 172–78, 198, 199;
  and Monetary Control Act, 180;
  and political manipulation, 82;
  and racial discrimination, 33; and
  Reagan, 205; and resources, 207;
  and Roosevelt, 63, 79; and Truman,
  23, 25
Newfield, Jack, 101
New Hampshire, 142, 185
New Left, 66, 71, 89, 94, 95, 97, 100, 101
New Republic, 98
New Right, 67, 81–82, 86–89, 92–98,
  101, 103, 106–7, 193, 253n3, 265n115
Newsweek (magazine), 49
New York, 68, 98, 194, 252n162,
  252n164
New York City Fiscal crisis, 76–78
New York Times (magazine), 44, 59, 68,
  70, 109, 146, 276n83
New York University, 38
NIE. *See* National Intelligence
  Estimates (NIE)
Nigeria, 118, 291n77
1933 Banking Act, 208
1944 State of the Union Address, 16
1948 Executive Order, 33
1972 Strategic Arms Limitation Treaty,
  112
1984 (Orwell), 202
1996 State of the Union, 208
Nitze, Paul, 122, 135

space mission, 112
special drawing rights (SDRs), 162, 297n129
Spirit of 13, 183
Spiritual Mobilization, 36–37, 231n108
Springsteen, Bruce, 189
stagnation, 72, 166, 205, 220n7
Stalinist era, 126
Standard Oil of California, 158
Standard Oil of Indiana, 70, 239n33
Stanford University, 8, 60
steel companies, 41
Stein, Herbert, 3, 51, 58, 74, 106, 154, 176, 203, 217n10, 245n98, 250n150
Steinem, Gloria, 100
Stigler, George, 38
Stiglitz, Joseph, 208–9
stimulus, 175
stock market, 144, 205, 234n134, 284n11
stock prices, 42, 234n134
stocks and bonds, 72
Strange, Susan, 167, 301n159
Strategic Arms Limitation Treaty, 131, 133
strikes, 24, 201, 305n47
strip mining, 173
Summers, Lawrence, 71, 208
Sun Oil, 53, 84, 248n129
Sun Tzu, 11
Surface Mining Control and Regulation Act, 173
Swearingen, John, 53
Sweden, 21, 49
Syria, 120

table tennis diplomacy, 112, 270n17. See also ping-pong diplomacy
Taft, Robert, 22–23, 227n74
Taft-Hartley Act, 24–25, 36, 40
Taiwan, 133, 270n18
tariff, 149
tax: capital, 28; import, 149; and Nixon, 149; poll, 44; property, 182, 310n93
taxation: as burden, 46; and Carter, 14, 177; and federal tax code, 205; and GI Bill, 31; and Libertarian Party, 89, 91; and NBER, 61; negative effects

of, 61; progressive, 2, 15, 31, 43, 46, 105, 177; and welfare, 15
taxation rates, 43
tax cut, 41, 43, 177, 182–83, 204, 234nn136–37, 304n43, 309n85
tax exempt: deep lobbying as, 8; religious schools as, 315n147
tax havens, 167
Taxi Driver (film), 99
tax increase, 44, 182, 235n146
Teamsters union, 90
Teeters, Nancy, 190
televangelist, 83
television, 59, 66, 68–69, 82, 86, 99, 259n58
Television News Inc, 70
Teller, Edward, 122, 131, 278n103
Tennessee, 176
Tet Offensive, 109
Texaco, 62
Texas, 68, 85, 274n56
Texas Rangers, 86
Thatcher, Margaret, 165, 251n158, 300n151
think tanks, 4, 8, 15, 35, 45, 48, 52, 58–64, 80, 90, 94, 117, 263n97
Third World, 118, 119, 157
3M, 66
Time for Truth, A (Simon), 184
Time-Life fortune, 183
Time (magazine), 49, 169, 192
Tisch, Laurence, 93
Title Insurance, 67
Tobacco Institute, 66
total factor productivity (TFP), 17
trade: with Soviet Union, 120
trade imbalance, 151, 157
Treasury Department, 28, 148, 151, 155, 159, 162, 165, 167, 187
Treasury-Fed Accord, 28, 30
Treaty of Detroit, 32–33
Trennert, Jason DeSena, 320n27
Trilateral Commission, 170–71, 297n129
trucking industry, 91, 180, 201, 260n67
Truman, Harry S., 23–27, 32, 33, 204, 225n54, 320n24
Trump, Donald, 204, 209–10, 320n24

TRW Corporation, 122, 278n103
TWA, 65
Twain, Mark, 87
Twenty-Fourth Amendment, 43

underemployed workers, 50
underemployment, 189, 313n125
unemployed workers, 50, 194
unemployment: and antibusing, 103,
266n121; and austerity, 28, 250n150;
and Boston controversy, 102; and
Carter, 166, 173–74, 174t, 176, 187,
195; and Humphrey-Hawkins, 104;
and inflation, 28–29, 105, 176; and
Phillips curve, 29; and Reagan, 195;
right to, 17; and stagnation, 166; and
Volcker, 188–89, 200–201
unionization, 18–20, 23–25, 40, 87, 95,
105, 144, 261n82
union membership, 18, 34, 40, 44, 74,
94, 201, 232n115, 253n1, 323n50
union movement, 15, 19, 21, 25, 27, 34
union protections, 34, 164
union rights, 18
unions: and AEI, 52; anticommunist
labor, 27, 95, 139; and antiwar
movement, 96; and Black caucus,
106; breaking, 65; as burden, 46;
and business-led mobilization, 94;
and Business Roundtable, 65; and
Carter, 170; Chicago School bias of,
39, 40; and class compromise, 18–19,
21–25, 27, 32–34, 36–37, 39–40, 42,
44, 46; corruption in, 36; declining,
74; and education, 92; evils of, 39;
and globalization, 95; influence of, 5;
and Kennedy, 41; leadership of, 36;
PATCO, 201; and shift to right, 79;
success of, 32; in Washington, 115;
weakening, 36, 40
United Auto Workers, 22, 32, 94, 106
United Church of Christ, 83
United Fruit, 48
United Nations Monetary and
Economic Conference, 142
United States: business in, 10; and
Cambodia, 126–27; and Carter, 166,

170; class compromise in, 15, 20,
22, 28, 31, 40; as conservative, 21;
conservative legal centers in, 67;
crises in, 198; and currencies, 143–
44, 145; and deindustrialization, 164;
and dollar, 186; economic analysis
in, 11; education in, 10; and energy
crisis, 154–57; and exchange rates,
143; floating exchange rate in, 6; and
Ford, 133; foreign policy in, 108; free
enterprise in, 67–70; and Friedman,
49; and human rights, 124; income
in, 206, 206t; and Indonesia, 127;
and Iran, 125; and Jewish population,
121; laissez-faire in, 47; and lobbying,
165; military Keynesianism in, 31; in
1979, 185; and Nixon, 111, 148, 151,
153; and Palme, 22; for right wing,
62; and Saudi Arabia, 158, 160–62,
295n108; security in, 128; social
classes in, 15; social structure in, 22;
and Soviet Union, 113, 129–32, 133,
136; superpower of, 142; and Taiwan,
133; unions in, 18; and USSR, 112;
and Vietnam, 113, 116, 126, 127; and
Volcker, 191; workers in, 115
United States-China relationship, 112
United States Steel, 39, 42, 48, 63, 66,
232n117, 239n33
United Steelworkers, 41
United Technologies, 69
universal health care, 177
universities, 8, 10, 199
University of Chicago, 10, 38, 48, 49, 51,
60, 150, 164, 232n114
University of Miami, 62
University of Notre Dame, 133
University of Pittsburgh, 10
upper classes, 21, 43, 45, 72, 80
U.S. Balance of Payments Policies, 147
U.S. Central Command, 202
U.S. Chamber of Commerce, 8, 22, 35,
37, 56, 57, 65–66, 68, 69, 90, 105, 171,
311n102
U.S. Constitution, 43, 88
U.S. Naval Academy, 169
U.S. News and World Report, 94

U.S. Supreme Court, 33, 66
U.S. Treasury Bonds, 157
USSR, 5, 113, 115, 120, 129, 136–37, 139, 282n152

Vaïsse, Justin, 129
Vanik, Charles, 120
veterans, 30, 100–101, 264n109
Vietnam, 54, 96, 109–11, 113, 116–17, 123, 126, 135, 145, 186, 270n24
Vietnam policy, 54, 253n7
Vietnam syndrome, 109–11
Vietnam veterans, 100, 264n109
Vietnam War, 44, 95–96, 98, 109, 112, 118, 123, 126–27, 148, 170, 235n144, 253n7, 262n88, 269n10
Viguerie, Richard, 85
Virginia, 86, 87, 193
Virginia Tech, 62
Volcker, Paul, 168, 187–91, 200–201, 205, 232n119, 285n15, 301n, 312nn112–14, 313n132, 314n133, 314n136, 314n138, 318n4, 318n6
von Clausewitz, Carl, 11
von Hayek, Friedrich, 4, 37–38, 49, 92, 197
Von Mises, Ludwig, 37–38, 146–47
voter registration drives, 193
voters, 37, 56, 80–81, 83–84, 89, 120, 169, 183, 193–95, 203–4, 208
voting base, 209
voting rights, 43

Wachter, Michael, 71
wage gap, 207
wages, 18, 30, 32–33, 40, 73, 76, 105, 144, 166, 178–79, 180, 189, 215n1
Walker, Charls, 128
Wallace, George, 102, 258n47
Wallace, Henry A., 15, 25, 46
Wall Street Journal, 34, 68, 77, 106, 136, 138, 176, 185, 196
Walmart, 87
Walters, Barbara, 156
Walton, Sam, 87
Wanniski, Jude, 77

War on Poverty, 43, 44
War on Terror, 122
Washington, 115
Washington, D.C., 8, 34, 52, 54, 61, 117, 143
Washington Post (newspaper), 58, 60, 66, 68, 69, 109, 128, 134, 135, 139, 146, 155
Washington Report (magazine), 69
Washington University, 58
Watergate scandal, 4, 55–57, 60, 85
Watt, James, 203
wealth: distribution of, 4; and GI Bill, 31; and income, 30
wealth concentration, 2, 7, 35, 80, 197, 199, 202, 207–8
weapons, 41, 112, 129, 131
weapons companies, 117
weapons manufacturers, 5, 118, 193
weapons procurement, 31, 139–40, 204
weapons production, 19, 109
weapons purchasers, 116
Weber, Max, 10
Wedemeyer, Albert, 183
wedge issues, 56, 80, 83, 88, 92, 101–3
Weidenbaum, Murray, 58–59
welfare state, 15, 34, 40, 46
West Virginia protests, 87
Weyrich, Paul, 80–82, 85, 88, 93, 97, 193, 198, 253n3, 253n5, 253n9, 254n16, 302n19
whites, 81, 88, 97–100, 102–4, 106, 169, 194, 203, 207, 301n1
white supremacy, 189
white workers, 18, 33, 107
Whitman, Marina, 162, 311n107
Whyte, William, 63
Williams, William Appleman, 110
William Volker Fund, 35, 37–38, 232n113
Wohlstetter, Albert, 122
Wolfowitz, Paul, 122
women: agendas for, 96; and Carter, 173; and Hicks, 102; and jobs, 95; and OPA, 19; and race, 102; roles